07 04 36

3990 6 3 9 1

Sharpbenders

Corporate Strategy, Organization and Change

Series General Editor
Andrew Pettigrew, University of Warwick

Associate Editors
Henry Mintzberg, McGill University
Peter Lorange, The Wharton School, University of Pennsylvania

Also in this series:

Strategic Change and the Management Process
Gerry Johnson

Management of Strategic Change
Edited by Andrew Pettigrew

The Dynamics of Strategic Change (forthcoming)
C. R. Hinings and Royston Greenwood

Sharpbenders

The Secrets of Unleashing Corporate Potential

PETER H. GRINYER
DAVID G. MAYES
PETER McKIERNAN

Basil Blackwell

Copyright © National Economic Development Office 1988

First published 1988

Basil Blackwell Ltd
108 Cowley Road, Oxford, OX4 1JF, UK

Basil Blackwell Inc.
432 Park Avenue South, Suite 1503
New York, NY 10016, USA

British Library Cataloguing in Publication Data
Grinyer, Peter H.
  Sharpbenders: the secrets of unleashing
corporate potential.
  1. Great Britain. Business firms.
Management – Case studies
  I. Title II. Mayes, David G. III. McKiernan
Peter IV. Series
658'.00941

ISBN 0–631–15304–7

Library of Congress Cataloging in Publication Data
Grinyer, Peter H.
  Sharpbenders: the secrets of unleashing
corporate potential.
  Peter Grinyer, David G. Mayes, and Peter McKiernan.
  p.   cm. – (Corporate strategy, organization and change)
Bibliography: p.
Includes index.
ISBN 0–631–15304–7
  1. Organizational change. 2. Organizational effectiveness.
I. Mayes, David G. II. McKiernan, Peter. III. Title. IV. Series.
HD58.8.G75 1988
658.4'063 – dc19   88–4958
            CIP

Typeset in 10 on 12 pt Ehrhardt by Columns of Reading
Printed in Great Britain by T J Press, Padstow, Cornwall.

Contents

Foreword   vii

Preface   viii

1   A Need for Action   1

1.1   Why Read This Book?   1
1.2   The Sharpbenders   2
1.3   Plan of the Book   5
1.4   The Structure of the Project   6
1.5   What is a Sharpbender?   9
1.6   The Process of Change   13
1.7   The Rest of the Book   17

2   The Causes of Relative Decline   18

2.1   Adverse Changes in the Total Market Demand   18
2.2   Falling Revenues due to Competitive Pressure   21
2.3   Lack of Marketing/Sales Effort   25
2.4   Poor Quality and Reliability   27
2.5   Poor Management   27
2.6   Inadequate Financial Control   31
2.7   Organization   33
2.8   High-Cost Structure Relative to Competitors   35
2.9   Acquisitions   39
2.10 Big Projects that Failed   41
2.11 The Combination of Causes   44

3   Triggers of Radical Change   45

3.1   The Need for a Trigger   45
3.2   Triggers found among the Sharpbenders   47
3.3   External Intervention   51
3.4   Change of Ownership   53
3.5   Injection of a New Chief Executive   54
3.6   Recognition by Management   56
3.7   An Overview of the Process of Triggering Change   58

4   What the Sharpbenders Did   63

4.1   Changes in Management   65
4.2   Changes in Organization   75
4.3   Stronger Central Financial Control   78
4.4   New Product Market Focus   81
4.5   Improved Quality and Service   86
4.6   Improved Marketing   89
4.7   Reduced Costs   91
4.8   Acquisitions   95
4.9   Debt Reduction   98
4.10 Windfalls   101
4.11 An Overall View   104

5   Characteristics of Sustained Improved Performance   109

5.1   The Relation between the Continuing Characteristics and the
      Steps Taken   110
5.2   Good Management   113
5.3   Appropriate Organizational Structure   116
5.4   Effective Financial and Other Controls   118
5.5   Sound Product Market Posture   119
5.6   Good Marketing Management   123
5.7   High Quality Maintained   124
5.8   Tightly Controlled Costs   125
5.9   Characteristics of the Sustained Improvement Considered   127

6   Unleashing Corporate Potential   130

6.1   The Initial Appraisal   133
6.2   Putting the Sharpbend into Practice   146
6.3   An Omission   149
6.4   Concluding Remarks   150

Technical Appendix   151

Vignettes of the Individual Companies   179

References   279

Index   283

Foreword

For one who usually dislikes management books and their pontificating style I compliment the authors on an excellently written and stimulating book. I believe it will be genuinely useful and valuable and the results of the studies on which it is based are well worth publishing.

The main lesson learnt is the need to adapt to changing 'externals'. Failure to do so is usually fatal whereas responding quickly and sensitively and in a sustained manner can lead to a 'bend'. As to what a 'bend' is, I suggest you read this book!

Sir John Cuckney
Chairman
3i Group plc

Preface

The aim of this book is to help UK companies improve their economic performance. The particular contribution of the project discussed in it is to focus on the behaviour of those firms which are already clearly identifiable as having achieved noteworthy rapid and sustained improvements in their performance. The task we set ourselves was to identify what had made these firms different from the general run of companies and to see if there were general lessons in behaviour which other companies could be encouraged to emulate.

At any time there would be an incentive to try to achieve *rapid* improvements in performance rather than slow ones; if, that is, they could be sustained subsequently without adverse consequences elsewhere in the economy which would nullify the gains. However, with high levels of unemployment, the need for rapid improvements is especially great.

Our first thought in contemplating this study was that there might be no specific ingredients which led to successful rapid rather than slow improvements. We thought we might find that these noteworthy companies had not done anything particularly different from their less successful competitors but had simply taken more actions and applied themselves harder. If that had been the case then there would have been no particular need to add to the traditional approach of promoting all the individual facets of behaviour which lead to improved company performance. However, an initial examination of one or two companies showed that these sharp improvements in performance did not appear to stem merely from a continuing pursuit of the various activities which are characteristic of success but from an explicit set of decisions and actions. It is thus possible to differentiate between what excellent or successful companies do and what companies do to *become* much more successful. We therefore decided to focus on this process of change and sharp improvement, which we have called 'sharpbending' to distinguish it from the related but conceptually different discussion of successful companies in the recent literature on 'excellence'. Sharpbending also bears some similarities with the process of 'turning round' companies but differs in that in turnarounds change is forced upon the company by extreme financial pressure. The sharpbending companies had a choice. They could have survived relatively unchanged but they chose to take the sequence of steps which led to their rapid improvement in performance. Why they made that choice when the large majority of companies in the country did not is in itself one of the major questions we study.

Thus the book concentrates not on companies which have been excellent for many years but on companies which have successfully adopted a series of measures which have transformed their performance for the better in a short period of time. The emphasis is thus on firms which took an identifiable set of actions, as a result of which they may of course indeed now be excellent companies. We argue that many companies have the potential for rapid improvements in performance, the problem our book deals with is how to unleash that potential.

The book is based on information and data resulting from a research project for the National Economic Development Office. Professor Peter Grinyer of the University of St Andrews was appointed as a consultant, and he, with his colleague Peter McKiernan, undertook the large majority of the fieldwork. David Mayes directed the project, building on the excellent work of many colleagues and assisted by several others, two of whom, Michael Bramson and George Gater, deserve particular note. Peter McKiernan was primarily responsible for the vignettes on each company. The authors record their gratitude to all those who helped, particularly those in the companies we studied, who gave of their time freely and generously despite the commercial pressures on them, in the hope that others could benefit from their experience.

The research project was carried out with the advice of a committee chaired by Sir John Cuckney, with membership drawn from unions, government and employers. The authors have found the comments of the committee particularly useful in keeping their ideas and conclusions on a practical track.

The resulting book is of course the responsibility of the authors and it should not be taken to represent the judgements or opinions of the National Economic Development Council or Office.

Peter H. Grinyer, David G. Mayes and Peter McKiernan
17 July 1987

1 A Need for Action

1.1 Why Read This Book?

This book is unashamedly intended to improve the performance of British companies. To do this it both recounts and analyses the experiences of a group of companies we have labelled 'sharpbenders'. These are characterized by the kind of dramatic reversal of performance illustrated in figure 1.1. A period of stagnation or decline relative to competitors in their industries was in each case followed by a dramatic and sustained improvement which resulted in their outperforming their rivals. Our study is about the process of turning losers into winners.

Our investigation of 'sharpbending' addressed a series of questions. These are best considered in detail in subsequent chapters but relate to five main issues:

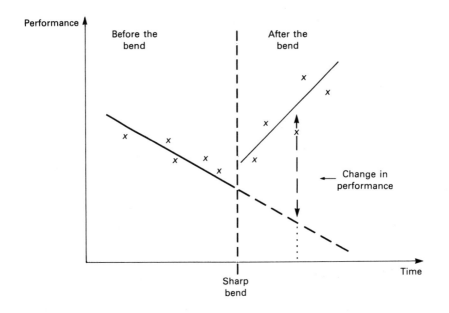

Figure 1.1 *Measuring changes in performance*

Why were the companies stagnating or declining?
What events or forces triggered the dramatic change in performance?
What did senior management do to achieve these marked sustained improvements?
What are the continuing characteristics of such companies?
How are the answers to the above questions interrelated?

Only the irredeemably complacent or consistently outstanding can afford to ignore the answers to such questions. The former will not be stirred to action and the latter presumably already know the answers.

Hence the lessons distilled from the experience of our sample of sharpbenders should be of importance to all those with a strong interest in the health of companies. Among these we would include:

company chairmen;
chief executives;
executive directors;
non-executive directors;
senior managers and those who aspire to reach such positions;
trade union officers;
consultants;
major shareholders;
bankers and major creditors.

Above all, it is directed at those who are dissatisfied with the performance of their companies, or those in which they have a significant involvement, and are resolved to do something about it.

However, the opportunity for sharpbending is not just restricted to those companies that were in relative decline as shown in figure 1.1. Some were performing quite steadily before their improvement (figure 1.2a), while others were already doing very well (figure 1.2b). Indeed one might argue that firms which succeed in arresting their rate of decline sharply (figure 1.2c), were also sharpbenders. They certainly contribute to the recording of a markedly higher average rate of performance in the period after the bend compared with that beforehand. Nevertheless, without in any way belittling the efforts of such companies, we restricted our research to those companies whose average performance improved after the bend as this is a more attractive goal for other companies to aim at.

1.2 The Sharpbenders

'Sharpbenders' are defined by us as companies which have been in decline relative to their competitors, which have then exhibited a marked, and often

Performance

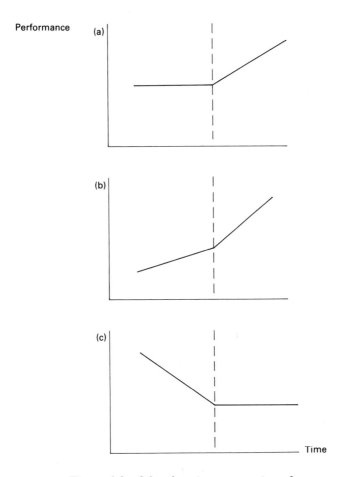

Figure 1.2 *Other sharp improvements in performance*

dramatic, improvement in performance; and which have sustained that high relative performance over a reasonable period of time and so are now regarded as outstanding in their industries.

Such companies may be small, medium or large. Indeed, Macallan-Glenlivet, the smallest of our sample of 'sharpbenders', has only forty-six employees. At the other extreme, Ferranti has 19,000. They are in declining industries like jute, relatively mature industries like whisky, fertilizers or building, or rapidly growing ones like electronics. Although our sample comprises mainly publicly quoted companies, because of availability of financial and other data, one of the sharpbenders was a closely held family company and two were subsidiaries of a larger group. In many ways these companies, drawn from different segments of business, are very ordinary.

They are involved in an ongoing, unromantic, daily drive towards better performance.

Yet these in some ways ordinary companies are remarkable. Externally, they are noted for their impact on their markets; for the service they give their customers; for their high rate of growth of sales relative to their competitors; often for a strong growth in exports. In some cases, such as Don Brothers Buist, they are applauded for bucking the trend by taking over production plant being disposed of by competitors in a declining industry and making it economically viable. They are all exceptional because of their high level of profitability relative to others in their industry. For these reasons, they tend to have the respect of their competitors, suppliers and customers, and to find favour with the financial community.

When we visited the sharpbenders during our research we found them to be qualitatively different from many, possibly most, other companies internally too. This is a matter to which we return in later chapters. For the present, we would stress the sense of purpose, commitment, pride in achievement, and of vitality which tended to pervade the sharpbenders, at shopfloor level as well as in the boardroom. We have no doubt that this was in part a consequence of success, for winning is satisfying and brings its own psychic rewards. The energy generated by such a heady potion is itself a strong contribution to outstanding performance. Perhaps in both Britain and the United States, top management in too many companies has forgotten how to win, that though winning takes sustained effort it gives a great kick, and that once one starts winning it is easier to generate the enthusiastic, positive, direct action at all levels of the managerial hierarchy essential to keeping ahead of the field.

Having said what 'sharpbenders' are, let us distinguish them from other categories, to which they are related but from which we wish to separate them. First, though they are 'excellent' companies, they are but a sub-set of them. Companies classed as 'excellent' in the growing literature on this phenomenon are usually large, with household names, and have held dominant market positions for many years (see Peters and Waterman, 1982; Peters and Austin, 1985; Goldsmith and Clutterbuck, 1984; Clifford and Cavanagh, 1985; Inkson *et al.*, 1986; for example). Our sharpbenders are, by contrast, often small, sometimes not known to the general public, and have attained excellence in most cases only in the last seven years. Decades of excellence would not permit exploration of the *process* by which it is achieved by the previously more pedestrian. Second, companies which have been 'turned around' or which have been taken over as a prelude to spectacular recovery are excluded from our category of sharpbenders, despite the fact that they may exhibit many similar characteristics and experience similar processes of change (Slatter, 1984; Bibeault, 1982; Kibel, 1982; Grinyer and Spender, 1979a). Our reason for making this distinction is that change is *forced* upon companies in both of these situations by external bodies and is consequently more easily set in motion. In the turnaround situation, in particular, conservative forces within the company are confronted by the fact that survival itself clearly requires major change. Most companies are not in such a dramatic crisis. They jog along, earning reasonable but not outstanding profits, giving an adequate but not exceptional service to their customers, and content to stay with the pack rather than ahead of it. These 'average', ordinary companies have great untapped potential, like our sharpbenders before their 'bends', and our focus is on how this can be realized without the trauma of a takeover or of impending financial collapse.

1.3 Plan of the Book

In the rest of this chapter, we set out the background, how the study evolved, and what it did. The remainder of the book is divided into six parts. The first four look at the logical evolution of the sharpbend. Chapter 2 begins this by assessing the state of the companies before the bend. It considers what they were like, their difficulties, what they were doing wrong, and external reasons for relative decline. Chapter 3 then answers the question 'Why did they change, what pushed them into the sharpbend?' Chapter 4 is in many ways the most instructive, looking as it does at what the companies did which achieved the bend. Chapter 5 then examines the characteristics of the companies in their successful period after the bend and seeks to determine why success continued and what differentiates them from less successful companies.

These four chapters therefore examine the main evidence from the study. The final chapter takes this information and considers the question 'What can be done?' It makes practical suggestions for those who can influence the performance of the firm for the better, principally chief executives, directors, managers, other employees, shareholders, advisers and suppliers. There is a section for government, though one characteristic of the findings is that the role of government, certainly in individual cases, is limited. The government's main task is to avoid inadvertently inhibiting the process and to provide the conditions under which improvements can readily take place.

We have argued that the best way to see how to apply these lessons is by example. These are provided throughout and, to help readers, an appendix provides a vignette of each of the sharpbending companies, giving a brief description of the company and setting out its individual experience under the same four headings as chapters 2–5, *viz.* what were the causes of decline, what caused the company to change, what did it do to make the sharpbend, and what are the characteristics of the company's continuing success? A technical appendix also provides the methodological details of the study, where this is not included in the rest of this chapter.

1.4 The Structure of the Project

The project had three main phases, the first of which was largely exploratory. The second was a pilot survey of half a dozen firms to assess the methodology before finally undertaking the main research. It would not be valuable to chronicle the way our ideas evolved but our first phase largely concerned the definition and selection of sharpbenders; the second was mainly taken up with setting out the hypotheses we wished to test and establishing whether our research methods worked in practice with the pilot companies.

Our basic design was to select companies drawn from a broad cross-section of industries, concentrated in the manufacturing sector. The industries chosen are set out in table 1.1. However, we started by trying to find companies which had either shown the sharpest bends or were best known as having achieved sharpbends. It was thus a two-pronged process starting from published Extel data on the one hand and from the opinions of stockbrokers, investment analysts and institutional investors on the other.

However, within that framework we thought it important to provide a contrast between the sharpbenders and a group of control companies. One of the characteristics of much of the recent literature on management success is that it focuses on successful companies. It examines neither whether less successful companies do in fact have the same characteristics nor what measures other companies have taken in a failed attempt to become more successful. For that reason we paired the sharpbenders in each industry with another company of similar size in that same industry.

While this 'control' firm had similar characteristics in the period prior to the sharpbend it nevertheless failed to change its behaviour successfully. We asked each of the firms the same basic questions so that we could isolate the factors that lead to sharp change from any others which affect all companies in the same industry. We decided to reinforce this by trying to find two sharpbenders in each industry selected so that a contrast could be provided and separate views on the sharpbenders obtained from their competitors. In some cases this was not possible.

The companies chosen are set out in table 1.1, where the Stock Exchange classification of sectors is used. The control companies are not of course shown as this could be invidious. Furthermore, we did interview other companies so it should not be taken that any company we interviewed which does not find itself on the list of sharpbenders, must thereby be a control company. We interviewed some companies which were clearly benders and yet not suitable for inclusion in our sample because of factors such as a subsequent change of ownership or difficulty in finding a control company.

We had a very low rate of refusal to participate so the companies eventually reported on were almost the same as our first choice of sample. Three companies did not wish to have their names disclosed. We have therefore

Table 1.1 *The sample of sharpbenders*

Industry	Companies
1 Building materials and fittings	1 Rotaflex PLC
2 Pharmaceuticals/agrochemicals	2 Fisons PLC
	3 Glaxo Holdings PLC
3 Offshore oil installations	4 John Wood Group PLC
	5 UDI Group Ltd
4 Building	6 McCarthy and Stone PLC
	7 Countryside Properties PLC
5 Electronics	8 Ferranti PLC
	9 A
6 Plant and engineering	10 B
	11 C
7 Distilling	12 Arthur Bell & Sons PLC
	13 Macallan-Glenlivet PLC
8 Publishing	14 Collins Publishers PLC
	15 Associated Book Publishers PLC
9 Papermaking & converting	16 Associated Paper Industries PLC
	17 Whatman Reeve Angel PLC
10 Clothing	18 Ellis & Goldstein (Holdings) PLC
	19 Dawson International PLC
	20 Pringle of Scotland Ltd
11 Knitting wool	21 Sirdar PLC
12 Jute spinning & weaving	22 Low & Bonar PLC
	23 Sidlaw Group PLC
	24 Don and Low PLC
13 Footwear	25 Ward White Group PLC

eliminated all explicit reference to them. Since two of them are in the engineering sector we have added a further company, TI Group PLC, to the list of companies studied in detail. While it does not form part of our calculations it does provide a helpful insight into a more recent bend.

A description of each of these companies and of their sharpbend is given in the Vignettes section at the end of the book. In many ways this is the most interesting part of the book for readers as it sets out the actual examples of the general items we are discussing.

Our work began with a careful analysis of published information about the firm – accounts, Extel cards, brokers' reports and a Textline search of newspaper reports – before proceeding to a series of structured interviews conducted in the firm with the chief executive, other executive directors, including, normally, the finance director, other relevant directors and representatives from the workforce. On some occasions we were also able to interview the chairman where this post had a separate incumbent. As these were all busy people we usually spent no more than a day in the firm. All were most helpful and obliging, providing further data when required and being quite prepared to give more of their time if it seemed needed.

We found that the major reasons for this great cooperation were enthusiasm for the aims of the project and the wish to tell other people about what had been achieved. The firms were characterized by enthusiasm. This was brought out very clearly in the visit to the last sharpbender we sampled, which also happened to be the smallest, Macallan-Glenlivet. It has a beautiful position on the shoulder of a hill just outside Craigellachie and excellent weather on the day of the interview reinforced this attractiveness. The distillery is next to an old house which they had purchased and recently refurbished for offices and a reception area for customers. Conducting interviews in what was in effect a very elegant drawing-room was certainly a pleasure, the management fitted the surroundings, being relaxed, pleasant and efficient. What struck us, however, was the attitude of one of the secretaries and one of the manual staff from the main distillery operation whom we saw as representatives of the labour force. They were clearly proud of the firm and its recent acquisition. Indeed, having that house with a small firm clearly helped reinforce what was a 'family' atmosphere, although this is a public company and the directors and senior management did not come from the same background of family ownership.

The enthusiasm and commitment were clearest when we discussed staff turnover. 'People don't normally leave or if they do it is to have children and bring them up.' They were keen to show off the plant and a new computer room which had brought the company right up to date with the provision of immediate accounting, stock and order information, and word-processing. This computer-based system had been introduced quickly and smoothly with staff of an age when change on that scale could easily have been difficult – not quite what one would expect in the rural Highlands. The marketing director was eagerly on his hands and knees on the carpet spreading out the originals from some of their successful marketing campaigns, encouraging us to participate in a competition to think up a new amusing storyline for their next campaign.

Although several different interviewers were used during the project, two people were present on most occasions in each particular firm. We made sure we worked together to monitor each other's styles, a clear structure was followed in each interview, and the interviews were recorded so we could play them back to make sure that the interviewees had not been led or items forgotten. It also helped ensure the accuracy of quotations.

Everyone interviewed was assured that their comments were confidential and we have carefully cleared the whole of the text with the people concerned. Only one person ever objected to being taped although from time to time certain confidential passages had to be skipped.

The questions were structured into what we determined were the four phases of activity to be observed:

1 What were the causes of relative decline, before the bend?
2 What triggered the change?
3 What steps were taken to achieve the bend?
4 What are the characteristics of the continuing successful company?

The interviewing schedule is set out in the technical appendix and the hypotheses are discussed in the rest of the book. We adopted an agnostic approach in framing the hypotheses, compiling a list from our own ideas, those of business leaders on our advisory committee, and those which we had culled from a wide survey of the literature. Our resulting conclusions are therefore not so much a finely tuned theory as an empirical set of findings, related to the experience and other published results in the field. In the main this was a reaction to what we perceived as some somewhat strained previous attempts to force the complexity of experience to fit into a very simplified framework.

1.5 What is a Sharpbender?

We have defined a sharpbender as being a company which achieves a sharp and sustained improvement in performance. Clearly all these components in turn need a clear definition. Taking 'performance' first, we are offered a wide range of possible definitions, most of which are usually concentrated on profitability or stock-market valuations, the focus of interest depending upon whether one is trying to run the company or investing in it. These interests are often reflected in the form of some summary measure of financial performance such as Z scores, which are a weighted sum of the individual components (see, for example, Taffler, 1981; and Taffler and Sudarsanam, 1980).

Our interest in this research is with the wider task of improving the performance of the economy as a whole. We are therefore concerned with the welfare of all interest groups in the firm and not just that of shareholders and management. A helpful analysis of such interests can be found in Newbould and Luffman (1978) who identify four groups whose welfare is affected by the performance of the firm. Their list is not all-inclusive as the welfare of suppliers, purchasers and others with financial arrangements with the firm is also affected by the performance of the firm.

Adapting Newbould and Luffman we have added two further groups to shareholders and management: employees and what we have described as 'national economy' as set out in table 1.2. The detailed measures used could

Table 1.2 *Measures of company performance used*

Shareholders
I   Basic return to shareholders
(Operating profit after interest, tax and preference dividends/ordinary shareholders' funds)

Management
II   Profitability
(Operating profit before interest and tax/net assets plus short-term borrowing including overdrafts)
III Sales

Employees
IV Earnings per employee
(UK employees' aggregate remuneration/number of UK employees)
V   Number of employees
(UK employees)

National Economy
VI Labour productivity
(Gross value added/number of employees)
VII Capital productivity
(Gross value added/capital employed
VIII Export performance
(Exports/total sales)

Contraction Control
IX Anti-contraction ratio
(Fixed assets/shareholders' funds)

readily be debated but we have opted for robust measures which are representative of many of the main measures which could have been added, because we wanted to keep the picture as simple as possible. Hence measures I and II are the straightforward measures of the rate of return and profits. However, it is regularly argued that profit maximization is not the only aim of managers. The growth of the enterprise is also important as this affects the number of employees and their welfare as well as being related to both profitability and stock-market valuation.

These measures were not in absolute terms, otherwise our sample would be dominated by electronics companies and others drawn from rapidly growing sectors such as retail sales. They were all calculated relative to their industry. Thus sales are expressed as a measure of market share. It is not of course a total as imports and exports have to be taken into account, but for many industries it is a good indicator.

Newbould and Luffman also incorporated measures of variability as being a further important factor of performance. A shareholder is interested not just in the average rate of return but in its risk (or variance) for a number of reasons. Firstly, simply because expenditures tend to be fairly even and fluctuating returns mean fluctuating incomes. Hence the individual could be in difficulty in any one year if returns dropped very low even if the longer-run outlook were perfectly acceptable. Furthermore, from the point of view of management, wide fluctuations in performance may be unhelpful because they increase the threat of takeovers. In view of the strength of these arguments we excluded measures of variability reluctantly. Our main reason is simply that the shortness of the effective data period which would result in variation measures which were themselves estimates subject to wide variance and hence not good discriminators.

For employees we felt that two considerations were important, *viz.* pay and employment, while for the 'national economy' it is the return on all assets which is the major consideration. The first two measures (VI and VII) look at the returns on the two main factors in production, labour and capital. The larger these are the more efficient the use of resources. However, performance in the domestic market is only part of the interest from a national point of view as the external performance of the economy (in an open economy such as the UK) also acts as a constraint on growth and the rate of increase in overall welfare. Export performance is therefore considered explicitly.

The reader will also have noted that there is a fifth category somewhat enigmatically labelled as contraction control in table 1.2. This is simply to identify companies which have achieved their rapid improvement in performance purely by closing down large parts of their operation or selling them to others. From our point of view these companies are rather less interesting as they may not have changed their performance markedly but passed the problems on to others.

In our initial study of sharpbending we looked at the performance of 1200 of the UK's largest industrial and commercial companies according to the nine measures in table 1.2, where the information was drawn from EXSTAT, a computer database of company accounts. We restricted ourselves to companies which were in existence over the whole period 1971–9, recorded values for all nine variables for each year and were free of obvious error. (These conditions had a dramatic effect on the number of companies studied, reducing them by half to 607.) In subsequent analysis for individual companies using the Datastream database we were able to add further companies and to capture more recent experience by adding further years and comparing their performance with the appropriate industry average.

Our requirement for a sharpbend is shown diagrammatically in figure 1.1, where for any one performance measure the values recorded in each year are marked by an 'x'. We then compared performance in the period before the bend with performance after it. Provided an average performance was better in the second period and was not declining then we regarded this as an improvement in performance. The two periods had to be at least three years long (1971–3 or 1977–9) in the early analysis as a minimum and the computer selected whichever year (1973, 1974, 1975, 1976, or 1977) gave the greatest improvement in performance. (The trends in performance estimated for the two periods were fitted by ordinary least squares.)

It is not absolute performance in the second period which was measured but performance *relative* to that in the first period. Thus the change was measured as the difference between what actually occurred in the second period and what would have happened had the firm continued to decline at the rate it did in the first period. Thus for any given performance in the second period, the worse the performance in the first the sharper the bend.

Only a very few companies, of which Arthur Bell & Sons were the outstanding example, actually improved their performance simultaneously according to the large majority of our criteria. A major reason for this was the disastrous performance of British industry as a whole both in the mid-1970s and early 1980s. Any manufacturing company which increased its employment during those periods was doing very well indeed. We therefore had to accept the more limited definition of improvement according to a financial criterion (I or II) and a real one (VI or VII).

These difficulties led us in the second and third phases of this study to a more informal method of sample selection. Nevertheless, the relationships found between the measures of performance are of interest in their own right. Profitability improvements were fairly closely associated with labour and capital productivity increases and with improvements in the return to shareholders. Job security and labour productivity tended to be negatively related indicating that increases in productivity tended to have been achieved by labour-force reductions.

We thus have a set of companies which are very much the product of their era. They are not on the whole the grand success which characterized Peters and Waterman's (1982) book *In Search of Excellence*, nor their smaller American counterparts in Clifford and Cavanagh (1985). All but two are public companies, primarily because these were the only concerns for which data were readily available. The exceptions were Pringle of Scotland Ltd, which is a wholly owned subsidiary of Dawson International, and UDI, a subsidiary of John Brown. These two were included to examine the behaviour of subsidiaries and how they respond to an owner's pressures. A major characteristic of all the sharpbenders examined is that they are typical companies, not unusual examples. Other companies could follow their example as their success and change were not based on largely unrepeatable factors.

Three categories of companies which show marked improvements in performance have been excluded. First, we regret that small, unquoted companies could not be included because of the lack of publicly available information, yet they may form some of the richest ground for examining change and rapidly fluctuating fortunes.

Secondly, our selection method excludes firms which have tried to change dramatically and have failed and gone out of business altogether, such as those covered by Stuart Slatter's (1984) study of turnarounds. By definition such companies cannot be sharpbenders since they have failed to achieve sustained improvements in performance.

However, it could be argued that successful turnarounds do exhibit the characteristics of sharpbenders but we have deliberately excluded them because in a turnaround the company has no choice but to change. If it fails to change successfully, it goes out of business but then it does that anyway even if it does nothing. The companies in our sample, by and large, were not in that position even though some were confronted by declining markets, as with the jute spinners. Our focus was upon companies which chose and were not forced to take the risks necessarily incurred in making major changes.

Thirdly, we have excluded takeovers and mergers. Again this is deliberate. There are many books and articles written on the subject and the cases are well documented. The pressure for change in such cases tends to be external, except perhaps where the takeover was encouraged by the acquired firm, However, among some of the sharpbenders, fear of potential acquisition or failed attempts to acquire the company were found to act as a trigger for change and in others clearly influenced strategic decision-taking.

Some of our sharpbenders were taken over after the study was complete. Bell's, for example, was acquired, to quite a large extent, because in looking at the long run it had diversified by buying the Gleneagles Group. This purchase resulted in the need for investment in the hotels, particularly the Piccadilly in London which had to be thoroughly refurbished. Naturally this had a short-run impact on profits and gearing and as a consequence this aided their susceptibility to the Guinness bid. However, it was still too early to say whether Bell's diversification had been successful. Maybe that was too big a step. Certainly there were differences of view on this within the company.

1.6   The Process of Change

Change is triggered in companies because actual or anticipated performance falls below a level that is regarded as acceptable. This may be, as in figure 1.3, because of continued decline in actual or relative performance, which either falls below or is anticipated to fall below an existing level of aspiration determined by senior managers, directors, bankers or others who influence the strategic decisions of the firm. As illustrated by case A in figure 1.4, perceptive management may react before descent below the acceptable threshold of performance, and in doing so increase the probability of success because more financial and other resources are available to it before their erosion by poor performance. However, the acceptable level of performance in most companies lies well above that which would lead to failure, so that even

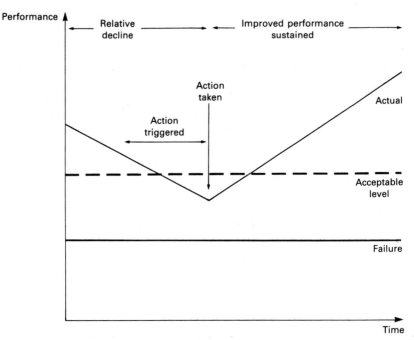

Figure 1.3 *Triggering action*

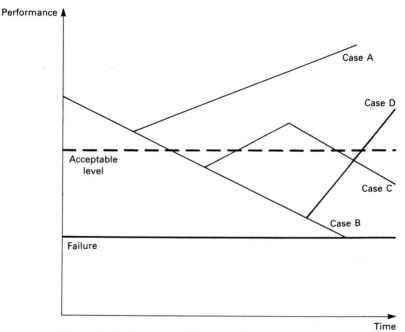

Figure 1.4 *Reactions to declining performance*

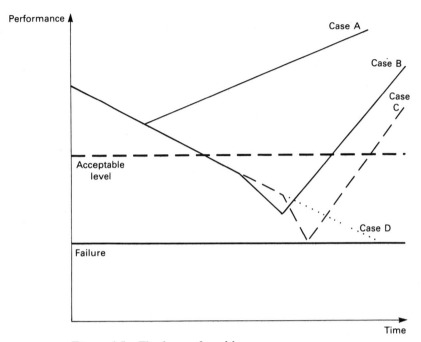

Figure 1.5 *The dangers from delay*

reaction to unacceptable actual, rather than anticipated, performance may lead to a sharpbend, as in case D. Case C illustrates an attempted but unsuccessful sharpbend. This may lead to the need for a turnaround. Equally, failure to react at all to an unsatisfactory trend in performance, as in case B, would force the company into a situation where only a turnaround could save it.

Clearly this simple model fails to capture adequately the dynamics of sharp change. First, it suggests either that the changes undertaken to generate a sharpbend produce immediate effects or that they are costless. In practice neither tends to be true and the actions taken to achieve a sharpbend may be expected to produce short-run deterioration in financial performance, which therefore dips below the downward trend before it is reversed. This is illustrated by cases B and C of figure 1.5. The latter illustrates the dangers of leaving action to correct the downward trend too late, for the company is in this case forced into a situation where a turnaround is required.

Second, the graphical representation in figures 1.3–1.5 suggests for ease of exposition that the aspiration or 'acceptable level' of performance is constant. This is clearly not so. In practice, it may be affected by actual performance, continued poor performance eroding expectations and aspirations and good performance increasing them. This is illustrated in figure 1.6. Moreover, observation of what others had done or perception of new opportunities, too,

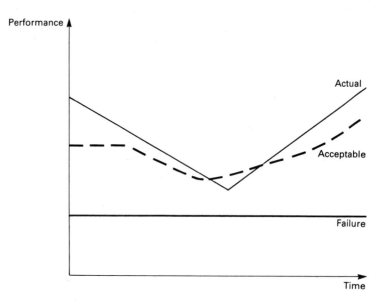

Figure 1.6   *Actual performance affects acceptability*

most certainly increased aspirations in some of the sharpbenders, in which a thrust for major improvement from a previously accepted plateau of performance was made by an unchanged team of senior managers, as in Ellis & Goldstein. Perhaps the most widely encountered cause for an increase in the acceptable level of performance, however, was change in corporate leadership. A new chairman or chief executive set himself a higher standard of performance than had been accepted as satisfactory in the past and induced the board and other senior management to accept it as both necessary and realistic. The company then sharpbent in response to new dissatisfaction with actual or projected performance. This is illustrated in figure 1.7.

The relatively simple model relating actual and anticipated performance to aspiration levels may therefore be extended to encompass the variety of triggers found in practice without losing its inherent simplicity. Moreover, this analysis suggests strongly why the trigger should be pulled because if it is delayed too long then the process of change is likely to be painful, involving redundancies and a major contraction before recovery is enjoyed. Furthermore it increases the risk that the result will be failure rather than a sharpbend.

In writing this book we are hoping to facilitate the process of sharp change, by showing how it has been done, and to encourage firms to *choose* to change; because if they wait until they are forced to, it may very well be too late. The incentive is clear. The sharpbenders have done very well, their management and shareholders have prospered. Benefits have been shared with the labour

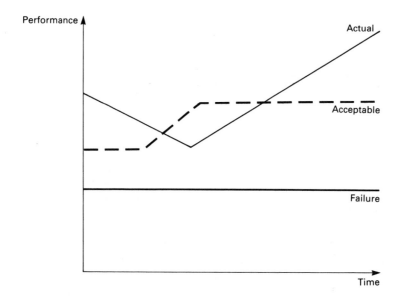

Figure 1.7 *A change in acceptability leads to a change in actual performance*

force and indeed employment has increased in many cases. The consumer has benefited through higher-quality and lower-cost products aimed more closely at his needs, and the economy as a whole has benefited through growth and through more efficient use of resources.

1.7 The Rest of the Book

In the chapters that follow we examine sharpbending in its four phases. The causes of decline (chapter 2), the triggers for change (chapter 3), the steps taken (chapter 4) and the characteristics of the continuing company (chapter 5).

2   The Causes of Relative Decline

To know what actions to take to improve the performance of companies we must first diagnose the causes of relative failure. Such causes are found both within the firm and externally. Almost by definition, such external environmental influences bear upon competitors as well. Success or failure turns on the ability of different companies to respond to the influences successfully and indeed where possible to change their environment proactively to their own advantage. Even in some of our leading companies, as in the case of Ferranti mentioned below, there has been failure to predict and to react to external and internal problems, which suggests either an inadequate diagnosis of causes of difficulty or failure to grasp the nettles.

Ultimately, therefore, relative decline tends to be due to a combination of external and internal factors. For example, by 1970 gross overcapacity in the industry had depressed prices and the level of business for Ferranti's transformer division. Between 1967 and 1973 it is estimated that over £20 million was lost, yet the division was not finally closed until 1984. This delayed closure occurred mainly because keeping the existence of division was a condition of government aid to the firm. Meanwhile capital and senior management time had been lost to the growth areas such as the electronics division. This example illustrates that lack of appropriate actions by managers, for understandable reasons, to deal with external pressures can ultimately lead to failure.

Among our sample of sharpbenders we found some general causes of decline (see table 2.1), the first two of which are clearly external and the remainder involve the behaviour of the firm to various degrees. Each firm will of course reflect these in some combination and although the table sets out the number of firms affected by each, this should be interpreted with care as the importance of the particular factor varies from case to case.

2.1   Adverse Changes in the Total Market Demand

It is no surprise that changes in overall market demand form by far the most important category of cause of relative decline as perceived by firms. In the downswing of economic cycles the spectrum of performance also moves downwards. Those who are at the lower end of it find that their position is

Table 2.1 *Causes of relative decline*

		% of sharpbenders citing this cause
1	Adverse changes in total market demand	75
2	Falling revenues due to more intense competition	60
3	Lack of marketing/sales effort	30
4	Poor management	45
5	Inadequate financial control	45
6	High-cost structure	65
7	Poor quality	10
8	Acquisitions	30
9	Big projects that fail	40

All figures rounded to nearest 5 per cent

approaching intolerable levels. The death rate of companies is much higher in recession. Thus we should expect to see simultaneous increases in the number of sharpbends, turnarounds and company failures as economic conditions worsen. Which of the three outcomes any one company experiences depends upon how badly the company is doing beforehand and upon the competence of management in tackling the problems. Those companies under the most extreme pressure fail, those under a little less can turnaround, and finally those where the pressure is strong but not overwhelming can sharpbend. It is for this reason that we find the sharpbends concentrated in the years immediately following 1974 and 1979.

However a very simple distinction can be made between a declining *trend* and the phenomenon of the general business *cycle*, as is set out in table 2.2. While cyclical decline is the cause cited most frequently there are clear examples of all the possibilities. In only four industries is cyclical decline not mentioned: electronics, offshore oil installations, knitting wool and footwear. The first two stand out from the pack as growth industries although the offshore oil industry was clearly subject to strong cycles. Sirdar suggested that knitting is relatively cheap and treated as a hobby by many, hence total demand may vary rather less with aggregate income as some people have more time to knit in a recession. The strong force of changing fashion may also help sustain demand. Although changing fashion also plays a role it is rather more difficult to explain what distinguishes footwear from the experience of most other industries and this may merely reflect the views of the particular respondents.

The form of the pressures under the other headings appears clear. Both electronics companies blamed changes in product technology for their period of relative decline while all three jute spinners blamed the introduction of new substitutes. Again it is clear that these pressures applied right across the

Table 2.2   *Reasons for a sustained drop in market demand*

		% of firms citing this factor
1.1	Change in product technology	10
1.2	New substitutes come on the market	20
1.3	Demographic changes	10
1.4	Changes in income and its distribution	10
1.5	Political changes	25
1.6	Cyclical fall	50
1.7	Other	0

industry. What distinguished the sharpbenders was that they subsequently responded to these pressures successfully.

Perhaps the most interesting example is Countryside Properties, where rates of net household formation are crucial to their work programme. Prior to 1972 the continuing excess demand for housing had meant that this particular reality of the market had not had a direct impact on the firm. Housing demand had risen with the income increases at the beginning of the decade but with the stalling of incomes in real terms, the high rates of interest and rapid increases in input costs the building industry was hard hit (see Mayes, 1979). All three building companies (Countryside Properties, McCarthy and Stone and the control) showed this strong cyclical pattern.

Some changes in the behaviour of the market were found to be caused by political decisions. These can be in the form of legislation or government action. W & R Balston, the manufacturing arm of what became Whatman Reeve Angel was working closely with NRDC on diagnostic enzymes and, with the promise of a large NHS contract, built a fully staffed and fully tooled plant at Maidstone. The government changed in 1970, altered the funding of NRDC and the NHS contract fell through. This was one of the three main factors leading to WRB's difficulties. Any firm supplying the electricity-generating industry is seriously affected by the fluctuations that have occurred in procurement.

Stuart Slatter (1984) has a very useful Table (2.1, pp. 26–7) deriving his own eleven causes of corporate decline from those of Argenti (1976), Schendel, Patton and Riggs (1976) and Sigoloff (1981). These causes are similar to our own, the major difference being one of extent as his companies were all involved in turnarounds (not all successfully). One well-known example of the problems of cyclical variation in market demand which he mentions (p. 42) is Hygena, the Norcros kitchen-furniture subsidiary, which expanded capacity late in the 1972/3 boom only to have it come on stream when demand had dropped drastically. This pattern is very well known on a macro-economic scale where investment surges in the upturn but because of

Table 2.3 *Reasons for falling revenues due to increased competition*

		% of firms citing this factor
2.1	Poor response to competitive changes	10
2.2	Failure to develop new products	10
2.3	Technological change lowers rivals' costs	5
2.4	Threat from substitutes keeps prices low	5
2.5	Removal of protection and other barriers to entry	10
2.6	High threat of potential entry	10
2.7	High exit costs keep competition intense in the face of falling sales	0
2.8	Lack of 'product market focus'	30
2.9	Lack of strong product differentiation	10
2.10	Lack of strong cost advantages	30
2.11	Other (e.g. low switching costs for customers)	10

the length of the time lag before it comes on stream (Mayes, 1981, ch. 4) much is too late to benefit the company as intended and supply surges ahead of demand, after the peak, leading to the usual stockbuilding cycle whose effects on production cause just such pressures as we have been discussing.

2.2 Falling Revenues due to Competitive Pressure

While the first group of causes affects the size of the market as a whole, the second group relates to the firm's relative position in the market because of changes in the way the market operates. None of these characteristics, set out in table 2.3, is as ubiquitous as the decline in market size but all feature in some measure.

The reasons set out in table 2.3 can be characterized into three groups:

1 *Those which relate to changes outside the control of the sharpbender:*
   (a) technological change lowers rivals' costs;
   (b) removal of protection and other barriers to entry.
2 *Others which relate to structural characteristics which* probably *already existed* but which made adjustment to the new, more hostile conditions, more difficult (this might include the declining trend):
   (a) threat from substitutes keeps prices low;
   (b) high threat of potential entry;
   (c) high exit costs keep competition intense in the face of falling sales.
3 *Indicators of failure by the sharpbender* itself *to respond* adequately *to the pressures* in this more competitive environment:
   (a) poor response to competitive change;

(b) failure to develop new products;
(c) lack of product market focus;
(d) lack of strong product differentiation;
(e) lack of strong cost advantages.

It is immediately clear from table 2.3 that it is the third of these categories which is the most important. Thus, although all facets are important and many firms cited factors in more than one category, it is clear that in the majority of respects there was scope for the firm to take action to offset this particular set of causes of relative decline. Hence it was not merely that circumstances were condemning them to ever-increasing problems – ways out existed.

In the traditional economics literature there are three possible forms of industrial structure, characterized as competition, cooperation and control. The structure of European industry under these three headings is summarized by de Jong (1987). His conclusions for the industries in this study which overlap with those described in his are set out in the Technical Appendix. The three areas picked out as exhibiting intense competition are semi-conductors and integrated circuits, textiles and pharmaceuticals. These three areas all feature in the report of competitive pressures, with the sole exception of Pringle of Scotland, while only seven other companies also report falling revenues due to competitive pressure.

Rivalry within the industry itself, the focus of de Jong's analysis of competitive pressures, is but one of five sources analysed by Porter (1980) each of which is reflected in table 2.3. The second source in Porter's framework, which is set out in table 2.4, is external, from new entrants or the threat of them. For a market to be efficient in competitive terms it is not actually necessary that it be contested by new entrants but only that those operating in the market believe that it is contestable (Baumol, Panzar and Willig, 1982; Bollard and Mayes, 1988). Interestingly enough only four companies cite removal or lowering of barriers to entry as a cause of competitive pressure and a further three quote the threat of new entry as a factor leading to their relative decline. For electronics companies the existence of such a threat came with the privatization of British Telecom and the ability

Table 2.4   *The competitive forces that determine profitability*

Rivalry among existing firms
Threat of new entrants
Bargaining power of suppliers
Bargaining power of buyers
Threat of substitutes

Source: Porter (1980)

of BT to buy supplies from a much wider range of sources. Even if BT do not exercise this ability they could do, and this increases very substantially the range of competitors and products over which a company has to be competitive in its telecommunications business.

Competition can also increase through growth of market demand, as this enables more companies to operate with the minimum efficient scale and hence attracts new entrants. Thus growth of market can have positive and negative influences. In a growing market all existing firms could gain but simultaneously new entrants are also encouraged by the prospects of growing turnover and higher profitability (a point which is covered well by Bain, 1956; Sylos-Labini, 1962; Modigliani, 1958; and Bhagwati, 1970). If one company can work out where market opportunities lie others can do the same. As Caves and Porter (1977) point out, rapid growth of market demand may also lead to more intense competition since the rewards from a larger market share are also increased. Furthermore, companies may believe that competitive moves by them are less likely to be detected by rivals since sales can be expanded without forcing contraction on a competitor.

Consideration of the possibility of entry leads one to question the general applicability of consulting firms' models, such as that of the Boston Consulting Group which suggested that there are clear advantages in getting into a market first. Such early entry and higher accumulated experience may give a competitive edge in some industries through lower costs, permitting a company to carve out a relatively secure market for itself. However, such cost advantages can often be overtaken by technological change. Markets tend to be relatively secure only where there are substantial barriers to entry.

To some extent this occurs where considerable product differentiation is possible, as in the case of Dawson International. Its relative decline in 1971–6 followed acquisitions in areas outside its own field of expertise and by overcentralization. Much of its subsequent success came from contracting back into business where it could exploit the potential for product differentiation as well as taking advantage of its experience of the business. Its famous brand names – Pringle of Scotland, Braemar, Ballantyne, Barrie, McGeorge, Glenmac and Gladstone – were promoted vigorously both at home and in export markets with conspicuous success.

Another example of a successful barrier to entry is that of Low & Bonar with their Flotex method of carpet-making. By obtaining the sole UK rights to the process from the French patent holder they were able to carve out a market share in a manner which could not be copied by their rivals. They were able to repeat this in other markets.

Some of the limits on rivalry between firms come from the costs to consumers of change. If one has a set of computers with a particular type of hardware and operating system, then although a rival company may be able to produce cheaper, more reliable machines and a more relevant set of software packages, it may nevertheless be uneconomic to change as all the equipment must be replaced rather than just some items at the margin. Some industries are more protected than others in this regard. Those with low product lifetimes and easy substitution by customers of one product for another, such as clothing or knitting wool, can be very susceptible to product changes by competitors and hence to sharp fluctuations in sales and profitability. It is perhaps for this reason that in both of these industries substantial expenditure is undertaken to establish and maintain a perception of differences between brands in the minds of consumers. When we are dealing with major items of equipment in electronics, telecommunications or heavy engineering this is much less true. A firm which becomes uncompetitive may continue for a while as it is difficult for purchasers to switch, but once they do this has long-run repercussions and it is very difficult for such firms to get back into the market.

This argument has introduced two more of Porter's (1980) influences on the competitive market. The first is the threat of substitutes. This can be within the industry, such as tufted instead of woven carpets, or between industries, such as man-made fibres for natural yarns. Not surprisingly the jute spinners emphasized the inroads made on their industry both from cheap imports from overseas and from new materials. They were thus driven out of the low-value-added part of the market both by competition from India and also by the use of artificial materials such as plastics for packaging.

The second influence on competition is the role of purchasers. Buyers' purchasing power can increase, perhaps because it becomes more concentrated, supplies being taken by only a few or even just one major company. For instance, the size of the contracts placed by Marks and Spencer and its major place in the distribution of clothing in the High Street is alleged to permit it to control specification, quality, cost and price structure of its suppliers. Nonetheless such control remains incomplete, which is a reason why some companies have purchased their suppliers. Such vertical integration has been practised by Dawson International, but in the period of relative decline it is the companies that are not taken over that suffer as potential purchasers satisfy their requirements elsewhere. Hence there are phases in market power as the direct pressure from a purchaser or potential purchaser increases with its market share and then changes as the purchaser is lost to the market having captured its own tied supplier. Competition among suppliers may have been reduced but so has competition for suppliers among the purchasers.

Some companies pursued this route for change of vertical integration in both directions: Bell's, for example, who bought a bottle-making plant by acquiring Canning Town Glass and a distribution company by purchasing Towmaster. In the period of relative decline it was actions like these by other companies which contributed to the sharpbenders' poorer performance.

The picture is completed by suppliers who can similarly become more concentrated and alter prices and availability and threaten vertical integration.

All these five features, rivalry within the industry, threat of new entrants, substitutes, purchaser and supplier power are reflected in table 2.4. We can see for example that economies of scale act as entry barriers in paper and board, and computers. PTT purchasers and national ordering in power plants exercises considerable control over the supplying industries. Textiles are protected and have been through the four Multi-Fibre Agreements. Most of the industries shown are heavily concentrated with the exception of textiles and paper and board, although the extent of such market control is often exaggerated as it does not allow for competition in export markets.

It is thus very clear that the way the firm can be influenced by competitive pressures in the period of relative decline depends very much on the market structure. The ending of cooperation agreements or the assertion of control can all have their adverse effects.

In our questioning we went on to try to determine the respects in which the competitive response had been weak. Lack of product differentiation was seldom cited but the lack of product market focus or strong cost advantages were much more widely found. In the former case the problem is simply a lack of focus. It is not so much a lack of good products but the inability to sell the right things to the right people at the right time.

2.3   Lack of Marketing/Sales Effort

It has been widely suggested that many problems facing UK firms stem from poor marketing. In our study we distinguished four aspects of marketing: (a) the sales force, (b) advertising, (c) market research, and (d) after-sales service. Other aspects such as distribution and packaging were not widely mentioned by firms. However, much effort on selling a product is wasted if the initial research on the nature of the market has not been undertaken. Equally, though, there needs to be effective selling and it is surprising how often in UK business selling seems to have been regarded as a vulgar activity. Thompson-McCausland and Biddle (1985) give a striking example. In their two-sentence mission statement for the company (the life assurance company, London Life) in 1985, the first began: 'to sell life assurance on competitive terms ... ' This apparently caused 'considerable disturbance ... a senior colleague took me quietly on one side and explained that in London Life selling was regarded as a dirty word'.

Interestingly enough our own sample suggested that these features were not very important in causing relative decline (table 2.5), yet most of the recent books on excellence stress the importance of getting close to the customer. Indeed they emphasize that marketing is a two-way relationship. The Midland Bank's slogan of 'the listening bank' is a clear example of trying to make this two-way relation explicit. Care of customers is one of the three main facets of Peters and Austin's (1985) model of the excellent company. The other two are 'people' and 'constant innovation' all set round a core of

Table 2.5   *Contribution of marketing to relative decline*

Lack of effective direction/control/use of	*% of firms citing this factor*
3.1 Salesforce	20
3.2 Advertising	10
3.3 Market research	15
3.4 After-sales service	0

'leadership'. Inkson *et al.* (1986) repeat the theme where 'Kustomer consciousness' (*sic*) forms one of the seven 'keys to excellence' in their 'Theory K'. The idea is probably summarized rather more clearly by Goldsmith and Clutterbuck's (1984) heading 'Market Orientation'.

Despite the low emphasis on marketing as a cause of decline there can be no doubt of its qualitative importance to marked improvements in performance of companies. As is shown in chapter 4, companies like Bell's, Macallan-Glenlivet and Sirdar changed markedly once vigorous action was taken to improve marketing.

A common cause of failure, in Rotaflex for example, was in not identifying the market segments where the firm's strength and abilities lay. A similar failure to focus can be seen in the Sidlaw Group in the early 1970s. We were conscious that after the sharpbend many of the firms were actively promoting themselves all the time. This importance of marketing has been noted elsewhere. In *Thrusters and Sleepers* (PEP, 1965, p. 165) one respondent put it that 'the job of the managing director is that of chief salesman'. Indeed, in their conclusion on the subject the authors quote one managing director as saying, 'But after all everything depends on selling. Without sales it is no good making anything anyway'. However, it is not just a matter of the quantity of the sales effort, advertising, market research, etc., which affects performance. It also depends upon how it is directed or controlled. In Bell's, after the sharpbend, Miquel took a close personal interest, having regular seven-weekly sales meetings where the performance of each sales area was examined thoroughly and 'public' examination of missed opportunities used to spur the group on to greater achievement. This sort of appraisal and experience was not usually observed in the companies in the period of relative decline.

After-sales service did not feature at all but this is perhaps a function of the small sample and its focus away from consumer markets, as it is clear from the work of the Domestic Electrical Appliance EDC that customers rate this facet of the product very highly and that UK companies' relatively poor record was an important contributor to import penetration (see NEDO, 1984). Sadly, however, it may reflect the continued failure of British management to recognize the importance of this factor in the analysis of past decline.

Table 2.6 *Poor quality and reliability as causes of relative decline*

	% of firms citing factor
4.1 Product or service sold	10
4.2 Documentation on product	0
4.3 Delivery times	0
4.4 After-sales service	0

2.4 Poor Quality and Reliability

Over the years, NEDO has stressed the importance of non-price factors in determining competitiveness. After-sales service is a well-known example but so are quality and reliability. Here again there was little evidence from our own sample of sharpbenders in the period of relative decline (table 2.6). Peters and Waterman (1982), on the other hand, have a section on 'quality obsession' which shows that the drive for ever-increasing quality is a central characteristic of many successful companies.

However, although low in terms of relative frequency, in those companies in which poor quality and reliability were cited as causes of decline their impact was clearly great. In Ferranti, for example, poor quality led to major difficulties for the firm. The company had succeeded in obtaining an important transformer contract with the Tennessee Valley Authority in the period before 1973, but the transformers supplied failed on impulse-testing – not meeting their required specification. Ferranti had to redesign and rebuild the machinery incurring heavy penalty clauses for late delivery. This not only caused a loss of £6–7 million but also laid them open to the charge of dumping as the equipment was supplied below cost and resulted in them being barred from the American market.

This can be contrasted with the opposite approach which was shown by many of the companies in their period of relative success. Sidlaw was able to compete in jute spinning by concentrating on the high-quality end of the market, and Bell's distinguished their product from other blends by selling it as a quality product attracting a higher price (and margin).

2.5 Poor Management

In one sense almost all reasons for relative decline in companies involve poor management because a good management team reacts to unfavourable circumstances and recovers. In this section therefore we have merely considered the general way in which management behaved as a cause of

Table 2.7   *Poor management as a cause of relative decline*

		% of sharpbenders citing this factor
5.1	Inflexible chief executive	10
5.2	Combined chairman and managing director	15
5.3	Insufficient executive directors	—
5.4	Insufficient non-executive directors	5
5.5	Non-executive directors not active	—
5.6	Directors hold few shares	5
5.7	Neglect of core business in diversification	5
5.8	Over-optimistic and incautious management style	10
5.9	Over-cautious and conservative management style	20
5.10	Failure to communicate effectively with management structure	30
5.11	Failure to communicate effectively with the workforce	15
5.12	Failure to create shared vision and values	30

relative decline rather than individual specific actions (see table 2.7).

Blame for management failure is frequently directed towards the top. Two issues have been frequently cited as contributing to the blame at this level, the first is the chief executive's management style and the second, the instances where the structure of the organization combines the role of chief executive and chairman, resulting in an overcentralization of power.

This is clearly not a universal finding as many success stories are heavily concentrated on the personality of the chief executive, take Raymond Miquel at Bell's or Philip Birch at Ward White, for example. The success of the company under these circumstances depends on the ability of the chief executive.

A highly able, forceful leader who combines the roles of chief executive and chairman may be able to respond entrepreneurially to changing market and internal circumstances more decisively and rapidly. On the other hand, where such a person is unsuccessful or too conservative it is more difficult for the executive or indeed non-executive to exert corrective influence effectively and things can go badly wrong. A particularly difficult situation is where a track record of substantial past success reinforces patterns of judgement which are no longer appropriate in changed circumstances and enhances the credibility and power of the combined chief executive and chairman, not only bolstering his belief in his own ability to handle the evolving situation in ways familiar to him but also making him unchallengeable until the failure becomes very clear indeed and possibly dramatic (Grinyer and Spender, 1979b).

As chairman and managing director, Miquel's predecessor was able to oppose the opening up of share ownership in Bell's prior to 1971. It was this widening which enabled the company to gain capital for expansion and acquire Canning Town Glass, a major move in the process of vertical integration which helped Bell's achieve its subsequent success. Similarly, the concentration of power of the chief executive and chairman in one person drawn from the family at Collins after 1969 was also said to have acted as a restraining influence on successful change although some of the problem in that case lay in lack of middle-management expertise. In the picture painted for us, top management were said not to have listened to middle management and middle management not to have listened to the workforce representatives. This seems in part to have stemmed from the almost military, hierarchical tradition of the old family firm. The family was said to have promoted faithful servants to middle-management positions on grounds of loyalty and long service. Many of the middle managers were thus still largely the sergeants serving the officer class (the family) but jealous of their own position *vis-à-vis* the ranks from which they had risen. Such sergeants did not challenge top management. To quote the union representatives at the Glasgow works whom we interviewed, 'until George Craig came no one would disagree with the family'. Trade-union suggestions to introduce new technology were actually rejected and by 1979 Collins was almost a decade behind the technology of its best competitors.

The nature of the management structure as a contributor to relative decline thus applies at all levels of management. We can relate this to the various headings set out in table 2.7 by grouping them as follows:

1   the role of the chief executive (5.1 and 5.2);
2   the role of the board of directors (5.3–5.6);
3   the attitude of top management (5.7–5.9); and
4   the ability of top management to communicate and motivate (5.10–5.12).

The experience of Collins is not unique to 'family' firms although similar remarks were made about the difficulties incurred by Sebastian de Ferranti's joint holding of the posts of chairman and chief executive in their period of difficulty before the sharpbend. However, in these circumstances the problem may lie not with the person concerned but with the organizational structure which allowed the circumstances to arise.

Our discussions with firms revealed differing views about the role of the board and of the individual directors. Some chief executives made it clear that they found little use for non-executive directors while others found them invaluable. Ellis & Goldstein Holdings had no non-executive directors on their board and their search for new products and ideas to revitalize the company's fortunes continued for a long time without success. That stimulation of external ideas and experience which can be available from non-executive directors might possibly have shortened the process and challenged conventional reactions effectively.

The facets of poor management which stand out from table 2.7 are those which relate to the general characteristics of senior management in terms of caution and optimism and to the ability to communicate and motivate within the organization. Only half as many companies cited over-optimism as a cause of trouble as caution leading to a failure to develop the opportunities available. Glaxo Holdings went through what was described as a period of complacency after a takeover bid by Beecham's in 1971–2 which failed. This was combined with factors we have discussed earlier: a worsening in competitive conditions through exchange-rate movements, a lack of an adequate marketing organization – in particular in those countries where demand was growing strongly, such as Japan, Europe and the US – a shortage of products to sell due to a lack of faith in the marketing staff – particularly no new substantial product to follow on from Ventolin, a highly successful drug in the 1960s. Together they led to the relative decline.

It is clear that issues related to adequate leadership are blurred with the organizational factors which form the core of section 2.7. Associated Paper Industries provides an example. While it was suffering from similar decline in its main markets with paper mills, it expanded into other areas such as coated laminates and stamping foils. However, prior to 1979 the group had a peculiarly weak structure. The central organization in 1970 amounted to a secretary sitting in a room in the offices of the Chairman, Leslie Farrow, in the City. No head office existed until 1979 when a small one with fifteen staff was set up by the present Managing Director John Graham. The lack of central direction was worsened because of the structure of executive management. There were two co-equal managing directors. One was responsible for the paper mills; the other, John Graham, was in charge of the remainder. Relations between the two seem to have been amicable but each represented a collection of vested interests and implicit bargains seem to have been struck between them with regard to items such as capital investment. With no central, overall, executive direction there was not the necessary means for pressing for disengagement from the increasingly unprofitable, general paper business.

In UDI the problem was that two of the three influential directors up to 1978 (John Hay and Ian Murray) were design engineers, people primarily involved with generating ideas rather than managing resources. The man in charge of administration, Peter See, faced a hard task on his own in the face of this combined interest and the company suffered from an excessive expenditure on product development. Again in UDI, after the takeover by John Brown it is clear there was confusion in the company between those who were trying to pursue goals set out by John Brown and those who were pursuing their own design objectives.

Many authors have stressed the importance of management creating a clear set of 'shared values' in the company. Thompson-McCausland and Biddle (1985) emphasize this in the context of London Life and indeed nearly half their book is about creating this jointness of purpose in the organization as a whole. It forms the core of the McKinsey '7S' framework:

Structure
Strategy
Systems
Skills
Style
Staff
Shared values

and is incorporated in the Peters and Waterman (1982) framework in the phrase 'Hands-on, value driven'. They say (p. 279) that if they were asked for 'one all purpose bit of advice for management, one truth (to) distill from the excellent companies research, (they) might be tempted to reply, "Figure out your value system. Decide what your company stands for. What does your enterprise do that gives everyone the most pride? Put yourself out ten or twenty years in the future: what would you look back on with the greatest satisfaction?"'

This failure to obtain a common set of beliefs is quoted in 30 per cent of cases and its existence is claimed as a reason for success among the sharpbenders. While this appears to be a less striking facet than in the US literature, nevertheless loss of morale and lack of enthusiasm are very obvious factors contributing to relative decline.

2.6   Inadequate Financial Control

One of the most obvious failures of management is in control of the business. Lack of financial control is a clear route to financial difficulty but in a less extreme situation it means that the firm cannot sort out what it does best, where it is losing money and what action should be taken. Almost half the sharpbenders cited this group of factors among the causes of their relative decline, although only one individual item, shown in table 2.8, was quoted by a quarter or more of the firms.

There is a distinction to be drawn between a lack of appropriate information and the inability of the firm to use the information that it does have. In some cases the two are related. For Collins, production and stock-control methods were loose and rather ineffective, which meant delivery delays and higher work in progress. They also burdened themselves with high interest costs as a result of financing a new factory by loans rather than a rights issue. This position was worsened by the practice of running large

Table 2.8   *Causes of relative decline from inadequate financial control*

	% of firms citing this factor
6.1 Lack of cash-flow forecasts	15
6.2 Lack of costing systems	5
6.3 Lack of budgetary controls	10
6.4 Management accounting information for top management too infrequent or late	25
6.5 Management accounting information: too voluminous/complex/irrelevant/wrong	10
6.6 Top management not 'numbers-orientated'	5
6.7 Costs distorted by arbitrary allocation of overheads	0
6.8 Failure to control working capital	15
6.9 Other (for example, asset-valuation problems)	10

editions, to get economies of long runs, which often did not sell leaving large sums of working capital tied up in stock that was sometimes obsolete.

As the case of UDI illustrates it is not just having accounting systems which matters, they have to be relevant and effective. When John Brown took over UDI in 1978 various plans and accounting techniques were introduced but staff changed rapidly. The firm lost John Hay, one of the original founding members, because he found the various disciplines required constrained his development of ideas; nevertheless this did not arrest the large sums of money that Seabug, their seabed-crawling vehicle for surveying pipelines, was absorbing, sapping the viability of the company. In the twelve months to December 1978, the date of the takeover, UDI made a loss of £191,000, whereas in the fifteen months to March 1980 this rose to £870,000 (an increase of more than three times on an annual basis).

Stuart Slatter (1984) gives a clear survey of most of the requirements and failings with respect to financial control. Many firms, particularly small ones, have failed to provide up-to-date information on their cash position. Yet it is negative cash flows not annual profitability which lead to insolvency. Moreover, monthly management accounts can signal impending problems and pinpoint causes of difficulty long before annual reports are produced in arrears by auditors. Secondly, in undertaking contracts and in pricing a firm needs to have a clear costing basis so that an adequate return is made on every item of work. Furthermore, it is clear that the firm needs to have a clear system of budgets, setting out what it is expected to achieve.

These alone are insufficient as there need to be means of assessing performance against targets and then taking effective action in the event of any warning signals. Such action is less likely where management has too much information as well as too little, when signals to top management on impending problems and need for action can be obscured by the welter of detailed, complex or barely relevant data. Similarly, control information can be too late as in Countryside Properties which had a manually produced cash-flow forecasting system as early as 1968. Preparation of the accounts took sufficiently long that the results tended to be overtaken by events, especially in periods of rapid change.

2.7 Organization

There is a large literature relating the organizational structure of companies to their environment, characteristics and success (see, for instance, Child (1984) for a useful synthesis and discussion). Much of this has involved the advantages and disadvantages of using bureaucratic devices such as job definitions and use of specialist staff as a strategy for control of lower-level operations. A certain amount of research by organizational theorists suggests that the formal aspects of such bureaucracy, which are by nature inflexible, are inappropriate when a company is operating in a dynamic, unstable, changing market (e.g. Burns and Stalker, 1961).

The substitution of formal, written controls and communication for the spoken word in face-to-face contact is the aspect of bureaucratic structure which most offends the proponents of the recent 'excellence' theories. It is clear from Peters and Austin (1985) that they feel that bureaucratic structures are the enemy of excellence and in private conversations more recently Tom Peters had been adopting a much harsher attitude as this quotation from a letter dated 20 August 1986 indicates:

> In short when I look at the US manufacturing picture in particular, I still see (1) absurdly heavy management bloat, (2) across the board questionable (i.e. shoddy) quality, (3) service that is laughable, (4) a lack of innovativeness/flexibil-ity/responsiveness (off the needed pace by perhaps a factor of 10), (5) pathetic international exporting skills, and (6) portfolios still loaded with odds and ends whose being under the same roof makes no sense whatsoever (except in the egotistical quest for size for size's sake).

The problem as Peters and Waterman saw it was a tension between maintaining enough control and information to be confident that junior managers were doing their job effectively to achieve the objectives of the company, while simultaneously trying to allow them the freedom to use all the flair and innovative skills they could muster. Three of Peters and Waterman's eight points which characterize excellent American companies apply to this tension in organization. They are: 'autonomy and entrepreneurship, simple form lean staff, simultaneous loose–tight properties.' To get the best out of people they have to be given their head but, as we have seen in the previous

Table 2.9   *Causes of relative decline from organizational structure*

	% of firms citing this factor
7.1 Centralized organization structure hindered effective allocation of financial responsibility to operating management	20
7.2 Centralized organization structure slowed response to changing market conditions	15
7.3 Too decentralized decision-making without adequate controls led to lack of coordination and control	20
7.4 Too formal and bureaucratic management systems slowed rate of response to changing environmental conditions	5
7.5 Head office too large and expensive	10
7.6 Other	5

sub-section, subject to certain controls. Peters and Waterman clearly suggest, from all but one of the remaining eight characteristics, that much of the direction and control of the company should be by means of common values which will drive performance, *viz.* a bias for action, closeness to customers, productivity through people and hands-on orientation (as is set out below).

The Peters and Waterman eight characteristics of excellence

1 A bias for action.
2 Close to the customer.
3 Autonomy and entrepreneurship.
4 Productivity through people.
5 Hands-on, value driven.
6 Stick to the knitting.
7 Simple form lean staff.
8 Simultaneous loose–tight properties.

Clearly, organizational weaknesses can compound the effects of poor financial control (see table 2.9). When Fisons was finding that it could not compete with fertilizer giants such as ICI with their special access to low-cost inputs, the position was accentuated by poor financial control which led to a rapid build-up of debts and substantial overgearing. Inhibitions to communication acted as an effective barrier to change at Collins.

The tension between tightness and looseness is shown most clearly by the fact that virtually equal numbers of sharpbenders suffered relative decline because of overcentralization as from over-decentralization. We would not infer from this that there is some happy halfway house, but rather that there is an appropriate degree of centralization for each individual company which is often not achieved. What is appropriate for a firm is contingent on the nature of its products, its markets and their location, its technology and size and the abilities of its managers. Moreover, most successful arrangements seem to incorporate elements of both centralization and decentralization.

They key issue is what decisions should be centralized and what decentralized. For instance, Ward White have tight central control over financial aspects of their business but have organized the individual component firms into industry divisions to ensure focused management. As Dawson International expanded after the purchase of Pringle in 1967, it purchased further companies in the same industry with names such as Braemar, Glenmac, McGeorge, Barrie, and Ballantyne, and centralized marketing as well as financial decisions. Particularly after it expanded into areas outside textile manufacturing between 1971 and 1975, centralized marketing was found to impede rapid reaction to changing market conditions and led to poor decisions. Excessive centralization, by removing authority and responsibility from the general managers of the subsidiaries also blunted the capacity and will of the subsidiary general managers to take either hard or entrepreneurial decisions. Yet a system of centralized financial control is critical for the coordination of activities.

One organizational problem observed from our fieldwork but not captured by table 2.9 is that of speed or organizational change. In the case of UDI it was not just the new structure introduced after the takeover by John Brown in 1978 which contributed to the problem, bogging down what had been a small organic company in a tight, formal planning mechanism, but the fact that 'too much was imposed on us too quickly', in the words of the current Chairman, Michael Hosking. Thus change in organizational structure as well as the structure itself can contribute to relative decline. This must be borne closely in mind in the context of a sharpbend. While a change in organizational structure may contribute to the successful bend such changes can also have the opposite effect. They are neither sufficient nor always necessary for the bend.

2.8   High-Cost Structure Relative to Competitors

A further major cause of relative decline was simply poor cost competitiveness. (Non-cost causes of failure to compete effectively such as poor delivery, marketing and after-sales service have been examined in the earlier sections of this chapter.) Table 2.10 shows the reason. Two stand out, *viz.* excess capacity and high interest/capital costs. These are very much the reflection of the periods before the sharpbend in macro-economic terms where the economy was in decline leading to a fall in demand and excess capacity, but also where

Table 2.10   *Causes of decline from high-cost structure*

	% of firms citing this factor
8.1 Market share too low to exploit economies of learning and scale	15
8.2 Competitors have 'absolute advantages' such as	
(a) tied suppliers of cheap raw materials	10
(b) immobile/superior R&D or managerial staff	—
(c) immobile, cheap or higher-quality labour	15
(d) proprietary production technology or know-how	—
(e) favourable location	5
(f) tied, superior, channels of distribution	5
8.3 Poor production control	5
8.4 Poor plant layout	5
8.5 Low labour productivity	
(a) morale	10
(b) inflexible job demarcation	5
(c) opposition to new practices	10
8.6 Excessive levels of wages	5
8.7 Strikes	—
8.8 Excess plant capacity (high fixed costs)	30
8.9 Difficulties with raw-material supplies	—
8.10 Bargaining power of supplier inflated costs of raw materials or components	—
8.11 Poor financial policy	10
8.12 Capital overgearing, inflated interest charges	25
8.13 Operational gearing too high	10
8.14 Other	15

policy measures had to be introduced both to reduce inflation and contain demand which necessarily raised interest rates. Thus several companies were in the unhappy position of being both over-capitalized and having to pay heavily for the privilege.

The jute spinners reported over-capacity as did the two plant and process companies. Gearing had also increased in the jute industry making diversification more difficult. In a sense, therefore, these problems are largely the upshot of the secular and cyclical declines in market demand.

Many of the remaining issues brought out in table 2.10 also refer to explicit cost problems. It is noticeable that none of the companies encountered heavy costs because of strikes. This is not because strikes were not a feature of the period we are examining. Particularly in the 1970s they featured strongly in industrial behaviour. While this could be a random finding it may indicate that firms which suffered from severe labour problems were by and large unable to become sharpbenders. There are notable exceptions. Major changes have proved possible in British Leyland and British Steel. Before its recovery, the former was plagued by strikes, both among its own labour force and by suppliers; while in the case of British Steel a major strike had to be endured before the changes could be fully implemented. By contrast, the characteristic of many of the firms that we visited was that they had good and constructive relations with their labour force and trade unions. Ward White was a particular case in point. This absence of importance of strikes as a determinant of decline is echoed in Slatter (1984).

Cost disadvantages can occur for many reasons, one of the simplest of which is size. In an industry with economies of scale, which characterize a lot of manufacturing, unit costs will be higher for smaller companies as their overheads are spread over a smaller range of output and they have less bargaining power both as a buyer and as a seller. Fisons quoted this very clearly in comparison with ICI and other fertilizer giants. The position is of course exacerbated if plants are not operating at full capacity. Such higher costs result in lower profits and hence a reduced ability to invest in machinery to produce at lower cost or in marketing to increase the scale of operation. There can thus be a vicious circle of high costs, lower investment, older equipment and hence higher costs, particularly for smaller companies which can neither exploit economies of scale nor move profits between activities and hence cross-subsidize those areas which are in difficulty.

There are other features of the environment which may lead to higher-cost structures. However, the extent to which these 'environmental' factors can be viewed as being outside the firm's control is always debatable. Indeed, it was changing many of them which enabled sharpbends to be accomplished for several of our sample. A major difference between the successful and the less successful is the extent to which factors which affect the firm are regarded as alterable by the firm's own actions or as a fixed part of the environment in which they operate and facts of life which have to be lived with. Location is a simple example. Low & Bonar with a Canadian paper- and textile-bag manufacturing company found that they could not break into the lucrative US market. A component of the sharpbend was the change in the nature of the product, by moving into plastics, and the change of location of its production by moving into the US from Canada.

Collins on the other hand showed that a change of location could actually misfire. Prior to the 1970s their printing and binding activities were located in old premises in Cathedral Street, Glasgow. Machines were somewhat antiquated. The building was multi-storey, different levels being called 'flats', and hence physical movement between stages of production was more expensive. The disadvantages were clear. The company therefore moved to a 'greenfield' site at Westerhill outside the city centre. However, the move misfired because the workforce had to be transported out from the city which took longer and was less convenient. It was no longer possible to slip out to the shops to buy food or have a haircut at lunchtime. The division of the workforce into groups by the flats had developed good social and working relationships which were broken by the unified works. Thus location or other 'environmental' factors alone are not always the explanation of the company's difficulties; it depends how they use them.

Sometimes location of factors cannot readily be changed. A close comparison of British Steel's plant at Ravenscraig with Hoogovens in the Netherlands (see Mayes, 1983) undertaken by NEDO showed that the setting of the Dutch plant, with ready access to the inward supply of new materials and outward delivery of the finished products, had made a major contribution to the Dutch plant's lower costs. Moving Ravenscraig would have been financially impossible. The cost differential therefore had to be overcome by other means. This particular comparison also revealed further 'environmental' advantages for the Dutch plant from higher-grade ore and from larger-scale equipment. There is thus a continuum of alterable and inalterable 'environmental' factors with no clear distribution between the alterable and the inalterable.

This dependence extends to raw materials as was noted in the case of Fisons, with the lack of such favourable access as its major competitors. Energy is a commonly cited example. One of the most extreme examples of this worldwide is the aluminium smelter at Tiwai Point at the very south of New Zealand. There the ore is shipped 2000 miles from Australia, smelted and then most of the product is shipped overseas again, all purely to take advantage of New Zealand's ability to produce cheap hydroelectricity as a major input to the smelting process. It was actually worthwhile constructing an elaborate hydroelectric system purely for the smelter involving an underground power station hewn out of the rock and a long tail race to take the water from Lake Manapouri out in the opposite direction from the natural flow under the main divide to the remote west coast of Fiordland.

Interestingly enough, none of the companies cited differences in R&D or managerial resources as a cause of the relative decline (the remarks on poor management made earlier apart). This is somewhat surprising, as a number of companies which have effected sharp improvements in performance through the takeover route – such as the Hanson Trust – are thought to offer superior management skills. Similarly with R&D it is suggested (Commission of the European Communities, 1986) that small firms have a relative disadvantage through high R&D costs and that UK industries which devote relatively more resources to R&D than their overseas competitors have a relatively better export performance (NEDO, 1984a). This is also likely to apply to the individual firm. It is the absolute amount as well as the relative amount of R&D which helps determine its success.

It is similarly surprising that no firm quoted the lack of proprietary production technology or know-how as being a cause of relative decline. Low & Bonar clearly pointed to the reverse as a contributor to their relative success with the Flotex carpet-making operation, licensed from France. Indeed such proprietary knowledge is an essential ingredient for success for any company like Fisons involved with the pharmaceutical industry.

Characteristics of the labour force were, however, noted in a number of cases. Low & Bonar and the Sidlaw Group both faced difficulties in trying to diversify in Dundee. Those in textiles found that in many areas there was no way they could compete with cheap imports from low-labour-cost countries overseas and hence like Ellis & Goldstein they turned more towards imports.

However, it is not just the availability of resources which leads to high costs but also the way in which they are used. Collins, for example, clearly suffered from poor production control as runs tended to be too long (through attempts to capture economies of scale) and hence unsold stock exacerbated storage problems and the ability to respond flexibly was reduced. Causes 8.5–8.7 in table 2.10 deal with the role of the labour force in relative decline. We have already noted that strikes had little role to play, however various other facets are noticeable. Ferranti, for example, suffered a very considerable loss of morale, not aided by resistance to change and difficulties in flexibility caused by rigid job boundaries. When matched with the sort of financial difficulties that have been mentioned, the opportunity for a firm to collapse quite rapidly is very high.

2.9 Acquisitions

Most of the causes of relative decline we have considered so far tend to have stemmed from inaction. It is in this mould that *Thrusters and Sleepers* (PEP, 1965) was cast. At that time some firms could be clearly identified as go-getters while others were more concerned with a relatively less stressful, quietly successful approach. This second group tended to miss the opportunities available and hence do relatively badly in comparative terms. In this and the following section, however, we consider two examples where firms have come unstuck because of action rather than because of the lack of it. Action is not a guarantor of success although prolonged inaction almost invariably guarantees relative failure.

In this section we see examples of where the path forward is hindered by poor acquisitions. Although many firms like Ward White, Fisons, and Low & Bonar have based much of their success on a policy of careful acquisitions it is also clear that poor acquisitions can bring a firm down. Stuart Slatter (1984) emphasizes this in his book on turnarounds. There he identifies three ways in which an acquisition can help bring the acquirer down, first because the acquired company is weak, second because too high a price is paid and last because the acquirer fails to turn the new business to his advantage through poor management. These factors are brought out specifically in table 2.11.

The frequency with which acquisition of a competitively weak company was

Table 2.11   *Poor acquisitions as a cause of relative decline*

	% citing this factor
9.1 Acquired companies with weak competitive positions	20
9.2 Paid too much for acquisition	5
9.3 Poor post-acquisition management	10
9.4 Other	10

noted as a cause of relative failure is instructive. In some cases this was due to lack of understanding of a business into which the acquirer was diversifying, which resulted in failure to understand the competitive position of its acquisition (see below). On occasion, lack of access to information internal to the intended acquisition created difficulties obscuring changes in relative costs. There was perhaps too often an assumption that trends would continue without a fundamental study of changing market conditions. However, it could well be that some at least saw competitive weakness as an opportunity to acquire assets at a low price, a policy that can be disastrous unless the acquirer has available management personnel with the skills, experience and personal qualities required to transform a competitively weak to a strong subsidiary, and is willing and able to back this new management with the necessary capital.

There are, however, some general themes running through this subject as enunciated both by Slatter (1984) and by Peters and Waterman (1982). A major reason for acquisitions failing is that the acquirer knows too little about the business. Peters and Waterman therefore recommended 'sticking to the knitting'. However, this precept runs contrary to the whole formula of success of companies such as Low & Bonar which diversified out of a declining industry or of those such as Hillsdown Holdings which have made their main advances largely by arguing that they would manage other companies better. Even the Sidlaw Group, which was rather more cautious, pursued careful diversification into hardware, hotels and oil support businesses.

Low & Bonar are a very good illustration of the advantages and disadvantages of acquisitions. Their downturn in 1980 was accentuated by the acquisition of Nairn Travel, a company which was in a very different industry from their main lines of business. Although the branches were concentrated in the part of Scotland where much of Low & Bonar's business lay, this was an insufficient link. Low & Bonar entered the industry at the peak of a boom. They discovered that firms with fewer than 200 outlets could not get the maximum discounts from travel operators and hence were at a disadvantage. Fortunately they were able to achieve a quick exit and merged the business with a specialist travel firm, A T Mays, which took a 35 per cent share and provided the management.

Acquisitions in engineering also provided difficulties in this case largely because of the depressed nature of the industry. Low & Bonar acquired the GHP group in the 1970s. This included Hugh Smith, which made hydraulic presses and sheet-bending equipment, and Brentford, a company involved in alloys and special pumps. Brentford relied on sales to the oil and petrochemical companies, while Hugh Smith specialized in large machines often costing £1 million each. Both suffered in the recession and had to be closed down. Hugh Smith also suffered because their main competitor was a state-owned Swedish concern which was being heavily subsidized.

However these difficulties stand in clear contrast to Low & Bonar's success, which has been mainly through acquisition in a diversified manner both domestically and overseas. Indeed the organization was changed to a regional, rather than an industry, basis in the early 1980s so as to encourage the establishment of well-diversified companies in each individual market, 'miniature Low & Bonars' as the finance director described them.

The over-pricing of takeovers is well known and has been shown for the US and Australia as well as the UK. The major beneficiaries tend to be the shareholders of the acquired firms. Slatter advises sensibly that there are two routes which are likely to succeed: the first where an acquisition can offer specialist support in a related business which the existing management does not possess and, the second where an acquired firm may be in an unrelated business but has all the hallmarks of potential success. Clearly the latter are difficult to define but reflect the characteristics of the successful sharpbenders discussed in chapters 4 and 5.

One of the problems with acquisitions is that the expenditure rarely stops with the acquisition itself, unless major reductions in the size of the business are envisaged, and hence the problems of paying too high a purchase price are compounded. Associated Paper Industries acquired George Whiley in 1978. It had a strong market position and looked as if it would do well in the future. In fact it did worse, contributing to heavy cash-flow losses in 1979 and 1980. Technical expertise was lost because skilled personnel were reluctant to move to Scotland and top management seemed to be unable to cope with the problem. In the sharpbend, this was resolved by changing top management and getting rid of a number of loss-making facets both at home and overseas.

In summary, it can be seen that acquisition is clearly a difficult area but one which can feature strongly in both success and failure.

2.10 Big Projects that Failed

Another contributor to both successes and failures has been big projects. Indeed some acquisitions are in effect big projects. If a company attempts anything large relative to its own size then the risks of failure necessarily become much more important. What would be an irritating short-run setback

Table 2.12 *Big projects that fail as a cause of relative decline*

		% of firms citing this factor
10.1	Failure of big project	30
10.2	Reasons given for failure	
	(a) poor cost-estimating	10
	(b) poor project control	10
	(c) design changes	10
	(d) start-up difficulties	15
	(e) high market-entry costs	10
	(f) capacity needs overestimated	10
	(g) other	10

for a large company can erode corporate performance badly and even lead to insolvency for a small enterprise. On the whole, small ventures have too little impact on corporate performance to warrant expenditure of senior management time. Clearly, the concern should be to ensure that big projects are successful rather than to avoid them.

From table 2.12 it can be seen that, in 30 per cent of the firms, failure of such big projects contributed to relative decline – one of the largest single causes of relative decline. The reasons for the failures, shown in table 2.12, may be summarized as poor design, poor planning and poor control. Sometimes, as with start-up difficulties with Flotex at Low & Bonar, there were technical difficulties which could not be foreseen. Recovery depended in these cases on energetic action. In many cases, as with Seabug at UDI, once successful, the big project contributed powerfully to the sharpbend. The Seabug example is instructive.

Over the period 1975–80 the development of Seabug, a seabed-crawling vehicle for surveying pipelines, dominated the fortunes of UDI. Its development required a major investment in design and the recruitment of an engineering team. It consumed cash at a rate the firm could not afford and by 1978 the firm was in severe financial difficulties and was not able to sustain continued independent existence. It was taken over twice, first by an insurance company, and then by John Brown in December 1978, because they felt that UDI had a sound design team with a potentially successful product in Seabug.

However, change in ownership did not solve the problem. Still more money was ploughed into Seabug. As mentioned earlier in this chapter, there was a welter of new executives, while plans and accounting techniques were introduced by John Brown which served rather to confuse and demotivate than bring the project·under effective control.

Between 1975 and 1980 Seabug consumed over £2 million in development funds compared with a turnover in 1980 of only £2.3 million for the company as a whole. Expenditure was not monitored closely, in the early days because the developers were the main figures in the company. At the same time other development projects were under way on various sonars and TV equipment, also with no real monitoring of expenditure. The actual path of development was further hindered by the pursuit of government grants whereby research was undertaken in part because it would attract the grants rather than because it would advance the project itself.

It was not until Michael Hosking was brought in as Managing Director, in February 1980, to oversee the Seabug project and pull the company together, that the necessary rationalization and consolidation took place. Effort was concentrated on the Seabug rather than the multiplicity of bright ideas that had characterized previous periods and within several years it was generating substantial profits. These in turn were then used to develop new products.

UDI thus exemplifies several of the characteristics given in table 2.12. There was poor estimating of what the costs were going to be, and poor control of the project thereafter. The design was changed on a number of occasions. Because of the nature of the product, the market-entry costs were very high as the development had to take place first.

Some industries are more prone to the risks associated with projects than others. We have already noted the vulnerability of companies to changes in the demand for electricity-supply capacity, especially in the nuclear field. Similarly, some of the electronics projects can be very substantial as is evidenced with respect to telecommunications equipment. The same can be said of defence contracts, something which has affected Ferranti and more recently GEC, in the case of the Nimrod airborne early-warning radar.

Problems of big projects failing to perform to specification, in particular start-up difficulties, were the single largest cause of failure of projects and among the most costly. Ferranti's problems in its transformer contract with the Tennessee Valley Authority, where in retrospect the initial costs had been underestimated, also provides an example. Because the equipment did not perform to specification, major changes were required which delayed delivery and penalty clauses were invoked. This resulted in a loss of £6–7 million on the project. A cash-flow problem ensued which was exacerbated by the dumping suit which effectively closed the US market to Ferranti. Another example which we have also already noted briefly is Low & Bonar's problems with the Flotex carpet-making operation. Not only were there the initial problems in 1973 when Brian Gilbert took over, with the company losing £700,000 a year, but in 1979 it was decided to put a new line on to Flotex. This took eighteen months to arrange and although proven technologies were used they were applied in a unique combination. The printing process did not work well and in one month the company lost £250,000 on the operation. For the year as a whole this turned a £700,000 profit into a £300,000 loss. Thus although Low & Bonar had spent $3 million on obtaining the Flotex plant and licences in the first place and had had difficulty starting up, they still, even as a successful sharpbender, encountered further difficulties with the same large project. Nevertheless, in the long term this was a successful operation, having earned around £1 million profits in 1984.

The problem for most companies was that although the big projects on their own would have been surmountable, these problems occurred in combination with other causes of decline – usually a cyclical downturn in business as a whole. Indeed, the cyclical downturn could be a major reason for the difficulties with the large project, because demand was depressed when the capacity generated by a big project came into operation.

2.11 The Combination of Causes

It was rarely the case that any one cause was sufficient to lead to relative decline. It was the combination of them which undermined the performance and in some cases threatened the long-term survival of the company. Thus, for Low & Bonar in the mid-1970s it was not merely Flotex which provided the problems, there was also an earlier lack of management accounting with no budgets or monthly accounts. The management was highly centralized with detailed decisions being made by the parent board when it met in Dundee every Monday morning. Some other constituent firms faced major strategic difficulties – Bonar Long because they were in an industry with over-capacity and the Canadian paper- and textile-bag company because it was restrained from entering the potentially lucrative US market – but these were obscured by the amount of detailed information yielded by a control system designed for the week-to-week operation of a textile business.

Each case is different and the reading of the vignettes on each company at the end of the book will help to provide the flavour of the combinations that occurred in practice. If we return to table 2.1 for a moment we can see the way in which the picture is built up. Most companies suffered from (a) adverse changes in total market demand, (b) falling revenues due to more intense competition, (c) a high-cost structure; while nearly half the companies suffered from (d) poor management, (e) inadequate financial control, and (f) big projects that failed. Thus most companies exhibit several of these major characteristics.

This tells us that the recipe for a successful sharpbend is not a simple one. Several major factors of the firms' behaviour will need to be changed radically. The changes that need to be made will depend on the nature of the causes of relative decline. Thus in the chapters which follow we link the triggers to change, the steps taken and the characteristics of the continuing successful business, to the original causes of decline, and see what responses appear to be successful in each circumstance so as to be able to provide a guide to the appropriate action for other companies.

3 Triggers of Radical Change

From chapter 2 it may be seen that the causes of decline of most of the companies visited seemed clear with the benefit of hindsight. Retrospectively, it is fairly easy to point to actions that would better have been avoided and indeed to suggest strategies which would have prevented some of the problems and would have resolved others. At the time things were not so clear. For instance, it is always a difficult judgement to decide whether a fall in demand is a temporary cyclical decline, part of a long-run secular trend or the result of uncompetitive prices, poor quality or inadequate marketing.

A wrong diagnosis, leading to inappropriate action, can compound a relative or absolute decline. Perhaps, for this reason many companies respond to mounting difficulties by implementing the well-tried strategy more vigorously and by trying harder rather than making fundamental changes to meet changed environmental and market conditions.

In contrast, the sharpbenders took identifiable actions which radically changed their situations. This raises the question as to what triggered them. The pattern of action which emerges has lessons for others who would also like their companies to sharpbend.

3.1 The Need for a Trigger

In chapter 1 we suggested that during the period of relative decline firms sometimes seem to adjust downwards their expectations of what constitutes a satisfactory performance, thus postponing the point at which they decide to take action. Once performance is unsatisfactory in the eyes of the firm itself then the chance of major steps being taken to rectify the position are increased. Nevertheless, there has to be some particular set of circumstances which stimulate the firm into taking radical enough actions to achieve a sharpbend.

From the experience of the companies in our sample it appears that many factors can contribute to provide the initial push. The simplest circumstance to understand is the turnaround. Here it is obvious to all concerned that unless the firm takes action it will go into liquidation. It may be the threat of going into receivership imminently or the refusal of an increase in lending by the bank which is the last straw but the essence of these circumstances – as described by Stuart Slatter – is that there is a crisis.

In a crisis people act and act quickly. However, if they wait until the crisis is upon them then their scope for action may be severely limited. If the main way out is to invest in new products and processes the company which waits until its reserves and borrowing power are exhausted will find it much more difficult to institute successful changes. It is considerably preferable to diagnose a problem early on and act upon it in a swift but considered manner, and it is this characteristic which distinguishes the sharpbend. But what induces companies to undertake such an analysis and subsequent action when they are not in any danger of going out of business? The sharpbenders, for instance, were merely in *relative* decline and in some cases could have carried on, largely unchanged, almost indefinitely.

There are other reasons why acting earlier is to be preferred to waiting for a crisis. In a crisis people may react inadequately and take poorer decisions; moreover as Slatter points out there is going to be a tendency for firms which are not good at making decisions to end up in crises. Crisis management requires considerable talents – as Slatter puts it 'beyond a certain point stress becomes anxiety-producing rather than motivational'. However, he also argues that it is generally recognized by students of organizational behaviour that some degree of stress is a necessary prerequisite for problem-solving, for without it there is no motivation to act.

It is thus clear that a wider explanation is required for sharpbends. The chance of a sharpbend increases as the gap between actual performance and aspirations widens. The gap can thus widen if aspirations rise just as it can if performance worsens. The speed of widening will also affect the outcome. A sharp upward leap in aspirations, say from the arrival of a new chief executive, is more likely to generate a sharp response, than is a steady rise in the level over a longer period of time. This mirrors the effect of a sharp deterioration in performance.

Although sharpbends appear to be stressful they have a better chance of success than a turnaround because they lack the pressure from having to finance massive debts and often having to try to recover in the face of a substantial contraction of operating assets. More than this, in the case of a turnaround, there is a problem of credibility with customers who have some doubts about the company's survival and with suppliers who fear bad debts and may impose more severe conditions of payment.

In this chapter we examine what the triggers for change actually were, but the much more exciting question is what they could be. What can each of us realistically do which will cause companies to improve their performance? We do not even have to work for them, let alone run them, to have some impact. Simply pointing out to the seller of a product or service that it is deficient in some respect and can be improved is of some use. As a result of the analysis in this chapter we suggest what these routes are for encouraging radical improvements in company performance.

Table 3.1 *Triggers for sharpbending*

		% of firms citing this factor
1	Intervention from external bodies	30
2	Change of ownership or the threat of such a change	25
3	New chief executive	55
4	Recognition by management of problems	35
5	Perception by management of new opportunities	10

It is clear that change takes effort, involves cost (both human and financial), disrupts well-worn practices and involves risk in so far as new ventures are involved. Hence there are strong forces for inertia. To produce action-generating change means that senior management must either recognize its need or be forced to undertake it by some external pressure. Such pressure can occur short of a crisis and this is the focus of our analysis. We concentrate on the factors which *impel* companies to change. These include:

1 crisis (real) as with turnarounds but not sharpbends;
2 crisis (perceived, or even 'manufactured' by senior management to stimulate change);
3 external investors'/lenders' dissatisfaction with results which forces management change;
4 injection of new chief executive or senior management keen to act and achieve change;
5 some experience, as with Ellis & Goldstein, which arouses senior management's awareness of new threats and opportunities;
6 threat of a takeover; and
7 an actual takeover.

3.2 Triggers found among the Sharpbenders

Our analysis suggested that there are five main sources for triggers (as shown in table 3.1). These five have very different implications for the way change might be triggered in other companies. Between them they covered 90 per cent of the cases we looked at, but in some companies there was more than one trigger.

The change in the chief executive stands out as being a characteristic of over half of the sharpbenders. However, it is important to question closely whether this change merely provided the catalyst for improvement or whether in fact it was the original stimulus. A firm in trouble is likely to change its chief executive. If the replacement performs the sharpbend then it is the action of deciding to have the change which matters and we must ask what the stimulus for that was. But if the change came about through the retirement or death of the incumbent then the focus is more likely to be on the new person directly as the stimulus to action.

Change of ownership has an artificially low rating as a trigger in table 3.1 because we deliberately excluded most takeovers from our sample; in part because of the statistical problem of measuring subsequent performance when the original entity has been absorbed into a wider enterprise. The trigger in such cases is very much outside the existing organization unless it is a voluntary takeover, seen by the acquired firm as the best way forward. Our exclusion of much of this category does not in any way imply criticism of the takeover route to change. Adverse criticism of individual takeovers may indeed be warranted but equally there have been examples of substantial beneficial effects in others, as with the early history of the acquisition of the Newton Chambers Group by Central and Sherwood (see Grinyer and Spender, 1979a). While the weight of statistical evidence is that takeovers on average do not lead to improved performance, there are still outstandingly successful examples.

Where existing companies fail to grasp the opportunities open to them, then it is in the interests of most of the four groups we identified in chapter 1 (shareholders, employees, management and national interest) for a change in ownership to take place. Relative decline is otherwise likely to continue. Set against this, the threat of takeovers tends to lead companies to take short-run measures to protect themselves, which are not necessarily in their long-term interests and may inhibit the process of sharpbending. We mentioned the case of Bell's in chapter 1, where major investment to diversify harmed the short-run cash flow and hence the valuation of the firm. In this chapter we examine two companies which have sharpbent through being taken over, Pringle and UDI.

The artificially low incidence of change of ownership as a trigger through the choice of the sample will at the same time increase the apparent relative importance of the other triggers. Thus the significance of recognition by the existing management, which featured in over a third of the cases may be overemphasized. Yet despite the bias there is very considerable evidence that firms can themselves recognize and engineer the changes necessary for a successful sharpbend. In a small number of cases, while the existing management was the trigger, they brought change about through seeing new opportunities rather than recognizing the sources of existing problems.

The remaining triggers shown in table 3.1 are from external influences, which in turnarounds is usually the most common stimulus to action. Indeed, the action can be enforced through compulsory receivership. It is a clear indicator of the differences between sharpbenders and turnarounds that it did not feature more strongly here in our study.

However, the striking point about table 3.1 is that more than one trigger for change took place in many cases. Indeed, even for the influences which are identified, these often acted in what was already a fertile environment for change. There are thus two stages in the triggering of a sharpbend. In the first phase the aspirations in the firm rise relative to existing performance either through a fall in performance, a rise in aspirations or some combination of the two. Dissatisfaction with the status quo mounts, making the occurrence of a sharpbend much more likely. In the second phase some event or set of events triggers off the radical changes. In this second phase the firm is ripe for a sharpbend but the particular run of circumstances determines whether and when it occurs. Thus for example, Ellis & Goldstein had already recognized the need to change and expand their product range, when they came across 'active leisure wear' in New York. It was this discovery which was the trigger for the sharpbend but had they not been actively seeking a new way forward they might not have come across the idea. Also, of course, they might have come across a different promising idea first and pursued that as the route forward to the sharpbend.

Put the other way round, if we are seeking triggers to induce companies to undertake sharpbends, we do not have to look for a single route. External intervention, internal recognition, the acquisition of new blood, and the threat of change of ownership could all result in action. The one which is the deciding factor could be very much the result of accident. Indeed, if the appropriate critical stimulus is not found the opportunity to sharpbend may pass. The level of aspirations may fall again relative to performance, say because market conditions improve and the firm picks up, and hence the susceptibility of the firms to respond to an opportunity also falls.

While there could in theory be many triggers for change our research suggests that the nature of the causes of relative decline makes some triggers more likely to occur than others, as is shown in table 3.2. The simplest example is that where it is the existing chief executive who was contributing to relative decline. The problem is addressed either when he is replaced or the ownership of the firm is changed, which is likely to alter his powers and the constraints under which he operates.

Four features stand out from table 3.2. First, our statistical analysis shows that it is only a worsening of the general market situation which is particularly associated with external intervention. This general decline in the market will be clear to everyone and does not require any detailed knowledge of the internal operations of the firm; this is consistent with the 'arms-length' approach to the management of the firm that seems to be favoured by external institutions in the UK.

Since 'ownership change' in the context of our sample normally meant an unsuccessful attempt at takeover this very threat was significantly related to *internal* weaknesses in the company. Acquisitors were not looking to enter declining markets where competitive pressure was strong but to take over

Table 3.2   *Relations between causes of decline and the triggers of the sharpbend*

	External intervention	Ownership change	Change of chief executive	Recognition by management
Decline of market	X			
Competitive pressure				
Inflexible autocrat		X	X	
Poor communication and vision creation		X	X	
Overly centralized		X		
Poor financial control systems		X	X	
High-cost structure		X	X	
Poor quality		X	X	
Failed acquisitions		X	X	X
Big projects failed		X		
Bureaucratic systems and large head office			X	

X denotes that there was less than a 1 in 20 probability that the association found was due to chance, i.e. the correlation was significant at the 5 per cent level.

companies where a change of management could lead to substantial improvement in performance without exiting the established business. Those involved in takeovers were more perceptive of the potential for improvement from change in management and this result supports the idea of potential takeover being a source of beneficial change when management has been weak.

Similarly a change in the chief executive (CEO) is associated with internal problems which are attributable to management. This association could have several explanations. In some cases recognition of managerial weakness could have led to early retirement, a move to another job, or even ill-health or dismissal of the previous CEO. In others, the causes of decline may have been seen only subsequently, i.e. the changes made by the new CEO threw into relief the shortcomings of old systems.

Lastly, the fact that recognition of problems by existing management is associated significantly only with failed acquisitions is an indictment against management. A failed acquisition is such a major matter for most companies that it can scarcely be overlooked. One must ask why they did not recognize major internal problems of poor quality, lack of cost competitiveness, etc. The lesson is that management must be self-critical and compare themselves with the best practice of their competitors.

3.3   External Intervention

We can note immediately that the frequently aired view, that institutional investors have little impact on the companies they have major holdings in, is borne out by our sample (table 3.3). These investors do not appear to have been instrumental in stimulating any of the sharpbends. Indeed, the role of non-executive directors – another favoured route for influence, as is witnessed by the setting up of Pro-Ned by the Bank of England quite explicitly to encourage and facilitate the appointment of non-executive directors – is only mentioned by one company, Collins. However, the Chairman of the Sidlaw Group, Sir John Carmichael, who introduced change in the early 1970s was introduced first to the board as a non-executive director. This finding, therefore, may be merely one of extent. While non-executive directors may have exercised a beneficial influence, it might not have been, by itself, sufficient to trigger change. It might, for instance, have led to management recognition of problems or early retirement of the CEO.

Where the company was independent the major impetus came from financial backers although this was still infrequent. In the case of Ferranti, the trigger for the bend came from the National Westminster Bank which declined to recommend an increase in the company's borrowings in September 1974. This came as a surprise to the Ferranti family, who had had every confidence that their bank would support them. It came as much less of a surprise to many of the executives in the company who had seen borrowings rise from £12 million in 1973 to £20 million in mid-1974. Indeed the fact that a crisis had occurred was welcomed by some as it forced the company to change. When the bank declined to increase the borrowing limit the company was faced with the prospect of receivership. This instance, therefore, is really an example of a turnaround. The company had no choice but to make drastic changes. They had choices over the form these could take and it is instructive that their first step was to seek an alternative source of finance by approaching

Table 3.3   *Triggers from external intervention*

	% of firms citing this source
1.1 Bank or source of finance	10
1.2 Institutional investors	—
1.3 Non-executive directors	5
1.4 Group (if a subsidiary)	10

the Department of Industry as the new Labour government had a commitment to industrial intervention.

A rather different intervention occurred in the case of Macallan-Glenlivet. The demand for whisky peaked in 1974 and simultaneously the company lost its largest customer, who took 30 per cent of output. It reacted to the crisis by trying to increase sales of bottled whisky, and cutting back on labour and energy costs – the first oil crisis coincided with their other problems. However, to make the investments necessary in capital equipment to cut labour and energy costs, they needed to borrow. This was clearly too big a proposition for the local branch office of the bank and was even beyond the limits of the area office in Aberdeen. This meant that they had to deal directly with the head office and as a result got considerable help in reorganizing the company. For such a small company it is unrealistic to expect that all the necessary skills would be possessed by management. Willie Phillips, the current Managing Director, had only just arrived in the company, as Management Accountant, at the time of the bend and clearly appreciated the bank's help. The bank thus acted as a catalyst rather than the very first trigger as that was provided by concern with the result of the decline in market demand and Macallan's share of it.

Whatman Reeve Angel achieved its sharpbend in part through the influence of Reeve Angel in turning around W & R Balston as a result of the merger of the two companies in 1973/4. RA's main contribution was, in the words of the Managing Director, cash, financial, flair, objectives and management. They also provided an established presence in the USA. WRB, on the other hand, had products, brand names, management accounting and other latent capable management. Again this was not a matter of the banks providing the initial stimulus but of being an essential contributor to, and facilitator of, change.

Subsidiaries such as Pringle (of Dawson International) clearly received help from their parent groups, not just in terms of guidelines for trying to achieve change but in terms of practical managerial help to achieve it. That pressure from the group in itself was a stimulus, although the subsidiary would have liked to run itself given half the chance.

Then in a group there can be a continuing pressure which is not applied to the boards and managements of independent companies. Such pressures can sometimes be stultifying rather than a source of high performance. Nevertheless, the independent company lacks the threat of intervention from such an effective source. As Williamson (1970) has argued, external capital markets tend to have less direct and powerful impact on management of enterprises than central control within a group of companies because takeover bids and shareholder revolts are expensive to mount and uncertain in outcome.

3.4 Change of Ownership

As we have noted already, by design this source of stimulus lies almost entirely outside our sample of companies and hence its apparently low frequency (shown in table 3.4) is an understatement of its potency in the economy at large.

However, our sample does give two rather different examples of the influence of new ownership on the acquired company, in both cases through an uncontested bid. The first instance is UDI through its acquisition by John Brown. Without John Brown, UDI would have gone under because it did not have the financial resources to finance the research necessary to develop its sophisticated and expensive products. John Brown were not initially able to provide the stimulus for change despite frequent changes of senior management, plans and financial control systems. However, they persevered, and, in the appointment of Michael Hosking, found the right means of pushing UDI forward.

There are some similarities with National Enterprise Board involvement in Ferranti. At the initiative of the company the NEB bailed the company out by buying a majority shareholding in 1975. The NEB then insisted upon a new structure, Derek Alan Jones was appointed as the new chief executive, proper financial control systems were established and regular planning and review meetings at all levels of management were introduced. There was a wider realization that hard decisions had to be made and recognition that even operations deeply imbedded in the history of the company must go where they persistently lost money.

Given the playing down of the role of actual change in ownership, it is not surprising that it was the threat of such change which resulted in action. The threat for Dawson interestingly was not that others wanted to buy it up but

Table 3.4 *Triggers from change in ownership*

	% of firms citing this factor
2.1 Unsuccessful contested bid	20
2.2 Contested acquisition	—
2.3 Uncontested acquisition	10
2.4 Inherited by new owner or divested by old owner	5
2.5 Management buyout	—
2.6 Bought by another firm	—

that competitors such as Courtaulds were buying up other independent firms such as Lyle and Scott. If Dawson was to maintain its market position it had to embark on the acquisition road too, thereby altering the structure and operation of the company markedly.

However, these takeover pressures can act the opposite way. Glaxo, which was faced by a takeover bid from Beecham in 1971–2, appears to have become rather complacent after a successful defence. Beecham felt that Glaxo had a sound research past but poor marketing and thought it could harness the former, eliminating duplication of its own resources, and improve the latter. As the bid failed the improvement did not take place at that time.

3.5 Injection of a New Chief Executive

To be effective, a chief executive must believe in the importance of his role in the company, and so of achieving a sharpbend during his time of office. Similarly, close colleagues may wish to support their chief executive in view of his power to influence their lives. Hence, despite the promised confidentiality of the research interviews there may have been a tendency to speak unduly favourably of the chief executive's role. We have therefore interpreted the comments on the role of the chief executive as a trigger with caution because we recognize the likelihood of bias in some of the views expressed. Indeed, we believe that in many cases change of the chief executive was an instrument of change already triggered and even in part a sign that such change was taking place.

Even when allowing for such reservations, in over half the sample we examined change in the chief executive appeared to be a trigger for change (table 3.5). A chief executive is appointed because he is expected to be a

Table 3.5 *Triggers for new chief executives*

		% of firms citing this factor
3.1	Due to external pressure or management change	10
3.2	Due to death or retirement of previous chief executive	40
3.3	On voluntary move of chief executive to a new job	5
3.4	On pressure from non-executive directors	5

potent force. If there are no achievements then the appointment will tend to be seen as a failure. To make an impact a new chief executive has to be seen as a force for change. He needs to stand out from his predecessor's actions. There is no guarantee that this change will be for the better, although that is always the intention.

Many of the chief executives in our sample are nationally known figures and cited regularly in profiles of the country's most successful chief executives. However, the extent to which their achievements are well known in part reflects the size of the company they are running. Their management styles varied very considerably from the highly centralized and personal role of Raymond Miquel at Bell's to the more decentralized arrangement of Low & Bonar under Brian Gilbert. The chief executive does not necessarily have to be a strong autocrat to be an effective trigger. However, firm and decisive action is required.

These new chief executives mostly came from within the firm, as is the case with Paul Girolami at Glaxo, John Kerridge at Fisons, Ian Wood at the John Wood Group, Philip Birch at Ward White, John Graham at Associated Paper Industries, Raymond Miquel at Bell's, Michael Walker at the Sidlaw Group and Bill Low at Don Brothers. Some such as Brian Gilbert at Low & Bonar came from outside the firm. Thus, unlike many turnaround examples, there is no consistent history of looking outside the company to bring in the charismatic figure who turns it round. Stuart Slatter (1984, p. 78) begins his analysis of successful recoveries by saying, 'Most, but not all, turnaround situations require new chief executives, since inadequate top management is the single most important factor leading to decline or stagnation'. This is true of our sharpbenders; indeed if we add to this the number of companies which changed their chief executive as part of the process of change (see chapter 4), there were relatively few companies for which a change in chief executive was not an integral part of the bend.

In several of the remainder the chief executive was a seminal figure in the process of change even if he was not the prime trigger. It is always difficult to discern the trigger. In the case of the John Wood Group, for example, it is by no means clear what would have happened without the discovery of North Sea oil. The company happened to be sited at Aberdeen and hence was ideally placed; yet without the appropriate direction it might not have taken advantage of the opportunities made available.

The role of the chief executive forms the centrepiece of Peters and Austin (1985). Indeed the discussions in Peters and Austin and in Peters and Waterman (1982) are very 'personalised', concentrating on the achievements of the individual as leader of the company, although in Peters (1986) 'leadership' is bracketed with 'organizational integrity' at the centre of the triangle of 'obsession with customers', 'continuous innovation' and 'all people as partners' which sums up his approach. However, to be fair to Peters he is concerned with leadership at all levels of the firm and not just at the top.

The important facet of a change in the chief executive is that this tends to entail a reappraisal of the company's objectives, structure and operation, as almost all new incumbents will wish to go through that process. There is a good chance that this in itself will generate change. In a company which has been in relative decline this can be the first step to a sharp and sustained improvement in performance. What should be stressed is that this impetus can come from within the firm itself. A newcomer brings a new perspective and has no commitment to past businesses, systems or values. However, a new chief executive who has had the opportunity to get to know the firm, its products, its staff and its opportunities may sometimes stand a better chance of improving the company's performance than someone just brought in, provided that he has the capacity to throw off the constraint of past practices and modes of working. On the other hand, an internal promotion based on effective working of the existing system, rather than a challenge to it, is unlikely to achieve a sharpbend.

The internal pressures which lead to a change in managing director, such as those at Collins in 1978/9, which led to the replacement of Jan Collins by Ian Chapman, may themselves reflect a necessary change in attitudes leading to the sharpbend. The change in managing director can thus be not only a step in the process of sharpbending but also a signal of such fundamental underlying changes. The new chief executive may then be swept into power by a newly influential coalition. At Collins, Clarke Paton, the current Managing Director, and George Craig, whom he saw as the main protagonist for change, had been in the company since 1975. They joined with Ian Chapman to introduce change and to achieve corporate leadership and this helped see through the sharpbend.

3.6   Recognition by Management

It is clear from examples such as Collins that companies can often achieve their own sharpbend without outside intervention. In many cases (see table 3.6), the management itself took action. However, it does appear that it was

Table 3.6   *Recognition of the problems by management as a trigger to sharpbending*

	% of firms citing this factor
4.1 New directors persuaded board	35
4.2 Other identified sources	—

new blood which acted as the stimulus. This underlines the importance of fresh perspectives on the business even if not necessarily in the office of the chief executive. Recognition of problems by management and change of chief executive are often related in a dynamic process within the early stages of triggering and introducing change. This is illustrated by the history of Sirdar. Sirdar's principal activity is the manufacture and distribution to retailers of hand-knitting wool and related products. The current Chairman, Mrs Tyrrell, is a member of the family which founded the company in 1870. Although it went public in 1954 she took over from her father on his death in 1960. During the period 1960–70 difficulties steadily accumulated and by the 1970s profits were down to only £70,000. Technology had been changing as synthetic yarns increasingly replaced wool. Nylon fibres cause more wear and tear on the machinery and are susceptible to 'climatic' changes. These problems were compounded by personality clashes, which Mrs Tyrrell says she was unwilling to resolve, primarily between the production and marketing sides of the company. Marketing criticized product quality and production blamed failure to sell.

This company's answer to the mounting difficulties was to bring in consultants. As a result of their report the managing director was replaced. Ironically, it was he who had advocated the use of consultants. His successor in 1970 was Mr Palmer who, in the next three years before his death, managed to bring together the strong team of people who provided the technical and marketing competence the company needed. Thus the company recognized the problem, the consultants diagnosed what was wrong, and the new managing director got on with the job.

Recognition is not an easy concept since while a problem may be recognized it does not imply that it will necessarily be acted upon. Don Brothers Buist, for example – which was formed in the early 1960s from the takeover by Don Brothers, a speciality manufacturer of jute textiles, of Low Brothers, its main merchants and distributors and Smarts, another manufacturer – realized that jute had no long-run future and that a capital-intensive substitute which could compete with low Indian wage costs was required. The younger generations of the founding families, Bill and Peter Low, Michael Hill and John Smart, saw the future to lie in woven polypropylene and believed that Sulzer looms could be used successfully for this purpose. The Chairman and Chief Executive, Lord Tayside, was more cautious about this possible solution. It was not until Bill Low succeeded Lord Tayside as Chief Executive that the company proceeded with this change in direction on which its subsequent growth and profitability was built.

At Associated Paper Industries, the problems were recognized, too, but it was not until Charles Rawlinson, who was a non-executive director, was persuaded to take over as Chairman in 1979 after the untimely death of his predecessor, Pat Young, that the action actually occurred. Rawlinson wanted things to happen and insisted that problems be confronted.

Thus an effective trigger for change requires not just recognition of the problem but recognition of a suitable solution, and the drive and willingness to try to carry it out.

3.7   An Overview of the Process of Triggering Change

In this chapter we have in the main considered the major events which were the stimulus to change – the intervention of the bank at Ferranti, the new chief executive at Low & Bonar, the finding of a new product area at Ellis & Goldstein and so on. However, as suggested earlier, many factors contribute in an interrelated way to the triggering and its timing. What actually sets the process in motion may be just the last in a whole stack of factors pushing for change. Contributing only a small part to one of them may be enough to tip the balance.

There is, however, a dilemma for anyone involved, because triggering the sharpbend and undertaking an improvement are different things. Improvements in product design, quality, production processes, marketing and financial systems, for instance, are all desirable in themselves and should improve profitability. Where the senior management and the strategic posture of the company are basically sound they may produce a marked and even sustained improvement in performance. However, they also relieve the pressure for change and so may postpone a sharpbend in a company which has fundamental strategic problems. In such a case they can produce no more than an upward shift of a declining trend of profit and sales.

The question is, therefore, 'Is it necessary to provoke a crisis?' Within the literature on organizational change there is strong support for the idea that a crisis is necessary to overcome the inertia inherent in old patterns of values, beliefs and working practices grounded in the existing way of doing business. In the context of the corporate turnaround Donald Bibeault (1982) suggests that there is usually a crisis or 'moment of truth'. Stuart Slatter (1984) takes the slightly broader view that companies can be turned around before the onset of the crisis. Our own fieldwork suggests that pressure, however generated, is required to initiate radical changes but that this can be well short of that associated with an ultimate financial crisis as in a turnaround situation. However, companies that were in absolute as well as relative decline would have reached that crisis point sooner or later. Internal and external pressures in such circumstances can be generated by anticipation of such a crisis unless major changes are made. On the other hand, a company which is still growing and making profits but at a lower rate than the industry as a whole, may be able to continue indefinitely if it has a market niche with effective barriers to entry from competitors.

Our findings provide pointers on this issue. The triggers we have identified in our study are:

external intervention;
change of ownership;
new chief executive;
recognition by management; and
finding new opportunities.

These events added sufficiently to existing pressures for change, both internal and external, to trigger radical action. In terms of our model (see section 3.1), this is reflected in changed levels of aspiration. Due to these events or changes in leadership, levels of performance were seen to be very unsatisfactory compared to what could be done.

For most writers the 'key' is leadership. The effective leader not only triggers change, he changes the climate of the company, its vision, and gives it a new direction. Inkson *et al.* (1986) put their whole emphasis on leadership. They put forward as their example, Bert Macartney, Managing Director of Healtheries of New Zealand Ltd, with the words:

> [The CEO] *is* the company. He has the entrepreneurial knack, intuition and vision ultimately translated into action to look ahead and position himself to be in balance with the consumers' needs at an appropriate future time . . . and the ability to communicate that vision . . . he is the dynamo, his people see him leading from the front . . . others reflect his energy . . . he is an enthusiast, a believer . . . where the company is today is largely as a result of his entrepreneurial skill and effort. (p. 31)

Peters and Austin (1985) have as their subtitle, 'The Leadership Difference', and leadership forms the core of their analysis of excellence. It is therefore no surprise that most of our companies showed a change in chief executive as a trigger for the sharpbend and when we include those companies that changed their chief executive as part of the achievement of the bend, we reach 65 per cent of the sample.

But we must take a step back. Eighty-five per cent of our control companies also changed their chief executive as part of their struggle to do better. The pressure for change there too had been high. The difference was that for a combination of reasons they did not achieve the increase in performance that they would have liked. Thus, while changing the chief executive is a way of achieving sharp improvements in performance, it is, of course, by no means a guarantee. Having a suitable person at the top is clearly a necessary condition for a sharpbend but not a sufficient one. Success requires appropriate action, too, a matter to which we turn in the next chapter.

But the message is not that one should necessarily change the CEO, as in a third of the cases change came without a change in the chief executive. In many others the motivation for change in the chief executive was not to achieve a sharpbend, it was just natural evolution. Indeed, if we took any period of ten years, most companies would have changed their chief executive, many of them more than once.

Some triggers come ultimately from the environment – falling demand, competitors' actions, a new discovery – which cause mounting pressure for change as performance falls below aspiration levels. Such triggers are either beyond our control or in themselves highly undesirable. But in this chapter we have seen those which can voluntarily have an influence from outside:

bankers;
consultants;
suppliers;
purchasers;
competitors;
non-executive directors.

Several of the mergers between companies such as those of Don Brothers and Whatman Reeve Angel, whether horizontal or vertical, were by mutual agreement. Thus arrangements with suppliers, purchasers and competitors by their initiative were contributors. For a firm in difficulty, a change in market position by merger or acquisition is often a route to better performance, as we shall see in the next chapter. Sometimes it is part of the sharpbend but it is also a clear trigger. This is clearest for the acquired firm, where senior management may be replaced and a new strategic thrust imposed. However, it may be the trigger for the acquirer as well as the acquired. Management personnel are a key part of the acquired firm. In the case of Don Brothers Buist it was the two other firms, Low Brothers and Smarts which came to join Don Brothers, which provide the chairman, chief executive and joint managing directors. (Since then Don Brothers has been acquired by Shell and there have been a number of board changes including the bringing in of a new managing director.)

It is thus important for each of these external groups, which can act as a trigger, to appraise whether these opportunities exist in any of the companies they associate with. Will harsh financial pressure provoke a change? Would possible mergers create major opportunities and stimulate change? Would a change of chief executive trigger necessary radical change in the company? What informal pressures and influence can be brought to bear on it? Should efforts be made to introduce an active, change-orientated, chairman or non-executive directors?

Much of the pressure for change comes from within the company itself and may prepare the ground for spectacular sharpbends. Self-examination and consequent actions may start some time before a bend becomes evident. Ward White for example, were involved in achieving a sharpbend from the late 1960s. When Philip Birch, the current Chairman and Managing Director, came to John White, a group mainly involved in the manufacture and distribution of footwear, in 1968, the company could be described as 'sleepy' and having slightly lost its way. Birch originally came to the company as a member of a consulting team brought in by the management and was later brought in to fill a vacuum left by the death of the chief executive. During the last few years there was vigorous cost rationalization and a continuing battle with rising import penetration. The management were 'dissected' and formed into a tighter, more aggressive team, to which Birch imparted his own highly motivated, entrepreneurial drive as its leader. It made two significant acquisitions – that of George Ward in 1972 (hence Ward White) and G B Brittan, makers of Tuf brand and safety footwear, in 1973. Despite an initial sharp recovery in profits in 1972 the firm was hit badly by the 1974 recession. However, with that groundwork it had a good basis to stage a recovery. Thus while the bend may have been preceded by the external decline, previous internal actions meant that a sharp recovery could be undertaken by the existing management thereafter. No additional trigger as such was required. The combination of the existing pressures for change and the environment was enough.

Rotaflex has a very similar story. This international group, whose main business is lighting, is involved, through its subsidiaries, in the manufacture of bathroom and shower appliances. While the company had a good reputation when Michael Frye, the current Chief Executive, came in 1976, it lacked a strong profit orientation, effective information systems and an appropriate management structure. Accounting and financial reporting was only half-yearly and control of overseas subsidiaries was largely left to the subsidiaries themselves. Frye introduced new management information systems and a rationalization plan. Growth segments of markets were identified but the company was caught by the 1980 recession as rationalization was slow to have effect. However, the tools had been developed and the experience gained. The second round of tightening up and rationalization after the recession generated the sharpbend. The tools and ideas already existed. It was a matter of their effective operation.

In the case of both Ward White and Rotaflex the initial steps had already been taken. It was the external market demand which precipitated the sharpbend. Thus pressure in the company to change and development of the structure which facilitated change were necessary precursors, although not as such the triggers of the sharpbend.

With the right structure the bend can take place. Both companies were on the way but had not yet succeeded. Rotaflex was caught in 1979 with high capital borrowings to develop a new site but without the premises yet constructed to produce the products required. The management changes were still in progress but more remained to be done.

Recognition by management is thus a trigger for change although the sharpbend itself may require a further trigger. Ellis & Goldstein are a good example as we have noted. The management knew it had to add something to the product range. The sharpbend occurred when they came across something suitable (fashion leisure wear). However, the management appreciated its potential when they saw it and had the drive to proceed with the exploitation rapidly; as the managing director put it, the idea of the Dash chain of shops 'was born out of shoe leather'. All this required the steps which form part of the sharpbend. The seeking of opportunities, the bias for action, and factors which form part of a successful sharpbend, do themselves form part of how an existing management can contribute to triggering such a bend. Nevertheless it remains that external pressure was by far the major influence on timing.

Therefore the appropriate answer to 'How can I be a trigger for change?' lies in the answer to the question 'What steps are necessary to achieve change?' which is dealt with in the next chapter. A firm which is pushing and being pushed in the direction of change is prima facie more likely to act. The wider the range of these pressures, the more likely the firm is to take major action, and the greater the chance of triggering a sharpbend.

These pressures are in themselves the product of a complex interrelated set of internal, external and market factors. But, as recognized by Pettigrew (1985), to effect change requires 'champions' to push for it and these may be in middle as well as senior management. Ultimately, in terms of our model, management must have high aspirations, be dissatisfied with performance and have the courage to press for something to be done about it.

Only key people can force sharp change in a company, but everyone can contribute to engendering an atmosphere in which change is encouraged and thereby increase the chance of its taking place. Even small and slow improvements should be encouraged. Rapid improvements, if successful, will clearly be even better but it will depend upon the particular company whether it can follow a fast or a slow path to better performance. Here we are interested in the fast path.

4 What the Sharpbenders Did

This chapter is the central one in the book as it sets out what sharpbenders actually did. This provides the groundwork which other firms can observe, relate to their own businesses and then use in formulating strategies for themselves.

In one rather elementary sense a large portion of what the sharpbenders did to achieve their success was to reverse the cause of their previous relative decline, where this lay within their power, and to change the way the firm reacted when it was not. Thus, firms with poor management changed it, firms with poor control systems improved them, and firms in declining markets altered their product market focus on to growing areas of business. Therefore, in so far as the particular mix of causes of the relative decline were different so too were the steps taken, because the needs were different. The form of the trigger for the sharpbend also matters, as a firm which sees new opportunities for the future, say, through the invention of a new product or the advent of North Sea oil, will behave in a very different way from one which has had a new management imposed on it as a result of a takeover or intervention of an institutional investor.

Therefore the twelve sets of steps taken to achieve the sharpbend which we have identified reflect in part the ten sets of causes of relative decline set out in chapter 2. These are set out in table 4.1. Six features stand out as the most commonly cited factors, namely:

reductions in production costs;
changes in management;
windfalls;
stronger financial controls;
new product market focus; and
improved marketing.

Firms took many steps and not just a few. However, as the second column in table 4.1 shows, so did the control companies. The actions described are common to many companies, but the sharpbenders succeeded because of the range and effectiveness of measures they used and their timing of them.

Eighty-five per cent of the sharpbenders and nearly as large a proportion of the control companies experienced windfall gains (category XI) where these

Table 4.1   *Steps taken by sharpbenders (controls)*

		% of firms citing this factor		
		Sharpbenders (a)	*Controls (b)*	*% difference (a − b)*
I	Major changes in management[1]	85	(30)	55
II	Stronger financial controls	80	(70)	10
III	New product market focus	80	(80)	0
IV	Diversified	30	(70)	−40
V	Entered export market vigorously	50	(30)	20
VI	Improved quality and service	55	(50)	5
VII	Improved marketing	75	(30)	45
VIII	Intensive effort to reduce production costs[1]	80	(30)	50
IX	Acquisitions	50	(80)	−30
X	Reduced debt	50	(80)	−30
XI	Windfalls	85	(70)	15
XII	Other	25	(20)	5

[1]   Fifty per cent of the sharpbenders took at least four steps in this category.

are defined as beneficial events not caused by the firms' own actions. However, it was the other actions taken which allowed the sharpbenders to capitalize on the windfall. Sirdar's Managing Director, Mr Lumb, reflected this when he said, 'the route to success is always luck and timing and taking advantage of what happens'.

As may be seen from the analysis in the appendix the sharpbenders stand out significantly from the control companies in three respects:

1   more of them improved their marketing (step VII);
2   substantially more of them reduced their production costs (step VIII); and
3   fewer of them pursued the acquisition route to change (step IX).

These three paint an interesting picture as they suggest on the one hand that the differentiating factors are that the sharpbenders put more effort into trying to produce what the customers wanted and into the focused selling of their products. They also concentrated on improving their cost competitiveness rather than purchasing other companies to try to change the structure of the business. This is not to say that the sharpbenders did not acquire other companies. We can see from table 4.1 that half of them did as part of the strategy to change their structure. It is merely that, relative to the control companies, they put much more emphasis on solving their own cost problems.

Facing the hard issues squarely is an essential characteristic of sharpbenders which struck us time and again when visiting them.

Secondly, our analysis suggests that five of the steps are not particularly associated with any of the specific causes either positively or negatively. This implies that companies in all sorts of circumstances changed their organizational structure, improved quality and reliability, reduced production costs, reduced debt and enjoyed windfalls. Indeed it would be rather strange if windfalls were not fairly randomly distributed across the whole range of companies, whether sharpbenders or not, by virtue of their very nature as an external event beyond the firm's control.

The third noteworthy feature of the analysis is that most of the relationships shown up make good sense – that firms with poor marketing should improve it, that firms facing sustained fall in market demand should adopt a new product market focus. However, some, although not contradictory to common sense, appear to have no particular rationale. It is not clear to us, for example, why poor marketing should be associated with stronger financial control rather than some of the other causes of relative decline.

We may learn too from the absence of relationships between causes of decline and specific steps taken. Clearly, a number of steps were general responses to poor performance rather than specific ones to be identified with particular causes of relative decline. Thus, except where the needs from the causes of relative decline are obvious, firms seem often to undertake a wide range of measures to achieve a successful sharpbend including some not obviously dictated by their particular prior circumstances.

We therefore now consider these steps in turn.

4.1 Changes in Management

Leadership emerges as a key feature of sharpbending. Sixty-five per cent of the sharpbenders changed their chairman or chief executive as part of the sharpbend. We have already noted that for others a change in the chief executive was the trigger for the sharpbend and so preceded it. This is consistent with the widely held belief that 'people' are a key element in the successful company. Peters (1986) phrases it more strongly 'Human Capital – that is people – is the key'. Inkson *et al.* (1986) develop this concept further by distinguishing the leader – the keyholder – from the value of people in general which they label 'kith and kin' to fit in with their 'Theory K' concept. However, they argue that different types of leader are required for different circumstances and in particular that 'in organizations making a successful recovery from a long period of moderate performance the keyholder is always primarily a transformational leader'. By comparison a mature successful company in their view requires a 'transactional' leader, who will sustain effective operations rather than introducing disruptive change. Stated in this bald fashion this statement seems to be no more than a truism. A company which needs to change needs a leader who is good at changing things. The significant questions relate to the characteristics of such 'transformational' leaders, how they are developed, identified and placed in positions in which they can generate change. Moreover, it has to be asked whether such characteristics are general or specific to industries or even situations within industries.

In the case of turnarounds the need for a transformational leader is clearly accepted with the growth of 'company doctors' who specialize in performing successful turnarounds. This is not the case for our sharpbenders. Many chief executives have emerged from within the company and in some presided over both the relative decline *and* the subsequent sharpbend.

Our interviews with executives in the twenty-five sharpbenders suggested some of the characteristics of such transformational leaders. It is clear from table 4.2 that the new top management was first, committed and positive

Table 4.2   *Changes in management undertaken to achieve a sharpbend*

		% of sharpbenders citing this factor
1.1	New chairman or chief executive	65
1.2	Change in executive directors	(30)[1]
	(a) marketing or sales	20
	(b) finance	15
	(c) production	5
	(d) R&D or technical	15
	(e) other	10
1.3	Injection of non-executive directors	10
1.4	Creation of more balanced board of executive and non-executive directors	10
1.5	Key executives buy shares or given strong profit incentives	15
1.6	New top management is committed, positive, with a bias for action	60
1.7	New top management injects new values, or vision which drives the company	40
1.8	New top management believes in stimulating innovative, entrepreneurial behaviour throughout management	40
1.9	New top management creates climate of 'productivity through people'	35

[1]   Number of firms citing at least one item in this category.

with 'a bias for action'. The workforce representative at Macallan-Glenlivet, when describing the actions of management, put it 'they never sat down'. They were out trying to drum up sales and actively trying to implement change. In sharpbender after sharpbender we found a similar perception of energetic pursuit of effective change. Sometimes this involved hard decisions, or 'nettle-grasping', as at Pringle where extensive redundancies were declared among management as companies were merged and antiquated mills closed.

A change in chief executive was frequently associated with the introduction of new functional executives. The new chief executive clearly needed executives who would manage change effectively, share his vision and whom he could trust. This follows naturally from the widely perceived emphasis among the sharpbenders on having the right management team. This is illustrated by the view of David Evans, Deputy Group Managing Director at Associated Book Publishers, who simply said that 'success comes from recruiting the top people'. A major contribution to ABP's sharpbend came from the recruitment of Alan Miles as Managing Director of their UK division. Not surprisingly, the most frequent changes were of the marketing or sales director, reflecting the importance of marketing in the overall success of the operation. For example in the case of Macallan it was central; before Hugh Mitcalfe came they had not had a proper marketing director. The Chairman's brother had hoped to take on the marketing role but rapidly became too ill to do so. When Mitcalfe filled this gap he was able to increase sales by 30 per cent a year for five years. However, in large companies at corporate level, marketing directors are sometimes seen as less important. Company A actually dispensed with a marketing director and devolved the marketing functions to the subsidiaries – 'we have no second-guessing in the team' as the technical director put it.

In many of the companies we visited the introduction of a new finance director was of at least equal importance. Dawson International took on two new recruits who are now marketing and financial directors but they dispensed with the posts of production and personnel directors in cutting the headquarters down to a more satisfactory size. It was he who was responsible for the new systems of financial control for management information and monitoring and, as Walter Telfer made clear at Low & Bonar, could create a second channel of information to the board in addition to the usual management chain through chief executives of subsidiaries.

Clearly, the emphasis in recruitment of the new team depends on a variety of factors, including the abilities of executive directors inherited, perceived needs of the business, nature of the industry, organizational structure and hierarchical level within it.

This idea of an effective management team was extended in some cases by having new active non-executive directors on the board. This was emphasized at Dawson, for example, where the management change at the top had been a little unusual with the removal of the managing director and his replacement by the chairman, who resumed his former role. However, this role of new directors is related to the organizational changes considered in the next section.

What stands out from table 4.2, however, is the importance of what a managerial team stood for, in addition to being 'committed and positive with a bias for action'. They injected a new set of values or vision which drives the company, stimulated innovative entrepreneurial behaviour throughout management, and created a climate of productivity through people. These themes are resonant of the 'Excellence' literature. Inkson *et al.* (1986) summarize this most clearly,

> . . . if it is the keyholder who breathes life into the organisation, fires the imagination of others and draws the best out of them, he or she is able to do so only through the use of the *kite*, the organisational purpose or mission. Keyholder and kite form a unity, a symbiotic relationship in which each draws nourishment from and gives strength to, the other. The most talented, transformational leader without a kite would be like a splendid ring master with no circus. (p. 49)

Like so many of the ideas presented in the literature on corporate excellence we find that this is an exaggerated claim. Companies need to have clear objectives, people need to be motivated but those needs are often met by more familiar goals and less tangible, more subtle values within a strongly established corporate culture than a few attention-riveting, simple statements. The list of companies without any *new* value system or vision is longer than that of those with one. Even so, there is no doubt about the galvanizing effects of the creation of a shared vision by an energetic and charismatic figure in some of our sharpbenders. Moreover, where the nature of the business needs to change radically a new kite may be essential to breaking old patterns of beliefs, values and methods of operating within the company. Perhaps we can illustrate the power of a new corporate kite by reference to a sharpbender which was not in our sample, London Life. When Ben Thompson-McCausland was appointed Managing Director the company was stagnating. He set about 'energizing' it and consciously sought to create a shared set of values, upon which what he called the 'corporate mind' would be focused. The corporate mind in his view is composed of the brains, experience, effort and values of the people in the company. If this is focused it can be directed to four channels:

confidence;
energy;
achievement; and
teamwork.

Ben Thompson-McCausland's four objectives are certainly important to success but they are more abstract and general than most kites which have a strongly operational flavour. The key question is the same in each case, however, namely how do such kites become strongly motivating and guiding value systems. In Ben's case it was clearly an example of the inspirational leadership we have discussed. He had an outline vision of what he wanted to achieve. By discussing the ideas with his colleagues and bringing them along with him – those who would not come left the company – he was able to refine the ideas and develop a general enthusiasm for these objectives. Most important of all he was a living example of his vision of energy, confidence, achievement and teamwork. Vision is clearly communicated effectively by example and behaviour even more strongly than by words. London Life illustrates the fact, however, that the kite may be inseparable from the new leader. We suspect that the company would have been transformed even if Ben Thompson-McCausland had adopted a different kite. The interesting question is whether he could have wrought the changes without any newly articulated mission or vision.

Of the companies we visited, 'A' had probably got the most developed 'philosophy'. It produced a book which each employee is given and which communicates the company's vision. This was introduced as part of the sharpbend to help motivate the employees and involve them in the company's aspirations and future. It was supplemented by a careful system of making sure that all employees were kept informed of what was going on both through meetings and through publications. In most of the sharpbenders the approach was less formal, particularly among the small companies. Even for Bell's, which projected its message that 'Bell's is best' very aggressively to increase and then maintain its market share, the picture presented of the company was largely for outside consumption rather than to motivate internally. The latter was achieved more directly by providing good conditions for the workforce with free meals, pensions, insurance, sports facilities, transport and a share-participation scheme. The importance of commitment, hard work and quality was also communicated by the Chairman and Managing Director, Raymond Miquel, orally and by example. Moreover, these qualities were evident, even in middle management. For instance, in the bottling plant, the shop steward interviewed commented that management was always there after the workforce left at night and in before them in the morning, problems being resolved before work was due to commence. Clearly belief in, and commitment to, the company had permeated the workforce to a large extent as labour turnover was low and there was considerable loyalty.

The most appropriate means of communicating the vision is partly a matter of personal style of the leader but turns crucially on size and complexity of mission. Small companies can communicate vision by informal means. In large companies more formal, bureaucratic devices (including annual 'strategy' conferences) are necessary to project top management's vision to the lower managerial ranks as most members of the company are far beyond the direct personal influence of the leader. Where the business is simple as with a small product range the communication of the vision by informal means may again be easier. It is difficult to get a feel for the nature of 'vision' and its means of implementation without fairly detailed examples. We now therefore look at Bell's in order to try to generate an impression of the 'atmosphere' created, as this was a striking example.

The major drive at Bell's clearly derived from the forceful personality of Raymond Miquel first as Managing Director and later as Chairman as well. He had always worked long hours and expected it of his colleagues. He is an enthusiast for physical fitness and has tried to instil that in the firm as a whole through competitions and sports days. There is no doubt that Miquel has been a 'transformational' leader in all the senses of the word. Jack House reports in *Pride of Perth*, a history of the company, commissioned by Bell's in the early part of the sharpbend, that the previous Managing Director's motto was 'hasten slowly' (p. 104). That certainly could not be said of Miquel who believed in driving forward – hard.

On our visit to Bell's we found Miquel's beliefs in effectively projecting the image of the company, operating with meticulous tight efficiency, personal physical fitness, complete dedication and unremitting labour for the firm, permeated all levels of management and clearly shaped behaviour. Again the message was communicated by both word and behavioural patterns.

The company is sales-orientated. In addition to the two editions of *Pride of Perth* it has also produced two films/videos about the company, the first called 'A Proud Heritage' and the second, which we were shown, 'Whicker in Bell's World'. This latter had Alan Whicker narrating what the company did and had done and walking round the various sites and gatherings talking to employees and others about the company. It is very effective; indeed the whole approach of Bell's in selling the 'image' is very well done. Although it may seem a minor matter, it is perhaps indicative that they handled us hospitably and efficiently, with a schedule, announced beforehand, which was not only followed but covered all the requests we made.

We gained a strong impression that the company projects a careful and very effective image to all customers and visitors. They have a magnificent reception centre at Cherrybank next to their head office in Perth which was opened in 1980 with the full panoply of publicity by Prince Philip. There is also a visitor centre at their Blair Atholl distillery. The aim of this approach is to build goodwill among both immediate and ultimate customers. Miquel's great step forward was to realize that the licensed victualler was the crucial person in the purchase of whisky rather than just the traditional market of main breweries and larger chains. From this developed the need to attract them, by incentive schemes and visits to Perth. Bell's now have a large programme of donations and financial support for worthy causes, such as the

Arthur Bell Estate at Blair Atholl, for the Licensed Victuallers' National Homes and the Perth Lawn Tennis Club.

All this and the well-organized sales events with brightly jacketed staff 'uniforms' amount to a major effort which we have done no more than summarize. Its effects on sales were strongly beneficial but within the company are mixed. East Mains where Bell's has its bottling plant lies in a traditional coal-mining area and some of the labour relations reflect that background. The cooper whom we saw as a labour-force representative made it clear that many employees viewed the share-participation scheme purely as a financial benefit – and indeed sold shares when they could – and not as some greater incentive to commitment to the firm. Yet he himself viewed the sustained growth of sales, the security of employment so produced and the associated commitment of managers as very much in the interests of the workforce. Despite some reservations based on attitudes inherited from their local background the workforce appeared, in part at least, to share the vision of 'Bell's is best'.

The total package is thus complex. Miquel's drive is clearly the important factor in the achievement. He remarked proudly in passing about the East Mains plant that the former Chairman had agreed to move out from the cramped premises in Leith if a greenfield site could be found which was level, next to a main road and a railway, and near an airport. This difficult requirement was possibly intended to try to inhibit the move but East Mains actually has all these characteristics and is near enough to Edinburgh for it to be possible, though difficult, to transport the existing workforce out to the new site. The drive and success were typical of Miquel's approach.

In Bell's case there was certainly a committed, positive top management with a bias for action, which injected new values and vision and put an emphasis on people, but the whole approach revolved round what is virtually a single product, Bell's whisky. (Although Canning Town Glass and Towmaster were separate operations they were really a form of vertical integration into the provision of bottles and delivery.) Shortly before we visited the company it had diversified into hotels by purchasing the Gleneagles Group. Our impression was that the Bell's vision at corporate headquarters had not evolved to accommodate this change. Certainly the acquisition facilitated the successful takeover of Bell's by Guinness. First, it meant that Bell's had to undertake major investments in the hotels before they could start earning their revenue potential and so depressed its profitability at a crucial stage. Second, it introduced a division into the board of directors, for the former head of the Gleneagles Group did not share fully Miquel's vision, which might not have been as appropriate for his area of business and he sided with Guinness at a crucial stage of the bid.

The experience of Bell's with the acquisition of the Gleneagles Group is thus very illuminating. Success over a period reinforces the vision, giving great confidence in it; but because it becomes such an important article of faith as a basis for operations it may in turn become a powerful impediment to evolution into a new type of business where it is not fully appropriate. The more powerful the vision the more it may blind its adherents to new and different business realities. Those who must contend with these business realities are then more likely to find themselves in conflict with the old leadership which saw the vision as central to its success. The central place for such vision, which in its operational form Spender called 'recipes', within the dynamic process of change, success, relative stagnation and subsequent change is explored in Grinyer and Spender (1979b). The point we wish to stress here is that whilst a new vision may be a powerful force for change its very success tends to ossify it, making subsequent evolution less likely unless corporate leadership understands the nature of the dynamic social process of which it is a part. Hence, in time, strong sources of successful change can become a major reason for stagnation.

The example of Bell's also illustrated for us how one man's vision can be particularly potent in a small or medium-sized organization. In 1984 employment in the whisky division was only 626 and 1989 in the group as a whole, despite a turnover of £221 million and profits of £34.6 million in the whisky division.

Throughout the whisky division but not we suspect the hotel one, Raymond Miquel's influence was felt strongly and in a personal way. He was seen often, his behavioural pattern was noted, he was the subject of company myths.

This effect of size can also be seen at Macallan where, with only forty-six employees, there was more of a family atmosphere and not the elaborate structure required for a large enterprise. By contrast, in a very large firm, while the CEO may have an impact in a personal, informal way primarily on his corporate executive directors and general managers of the divisions, more indirect and indeed formal methods are needed, as we have seen, to reach the wider ranks of management and workforce. It must be harder to sustain a widely held vision within the company where its communication is necessarily via several echelons of management and less personal means.

A final impression that we wish to impart from the example of Bell's is that the central theme may be different from and is more complex than those suggested in the literature on excellence. While some firms stressed the importance of innovation, Pringle for example suggested that 'the market place is a living thing', the emphasis was not as strong as is implied in the excellence literature. Some firms such as Ellis & Goldstein are in a highly innovative industry. Designs change all the time and any one item may have a shelf-life of only six weeks.

There is more than one set of concepts bound up in the idea of the values of the company or its philosophy. This is the distinction between the objectives of the company, the path to their achievement, and the general

Table 4.3 *Corporate cultures*

General group	Culture	Description
I Energetic	1 Competitive	aggressive, ambitious, confident, positive, winning
	2 Committed	hard working, dedicated, consistent, enduring
	3 Exciting	enthusiastic, stimulating, fun
II People-orientated	4 Teamwork	team, team spirit, cooperative, partnership
	5 Leader	charismatic, driven from the top
	6 Family	caring, supportive, people-centred, considerate
III Change	7 Adaptive	flexible, adaptable, changing, dynamic
	8 Innovative	creative, entrepreneurial, searching
	9 Expanding	international, expansive, growing, diverse
	10 Visionary	forward-thinking, progressive, future-orientated
IV Results	11 Rational	precise, efficient, lean, planned, disciplined
	12 Performance	goal-directed, profit-orientated, results-orientated, financially driven
	13 Customer	quality, sales-orientated, service
	14 Conservative	traditional, formal, loyal
	15 Honourable	integrity, respect, responsibility

Source: Inkson *et al.* (1986).

atmosphere or way in which the company operates. We have seen all these at work in Bell's. It is the company atmosphere, or 'culture' as it is frequently called, which is easiest to oversimplify. Inkson *et al.* (1986) suggest a fifteen-fold classification of cultures (see table 4.3). However, the table concentrates on positive cultures while many companies have unwittingly managed to develop negative or depressing cultures, which are very difficult to change.

It is instructive to try to fit our sample of sharpbenders into Inkson's categories. We found that in most cases none of the fifteen types of culture adequately described the company. Each had in some respects a unique hybrid between these stylized cultures. The importance of this framework is hence not so much in its categorization but in pointing out that there are many corporate cultures associated with successful sharpbenders. To give just one, Bell's has gone to a great deal of trouble to emphasize its heritage, the basis of the company in the careful skills of developing the product over 150 years so possessing qualities of conservative culture (culture 14). It is customer- and sales-orientated with a stress on quality (culture 13). It had a strong leader and made an effort to create what in the Inkson framework can best be described as a 'family' culture (culture 6). Similarly it was most certainly committed (culture 2) and competitive (culture 1). Its success lay in its unique blend of these elements of different cultures and the way the elements interplayed and balanced each other which was effective given the personalities involved, the cultural background of managers and workforce, the nature of the business and the stage in the development of the company and its markets.

A further weakness was that we found Inkson's list of fifteen cultures insufficient to describe some firms adequately, even when used in combination. The fact that simple or even extensive categorizations of cultures cannot adequately represent cultures encountered without development of complex hybrids raises the question as to whether it is possible to isolate the cultural elements of success on the one hand and to replicate them on the other. Our fieldwork suggests that the answer to these interrelated questions is complex. Each company certainly had a mix of beliefs, values and operating practices which could be called a culture, but as we have seen most were hybrids of stylized types. Clearly, to be successful the different elements had to be coherent, rather than conflicting, and appropriate to the size, nature of business, technology, stage of evolution and markets of the company, and this we found. Yet the very complexity of the hybrids found and the problems of relating them to such contingencies suggested that adequate analysis was virtually impossible. Moreover, conscious design of company cultures *in toto* struck us as impossible, making replication of successful hybrids out of the question. Each culture was the result of enduring experience, the contribution of sometimes many generations of managers, small as well as great, and also of the local industry and market environment. Cultures had evolved rather than been designed. This is not, however, to deny that leaders may radically change them in important respects, and this is frequently necessary where the company must be regenerated. But in doing so they reshape part only of a more complex set of beliefs and values.

Our feeling therefore from the results of the study is that, while clear objectives are necessary for the successful sharpbend, accompanied by the drive to achieve them, the culture as such does not need to and indeed often cannot be specific, although articulation of certain key elements clearly helps in some cases. What is required is a well-motivated courageous, committed, hard-working, innovative and positive management and workforce and this can be achieved through many routes – by example and personal identification with the goals, by loyalty to and care of staff, by oral and written communication by senior managers, through the operating rules of the system, through incentives, or by appointing new executives who have those qualities and share the corporate vision. By looking back to table 4.3 we can see that 85 per cent of firms made a management change and 50 per cent made four or more changes. New management is thus an important step in achieving the sharpbend, provided it possesses the right qualities.

In the sections which follow we examine the steps that the management, whether new or not, have taken.

4.2 Changes in Organization

The appropriate organizational structure is a widely debated area in the management literature. There are also arguments within firms about whether they are too centralized or decentralized, whether they should retain a purely functional structure or adopt a divisional one, and whether divisional structures should be on a product or geographical basis. 'Contingency theorists' such as Burns and Stalker (1961), Woodward (1965) and Katz and Kahn (1966), who think that organizational structure is dependent on specific contingencies such as size, technology, the people involved, internal political factors and the nature of the environment, would argue that the firm is the appropriate forum for such a debate. They would not be surprised by table 4.4 which shows that some firms decentralized operating decisions while others did the reverse. This, no doubt, reflected the perception by some companies that they were too centralized and others too decentralized (see causes of decline above). The need for centralization or decentralization as one aspect of design can clearly change over time. Mr Matsushita, the founder and President of the giant Japanese electronics company Matsushita, quite deliberately introduced phases of centralization and decentralization, arguing that needs change, depending upon the fortunes of the company, the people and the phase of technological development.

Clearly, within any company some decisions will remain centralized and others will be decentralized. The key questions relate to which decisions and how many of them should be taken at the top of the organization rather than at lower hierarchical levels.

The Peters and Waterman views on this matter contrast with those of the contingency theorists by being prescriptive. They claim that centralized control is required to ensure financial performance and quality, and to avoid unplanned competition between different parts of the group, while decentralization is necessary to give sufficient scope for the exercise of subordinates' flair and to give them motivation. They label this 'simultaneous loose–tight

Table 4.4 *Changes in organization taken to achieve a sharpbend*

		% of sharpbenders citing this step
2.1	Decentralization of innovative and operating decisions	35
2.2	Reduction in size of headquarters	30
2.3	Centralization to tighten:	
	(a) financial controls	10
	(b) control of key values of company	15

properties'. An example of 'loose' properties is given by Jeremy Leigh-Pemberton, the Managing Director of Whatman Reeve Angel. He said that he was 'a shoulder to lean on' for the chief executives of the subsidiaries to whom operating decisions were delegated. His aim was to 'try and provide the environment in which they [the subsidiaries] flourish most, 'an elder brother relationship rather than a father one'. We see in this case therefore a fair degree of autonomy. This was supplemented, however, by strong, central, financial controls providing the 'tight' property. Bell's was the exact opposite. The board discussed in considerable detail, for example, all capital projects over £1000. It was relatively isolated from the rest of the group except for regular visits to plants and customers. Other staff did not come to the directors' floor except by invitation. There was tight central control of virtually all aspects of the business.

Philip Birch at Ward White described the management style as 'hands-off operation' to give autonomy to the operating companies. What he was looking for was flair. However, Ward White's success has come from accomplished expertise at acquisitions. They are good at identifying suitable companies for takeover and find that the overnight introduction of proven managerial controls pays off. To be attractive, potential acquisitions must first complement Ward White's existing operations and, secondly, require only limited attention before they make a positive contribution to the success of the group. Take Halfords, the motor accessories and cycle retailer, which Ward White acquired in 1984. The management was reorganized immediately, the control system introduced, points of sale computerized and consequently a year later Halfords was contributing to Ward White's overall success. Here, therefore is a balance between the loose and the tight properties.

Dawson also practice such a mixed approach with their subsidiaries, which we were able to look at from both the group and the subsidiary's point of view as Pringle is also one of our sharpbenders. Before the bend, Dawson was overcentralized, even the marketing decisions for subsidiaries being taken at head office. During the sharpbend, such decisions were decentralized to the subsidiaries whose chief executives were given considerable autonomy. Key controls do, however, remain. Subsidiaries prepared two key documents and kept them updated. The first was a formal business plan looking three years ahead and the second an annual budget. From what we were shown these were substantial and closely argued documents, whose format is set out by Dawson. These are then discussed by the group finance and marketing directors with the subsidiary on the subsidiary's home ground. This discussion is not a formality – it was described to us as an 'inquisition' at one stage – however, managing directors are not ordered to do anything, although they are sometimes advised to adjust their plans or their budgets.

Moreover, ambitious targets for return on capital employed and growth are set by the centre for the subsidiaries and these form the basis for incentive payments for the senior managers of the subsidiaries which can range up to 50 per cent of annual salary. Underlying the whole of the approach and pinning it together are the personal relationships between the chief executive, marketing director and finance director of the group and the senior management of the subsidiaries. At the time we interviewed them Ronald Miller was Managing Director. He has since become Chairman. In that capacity he spoke frequently to his subsidiary chief executives as well as visiting them several times a year. Any major strategic decision tended to be brought to him for discussion to permit the subsidiary chief executive, who would make it, to share responsibility with head office. Care was taken, however, to ensure that the decision remained with the subsidiary. Operation of this informal, oral network of communications had not only a strongly motivating effect but also allowed the quicker transfer of good ideas between subsidiaries. One interesting point relates to treatment of 'failed' subsidiary chief executives. Dawson is in no doubt that they must go. However, to make this possible corporate management find it necessary to 'distance' themselves from the failed individual, the warm, oral communications with head office becoming increasingly chilled and formal. It is hard to dismiss a friend.

Both the literature on turnarounds, ably summarized by Slatter (1984), and Peters and Waterman (1982) stress the importance of lean head offices and simple form (of organization). It is no surprise, therefore, that the head office was reduced in size by 30 per cent of the sharpbenders. However, half the control companies did the same. Indeed it is worth noting that the control companies in general tended to make more organizational changes than the sharpbenders. Clearly, although slimming the head office should cut overheads and may avoid all but the necessary financial bureaucratic checks on subsidiary entrepreneurial decisions, it is not in itself a sufficient route to improvement. Moreover, it may delude management into thinking that it has a solution when it has not tackled fundamental problems like product market focus and production costs.

This note of caution should not, however, lead us to reject such organizational changes as unimportant contributions to beneficial, radical change.

A striking example of such a move to a lean headquarters is provided by Low & Bonar which has a pleasant new building on the outskirts of Dundee. This was designed to house the head office as it then existed; but by the time it was completed and ready to move into, the head-office staff had been cut from fifty-four to about twelve and as a result it now occupies part of one floor, the rest of the building being used by one of the operating divisions. Like many other firms in our sample the recession after 1979 convinced top management that cuts in corporate overheads had to be made and could be achieved most readily by shrinking head offices. Like others before them they recognized that there was no need to try to second guess the management of the subsidiaries all the time if the essential control systems were good and they had appointed the right divisional and subsidiary chief executives.

From the literature and our discussion of examples above, it would seem that strong financial controls need to remain central even when operating decisions are decentralized. Consequently, it is rather surprising that more sharpbenders did not take steps to centralize their financial controls. One possible explanation is that many already had effective, central, financial controls and did not need to take further action. An alternative reason could well be that any move to centralize financial controls was outbalanced by decentralization of operational decision-making. Certainly our field work suggested that both explanations were valid.

4.3   Stronger Central Financial Control

In common with many other companies in the UK our samples of sharpbenders and control companies alike had made improvements to their methods of financial control over the previous fifteen years. In part this was because the means of improvement has been developed with the rapid rise in the availability of computer hardware and software and their similarly rapid fall in price which has brought them within reach of even the smallest business. It might also be seen as a response to more difficult financial conditions in the mid-1970s and the early 1980s. The greater emphasis on control of overheads and cash flows in table 4.1 no doubt reflects both these conditions and aspects of control which had achieved less attention in the past. Eighty per cent of the sharpbenders and 70 per cent of the control companies tightened their financial controls during the period of the bend. Almost all of the remainder of the sharpbenders had tight controls already and only minor improvements were made during the bend itself.

As is clear from table 4.5, the changes employed run across the whole range of normal financial measures. Not only were information flows improved in the sense of collecting the necessary data in the first place, but helpful methods of summarizing it were employed to enable managers and the board to make early decisions on where problems and opportunities lay and to act upon them. Improved control systems and monitoring arrangements meant that it was less likely that subsidiaries or sections would get into serious trouble without the senior management knowing.

Several of the companies took us through their financial information and control systems very closely. Walter Telfer, the Finance Director at Low & Bonar, was particularly helpful. He was brought in by Brian Gilbert, soon after he was appointed Chief Executive and set about establishing an effective and efficient accounting, information and control system. The company applied a regime of strict cash management. Each of the many subsidiaries had cash limits and Telfer claimed that by 9.30 in the morning he knew what each subsidiary's cash requirements for the day would be and could hence manage the flow very tightly. The holding company thus acts like a bank for

Table 4.5 *Stronger central financial control as a step to achieve the sharpbend*

	% of firms citing this step
3.1 Cash-flow forecasts	45
3.2 Budgetary controls	35
3.3 Management accounting data on production	35
3.4 Capital budgeting system	35
3.5 Tight control of overheads	55
3.6 Key financial ratios to chief executive and board more frequently	30
3.7 Improved quality of information	30

Note: Some companies improved financial controls in more than one respect. In all, 80 per cent of the sharpbenders introduced at least one improvement during the sharpbend.

the subsidiaries although this role is somewhat reduced for the enterprises overseas. Each subsidiary has limits for capital expenditure and close telephone contact is kept in order to question closely.

At the same time the quality of control information was improved. Before Brian Gilbert joined the company, in the mid-1970s, a very detailed system of control designed for the textile business was applied even to the diversified subsidiaries. This was pruned and reshaped but the monthly board meeting still receives detail on each of the subsidiaries. This includes a statement giving the profit-and-loss account compared with the budget, showing materials purchased, production overheads, sales, direct labour costs, gross margin and a balance sheet. There was also a forecast for the three months ahead, with the usual calculation of the main financial ratios. These were also summarized and consolidated accounts produced for the group and its divisions.

This improvement in financial control was certainly a contributory factor to the company's sharpbend in the mid-1970s. It did not prevent the company getting into financial trouble in 1980–2 although they no doubt assisted the rapid recovery that was then made. This example illustrates that whilst good financial controls may be necessary for success, they alone are not enough to avoid problems caused by a combination of other factors. The company had grown steadily after 1974, largely by acquisition, continuing the trend of diversification set by Herbert Bonar, Brian Gilbert's predecessor. The 1980 recession caused sales to fall at home and particularly abroad as sterling rose. The combination of the rise in interest rates and the rise in the pound meant that a large $11 million American loan which had been raised to buy out the US partner in the Canadian packaging business became increasingly expensive to service. Two major projects went wrong. Nairn Travel had been purchased at the height of the 1979 boom and then proceeded to make heavy losses, consuming £3–4 million of the firm's resources. The Flotex project also went wrong after a major investment and also made losses.

The availability of extensive management accounting data at Low & Bonar, however, permitted a rapid diagnosis of the sources of the major problems and early identification of the steps to be taken. The strategy for reversing the negative flows was as follows:

1   take energetic steps to resolve the cost problems in basically sound businesses – this was particularly true in Flotex where outside technical consultants were brought in;
2   contract, close or sell loss makers – within the engineering division foundries were closed with the aid of the Lazards scheme for encouraging rationalization of the industry; Hugh Smith, a producer of special pumps, was closed, together with most of Langley Alloys, and in the packaging division the older UK plants were closed;
3   tight cost controls were imposed on profitable but mature businesses and no new investment was permitted;
4   steps were taken to reduce indebtedness; and
5   head office was cut drastically as was described in the previous section.

The extent of the crisis was clear – dividends were suspended in 1981 and the share price plunged from 214p to 54p.

Two lessons are worth extracting from this experience. First that there is a range of emergency cash-flow measures which can be applied, but that a thorough change takes longer. Nairn Travel was not merged with A T Mays until 1983 (to reap the benefits of larger scale and the management expertise of A T Mays in the travel field). The 50 per cent share in the South African subsidiary was not sold until the same year – releasing a much needed £4.6 million – and the flotation of the Canadian company to eliminate the $11 million loan was not organized until late 1984. The second lesson, reported by Walter Telfer, was that it emphasized the importance of paying attention to the cash consequences of actions, particularly acquisitions. 'Acquisition is more exciting than organization' so one tends to pay too little attention to organization. That attention was paid very closely as an important contributor to the sharpbend.

The five measures taken by Low & Bonar are in many ways reminiscent of those typically found in a turnaround where there is always the need for immediate, drastic measures to boost cash flow, and which depend critically on financial data, analysis and control. These include expenditure-reducing measures, putting off all non-essential purchases, centralization of spending to improve control, stopping expansion or job replacement, improved management of debtors and stocks, and strict control of wastage. However, this is only one side of the account and steps need also to be taken to improve revenues. Such steps are inevitably rather slower to employ as this requires an evaluation of the firm's product markets (as will be seen below), but in the longer term they can be of greater importance.

Furthermore, drastic changes were required following a second sharp shock to the company in 1984–5. Brian Gilbert retired and was replaced by Roland Jarvis who has undertaken a major restructuring of the company, focusing on four business areas where the group has a technical edge as is described later on. However, he described the whole process as 'revolution followed by evolution'. The revolution was the original sharpbend but further substantial changes had been required. The sharpbend did not provide a once-and-for-all solution.

Unlike turnarounds the sharpbend does not usually involve quite the same degree of urgency, and short-term acts which harm the long-run viability of the business may be more easily avoided. Moreover, there can be a greater emphasis on changes of longer-term strategic importance. Michael Frye's package of actions at Rotaflex is more typical of the sharpbenders' approach; it consisted of three main steps:

1 he introduced management information systems to get frequent, speedy financial reporting from the subsidiaries;
2 he set up a rationalization plan aimed at consolidating the group's activities; and
3 market growth segments were identified.

The financial controls were thus very much part of a wider process of change, ensuring a focused and well-informed strategy. A good set of financial controls is viewed as an essential part of a well-run company and not something which is static. Countryside Properties had a set of reports and controls from the early 1970s. These were maintained through the bend in 1974–5 and computerized in 1976. Since then they have been upgraded twice and the most recent system has personal computers for spreadsheet work and a mainframe for a highly sophisticated contract-handling package. However, a further upgrade is being introduced in 1987. Clearly this contract-monitoring and budgetary facet is particularly important in the construction industry. McCarthy and Stone and our control also had careful computer systems for this function – in the last case including hand-held computers which can be used on site and also linked into the mainframe when required.

4.4 New Product Market Focus

One way and another all the sharpbenders adopted a new product market focus (in table 4.1 diversification was treated separately), but then so did all but one of the controls. The 1970s and early 1980s were a period of pressure

Table 4.6 *New product market strategy as a means of sharpbending*

	% of firms citing this step
4.1 Analysed existing and alternative product market postures and determined corporate plan	55
4.2 Cut back to profitable core business by:	
(a) closure	50
(b) sale of weaker business	45
(c) raised prices and squeezed costs to 'harvest' competitively weak business prior to closure	5
4.3 Divested business company did not know well	20
4.4 Focused on specific market segments by differential prices, sales emphasis and product qualities	50
4.5 Differentiated products to raise profit margins	30
4.6 Gained cost leadership by:	
(a) developing economies of scale	10
(b) developing economies of leasing	—
(c) tight control of marketing costs	15
(d) discouraging high-cost customers	5
(e) tight control of production costs	45
(f) tight control of energy and material costs	30
(g) tight control of overheads	45
(h) investing in new technology	60
4.7 Raised customer switching costs or other barriers to entry	—
4.8 Diversified into related businesses	30
4.9 Diversified into unrelated businesses	10
4.10 Invested in new plant to enter new markets	25
4.11 Mergers and cooperative supply agreements to reduce capacity and competition	5
4.12 Turnkey operations in LDCs	10
4.13 Secured supplies by backward integration	10
4.14 Warned off potential entrants and competitors by 'market signals' e.g. threats to expand	—
4.15 Entered export market vigorously via:	
(a) sales subsidiaries	15
(b) overseas agents	30
(c) home-based export salesmen	20
4.16 Other	—

and change hence there was a need for most companies to reappraise their market position. From table 4.6 it can be seen that 55 per cent of the sharpbenders did so consciously, analysing the existing posture and alternatives and determining a corporate plan. In many other companies the process was less formal, but this does not seem to have inhibited major changes. The major features which stick out in the sharpbenders' appraisals is that they:

1 invested in new technology;
2 focused on particular market segments;
3 cut back to a profitable core business through closure and sale; and
4 gained cost leadership through tight cost control.

For the control companies there was more emphasis on sale and closure and divesting rather than investing.

A clear example of such a strategic appraisal is given by the Sidlaw Group. Sidlaw was the largest jute-spinning company in the western world and until the late 1960s it was entirely involved in textiles. When Sir John Carmichael became Chairman (he was previously Managing Director of Fisons in the period well before the sharpbend) he realized that diversification was essential to avoid decline. This took the form of acquisition of a hardware wholesaler, an investment in Aberdeen hotels, the setting up of an oil support business called ASCO, and an investment in up-market weaving in wall and floor coverings. All this happened before the bend, which was precipitated by a serious collapse in the textile business and losses by the hardware firm.

Sidlaw achieved the bend by:

1 selling the hardware business to GKN;
2 closing the weaving plant and concentrating in textiles on fine jute yarns, synthetic carpet yarns and merchanting;
3 cutting the head office;
4 developing the oil interests as rapidly as possible and expanding internationally; and
5 a small new expansion into the distribution of microcomputers and software-related services which exploited internal skills.

Thus the company turned away from declining markets and towards rising ones, altering the balance of its products. Loss makers were sold or closed and in the traditional textile areas production was focused on niches which could continue to remain profitable. Focusing on the fine yarns, which they already produced, was a good move, first because producers in the Indian subcontinent could not achieve those levels of quality, and second because the major European competitors went out of business. Sidlaw now has some 40 per cent of the western market for fine jute yarn for woven carpets, with a rapid growth of exports from 5 per cent of turnover in 1981 to 40 per cent in 1985. The focus on high-growth areas was both within the existing business in oil support and outside it in computers, again using both acquisition and direct investment. The cutting of head office and tight cost control meant that items such as the fine yarns remained cost-competitive despite low labour costs overseas.

We can therefore see that although Sidlaw correctly identified the problems as early as the late 1960s, initial steps included a number of mistakes and it was not until the pressures after 1979 that the business was successfully reorganized on a longer-run basis. In Sidlaw's case the major financial control systems had been introduced in the 1970s so the company was in a good position to be able to mount a sharpbend. While each of the businesses is a separate profit centre, it is run according to different criteria. The oil businesses are encouraged to be forward looking and innovative while the textile business is subject to close cost controls and is not geared towards major investment or expansion.

Sidlaw's experience also illustrates the risks inherent in entry to such a high-growth sector. By 1986 the oil-related business had become its main generator of profits. With the collapse of oil prices in 1986 and cutback on North Sea exploration by the major oil companies, Sidlaw's profits plummeted. The effectiveness of other actions taken limited the extent of the fall, profits from fine yarns sustaining the company at a time of considerable difficulty.

In the case of companies like Ellis & Goldstein and McCarthy and Stone the change in product market focus was sharp, striking and clearly the major source of their success. McCarthy and Stone had been acquiring land steadily for building development in the early 1970s and were hit hard by the 1974 recession. Even though it sold some of its land stock it had no need to make further purchases until 1977. The change in product market focus was to some extent fortuitous.

They had acquired in 1972 a site called the Waverley near New Milton in Hampshire. Various attempts were made to get planning permission for a development which McCarthy and Stone felt was financially viable, But it was not until 1977 that permission was eventually received – for a development of 'sheltered housing' for the elderly. Density could be higher with lower requirements for parking. The development was completed in seven months and a second, similar, project embarked on which also sold well. From that point the company never looked back, and while it had drastically reduced from around 100 to six employees plus the two directors in 1974 it picked up to 600 by 1984 and from nothing to a £7 million profit over the same period.

The company had identified a market which was capable of sustainable growth over many years as the proportion of elderly people in the population grew. It was also one where there was little competition and for which there was a great deal of government approval and encouragement. This was not, however, the sole source of McCarthy and Stone's success they also had:

1 a technically refined and well-designed product to high-quality specification and strict budgeting cost controls;
2 good marketing, liaising well with potential purchasers and local authorities before development started;
3 good management of the land bank after the disastrous 1974 experience; and
4 an ability to appoint good people who were well motivated and worked together well in teams to enable smooth operation on the sites.

Ellis & Goldstein on the other hand had been looking for suitable new ideas and products for some time, having recognized that some of their strong brands were mature, cash flows were strong but a new vehicle for growth was needed. With this in mind they scoured the market at home and overseas for a new opportunity. They found it in New York, where a brand of leisure wear, sourced from Hong Kong was on sale. Before Alan Philpot left New York, he had established contact with the suppliers, Richard Harvey, and plans were then made to market the range under the name DASH in the UK via Ellis & Goldstein. An extension of their range to include fashion leisure wear, targeted at the twenty- and thirty-year-old woman and since expanded to service the young market including both children and men, was a dramatic change for a firm specializing in tailored women's wear for the middle to upper range of the middle-aged, middle-class market. In their case, success also came from tighter financial control particularly over cash, and the ability to react quickly in a fast-changing market.

Their major assets were strong stock-control and distribution systems, an understanding of the market, a flair in producing ranges of coordinated products in a variety of fabrics, an exclusive access to design and manufacturing agents in the Far East and strong credibility with the stores which permitted them to establish DASH shops within stores quickly. On this basis, they have expanded sales through DASH shops within stores at an impressive pace, established their own DASH shops and more recently started franchising DASH throughout the country. With expanding sales and profitability they have themselves made an increasing contribution to the design of DASH products, which has established a strong market image in the UK.

The example illustrates the fact that a new market posture often gains more from a wide-ranging search, frequently overseas, for opportunities which would permit existing strengths to be exploited rather than by exhaustive desk research and analysis. Analysis of sales potential and financial implications of potential projects is clearly a necessary check on intuitive, judgemental decisions but the critical ability is either to perceive or to create opportunities which the human, financial and other resources and strengths of the company permit it to exploit at least as well as, and ideally better than, other companies.

Fisons, too, provides an example of a change in product market posture. Like many others it confronted financial decline by a battery of measures to reduce costs and control them. Tight cash controls were introduced within the management accounting package; there was a substantial shake-up of management; the head office was slimmed; a five-year rolling corporate plan and annual detailed budgeting were implemented; senior management were given bonus incentives dependent upon cash as well as profit achievement; also divisions were made to run their own affairs within general and financial constraints. The underlying problem was the product market position of the company. Several businesses were making losses and had little prospect of substantial return from a major investment of corporate time and money. Even a core business, fertilizers, was in this position, for fertilizers had become a commodity business in which production and marketing economies favoured the giants like ICI. The key steps which were to lead to sustained recovery were, consequently, related to this fundamental problem. Loss-making businesses with poor prospects, including the fertilizer division, were sold, and others acquired to strengthen those aspects of the company thought to have strong prospects.

A major feature to notice from the way in which the product market focus changed for the sharpbenders was that it was frequently into quite new areas, outside the existing business of the firm. However, it was not usually into a range of unrelated products but into ones which could be grouped or exploited in a coherent division. Many firms had to turn away from their existing businesses because they were in decline. 'Sticking to the knitting', to quote the Peters and Waterman phrase, would have been disastrous. As we noted earlier, even the control companies realized this, and attempted to develop new businesses. On the whole, their switch in focus was either less expertly executed or not combined with enough other supporting factors.

4.5   Improved Quality and Service

We have noticed in the previous section that both McCarthy and Stone and Ellis & Goldstein stressed high quality as one of the elements leading to their success. The single most important step to improve quality among the sharpbenders as shown in table 4.7, was improvement in design but not all sharpbenders followed this route. Where the sharpbend involved surmounting major financial difficulties, design costs were sometimes cut, together with other overheads. Despite such exceptions, design remains the most general and important of quality-enhancement factors among the sharpbenders. Perhaps the most striking example is Countryside Properties. Like McCarthy

Table 4.7 *Improved quality and service as steps towards the sharpbend*

		% of firms citing this step
5.1	Better product design	40
5.2	Introduced or improved quality control	20
5.3	Introduced quality circles	5
5.4	Reduced delivery delays by:	
	(a) better production planning	15
	(b) bigger finished goods stocks	10
5.5	Introduced or improved after-sales service	10
5.6	Other	10

and Stone they were caught by the 1974 property crash. In the period prior to the crash they had paid too highly for building land and lacked the tight financial controls and cash-budgeting necessary for circumstances which did not involve rapid growth. They had started making changes in 1972 in both cash-flow forecasting and, principally, marketing and rationalized the business into three divisions: residential, commercial/industrial and property investment; but these steps alone were not enough to halt their relative decline.

Their striking success was to take seriously the Essex Design Guide, produced by the county planning department in 1973, and to implement it in their proposals. Alan Cherry, the Chairman and Managing Director, had been involved in the production of the guide and recognized the importance of design and its crucial role in successful marketing. Following the guide's precepts meant that planning permission was readily achieved, hence giving the firm market leadership for several years before other firms recognized the advantage. By having excellent designs and a good site at Brentwood for the first scheme under the guide, they provided such an excellent illustration of what was wanted that for three years the county planning department took visitors round Countryside's developments to illustrate what was intended. Their designs have continued to win awards and credits in various competitions and have received the accolade of being copied by some of the large building firms. However, the company has worked on their success, working with other planning authorities in bringing out similar guides and earning a reputation as a 'caring and conservation-conscious builder' by trying to blend developments into the existing landscape rather than just bulldozing the green spaces and trees.

Countryside Properties made other changes, too, to capitalize on the success of their designs: they widened their product range, acquired a good management team and built up the specialist skills necessary for the trade, rather than buying them in for each development. Hence, they have moved in exactly the opposite direction to the trend revealed in section 4.2 by increasing rather than reducing the size of their headquarters. By standardizing their designs they have also made major economies in the purchase of materials.

Design also featured strongly in the success of company 'C' who on their engineering side had made great steps forward in efficiency by thorough application of computer-aided design and manufacturing (CADCAM). The group primarily concentrates on manufacturing machinery for a number of industries. It is particularly clear in this case that improving design involves investment. Cost-cutting strategies, which affect what in the short run may appear to be overheads, can seriously prejudice future developments and mean that the sharpbend does not result in the continuing good performance that is the subject of our inquiry. Rotaflex among our sharpbenders did actually cut its design team from twelve to two to help them get through the worst of the downturn, but as a result it was not until three to four years later in 1983/4 that the new designs started coming through again. However, the company was sustained in part because it had a high reputation for design flair and product-pioneering and hence had a stock to help sustain it through a difficult period.

Whatman Reeve Angel followed a strategy to exploit different markets by using the high reputation of the Whatman name. Customers expected a higher quality and higher price. They introduced very advanced computerized processing and monitoring equipment in papermaking and conversion, which not only sped up production, allowing them to respond more quickly to market movements, but increased productivity, reduced most costs and improved quality and consistency. They thus improved the standing of the Whatman name still further, improved profitability and expanded capacity all at the same time. This again involved heavy investment and hence tight controls in the short run. Everything possible was done to keep the Whatman brand name synonymous with quality, consistency and service.

This idea of trading on 'quality' was common to several companies. We have already noted it for the two distillers in their different ways: Macallan as a connoisseur's product; Bell's, in the blended market, being able to generate a margin over its rivals which in turn enabled it to put more effort into marketing and a close relationship with customers which further enhanced their market share.

In the clothing trade, design is an essential feature for success, and we saw in the last section how in its switch to fashion leisure wear Ellis & Goldstein put a premium on design and flair in coordinating colours and fabrics. Dawson International added a strong emphasis on quality with their Scottish knitwear brands aiming for the upper part of the market. In many cases there was not the 'obsession' with quality which is said to characterize some of the best American companies but there is certainly a sustained emphasis. Some like Sirdar further enhanced their position after the sharpbend by devotion to continuous technical improvement and innovation as part of a general strategy to move into the high-value-added products. At Don Brothers, now Don and

Low, we were told 'we are not the cheapest on the market but we are the most efficient . . . One of the things people have under-estimated is quality control'.

Bill Low and his colleagues at Don Brothers recognized clearly that because a fault in yarn or backing, which represents a low proportion of the total cost of manufacturing a carpet, can cause rejection of the whole carpet or difficulties in its production, consistently high quality is a critical factor. They introduced 100 per cent inspection of the product by installing computer-controlled electronic devices on each loom. They retained a final manual inspection too. This increased quality and at the same time reduced costs dramatically by allowing each operative to run many more looms. When a fault (break) occurs the loom stops automatically.

4.6 Improved Marketing

Marketing, in the sense of getting 'close to the customer', is one of Peters and Waterman's eight characteristics of the excellent firm. In the more recent work with Nancy Austin (Peters and Austin, 1985), it is one of the three facets of excellence with which he surrounds the core of leadership. Indeed, in the latest version (Peters, 1986), it is labelled 'obsession with customers'. A similar note is sounded by Goldsmith and Clutterbuck (1984). We explored this 'customer-first' mentality with each of the sharpbenders and, as is shown in table 4.8 (item 6.10) nearly half of them had deliberately tried to develop close relations with their customers as part of the sharpbend.

The best example was very clearly Bell's with the pursuit of a detailed, almost family, relationship with the licensees. However, it is clear that the nature of the relationship depends upon the type of industry and number of buyers. The domination of a large part of a company's business by single customers – such as the Central Electricity Generating Board or, with the sales of telephone exchanges, by British Telecom (and its antecedents), or for Ferranti by the Ministry of Defence – could affect the viability of the enterprise very substantially. Clearly a very close relationship is required in such cases and indeed it is usual for the customer to have a major say in the development of the product and its detail. The involvement of British Petroleum in the development of Seabug at UDI was a further instance.

Such a close relationship is not always welcomed, particularly in industries where domination by a single customer is not a necessary outcome. Ward White, for example, explicitly sought to avoid such dependence on a single or a few major customers. Indeed, the way they tried to get closer to the ultimate customer was by moving into retailing rather than concentrating on manufacturing. One of the problems facing a manufacturing firm is that its customers are not necessarily the ultimate purchaser and hence the firm is dealing with an intermediary such as a further manufacturer, wholesaler, retailer or shipper. In those circumstances the relationship between the

Table 4.8   *Improved marketing as a step to sharpbending*

		% of firms citing this step
6.1	Prices raised where demand is inelastic	15
6.2	More competitive discounts	—
6.3	Rationalized product range within existing markets	15
6.4	Improved distribution channels	20
6.5	Focused on more profitable customers	15
6.6	Optimized after-sales service	15
6.7	More cost-effective advertising and controlling salesmen	15
6.8	Better finished-stock levels	10
6.9	Improved marketing information supplied frequently to board	20
6.10	Stressed 'getting close to customer' in company value system	45
6.11	Rationalized sales staff and delivery journeys	15
6.12	Other	30

ultimate customer and the producer can be much weaker and the necessary feedback of information from them more difficult to obtain. Peters (1986) puts the emphasis on after-sales service, but it is noticeable from table 4.8 (item 6.6) that this emphasis is not shared by the sharpbenders. To some extent this is because of the products involved. Not surprisingly, both builders. Countryside Properties and McCarthy and Stone, paid special attention to after-sales service. In some cases of residential housing such a service is actually compulsory under the conditions of the NHBC. However, as both companies recognized, marketing is a far wider problem than dealing with customers. The development has to be 'sold' to the planning authorities before it can take place, and in each case the companies had managed to develop close ties with various local authorities which helped them steer their developments through. It is also important in that industry to find a buyer before the property is completed so that the capital is tied up in the buildings constructed for as short a period as possible.

Publishers also have a second type of 'customer'. A successful publisher has to be able to field a good string of authors in order to be able to generate the necessary books to sell. Thus, it is perhaps even more important for them to nurture authors than the customers for the books themselves. '[Editors] have to embrace authors; it's no Monday to Friday for a good publisher. Whether it is something obscure like embroidery or areas like Monty Python or children's books, you really have to know your authors, assess them, know them, their wives, their children, their dogs, their holiday plans, their interests, quirks, birthdays, and you have to share enthusiasm and interest with them. This is the only way you get the right people for the right subject and get them to write books' according to David Evans, Deputy Group Managing Director at ABP.

Whilst the precise emphasis of the marketing changes made by our sharpbenders varied according to the nature of their business, as is evident from table 4.8, there can be no doubt of the importance that most of them attached to marketing. We have already noted how, for instance, a marketing director was appointed to Macallan because the company 'had to get the consumer' for bottled malt whisky as the demand from blenders was contracting. Here as in other companies high pressure forced companies closer to their customers. Taking this further, the company which voluntarily gets close to the customers will tend to have a competitive edge over other firms in the industry.

4.7 Reduced Costs

Reductions in costs clearly play a central role in the achievement of a successful sharpbend. Not only is reduction in production costs one of the main features which distinguishes the sharpbenders from the controls but it is the step with the most clearly defined antecedents in the period of relative decline (see appendix). Companies which previously had poor financial control mechanisms found when they tightened up that there were many areas in which costs had not been controlled as they might have. However, more generally, attention to costs is a major response to pressure, either from increased competition or from a general decline in market demand. In slacker periods it appears that there is a strong temptation not to apply the same scrutiny to costs at every level.

However, one feature stands out in the opposite direction. Companies, whose relative decline was attributed in part to poor quality and reliability, put significantly less direct pressure on cost reduction. Here their problem was to improve the product and that frequently involved extra immediate expenditure rather than reduction in it. However, improved quality-control measures often reduced wastage, the proportion of products returned and after-sales service, so creating in the longer run savings quite sufficient to outweigh these costs. At the same time, several companies benefited from an increase in sales stemming from recognition by the customer of the better-quality product or service.

From table 4.9 it is evident that many different actions were taken to reduce costs both in general and of production. As many as 65 per cent of the sharpbenders, twice the proportion found among the controls, cut production costs by investing in new plant and equipment. Second, 40 per cent of the sharpbending companies increased productivity by improving morale. It was

Table 4.9   *Cost reduction as a step towards sharpbending*

		% of firms using this step
(a)	*General*	
7.1	Introduced cost-reduction targets	30
7.2	Introduced zero-based budgeting	10
7.3	Introduced profit or cost centres	20
7.4	Cut head-office staff	45
7.5	Moved head office to cheaper premises	10
7.6	Cut working capital costs by reducing:	
	(a) finished-goods stocks	10
	(b) materials stocks	5
	(c) work in progress	10
	(d) debtors	10
7.7	Cut marketing expenses	—
7.8	Other	35
(b)	*Production costs*	
8.1	Increased labour productivity by:	
	(a) better training	25
	(b) improved morale	40
	(c) removal of job demarcation	15
	(d) work study	30
	(e) wage incentive schemes	30
	(f) consulted workforce on cost reduction	20
8.2	Reduced pilferage	—
8.3	Better quality control reduced wastage	20
8.4	Better production control	35
8.5	Better stock control	30
8.6	Improved utilization of capacity	35
8.7	Invested in new plant to reduce costs	65
8.8	Other	30

not just a matter of cutting back on employment. Certainly major labour reductions were necessary initially – McCarthy and Stone fell from 100 to six employees in the downturn but by 1987 employment has reached 2000. What is clear is that cutting production costs was associated with positive advances in technology, working practices, morale, planning and control, and not just with a negative, defensive, slashing of resources.

That cost reduction without a positive element is not a good strategy, is brought out very clearly by Stuart Slatter's (1984) study of turnarounds. Here 90 per cent of failed turnaround attempts pursued cost reduction while only 63 per cent of the successful cases did. Direct comparisons with the proportions in our own study are not possible because of the differences in definition but the contrast with the turnaround is clear. In the turnaround, according to Slatter, the most popular strategy among the successful companies is asset reduction. The problem for the company in serious trouble is damage limitation in the short run. For the sharpbender the position is much more equilibrious, with the striving for the new balancing the correction of the old.

The cost of the manufacturing side of Collins at Westerhill is a good illustration of this balanced approach. On the negative side, in the face of losses, employment was halved from 1750 in 1979 to 836 in 1986, entirely by voluntary redundancy. This was easily achieved in 1979 because many thought that the firm would fail. However, even when announcing the redundancies in 1979 an announcement of an investment of £1.4 million was also made. Since then the rate of investment in the latest technology has increased and was £10.5 million in 1984–5. As a result output actually rose, so productivity more than doubled – quite a contribution to reducing costs. Secondly, wastage was reduced and quality improved by putting the responsibility back to the journeyman who could lose his bonus if quality was poor. Improved production control reduced the amount of working capital tied up in work in progress, while improved and computerized finished-book stock control reduced the working capital tied up in stocks. The new technology made it more economic to have shorter runs for each edition, thus contributing, clearly to the reductions in stocks. The cost reductions were not restricted to production. There were early retirements and redundancies among middle managers and clerical staff. Indeed part of the office block was bricked off to avoid having to pay rates. In the group as a whole the prestigious head office in St James's Place was sold and the London office was also moved to smaller premises in part to signal the new spirit of austerity.

However, this major cost-reduction exercise was only part of the total package. The sale of the offices and of the three divisions of the American subsidiary not only cut running losses but realized capital which could be used to reduce debt. The management 'culture' was changed to a more open system which involved easier communication, an emphasis on getting able people and motivating them to achieve good results within a framework of controls and accountability. Management is very much directed to action. The printing works now handles 'contract work' from other publishers which accounts for about a third of the business. Later the position was improved still further by the acquisition of Granada and rationalization of the assets of the two businesses. This meant that capacity could be fully utilized and production costs cut still further. The strength that Collins regained so quickly meant not just that it was able to make a profit of over £1 million in 1980, within a year of embarking on the strategy leading to the sharpbend, but that in the following year it was able to mount a successful defence against a takeover bid by Rupert Murdoch's News International.

The extent of cost reduction which can usefully be employed obviously depends upon the circumstances of the firm beforehand. Pringle was making substantial losses in 1973/4 and had an overdraft of some £10 million. It had become a subsidiary of Dawson International in 1967 so, despite being a subsidiary, the sharpbend was not caused by the original takeover itself. Dawson did, however, take actions in 1974 to stimulate a sharpbend. Pringle of Scotland was centred on Hawick with two production plants and three marketing companies, each with separate managing directors and twenty-six directors between them. Dawson brought in a successful new Managing Director, Bill McEwan, from one of its other subsidiaries and not suprisingly he was able to make sweeping cuts to overheads. The existing structure was reformed, the twenty-six directors were reduced to six, one of the production sites was closed and production concentrated on the remaining one. Half the management were made redundant – a bigger cut than was sustained by the workforce as a whole which fell by 1000 to 1400. These cuts were obtained with the collaboration of the trade union (the GMWU) aided by the decision to have heavy and continuing investment in the plant which meant that new complex designs could be executed by machines. This, coupled with the introduction of more standard lines like 'sportswear' in addition to original high-quality cashmere products, meant that output did not fall and hence labour productivity was virtually doubled. This extension of the range of products also helped reduce production costs by overcoming the problem of slack summer sales. Control over costs was tight and detailed; for example, free tea and rolls were removed as fringe benefits for the whole workforce, including management, and working lunches had to be paid for.

These two companies, therefore, covered the whole range of cost-reducing measures suggested in table 4.9, each employing a large number of them, including the cutting of the size of the head office, which we have already observed was a frequent action.

Their behaviour was similar to that of other sharpbenders in the same industries, but was more extensive. Michael Turner, at Associated Book Publishers, told us: 'In the short term we were fairly bloody both to debtors and creditors and that caused quite a lot of pain – a difficult thing to force through for about nine to twelve months because it had not been our style. We were very prompt payers, we were renowned for our promptness. Many of our suppliers had relied on ABP cheques coming through dead on time.' His Deputy Managing Director, David Evans, described how the cost reduction applied in more detail at the production level: 'We stopped people using all kinds of exotic paper. Editors love choosing papers. I have attended editorial conferences in the mid-1960s where you spent the whole afternoon choosing whether the paper will be a particular kind of antique laid.' In ABP's sharpbend in 1980, they did not repeat the error of the previous downturn in the early 1970s when they cut back investment. Publishing of their kind often involves development periods of some seven years – you eat your seed corn at your peril.

4.8 Acquisitions

Acquisition as a step to sharpbending (see table 4.10) must clearly be treated with caution compared to many of the other steps which firms have taken because it was more popular with the control companies (80 per cent) than with the sharpbenders (50 per cent). It does not require much thought to see why. If we look back to the causes of relative decline we see from table 2.2 that 30 per cent of the sharpbenders were helped on the downward path by poor acquisitions. However, if poor acquisitions can be disastrous, well-chosen ones, subsequently properly integrated into the company and managed effectively, can make strong positive contributions. John Wood provides a good example. In the 1960s the company operated a fishing fleet and ship-repair business from Aberdeen. After Ian Wood joined the company it began to make some acquisitions: a fish-processing company in 1967, a sheet-metal company in 1968 and a joinery company in 1969. So progress in the period before the bend had been above average. Ian Wood was young, ambitious and keen to get the company to grow; even so, when the oil industry came to Aberdeen it took the company a year or two to realize the opportunities available (reinforced by a trip to Houston). They then began by buying in the specialist knowledge by attracting experienced staff away from Great Yarmouth-based companies, which had provided logistic support of operations in the southern sector of the North Sea and had now set up in Aberdeen. Wood's initial progress was steady but not spectacular, as it learnt the new business in this way and by joint ventures, which enabled it to acquire the necessary technology. At the same time it entered related businesses, such as painting oil rigs, which could be jointly marketed.

From this base it had begun, by 1975, to acquire small companies, previously established by entrepreneurial technologists who had already undertaken the early years of developing their businesses and had borne the heavy negative cash flows involved. They were frequently in financial difficulties and had often also revealed a lack of managerial ability. Half of the companies came to the John Wood Group for financial salvation and the

Table 4.10 *Acquisition as a means of achieving a sharpbend*

		% of firms using this step
9.1	To diversify	20
9.2	To increase market share	25
9.3	To secure suppliers	10
9.4	To secure distributive channels	25
9.5	Positive management action to integrate new acquisitions	15

others because of the extensive local knowledge of Ian Wood and his team. The recipe was to provide the financial backing of the Group, the greater security to clients given by a substantial company, and to bundle services so that more and less profitable services were provided to the same customers on the same rigs.

Ian Wood operated a managerial approach which stimulated initiative and application among lower levels of managers and foremost among the general managers of the operating companies, to whom all operating, but not major policy or capital-investment decisions, were delegated. He works long hours himself, believes that risks must be carefully evaluated but then taken to gain high returns, operates an 'open-door' policy to both his own managers and others who may bring intelligence about opportunities, communicates orally with his senior managers and is participative, while requiring short succinct, written statements of all proposals. He stresses the importance of looking beyond present operations to future opportunities. More recently this centralized approach became impossible as the company's size rose too far; so three divisions were created. Right through this period of rapid growth an effective financial control system was applied with centralized cash management on a daily basis. There was a corporate plan at Group level and the individual enterprises had to form business plans to fit in with it. Decisions on implementation were made after consultation with Ian Wood at Group Management (a head office of twelve).

Thus, the successful acquisition strategy was not only thought out carefully with a string of related businesses but was carefully managed, monitored and controlled thereafter, with each enterprise being firmly drawn into the Group. It was not a fairly random acquisition of firms which appeared a good buy and were then left largely with their existing management and systems intact.

Dawson International ran a similar acquisition strategy. Again they had been acquiring well before the bend – their acquisition of Pringle occurred some seven years earlier. The group had expanded from a fibre-spinning and merchanting base into knitwear. In this phase, the motivation had been largely defensive, pursuing forward integration to prevent outlets from being captured by rivals. However, many of these early acquisitions were shown to be successful.

The initial strategy was extended when the founder of the company became chairman and his finance director became chief executive. Headquarters were built up and the company tried to diversify into other areas such as hotels and leisure. The centralized system meant that the subsidiary directors had too little power to act while the group directors were often out dealing with one company or another and were difficult to contact – hence making communications and decision-making difficult. The new diverse subsidiaries were not well run and the group did not manage to correct this properly. Perhaps because of the rapid growth of Dawson

International as a group of diverse companies, head office lacked some of the key skills to manage such an undertaking effectively, and were not able to identify and correct the various management weaknesses of their new subsidiaries. This was the more serious because many had been vulnerable to takeover just because of their poor performance.

In the sharpbend, the top management changed with the chairman resuming the role of chief executive. Power and incentives were given to the subsidiaries – incentives relating both to group and subsidiary performance to discourage attempts by one part of the group to profit at the expense of others. Group management were then able to concentrate on strategy.

Delegating operating-decision-taking, including major decisions on new products and marketing, to subsidiary chief executives might seem to be a strange move given their earlier failure. One explanation of this apparent inconsistency is that where performance had been strongly deficient the problems were very great. Hence, while there were some personnel changes, and new management was brought in as at Pringle, many of the old senior management remained, but were now liberated from previous frustrating restrictions imposed by the group. They now had authority to make decisions but were fully accountable for them. This alone was said in Dawson International to have led to fundamentally new patterns of behaviour. Again, the company applied a wide range of the steps we have been discussing: stronger financial controls, new product market focus, improved quality, service and marketing, cost reduction – balanced by investment as we noted in the previous section. Loss-making subsidiaries that were unrelated to Dawson International's core business were sold. Once again acquisition provided a major thrust forward, with purchases of Haggas, a well-run textile firm (subsequently sold), KSW, a German spinner of hand-knitting yarns and J E Morgan, an American manufacturer of thermal underwear.

However, unlike in the early 1970s, in this second stage of growth Dawson have pursued exacting standards for acquisitions. First they have stuck to the textile industry, which they know, and have not diversified into 'fish farms and tourism'. Second, they required that the proposed acquisition be well run, in a country with a stable economy. As for its type, it needed to have good consumer ties, and have a strong production base which they could exploit with their marketing experience and techniques. Thus there was a clear strategy which has produced sustained growth in both sales and profits for Dawson International over a decade in which market conditions have rarely been easy.

However, not all acquisitions are intended primarily to add new markets to the parent company. The Collins acquisition of Granada in 1983 certainly added important authors, a range of paperbacks and a valuable publishing mark. It also brought in a new management team with a different philosophy which helped input new ideas. Nonetheless, the main logic behind the acquisition lay in more effective use of Collins's distribution and printing facilities. Collins were also able to tie the acquisition in with a rights issue which reduced debt and increased working capital.

Acquisitions can thus form not only a part of a successful sharpbend but also contribute to the sustained good performance over the future, as long as they are an asset which continues to generate a return on which further growth can be based, are well managed, and are well integrated into the control systems of the group.

4.9   Debt Reduction

We noted earlier that Stuart Slatter had found that asset reduction was the commonest step undertaken by successful turnaround companies with a view to raising cash to ease their debt and cash-flow problems. It was also clear in table 4.1 that debt reduction was much more common among the control companies (80 per cent) than the sharpbenders (50 per cent). Clearly, debt reduction in itself does not distinguish sharpbenders from other companies. Nonetheless, removal of a crippling burden of interest payments and restoration of a sound gearing ratio can certainly liberate a company to take positive steps to increase growth of sales and profitability. The direct effect of debt reduction by sale of assets must, however, turn on the relative importance of the profit-generating potential of these assets on the one hand and reduction in the cost of servicing debt on the other. (see table 4.11.)

The sale by Collins of their headquarters provides a useful illustration, as parting with the valuable, prestigious building permitted them to reduce their debts. Here they were disposing of an overhead, albeit a dearly cherished one, which had little direct effect on the generation of revenue. Hence the impact on profitability was strongly beneficial.

Similarly, asset-restructuring at Low & Bonar allowed pressure on the company to be relieved without apparent long-term damage to its revenue-generating capacity. By floating their Canadian subsidiary on the Stock Exchange they were able to pay off an $11 million loan and were able to retain

Table 4.11 *Steps to achieve sharpbends through debt reduction*

	% of firms using this step
10.1 Sale of subsidiaries	35
10.2 Sale of other assets	20
10.3 Sale of assets and lease back	5
10.4 Public flotation of subsidiaries	5
10.5 Rights issue	25
10.6 Going public (if a private company)	10

a major stake in a now-profitable company. Sale of their Zambian subsidiary had a purely favourable effect on cash flows within the group since Low & Bonar had been unable to repatriate the profits. What it generated had appeared from the accounts to be usable funds, but they had to remain in Zambia and could not be employed to help other parts of the group. This illustrates the fact found in many of the sharpbenders that the motives for the sale of subsidiaries may be complex and interrelated. Debt reduction may be only one. Since 1984 the new management at Low & Bonar has taken the restructuring much further, selling all African and Australian businesses and also the loss-makers in engineering. At Fisons, the sale of their fertilizer interests to Norsk Hydro in early 1982 may best be seen as part of a major break with the past and a reorientation of the business. Although the sale was perhaps the most externally visible and dramatic change, it was combined with other steps: management changes, accounting and tight cash control, slimming of head office, a cost-reduction drive, corporate planning and budgeting, cash and profit targets with incentives for management, and greater divisional responsibility. All of these also contributed to moving the company out of loss making and into the purchase of new businesses, particularly overseas. This change of focus provided the basis for the steady build-up of the business since 1981.

Sales of subsidiaries, such as Whatman Reeve Angel's biochemical division to a British subsidiary of the Genzyme Corporation, were in many cases as much to get rid of loss-makers, which of course contributed to increasing indebtedness, as to realize assets and to repay the debt itself. Thus there is a mixture of both profit and balance-sheet motives for many disposals. It is only in cases like that of Ferranti where the trigger for the sharpbend is the refusal of the bank or other creditors to allow the debt to continue or be increased that the primary initial motive must be debt reduction. Ferranti looked to the government for a substantial injection of funds to get them out of their financial difficulties, which they achieved when the National Enterprise Board acquired a majority holding in the company; but in this case the company was selling control of itself.

That route to debt reduction is obviously specific to the period when there was a policy of government intervention in industry. Other examples such as British Leyland are well known, although in the case of Rolls Royce the action had occurred earlier, rather against the grain of the prevailing policy which was opposed to intervention. Such an opportunity does not exist at present and if injections of equity capital are required this has to be achieved through the private sector. Although some routes of public sector help to achieving the sharpbend may be closed now, others are still open and should not be neglected. Examples of what was used are discussed in the next section, including the Wool Textile Investment Scheme which helped Sirdar restructure, research grants for UDI, and the Lazards scheme which helped Low & Bonar extract itself from the loss-making castings business.

Equity capital was raised by McCarthy and Stone in several steps, going to the Unlisted Securities Market in the first instance in June 1982, when they raised £1 million. They returned in December 1983 for a further £12 million and have since obtained a full market quotation, in January 1984, and raised a further £12 million to finance additional development. They, along with other construction companies, faced very considerable asset-structure problems when the housing market collapsed in 1974. Not only was the value of their land assets reduced but the value of the loans taken out to purchase them remained unchanged. Interest rates had risen rapidly, a major cause of the collapse of the market, and, of course, the land was not readily saleable at any reasonable price. The first step in changing the structure of their assets and debt therefore had to be the sale of such land as they could in order to finance keeping the business going at all. It was only when the sharpbend was well established that they could seek finance from the USM by approaching it as a thriving concern.

This illustrates a problem for potential sharpbenders wishing to alter their debt position by raising new equity. Mounting financial difficulties, where the company is in absolute decline, or lack-lustre performance where it is just stagnating makes a company's equity unattractive. Moreover, in general recessions, when industry as a whole is in difficulty, stock-market values are consequently lower. For both reasons any price–earnings ratio at which a rights issue is made is likely to be much lower than management believe would properly reflect potential for growth and level of profits. It is for this reason that sale of assets tends to be used as the only way out, although, in their history of the Newton Chambers Group, Grinyer and Spender (1979a) point to a radical way out used by Central and Sherwood after their takeover of Newton Chambers. Instead of selling the loss-making activities they sold Izal, which was doing very well, for a healthy £13½ million which enabled them to repay the main £12½ million bank loan which had seen them through the first crucial period of the turnaround. The strategy was to use funds from the strong parts of the business to invest in the weaker parts to make them in turn profitable. This is the complete opposite of the strategy employed by our sharpbenders where the tendency was to get rid of the loss-making subsidiaries. Dawson International and Sidlaw are clear examples. As Philip Birch of Ward White put it, their strategy was to 'eliminate all the fringe non-profit-making activities and concentrate on the core business'. TI's recent sale of its consumer-products businesses shows a further aspect of these strategies. While those subsidiaries were profitable and had contributed strongly to the success of the group, it was felt that the group needed to concentrate on its most promising growth areas so that it had sufficient resources to support the scale of investment necessary to enable those businesses to maintain their competitive edge.

Firms seeking a cash injection to get themselves out of debt problems had to look for harsh solutions. In some cases, as with UDI, this occurs through complete takeover, but the help can be partial as with the substantial holding of Rupert Murdoch's News International in Collins. Here this was the result of a failed takeover bid, which in fact turned out to be for the company's benefit. Obviously transactions in existing shares do nothing to reduce the company's debt as they are an exchange between shareholders. It depends on how the new shareholders are prepared to help the company.

Sharpbenders are thus clearly in a different position from turnaround companies but this is partly a matter of extent. Their basic viability is not normally in question and hence with a comprehensive, forward-looking package they have been able to finance their operations without having to resort to emergency measures. The measures of financial control, restructuring, changes in product market focus and cost-reduction strategies were essential parts of this. In periods when real and nominal interest rates were high it clearly paid to make debt reduction an integral part of the strategy also.

4.10 Windfalls

As we have noted from the remarks of several chief executives, luck apparently played an important role in many sharpbends. Indeed, according to table 4.1, 85 per cent of the sharpbenders benefited from windfalls of one form or another compared with 70 per cent of the control companies. Given that the relative decline experienced by most sharpbenders was associated with a recession it is not surprising that the recovery after the bend was also associated with the pick-up of demand (see table 4.2). Clearly that pick-up on its own is insufficient for a sharpbend as the whole industry is subject to the same cyclical forces. What it offers is the ability to finance the changes in structure and methods of operation through increasing revenues. Without this recovery the firm would be unable to move forward in anything like the same manner and benefit from the improvement in its competitive position relative to the others in its industry.

Since these are windfalls, not changes engendered by the firms' own actions, they represent a change in circumstances which aid the firm's own attempts to change for the better. This is the exact opposite of the causes of relative decline where cyclical decline, when added to the failings of the company, depressed company performance. We observed, however, that both decline *and* perception of opportunities created by windfalls pushed sharpbenders towards taking the radical steps necessary for a sharpbend – the pressures on the company 'crystallized the issues' as Philip Birch of Ward White put it.

As is clear from table 4.12, it is the factors which affect all companies in the industry, relating to the general conditions in the markets, which are the most widespread form of windfall. These comprise not just cyclical variation in demand but a more general secular change as well. Furthermore, given that

Table 4.12   *Windfalls as a step towards the sharpbend*

	% of firms taking this step
11.1 Cyclical upturn in demand	40
11.2 Secular upturn in demand	20
11.3 Government action	20
11.4 Operation of government agency	10
11.5 Falling costs of inputs relative to competitors	
(a) raw materials	—
(b) interest rates	—
(c) wages	5
(d) other	—
11.6 Exit of competitor	20
11.7 Action of competitor creates protective barrier for all	—
11.8 Fall in exchange rate making prices more competitive	30
11.9 Other	30

the UK had a floating exchange rate during the entire period of our study, quite large changes in relative competitiveness took place which also had an impact on the companies' sharpbends. This, of course, is related to the recovery from the 1974 and 1980–1 recessions after which the exchange rate improved. Indeed in 1980–1 the rise in the exchange rate – as a result partly of the exploitation of North Sea oil and partly of the government's monetary squeeze which drove up interest rates – was a contributor to causing the recession (see Aldington and Mayes, 1988). These fluctuations affect all firms dealing in traded goods and services, whether or not they are exporters, because they face competition at home from imports.

The second main area of influence is from the government itself either from specific measures, such as the aid to Ferranti, or from more general measures, such as regional grants from which a wide range of firms can and did benefit. Thirdly, the competitive position of firms in the market can change as a result of the actions of others – either competitors who may become less competitive in relative terms or even leave the industry altogether thereby reducing competition, or suppliers or purchasers who can affect relative costs by altering their own prices, product specifications, quality, reliability, or volume of purchases. There is also a large residual group of windfalls containing a heterogeneous set of factors, ranging from coming up with an excellent innovation, to happening to be in a sector of the market which takes off. For instance, the fact that the John Wood Group was sited in Aberdeen was purely fortuitous; if it had been based elsewhere, it would have found it much more difficult to benefit from North Sea oil and it could not have achieved the same spectacularly successful growth from its traditional fishing and related businesses.

Glaxo is a good example of a number of facets of external forces and lucky timing which helped the company achieve its sharpbend. The most important factor was the development of a new anti-ulcer drug, ranitidine, usually known by the name Zantac. This was launched in 1981/2 in the UK and Italy and in mid-1983 in the US. Its sales accounted for over 20 per cent of turnover in 1984 and at the time of writing it is still one of the top two or three most successful drugs in the world in terms of sales.

Second, since Zantac is an international product, Glaxo was aided in its successful marketing by the fall in the sterling/dollar exchange rate which continued from early 1981 right through to early 1985. The general recovery from the recession also aided demand for a wide range of Glaxo's products.

Zantac would have made a substantial improvement to Glaxo's performance without other radical measures. Glaxo is a sharpbender in the full sense, however, because of the other measures it took. The company had been steadily changing its focus towards a multinational one since 1963. This process was continued under the chairmanship of Sir Austin Bide and developed still further by Paul Girolami who became Chief Executive in late 1980 (Sir Austin continued as Chairman). The drive and determination increased with successive leaders. The UK operations were restructured in 1978 with all the UK companies being brought together under one operating company, Glaxo Pharmaceuticals. By 1980 the profitability of these companies had doubled.

Thus major steps had already been taken whose results filtered through and helped in the exploitation of Zantac. This increased profitability and activity, which in turn not only raised morale and increased the enthusiasm of the workforce but enabled Glaxo to put more resources into R&D to help ensure the continuing flow of new products, and into marketing which was reorganized on a team basis.

The major point therefore is not simply that Glaxo got windfall gains but that it was geared up to make use of them. The control companies also enjoyed windfalls but they were not able to capitalize on them with the same success as the sharpbenders as they had not, by and large, undertaken sufficient of the other steps necessary for sharpbending.

It is easy to see that timing can be fortunate or unfortunate. Associated Paper Industries felt there was no long-term future for corrugated paper without major investment in expansion, and recognized the increasing substitution of plastic material for this paper packaging. Since it had only one plant, Mallandain, from which it had difficulty servicing the country as a whole, it decided to sell the plant to Jefferson Smurfit in June 1980. It is fortunate they did so as profits soon slumped when the demand for corrugated paper plummeted in 1981. Similarly, McCarthy and Stone hit upon their winning strategy of sheltered housing as a result of a very fortunate combination of circumstances – they had a site which they had difficulty getting planning permission to develop. However, in 1976 the government Green Paper on housing requirements came out which permitted higher-density housing for elderly people and presented a viable way forward. Furthermore, the failure of an arrangement with a housing association meant that they had to organize the running of the development themselves which meant they could avoid a 5 per cent commission. This stroke of luck followed the Finance Act at the depth of the recession which permitted the offsetting of the inflation component of stock-building against tax.

Other events may be regarded as windfalls or the result of effort depending upon one's position. UDI, for example, who had developed scanning sonar for their oil-rig work were delighted to find that they had a lucrative military spin-off. However, they had consciously invested heavily in R&D and encouraged work on sonar, and a potential military market had also been recognized from the early stages of this work. The pay-off could be regarded as a normal reward for their efforts. Similarly Ellis & Goldstein were seeking opportunities when they came across fashion leisure wear. While the particular discovery was partly a matter of luck, if they had not been looking they probably would not have made it. Thus the sharpbenders benefited from windfalls in two senses; first they had more because in seeking opportunities they were more likely to come across a windfall; second, because they were taking many other measures which would aid a sharpbend they were more likely to benefit from a windfall if it occurred.

4.11 An Overall View

The major characteristic of the sharpbenders was that they were active on many fronts. Almost all firms took action in five areas:

1 there were major changes in management and often in organization;
2 stronger financial controls were introduced;
3 there was a new product market focus;
4 marketing was improved; and
5 there were strong pressures to reduce costs.

In this most were aided by windfall gains, which in particular contributed to the specific timing of the bend. In addition about half the companies:

6 sought to reduce their debt; and
7 made acquisitions.

These various actions can be grouped into three main categories. Most firms changed the people at the top and the way they were organized. They made major efforts to cut costs, particularly central overheads and introduced strong controls to manage expenditure and information flows to identify opportunities. Thirdly, they took positive action on a wide range of issues – investing in the future, re-orienting the product market focus, acquiring new companies to strengthen their favoured areas and divesting themselves of loss-making parts of the business. It is this positive bias for action which characterized most of the companies we interviewed. By and large this was not of the great outward, cultural variety commonly referred to in the American literature on excellence but a straightforward enthusiasm, commitment, determination to succeed, and courage.

The message is simple. Act. Try it. As Mrs Tyrrell at Sirdar put it, 'Success is what you make it'. Vigorous action was necessary to achieve a change. It was not achieved by people who flinched from the harshest decisions or at taking well-judged risks. This contrast between harsh measures to control costs, reducing overheads and getting rid of loss-making areas on the one hand, and forward-looking enthusiasm, with investment, acquisition, new products, innovation and a drive for quality on the other, is a difficult pairing to manage simultaneously. Michael Frye at Rotaflex thought it too harsh a combination, 'I could not be good and nasty at the same time', so he brought in McGrath from British Leyland to examine each of the plants and head office and make the necessary cuts. Four hundred and forty out of the total group employment of 1185 were made redundant. When the task was complete after twenty-one months in March 1980, McGrath left. Frye was therefore able to keep his own dynamic, forward-looking reputation intact and carry the group into the upturn. To help with this the company put an emphasis on keeping together a professional management team of young, dynamic managers or 'performers' as they were referred to.

This technique of employing the right people to make the changes ran right through our sample. While it is necessary to have clear objectives and a good operating strategy to achieve them, as Arthur Baker at Whatman Reeve Angel put it 'The plan is only as good as the people to carry out the plan'. It is necessary to have people who are good at management, 'You find a lot of professional people are very good at their job, but give them a managerial job requiring motivation of people and they are no good' (McCarthy and Stone). This was recognized by control companies as well. 'There is people in everything'. The successful sharpbenders had tended to be able to motivate their workforce even where it was by quiet enthusiasm and loyalty as at Macallan-Glenlivet.

There are clear difficulties in undertaking a sharpbend because, except in a few cases where the relative decline was due to factors totally external to the company, the company was doing various things wrong or badly. These required correction; people, therefore, needed to recognize they had made mistakes, admit them, and then behave differently in the future – by and large a tall order. Secondly, the business is likely to have been inefficient and steps are then needed to redress the problem. In a rising market that might purely entail getting more output from the same resources. However, sharpbends usually occur in recessions when demand has fallen or is still falling. Thus increasing productivity in those circumstances entails using fewer resources to obtain the same output. This inevitably involves reductions in employment. In the lucky cases this could be done by natural wastage – not replacing people as they leave – but in many cases redundancy was required. In all cases, the redundancies were obtained without strikes largely because the labour force and the trade unions could see that on the one hand such reductions were necessary to turn the corner and on the other, if the sharpbend was successful, employment would grow again.

Thirdly, the necessary acceptance of fundamental changes which disrupt working practices and people's lives is more difficult within a sharpbender, which by definition has not reached the point of crisis, than within a turnaround situation where survival is obviously at stake. For this reason sharpbending was often associated with an internally created, rather than externally generated, sense of impending crisis. Clearly this was more easily achieved the more marked the decline of the company, yet this decline in itself eroded the resources to make a sharpbend.

All this emphasizes the need for other companies to undertake their sharpbends voluntarily, and at as early a stage as possible. This means engendering a *wide* recognition of the existence and nature of weaknesses and acceptance of the need to act before being forced to by external pressures. A sharpbend which takes place in generally favourable conditions can be achieved with rather less anguish and considerably greater prospect of ultimate success. The experience of the sharpbenders suggested that the drive to achieve this recognition, acceptance of changes and then to implement them must come from the top, although pressure for change can be applied throughout the organization. For this reason it has often been associated with the appointment of new chief executives, often followed by some new executive directors, who see the company from a different perspective in the light of their prior experience and have a strong personal motivation to demonstrate their own success and to leave their mark upon the company. But many companies sharpbent without a change in chief executive.

Introduction of new top management was particularly important where sharpbending involved a re-orientation of the business and giving up long-cherished activities. For some companies this was breaking a century-old tradition or giving up the business one's parents or grandparents had spent many years of dedicated effort establishing. This was particularly painful and difficult for some of the old senior management of traditional family businesses who in some cases would have blocked change. It is not surprising that drastic changes therefore involved reductions in family interests in firms such as Ferranti, Collins, Bell's and even Macallan, in one of these cases after the family had lost control of the board after a bitter struggle.

This range, complexity and the balance between correcting the errors of the past and the drive for a greatly improved future are best illustrated by example. We have chosen two, Fisons and Dawson International. Fisons took nine main steps. They:

1   sold businesses which were either loss-making or with poor prospects (this included the fertilizer business which was very much at the core of the existing business – a difficult decision for some);
2   acquired new companies in established areas of business where prospects appeared good;
3   focused sharply on cash control within the management accounting package;
4   undertook a substantial shake-up of management;
5   slimmed head office;
6   undertook a cost-reduction drive;
7   introduced a five-year rolling plan and annual detailed budgeting;
8   incentive bonuses were set for senior management dependent upon cash as well as profit achievement; and
9   divisions were left to run their own affairs within constraints such as £100,000 per item limit on investment within the budget.

This brief list over-simplifies the strategic approach of the company which was divided into pharmaceutical, horticulture, and scientific divisions but it does show five of the seven main steps we outlined:

1   major changes in management;
2   stronger financial controls;
3   new product market focus;
4   strong pressure to reduce costs;
5   acquisitions.

Steps in the other two categories, reduction of debt and improvements in marketing were made but were not so central. They also had some 'windfalls'.

Dawson International took steps in all ten of the sections we have covered in this chapter.

1   *Changes in management.* The chief executive was removed, two central directorships – production and personnel – were abolished, new marketing and financial directors were appointed, the structure of non-executive directors on the board improved, incentives introduced with a distinct attempt to change management values and attitudes.
2   *Organizational change.* The principal factor that promoted the sharpbend

was *decentralization* for greater freedom to operate and reduce head-office functions, concentrating on the major issues.

3   *Stronger central financial control.* Precise objectives: a detailed plan and rapid reporting of a broad range of statistics enabled swift response where the onus for correction lay on the subsidiary in the light of advice from the group.

4   *New product market focus.* Divestment of non-textile business, concentration on high-quality end of the market, market orientation to ensure rapid response to opportunities.

5   *Improved quality and service.* Quality is a *sine qua non* (even within the organization) – the yarn spinners produced a fashionable and interesting colour range with adequate stocks to meet customers' demands.

6   *Improved marketing.* The theme is 'we listen to the market'. Marketing is a very costly and essential part of the business pursued separately by the subsidiaries with informal group links. Group concentrated on major customers and agents.

7   *Reduced costs.* Head office cut, operating costs squeezed, input purchases to be within the group where possible *but* no hesitation to invest where this is a route to cutting costs.

8   *Acquisitions.* A clear strategy of acquiring well-run businesses, related to textiles, which they felt they could improve by their marketing and management expertise.

9   *Debt reduction.* The main step to regaining financial health was to dispose of poor companies.

10 *Windfalls.* Improvement in sterling/dollar exchange rate, membership of the EEC as suppliers of final product and intermediate textiles within the tariff and quota barriers.

These two examples are typical, not 'the best', and they show that two companies which had good strong bases nevertheless had to undertake a wide range of measures. Neither had approached a crisis typical of a turnaround but the recessions, in 1980 and 1974 respectively, led to losses which pushed them into action. As can be seen the actions taken were wide-ranging, no single step alone generating the sharpbend. Indeed, in this again these two sharpbenders were typical, for in case after case we noted the wider range of actions taken by positive management which sought improvement and more effective operation in virtually all aspects of its business. Clearly, there is no magic in sharpbending but sheer, sustained, dedicated, unremitting pursuit of high performance.

5 Characteristics of Sustained Improved Performance

It is one thing to be able to make a short-run improvement in performance. It is quite another to sustain it. Sharp improvements in financial performance can be made by cutting out various areas of expenditure which relate to future success, such as investment in physical assets, research and development and human skills and by selling parts of the business. In the longer term, if the initial steps to improve the company's position have not laid the foundation for continuing improvements, the recovery will tend to be short-lived, indeed the company may be even worse off than before. A company experiencing a cyclical downturn may have no serious long-run problems; more drastic short-run measures may therefore create longer-run difficulties which need not have occurred. Our analysis in the previous chapter, setting out the short-run steps taken, includes only companies which went on to sustain their improved performance. Hence we are relatively unlikely to have included damaging short-run measures.

However, the major distinguishing feature of the sharpbenders is that a sharpbend is not a one-off set of measures which somehow enables the company to do better indefinitely. It is a change to a new form of behaviour. The characteristics of the company in the longer run after the bend are different from those beforehand. For some companies those changes were already taking place before the sharpbend. The bend was associated with a kick to complete the process.

From table 5.1 it may be seen that we analysed the characteristics of sustained good performance into seven groups. These are very general and are examined in detail in the sections which follow. However, we would expect these characteristics to be related to steps taken to achieve the sharpbend, such actions themselves changing the behaviour and characteristics of the company. This is found to be so in the next section. The major point to note is that continuing success relies on a range of measures, not just those in any one or two of a number of areas. Thus it is not just changes in management or organization or financial controls which are necessary but a combination of them.

Table 5.1   *Characteristics of sustained improvement in performance*

		No. of characteristics cited	% of firms cited
1	Good management	4 or more	90
2	Appropriate organizational structure	4 or more	75
3	Effective financial and other controls	4 or more	50
4	Sound product market posture	5 or more	45
5	Good marketing management	2 or more	55
6	High quality maintained	2 or more	35
7	Tightly controlled costs	3 or more	40

5.1   The Relation between the Continuing Characteristics and the Steps Taken

If we begin looking at the most frequently occurring relationships, it is immediately clear from figure 5.1 that the steps taken (shown in the boxes) contribute to the sustained improvements (shown in the circles) in performance in a complex way. First, four sets of steps:

new product market focus;
improved quality and service;
reduced production costs;
improved marketing;

each with an impact on a wide range of the characteristics of the sustained performance. This does not necessarily mean that they are the most important influences, merely that they have an identifiable impact on several areas. Take the new product market focus for example. We would have expected reappraisal of product market position to be associated with sounder market posture subsequently, although it is clearly valuable to know that this was found in practice. What is immediately obvious is that companies which reviewed their product market position were found to have appropriate organizational structures, maintenance of high quality, tightly controlled costs and effective controls more generally.

The reasons for these associations lie in the clustering of steps taken, revealed in the last chapter. A thorough, objective analysis of product market posture should reveal any relative cost disadvantages, relative quality of product *vis-à-vis* competitors and so suggest areas where action is required. Actions to reduce and control costs and improve quality can therefore flow from such an analysis as well as a fundamental change in products or markets. Equally, the analysis may suggest that either excessive centralization of

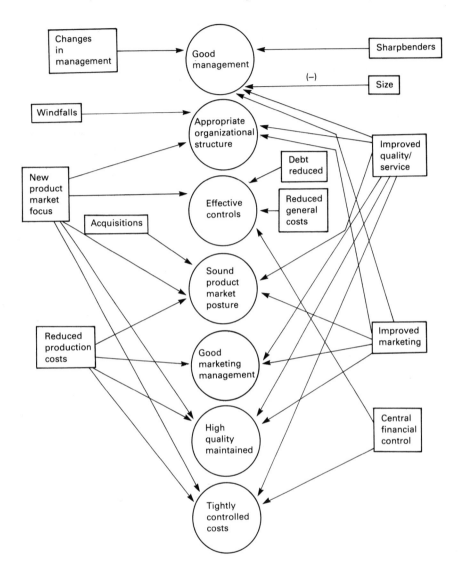

Figure 5.1 *Interrelation of steps taken and continuing characteristics of companies*

operations, on a functional rather than product basis for organization, or some other aspect of the organizational structure is preventing rapid and effective response to changing competitive opportunities and threats. Here again, effective management would respond to the perceived problem. Hence the very analysis of a company's place in the market relative to its competitors and of the trends within these markets, can stimulate actions beyond the domain of marketing and so establish longer-lasting strategies.

Similar themes can be developed for each of the main sets of steps taken. These are not necessarily causal links but groups of characteristics which all seem to go together. Thus improved marketing not surprisingly leads to good marketing management as a sustained characteristic, but it also contributes to a sound product market posture and the maintenance of high quality. A firm which is undertaking careful market research for its products will be able to identify what areas to concentrate on and the characteristics which appeal to customers. A company which can get these factors improved together is also likely to be well managed. As we can see from figure 5.2, the various facets of the sustained improvement are highly related. The light lines indicate significant relationships and the heavy lines highly significant ones (correlations significant at 5 and 1 per cent levels, respectively). Sound product market posture is associated with all the other factors except good management and all the other characteristics are related to at least three others. The stronger relationships are denoted by heavy lines.

We noted in the last chapter that the control companies also took many of

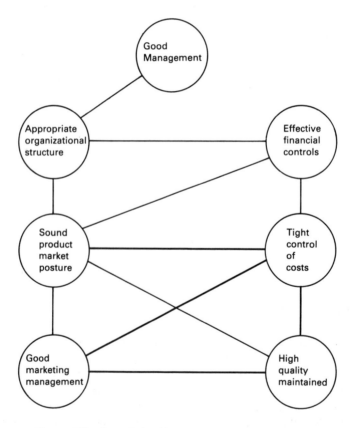

Figure 5.2 *Interrelationships among continuing characteristics*

the same steps as the sharpbenders, but that they employed a smaller range, and, in particular, undertook less of the steps that put an emphasis on the future, and hence on the sustaining of the bend. In figure 5.1 the one area where the sharpbenders are clearly different from the control companies is the first heading of good management. Even after allowing for differences in the steps taken the control companies still exhibited very considerably fewer of the characteristics of good management (see appendix). Good management also has one other strikingly different relationship with the steps taken compared with the other six sets of characteristics, namely, an inverse relationship with size of the company, whether measured by turnover or number of employees. This could merely indicate that it is more difficult to manage large companies well, but it could also indicate that large sharpbenders have behaved somewhat differently from their smaller counterparts. A third possibility is that what the existing literature classes, possibly arbitrarily, as 'good' characteristics are more frequently found more appropriate to small than large companies.

5.2 Good Management

Four characteristics of good management stand out from table 5.2 as being practised by the large majority of companies: their management is action-orientated, values people, has good internal communications, and the board and key executives have financial incentives. Furthermore, most companies can be described as being close to the customer, having strong company values, and a board which is not involved in the day-to-day operations of the company. If we list these characteristics:

    action;
    people;
    communication;
    incentives;
    customers;
    values; and
    delegation;

we can see readily that there is a close similarity between this list and the findings of the 'Excellence' literature. This should not be surprising as our companies have become above-average performers.

However, the list is not identical and the emphasis is different. It is noticeable, for example, that there is somewhat less emphasis on innovation – the third plank in Peters' (1986) refinement of his theory, after people and customers. The structure of the board and the relation between chairman and managing director seem less important. There are several examples among our sharpbenders where the managing director has gone on to become

Table 5.2   *Good management as a characteristic of sustained improvements in performance*

		% of firms showing this characteristic
1.1	Action-orientated management	85
1.2	Management 'close to customer'	60
1.3	Management fosters leaders and innovators and encourages risk-taking	40
1.4	Top management relies less on 'true and tried' products	20
1.5	Top management projects strong company values	55
1.6	Management values people	80
1.7	Good communications with employees and good industrial relations	80
1.8	Board members and key executives have ownership or other profit incentives	70
1.9	Chairman exercises controlling role over separate managing director	30
1.10	Balance between executive and non-executive directors on the board	30
1.11	Non-executive directors active	15
1.12	Board does not interfere with day-to-day operations	55
1.13	Other	30

chairman, thereby consolidating his position – Kerridge at Fisons, Girolami at Glaxo, and Miquel at Bell's, for instance.

The most important factor in the list and the one which impressed us most strongly in the interviews was action orientation. Sharpbending companies were not sitting on a constant product. They were changing all the time. Rotaflex for example was introducing one new product a week in 1985. The emphasis was on keeping together a professional management team, encouraging flair with young dynamic, aggressive manners. (They now look five or more years ahead in product development taking 'big risks' as Frye, the Managing Director, puts it). But in doing so they also tried to keep close to the customers, and at the beginning of 1985 they had just completed a comprehensive mail survey of future needs of customers, together with an on the road show to invited audiences round the provinces.

Companies like Rotaflex that are continuing to grow can sustain their rate of progress only by following a strategy of seeking out new markets. Philip Birch at Ward White also saw the need for organic internal growth to be supplemented by acquisitions, 'Be forever active in the continual assessment of opportunities but cautious in those eventually chosen – they should "knit-on" to the enterprise without too much reorganization time'. This action orientation extends into all facets of the business including organization structure (which is the subject of the next section). The John Wood Group realized that the rapid growth of its North Sea oil-related business was demotivating the traditional (fishing-related) business and so that was demerged. As the firm expanded it decided to spread the risk and operate outside the North Sea, first looking for high-value-added business in the US. A new 'well-drilling and production services division was set up to focus on these new high-value-added, high-technology industries'.

This continuing push forward does not mean that companies have to be brash or aggressive. Paul Girolami at Glaxo, who has recognized that when a company does very well it will eventually have to slow down a little and take some defensive steps, has described the approach, in an interview with *Financial Weekly*, as, 'This will not be aggression; that does not pay in this industry. It will be positive orientation.' He has endeavoured to set company values and goals, avoiding rhetorical phrases like being 'number one' in a particular area. Glaxo is particularly interesting because it is trying to secure a strong and sustained future for itself in the light of the precariousness of its position so heavily based on the performance of one drug, Zantac, which has been extremely successful round the world. Girolami's response to questions about his strategic approach are also telling: 'We are in a dynamic situation. If you ask me the same question tomorrow you may get a different answer. After all it is my job to ask myself that kind of question every day'.

The emphasis varies very much from company to company. In Ellis & Goldstein the strength of the management lies principally in its judgement and experience of the vagaries of the British fashion market. It is actively involved in influencing what its customers will be offered. There is certainly a never-ending probing of the market and assessment of changing fashions, primarily on a seasonal basis. It prides itself on keeping abreast of what customers are interested in, and what new developments are taking place around the world which might fit this. Thus we might put customers top of their list, but other factors are important, including communications and incentives. Care is taken with employee relations, which have always in consequence been good. Higher wages than normal in the industry are paid and a profit-sharing scheme has recently been produced. The company's performance is set out in a report to employees, aimed at being 'comprehensible but not condescending'.

The Managing Director at Dawson was kind enough to set out the five key characteristics in his view:

1 decentralization;
2 employ the right people for all purposes, including selling agents;
3 pay attention to the market place and be ready to innovate anywhere when market requirements dictate;
4 insist on quality in every respect: people, products and equipment;
5 have wide horizons – have a go anywhere in the world.

Some of these are familiar – people and innovation, for example – but this list is rather broader than management as such and is our cue to look further afield.

5.3   Appropriate Organizational Structure

As we have already noted in the previous section a good organizational structure aids management. However, in the same way a good management will develop the right structure. While the experience of the sharpbenders indicates there are some straightforward characteristics to what constitutes an appropriate organizational structure, the appropriate structure varies with the size of firms, the nature of the product market, the technology employed and the state of the environment.

There has been a tendency in recent years to try to seek simple statements which can be applied to all companies. There is a danger that they are either so general that they convey little information or that they have to be qualified to such an extent that they are rendered of little value. With this proviso in mind we note here what appear to us to be five general characteristics of an appropriate organizational structure which have been shown in this study.

1   It should be as simple as possible.
2   The head office should be no larger than strictly necessary.
3   It is advantageous to have profit or cost centres with operating decisions delegated to them.
4   In large firms a fairly formal strategic planning approach is necessary while the smaller organization needs regular but informal reviews.
5   A balance needs to be struck between giving divisions or subsidiaries the freedom and motivation to develop their sector on their own and making sure that they do what head office wants, particularly in regard to expenditure, costs, marketing, etc.

We noted the approach of Dawson International and Fisons in some detail at the end of the last chapter. Here, an interesting case is that of company 'B' which faced a highly cyclical demand for its main product and developed a flexible organization whose structure varies with the cycle.

Some companies went beyond setting up a more developed divisional structure, pursuing vertical integration in order to get control over the supply of raw materials, for example. Low & Bonar took the process of devolution further by reorganizing from an industry-based divisional structure to a geographical one. Deliberately trying to get each area to diversify and in effect to run local Low & Bonars. At the same time they dispensed with corporate planning on the grounds that a board which knew the business did not require a corporate plan, particularly as that tended to project the existing structure.

This divisional policy, with the subsidiaries having their own identity, has enabled them to be a focus of loyalty for the workforce. The management get direct incentives from being able to run the businesses readily and take operating decisions within the overall policy. Having separate companies has also helped to keep industrial relations problems localized and has permitted bargaining separately in each area.

The hard, action-orientated, entrepreneurial management style, which we described in the previous section, permeates the Low & Bonar group and instils the attitude of identifying, confronting and tackling problems even where this is difficult. The link with head office is largely by word of mouth to impart as much personal support as possible to subsidiary managers in the solution of their problems, even though this involves a lot of travel. This is combined with the effective financial and management accounting controls we deal with in the next section, giving a good example of the 'simultaneous loose–tight properties' referred to in table 5.3. It should, however, be noted that the structure of the company has changed again more recently with divisions based on four product groups.

The Sidlaw Group followed a similar strategy of devolution with each subsidiary as a profit centre. They stand or fall on their own achievements and the head office is little involved in operational matters, merely being available for consultation. Michael Walker, the Managing Director, spends a lot of time with the managerial teams and, interestingly enough, remarked that he felt that the head office had perhaps been slimmed too far because he was too involved

Table 5.3 *Organizational structure as a characteristic of sustained improvement in performance*

		% of firms showing this characteristic
2.1	Structure appropriate to size and product market posture	80
2.2	'Lean' head office	70
2.3	Simple structure	75
2.4	Profit or cost centres with operating decisions delegated to them	60
2.5	Formal mechanistic decision-making and control systems when product mature and market stable	20
2.6	Informal, organic decision-making systems when product young and market growing or unstable	10
2.7	Different types of manager in the business at different strategic stages	30
2.8	'Simultaneous loose–tight properties'	50
2.9	Strategic planning systems used in large organizations	40
2.10	Regular but informal review of strategy in smaller firms	55

with the subsidiaries to think enough about the future. Again there is a detailed management accounting system and annual budgets which are resolved in a 'confrontation' with the group managing director and finance director.

However, as with all good generalizations there are exceptions. Countryside Properties actually increased the size of their head office. This was in part purely because of the rate of growth of the firm but also to provide central cohesion and strong design, both necessary to keep site management in line with the latest ideas and subject to adequate controls. Moreover, it is clear that structure needs to evolve with size. When UDI reached 130 employees the eight department heads were put into a separate tier of management. Thus with around 155 employees at the time we visited them they had three such tiers. In book publishing the appropriate degree of centralization depends on the functional area. There are major economies of scale in warehousing and distribution; administration and support services can also be centralized but the 'people' side of the business, those who select topics and manage authors, need delicate handling.

5.4 Effective Financial and Other Controls

In many ways control systems are the least interesting area of study because all companies exhibited them in most respects as did the control companies (see table 5.4). These systems are not so much a distinguishing feature of sharpbenders as a characteristic of almost all companies that are showing reasonable success. It is thus not so much that the system exists which matters, but how it is used. Take Whatman Reeve Angel for example. They have tight financial controls based on proven standard cost-accounting and budget variance analysis which was installed in W & R Balston in the early 1970s. There are monthly reports to the board showing full profit-and-loss accounts at budgeted and standard exchange rates, balance sheets, analyses of

Table 5.4 *Effective financial and other controls as characteristics of sustained improvements in performance*

		% of firms having this characteristic
3.1	Timely production (of key ratios only) for MD and board monthly	65
3.2	Cash-flow forecasts and liquidity controlled frequently	70
3.3	Effective budgetary control system	85
3.4	Effective capital budgeting systems	85

variances, schedules of fixed expenditure broken down by departments (actual and budget), order-book position, work in progress, employee analysis by department, schedule of capital expenditure with a final report and prognosis. WRA are at the upper end in terms of detail. More typical might be Low & Bonar with a two-page summary of each company. On the whole the boards of the more diverse companies were looking for exceptions – variations in performance from those expected. Only in some cases like that of Bell's were there detailed central examinations of the work of each sales area.

However, control systems had two elements. One was simply the regular, usually monthly, budgetary assessment; the other was tight cash management. In some cases the cash would be held centrally with the head office acting like a bank, meeting the daily needs of the subsidiaries, as in the case of Low & Bonar. This meant that there was a second information route. However, it was the experience of the two recessions in 1974 and 1980–1 which brought it home to companies that the cash position was crucially important to their survival and effective growth. It was no good having profits tied up in non-convertible currency in Africa. That could not be used for sterling investments.

In many cases these control systems extended beyond financial variables into quality, for example. Don Brothers Buist took this further by monitoring delivery performance compared with the promises made. The major point of difference was how far ahead the companies looked. For many the closely defined horizon was only for the annual budget, whereas others looked three and even five years ahead. In part this depended upon the type of business. In areas where set-up costs were low and fashion highly variable, horizons were short – almost weeks in some cases – while in others such as pharmaceuticals where development periods could be as long as fifteen years, careful profiles had to be followed to try to organize a sequence of products.

5.5 Sound Product Market Posture

There are many well-known principles for assessing the appropriate product market, perhaps the best known of which is that of the Boston Consulting Group. They advise companies to adopt a two-dimensional approach to their actual and potential product markets by assessing their growth potential on the one hand and the company's competitive potential on the other. The area for concentration of new resources is product markets where there is not only strong growth potential but the company thinks that it has competitive advantages over other firms in the industry. Sixty per cent of the companies in our sample followed that strategy as an explicit aim, as is shown in the first line of table 5.5.

However, this is only part of the BCG advice. Firms should seek to extract themselves from competitively weak areas while they still have a viable

Table 5.5   *Sound product market posture as a characteristic of sustained improvements in performance*

		% of firms having this characteristic
4.1	Invest in growing markets where competitively strong	60
4.2	Continue to 'harvest' or divest competitively weak businesses	30
4.3	'Milk' competitively strong but mature businesses	30
4.4	In major businesses have	
	(a) focused strategy	55
	(b) differentiated products	50
	(c) cost leadership	30
4.5	Strong bargaining position in major businesses	15
	(a) *vis-à-vis* suppliers	—
	(b) *vis-à-vis* buyers	—
4.6	Company concentrates on businesses it knows well	70
4.7	Effective barriers to entry in major businesses	50
4.8	Company has relatively high market share in major business	65

business to sell. Nevertheless because there is the trade-off between competitive strength and growth potential a firm may find it worthwhile to continue. The third part of the strategy, also covered in table 5.5, is to get as much as possible out of businesses where the company is competitively strong but the market has reached a mature phase. This approach, therefore, also incorporates some of the ideas of the product cycle, with each product going through the cycle of concept, development, launch, growth, maturity, decline and withdrawal.

It is clear from table 5.5 that the growth focus is a more widespread strategy than the other two parts of the full concept, in part because divestiture may not be so explicitly expressed. However, there are other ways of looking at product market strategies and we examined those of Porter (1980; 1985) and Peters and Waterman (1982), where the latter suggested that companies should 'stick to the knitting' by which they meant 'concentrate on what they know well'. Again this was an approach which approximately two-thirds of the companies followed. However, as we have noted earlier, some firms like Low & Bonar have an explicit policy of diversification.

Glaxo is an example of the focused strategy. Despite their position as the fourth largest pharmaceutical company in the world they concentrate on relatively few business areas in which they have experience, but in those they market aggressively. They argue that the main reason for this lies in the product-development phase. In an industry where products are highly research-intensive, spreading resources thinly is a mistake. Concentrated drives in limited product areas are more likely to produce breakthroughs. While some discoveries are a matter of luck, on the whole they relate to the amount of effort put in (see NEDO, 1987 for a discussion of research and development in this context). We saw in the last chapter how Fisons, the other pharmaceutical sharpbender, had concentrated in its product market focus, by moving away from areas such as fertilizers, where it had no particular competitive edge, and into areas, such as pharmaceuticals, where it could exploit markets from its research base.

The nature of the strategy varies by company. Those with a limited product range like Macallan-Glenlivet clearly have to concentrate on picking the market correctly, while those like Dawson, who are in an industry where fashion changes rapidly, have to keep up a continuing stream of new ideas.

Associated Paper Industries is a good example of how these general strategies could be pursued. The company was starting from a mature, uncompetitive business, but while papermaking is still central to API's output they have sought market and growth niches in which they could secure higher profit margins. They started by strengthening their position in areas where they saw themselves as having strength and a good potential growth. This involved investment in stamping tools with a coater and a metallizer, in computer controls on paper machines and in a waste paper plant. They also diversified into related areas such as charcoal and silica-gel-based paper products, such as odour-eating material for shoe insoles and fridge fresheners. Their company purification products had no UK rivals and was expanding rapidly overseas. API also acquired Airpel which had a comprehensive range of liquid filters, used in water treatment, petrochemicals, offshore oil, process plant and other industries, but they planned to sell Airpel Hydraulic, which distributed hydraulic valves, as this did not fit into the pattern of their group.

Thus there tends to be a combination of the BCG product market appraisal methods with examples of concentration and diversification depending on whether the core business is weak or strong. Similar combinations of concentration and diversification can be seen at Collins which built on the profitable strength of Hatchards, the retail bookshop, with the expansion of book supply to schools and libraries, and diversified into home-computer software.

However, these approaches look at the problem from a different point of view from Porter (1985), who explicitly sets out appropriate strategies in terms of exploiting the competitive advantages that firms have. These can take a number of forms. The first is simply that the firm exploits any bargaining advantage it holds over its suppliers or buyers. Perhaps the best-known example of this is Marks and Spencers who are able to exercise very considerable power over their suppliers because of the importance that such contracts can mean. Partly as a reaction to this sort of result Ward White have as a matter of policy avoided getting themselves tied to any particular purchaser.

Porter is thus advocating exploiting market power. There are of course legislative limits to the exercise of such power, but half of the sharpbenders have established effective barriers to entry to try to deter other companies from entering their markets. Countryside Properties deliberately set up close relations with local authorities and following successful participation with the Essex County Council on the Essex Design Guide, 1973, helped set up further guidelines where they had the advantage of being on the inside. To be able to attract work it is normally necessary to be able to get on to approved lists so as to receive invitations to tender. Bell's purchase of Wellington Importers in the US in 1984 was in part to obtain the licences to sell their whisky in the US. Using distributors as the other route to breaking through the barriers had proved decidedly unsuccessful.

Porter argues further that there are specific routes towards getting a competitive edge in a market – first by focusing narrowly, second by trying to make products distinctive by differentiating them from those of competitors. Lastly, the edge can be obtained simply by being able to undercut the opposition through lower costs. This latter is particularly important when the product is relatively homogeneous and the purchaser tends to buy largely on price. It is very interesting that this last category occurs the least frequently of the three (see table 5.5). Bell's show one of the best examples of product differentiation. Although the standard Bell's whisky is a blend of normal age it is sold with a mark-up over the general run of whiskies by successfully claiming that it is of a higher quality. Hence it is bought by brand name rather than by generic name. In a pub, purchase by generic name takes the choice away from the customer altogether and leaves it with the bartender.

Ellis & Goldstein have similarly tried to produce distinctive products, concentrating within the market they know well. The most interesting cases, however, are companies like Sidlaw which run different parts of their business in different ways in order to reflect the differences in the product market. The oil-support industries are encouraged to look for new opportunities and invest in plant and people, while the textile subsidiaries are run on a tight rein with an emphasis on cost control, thus trying to reap as much as possible from an existing business.

These strategies of having an evolving product market focus can be achieved either by development of existing products and processes or by acquisition and divestiture. It depends very much on the scope for differentiation and the length of time over which it is needed to develop new products whether the first rather than the second route is used. Since change needs to be rapid, acquisition and sale has to be used in industries, where organic internal growth is necessarily slow.

5.6 Good Marketing Management

The good product market focus has to be accompanied by good marketing if it is to result in achieving the sales potential which is generated. The major characteristic of this marketing effort is continuous attention to the market and what the customers want (table 5.6). The techniques used varied, sometimes within the same firm. In Whatman Reeve Angel both the Whatman and the Balston divisions had a strong marketing orientation, but they applied it differently. Whatman International imposed the overriding condition that all laboratory products must be marketable by means of a catalogue and not require an external sales force. They therefore looked for products which improved the way laboratory methods could be practised rather than providing a full range and used the Whatman brand name to its full advantage. Their industrial products on the other hand used innovative technologies but again emphasized consumer allegiance to the Whatman brand name in their marketing.

The Balston group of companies on the other hand, while they were similarly market-oriented, used a very different selling arrangement which eliminated heavy overheads. They identified distributors within target markets and requested that one of the distributor's sales force became purely a Balston specialist. They were trained by Balston, visited the firm regularly and participated in decision-making. They thus felt as if they were Balston employees, yet they were employed by the distributors. This policy therefore produced well-motivated and well-trained Balston specialists at low cost, enabling the company to target specific markets.

This sort of divergence within a single firm is to be expected when the

Table 5.6 *Good marketing management as a characteristic of sustained improvements in performance*

		% of firms with this characteristic
5.1	Regular analysis of sales and concentration of marketing effort on high contribution markets and customers	45
5.2	Strong motivation and coordinating of sales force	30
5.3	Competitive discount structures	5
5.4	High margins maintained where company is dominant and demand is little affected by price	35
5.5	Management continuously monitors market for signals of threats, opportunities and competitive intentions	55
5.6	Management consults regularly with key customers and seeks to meet their needs	50

organization is decentralized. Each part of the firm will try to follow the marketing strategy appropriate to its particular product market focus. The extent to which these differences actually emerge depends on the functions which the group controls.

Dawson International are another group with a more complex marketing structure than might have been anticipated because they feel they get closer to the customer by letting each subsidiary do its own marketing. Their product market focus has been to exploit their position at the top end of the market using inputs from other parts of the group where possible. There is great emphasis on gaining the rewards of this high position by branding their consumer goods wherever possible and by concentrating selling on those foreign markets with high disposable incomes who can afford the product and on those firms which require high-quality inputs to meet their own output standards. The subsidiaries compete on quality and responsiveness to market needs rather than price, although it is the latter which determines the markets on which they can focus. The emphasis is thus on healthy diversity. The individual subsidiaries pride themselves on speed of response to market demands. The theme for the group, we were told, is 'We listen to the market'. They stress the importance of getting close to the final customer rather than to intermediaries such as overseas agents. Exchange of information between subsidiaries is informal. However, the group shares the intelligence it has received and any ideas it has obtained with the subsidiaries, and keeps some contact with the major customers.

As marketing is a costly exercise with huge bills for foreign travel and advertising it might appear that there was scope for economy here, but it is a reflection on the importance attached to the supplier having contact with their own customers that this reduction is not made. Pringle, the Dawson subsidiary which we considered separately as a sharpbender, described their view as 'The market place is a living thing. It changes all the time. You have to change all the time.' This last remark typifies the major characteristic of the sustained improvement in performance, namely *continuing change*.

5.7 High Quality Maintained

The pursuit of quality is a characteristic of Peters and Waterman's excellent companies. Clearly a successful company will be selling products which have a competitive edge over others in the market. This edge may come from offering the most attractive price. It may come from exploiting the various aspects of competitive advantage that Porter mentions – by differentiating the product for example, by restricting entry to the industry, etc. However, in a highly competitive industry where all have to conform to the market price to achieve sales, a firm will have to fight on the qualities of its product alone. This is even more true when there is major competition from cheap labour

Table 5.7 *High quality as a characteristic of sustained improvement in performance*

		% of firms with this characteristic
6.1	Quality control system operated	30
6.2	Customer complaints analysed and appropriate action taken	30
6.3	Top management monitors product quality, delivery times and after-sales service and takes appropriate action	30

sources. There, price competition is not possible; what gives a company the edge is quality. Sidlaw, for example, could not hope to compete directly with the products of the Indian jute industry, so it concentrated on the top end of the market on a quality which the Indians could not match because they did not have access to the skills and technology.

Similarly, although some trade in textiles and clothing is protected by the Multi-Fibre Arrangement, Dawson International reached their strong position by concentrating on the top of the market. Among the whisky distillers Macallan-Glenlivet also prided themselves on the quality of the product. Indeed it is difficult to think of examples where competitiveness has been achieved without a conscious effort at quality. Quality in this sense is as much a service as a facet of the product. An excellent washing-machine will not be purchased if there is no after-sales service, no delivery, unfavourable credit terms, etc. Don Brothers Buist placed a particularly strong emphasis on a high level of service. They had technically qualified representation who worked with customers to see how their specific needs could be met. Carpet textile technicians had been employed since the 1960s and with the introduction of geotextiles they employed a civil engineer. There was a strong commitment to delivery at the promised time, which involved close collaboration between marketing and production control. Standard products could be delivered from stock and the extent of the emphasis on maintenance of product quality can be judged from the fact that the chairman, Bill Low, received copies of all customer complaints and checked on the action taken. The quality of goods and services is thus the key to strong further growth (table 5.7).

5.8 Tightly Controlled Costs

This final area takes us back to the early steps of the sharpbend. Marketing may be a help in selling but without the right design sold at an attractive price many aspiring companies would have no future. Some of the competitiveness

Table 5.8 *Tightly controlled costs as a characteristic of sustained improvements in performance*

		% of firms with this characteristic
7.1	Cost control over	
	(a) raw-material costs	30
	(b) labour costs	30
	(c) pilferage	20
7.2	Production engineering, work study, etc., used to minimize production costs	30
7.3	Technology regularly reviewed to seek cost reductions	40
7.4	Productivity measured and reviewed regularly	20
7.5	Workforce consulted about improvements and their ideas sought	30
7.6	Marketing and distribution cost monitored and controlled	10
7.7	Firm makes good use of	
	(a) computers and office automation	50
	(b) OR and O&M	10
	(c) management training	15
	(d) NEDO and DTI advice and support	10

has to come through prices. While tight cost control features quite noticeably among companies (table 5.8), it is distinctly less important than the sharp cost-cutting exercises which accompanies the sharpbends themselves. Then almost all companies undertook a vigorous exercise, trimming their head offices, slimming the workforce, closing uneconomic plants and so on. After the bend, with the leaner organization, tight financial controls and a new operating framework, much of the cost control will come naturally from the other actions taken, which may explain the relatively small proportion of companies which stressed these points in our interviews with them. Interestingly enough, the proportion of control companies imposing tight cost control was actually larger, implying perhaps that the need to impose such controls reflected the failure of the other policies.

Some industries have more of a reputation for uncontrollable costs and it is thus not surprising to see that both McCarthy and Stone and Countryside Properties impose very strict controls on expenditure on their sites as the tendency of construction costs to rise and hence cut into profit is well known. The key to profitability is on the construction site and here McCarthy and Stone has exercised control over quality, costs and construction times by developing small teams who are motivated to do a good job and to stick together from one project to another. By being able to field experienced teams the company is able to benefit from their avoiding the mistakes of the past and doing things well first time.

Among the sharpbending firms, Rotaflex put cost control first among the characteristics of sustained improvements in performance, although for other companies such as Bent, a subsidiary of Ellis & Goldstein, keeping their cost structure as tight as they can manage is essential in the competitive battle for margins with the chain stores. Such smaller companies simply cannot compete by producing very long runs of standardized products and hence they have to put even more emphasis on the items they can control.

What needs to be offset against these cost-control measures is that the companies 'know how to spend'. Cost control is not enough. It is necessary to invest in new plant, machinery and technology, to train staff, and undertake research and development. Furthermore, marketing is usually an essential ingredient in success. It is not enough just to produce an excellent product; it needs to be marketed and that marketing tends to be very expensive. There is therefore the contrast of running a tight ship on current costs, production methods, stock control and overheads while putting sufficient emphasis on the future, both in finding the next generation of competitive products and services and in having an organization which can react rapidly and effectively.

5.9 Characteristics of the Sustained Improvement Considered

The important difference between achieving a sharpbend and sustaining it is that the initial step involves rectifying a lot of things which have been done wrongly as much as it does taking new measures correctly, whereas sustaining the performance involves continuing development of what is already good. In the sharpbend, drastic and strong action is usually called for with the need for many sacrifices to be made. A company cannot work in that way continuously, nor does it need to, as many of the steps taken in the bend are one-off or short-run measures. Once debt has been reduced it does not need to be reduced again, it needs to be controlled.

However, many characteristics of the sharpbend do continue. Achieving the sharpbend in the first place requires an action-oriented management. Keeping the process of change going requires such action as well. The market is continually changing; a company cannot rest on its laurels after the bend, it must continue to evolve. Similarly, we saw the crucial role of motivation, getting the necessary enthusiasm and commitment to make a difficult change. This also needs to be maintained. Maintaining success depends on the people who are there to undertake it. As Michael Walker at Sidlaw put it, 'You pick the team but it had better be a good one because your future depends on it'. He concluded that in their own case 'The result is quite simply: we have got the best team, and we have got a tighter ship on what we have got left'. This second remark fills in more of the picture – that the sustained improvement comes with effective controls, monitoring and strategic assessment of the way forward.

There is a tendency to try to distil the characteristics of continuing success further and further and produce a series of simple embracing 'truths' which are memorable and generally applicable. This is readily understandable in seeking to provide a clear message but in our view this has gone too far – the sharpbenders' study has shown three important things if nothing else. First, while it may be difficult to undertake a bend it is also hard to make the transition to sustain it. The initial impetus can easily wear off. The second is that it is a complex task involving many characteristics and the balancing of competing claims. There are no simple easily attainable recipes, otherwise they would have been undertaken long ago. Third, that the truly outstanding companies continue to put substantial effort into high performance in virtually all aspects of their business. They are not marked by single, dominating characteristics which others could imitate easily. Success involves continuous commitment, effort and restless hunger for yet more success.

The thirteen key features of the continuing business revealed by our study of the sharpbending firms are set out in table 5.9. They emphasize the need for action and the ability to change quickly, but they also express the importance of a strong and clear organization where strategy is reviewed regularly and responsibility is sufficiently devolved to give each subsector the motivation to compete and to seek to achieve good results. But running across this is a system of effective management information and financial and management controls, particularly in the management of cash and capital spending.

Nevertheless, however strong the system, success comes from the quality of

Table 5.9 *Key features of sustained improved performance*

1	Action-orientated management
2	Effective financial controls and management information
3	An emphasis on 'people' within the firm
4	Good internal communications and industrial relations
5	A simple organizational structure with a small head office
6	Incentives and motivation for employers
7	A clear product market focus with a deliberate concentration on what the firm can do best
8	An emphasis on customers
9	A strong marketing focus
10	A drive for quality
11	Delegation to responsible profit and cost centres
12	Regular reviews of strategy with formality increasing with the size of the firm
13	A forward-looking approach which invests in the future through plant, equipment, R&D and training

the people who run it. The selection and motivation of them play a pivotal role in continuing success. Again this is not a once-and-for-all selection of a team but the continual bringing forward of new talented people with new ideas.

However, the firms succeeded because they sold goods and services which the customers needed. This was maintained on the one hand by good marketing and information about the nature of demand and by keeping a competitive edge on the other. This edge was obtained first by concentrating the firm's product market focus where it was strong, eliminating activities where there was little potential. But it was also obtained by an emphasis on having new products, processes and ideas by striving for all the features of non-price competitiveness – quality, customer service, delivery, reliability, etc. – and price competitiveness itself through control of costs, in particular the elimination of unnecessary overheads. Various methods were used, such as quality circles, but there was no uniform recipe.

Indeed the variety of experience was a clear theme which runs right across this research. There are common features, but when it comes down to detail no two firms acted alike. Larger firms required more complex structures and more formal arrangements. Firms in declining industries need to diversify steadily and seek market niches in traditional businesses where a continuing competitive advantage could be obtained.

Between them our twenty-five examples cover a broad range of experience. No doubt there is considerable further richness to be obtained by studying other examples but these between them provide a broad spectrum on which other companies can base their own approach. This leads us therefore to our last and most important chapter which sets out what others can do – what firms should examine – how they can unleash the potential which exists in the skill of their staff, their accumulated knowledge and experience, their reputation, products and linkages with customers and suppliers. Some companies were in unusual circumstances or run by exceptionally talented people, but others had little to distinguish them from the general run of companies in their industries before the bend, except perhaps in some cases that their position was deteriorating. Yet they managed to grasp the opportunity for sharp and sustained improvement. That opportunity exists for others if only they will take it. Some will choose voluntarily. Others will be forced to do so by takeover, new people or creditors. If the trigger for change can be pulled then the potential for sustained improvement can be unleashed.

6 Unleashing Corporate Potential

In this chapter we confront you with the issues that the sharpbenders faced and the actions they took and ask you to consider the questions: 'How does this apply to my organization?' and 'What actions can I take?' This does not mean that every company is a potential sharpbender. Some will already be doing extremely well and the scope for improvement may be small. Others may find that the scope for noticeably sharp change is limited because the various beneficial steps that may be taken to produce change cannot happen together and hence the improvement will be more spread out. Moreover, external circumstances influence the ability of key people in the organization to introduce fundamental change, hence timing can be important. For instance, we noted at the outset that sharpbends tend to be concentrated in periods of general economic recession, because it is that which provides the trigger for action. Seeing rapidly sliding profits and a falling stock-market quotation is a much better spur to action than the hope of improved conditions in the future. Even so, we hope the experience of the companies we have quoted in this book may stimulate others into believing that they too could do as well without serious short-run difficulties to spur them on.

The companies we looked at were in relative decline, most with respect to the rest of their industry but some only with respect to their subsequent achievements. The John Wood Group, for example, could not reasonably be described as anything but successful in all of the periods we looked at. Where that decline is absolute as well as relative the company will have to take action sooner or later. However, most of the companies in our sample were growing in absolute terms. While short-run problems with profitability or cash flow may have triggered the wish to change, they could have weathered any short-run difficulty and continued in business with an adequate performance. We can say this confidently as a generality because we also examined a control company in each industry, which had a similar performance to our sharpbenders before the bend, faced similar external pressures and yet did not achieve the sustained improvement in performance that the sharpbenders did.

There is however, a continuum from companies such as Ferranti, which were compelled to take action because of the refusal of their bankers to increase their loans, to those with no such difficulties. At this lower end of the continuum therefore we have what is virtually a 'turnaround' where there is no alternative but for the firm to take major measures to alter the long-run potential of the company. Above that the decision to change is voluntary. However, all those in absolute decline will be forced into change at some stage. Those who wait either for short-run problems to force them into action or until they find they have reached the conditions of a turnaround find it much harder to achieve a sharpbend. According to Slatter (1984), three in four attempted turnarounds fail and the company goes out of business or is taken over. If the company is trying to change while it has cash-flow problems, is making a loss rather than a profit, and has accumulated major debts, it first of all has to generate the resources to change. Short-run salvation can be gained by sales or closure, redundancies, cutting of 'overheads' such as R&D, marketing and investment which are not directly part of current production but this does not help the long run, it makes it even worse. Changing the product market focus of the firm and developing and exploiting competitive advantage require investment in the future, in plant and equipment, in developing new products and in improving the skills and abilities of the labour force at all levels. This all involves expenditure but when a firm is in a financial crisis any extra expenditure may undermine its viability in the short run.

Thus the 'voluntary' sharpbender, which chooses the timing of its efforts to suit itself and not the demands of others whose interests in the success of the firm may be rather limited, will tend to find the process rather easier as it does not have as much pressure to cut back initially further than it would wish in order to create the headroom for the new investment in the future. However, a note of caution is required. Up until the 1980s the UK and indeed most developed countries were subject to economic cycles of around four to five years in duration. Attempting a major step forward at the wrong moment in the cycle could make the company much more exposed than if it had been much less adventurous and merely stayed within the existing business. Indeed some of the sharpbenders were already trying to change and had undertaken major investments which had not yet paid off when the cyclical downturn occurred. The resulting problem triggered the sharpbend by further heightening an existing willingness to change.

Achieving a sharpbend is a major effort for most firms, involving a substantial shake-up. While we claim that there is the opportunity for many firms to undertake a successful sharpbend we must stress that it is not without risk and anyone attempting it should make a very cool assessment of the risk they could face. That said we re-emphasize the advantages of undertaking a voluntary change.

One of the main stimuli for a sharpbend has been a takeover. Others outside the firm perceive the opportunity to make a marked improvement in the business and have the resources to do so. If the existing management does not perceive that opportunity they will tend to lose out and indeed may lose their jobs. A takeover may very well be for the benefit of the other interest groups in the firm. The existing shareholders may get a better price, either in cash or in shares of the acquiring firm than they would from the continuance of the existing business and hence improve their rate of return. The firm may pick up much more successfully, to the benefit of what we have described as the 'national interest' through increased output and all-factor productivity and to the benefit of the employees. Fewer jobs will be lost in the short run, more created in the longer run and higher pay rates achieved.

These gains to the other interest groups are possible, not necessary, outcomes. The new management may move in to improve its own market position or to reap a shorter-run advantage by divestiture of a large portion of the business, to the detriment of both managers and workforce. It is the shareholders of the acquired firm who seem most likely to gain. There is thus a very considerable incentive for management to act to make their firm secure before others seek to acquire it to realize its potential.

We do not suggest that there is any substantial group of firms who do not wish to change and do not perceive the risks from failing to change. The control companies took many of the measures that the sharpbenders did but without the same comprehensive approach and in general with less drive. There are many barriers to change, not least perception of the risk and uncertainty involved. This uncertainty is related to the fact that management must break away from old patterns of thought and methods of operation. This is always difficult, the more so because it may involve recognition of past failure, and is beyond many management teams. In some cases although management recognizes the need to change it is difficult to carry through a fundamental transformation, because workforce and customers either fail to believe in its necessity, or doubt the ability of the existing management to see it through. A track record of relative inertia or failure of past decisions does not engender confidence. It is partly for this reason that many sharpbends have been associated with a change in the chief executive. Not only will a new chief executive want to make a clear mark on the business but he or she may have been appointed precisely because of the contributions they could make to the successful development of the company. Hence both the very presence of new leadership and its freedom from association with the difficulties of the past will facilitate the fundamental changes in attitudes and behaviour. However, this is not to say that the recipe for sharpbending is simply 'change the chief executive'. There are instructive cases where this did not happen.

Most sharpbends we have examined have had a harsh side to them. Changing the product market focus means not just starting new products and processes but dropping old ones. Those in the declining areas will tend to lose out. Similarly a drive for increased efficiency and productivity is likely to involve economies even where there is also increased output. There will therefore be some job losses even if these can be met by natural wastage or by switching people within the firm. It is a noticeable feature of the sharpbenders that these changes were introduced without major strikes or labour disputes. When properly consulted trade unions and workforces could see the long-run advantages of the changes proposed, and although some of their colleagues/ members might lose their jobs in the short run the alternative would be worse. If the nettle of the unpleasant side of the change were not grasped the sharpbend would not be successful and might not occur at all, in which case the longer-run prospects for the rest of the labour force would be worse.

This harsh side tends to affect many categories of employees: management and head office staff often suffering more than the rest of the workforce given the tendency among the sharpbenders to trim the size of the head offices markedly and to simplify their management structures. Thus those who have to develop the policy may themselves find that they lose their jobs. We have already noted the example of the senior executive who strongly advocated the hiring of consultants only to find that they recommend his own departure. However, not all cost-cutting results in loss of employment. Other measures to cut costs – through reducing stocks and work in progress, reducing debt or improving production planning or quality, reducing waste – aid profitability and competitiveness directly. In the successful sharpbend it must be clear that the long-run gain outweighs the short-run pain and that must be believed by those concerned.

6.1 The Initial Appraisal

The major difference between a sharpbend and a turnaround at the outset is that in a sharpbend there is usually the time to sort out a coherent strategy rather than just needing to take emergency measures. In the experience of our sample, the first step is thus a careful appraisal of the business, based on the following seven factors:

1 the causes of relative decline;
2 product market potential;
3 sources of competitive advantage:
   (a) quality of staff and their skills;
   (b) sources of cost and price competitiveness;
   (c) non-price competitiveness including particularly marketing and quality;
   (d) goodwill associated with established products or services;
   (e) market shares and existence of effective barriers to entry;
4 appropriate organizational structure;
5 methods of financial control and management information;
6 a financial strategy and a time path for the achievement of change; and
7 the need for motivation and commitment.

The process needs to be undertaken promptly and the necessary actions taken firmly and swiftly thereafter. As Tom Peters (among others) has pointed out the propensity to prolong the process, to fail to take action, to tone down measures and to compromise is enormous. Excellent reasons can always be adduced for cautious inactivity. To counteract this he prescribes that the firm should set itself a harsh programme of targets for numbers of changes in each area of action to ensure that rapid progress actually occurs. The problem seems to be that having to act under the pressure of necessity seems to concentrate the mind very effectively and yet to await the stimulus of the accumulated effects of severe short-run problems reduces the prospects of success. Greater scope is offered by changing under conditions of strength. For this reason some incoming chief executives generate what may be seen in retrospect as an almost artificial sense of crisis.

6.1.1 The Causes of Relative Decline

It may seem a rather trivial observation but the appropriate strategy depends upon why the company had not achieved such good performance in the earlier period. Nine general causes have been suggested:

1 adverse changes in total market demand;
2 falling revenues due to more intense competition;
3 high-cost structure;
4 inadequate financial control;
5 poor management;
6 big projects that fail;
7 acquisitions;
8 lack of marketing/sales effort; and
9 poor quality/reliability.

The first two of these refer to changes in the environment which affect the firm. Some of these are permanent and some temporary. Half the sharpbenders were affected by cyclical changes in demand. These clearly require different responses – short-run problems can be offset by short-run measures – although since cyclical problems recur by definition the best means of offsetting them also recur automatically each time, either by diversifying into products or markets which have different cycles or by altering the structure of the business immediately.

Those longer-run changes where the market as a whole is in decline mean that the firm must change its product market focus. It must either move to subsectors of the market (often referred to as niches) where reasonable profit margins may still be obtained or to other industries altogether. However, it is a mistake to view this as a single adjustment, which when completed will solve the company's problems thereafter. The market changes all the time and existing products can face declining demand at any time as technologies change and substitutes come on to the market. The competitive firm is not merely responding to those changes but is at the leading edge of such changes, seeking new ideas and opportunities. It will therefore tend to be caught out less often. However, the protection offered by such a pro-active stance cannot be complete as threats may be posed by actions of others beyond the control of management. Governments lower protection, reduce subsidies or change regulations; exchange rates may change substantially; other firms may disrupt the market to create new competitive advantages for themselves. The company can clearly respond more rapidly and adequately to such externally induced changes when it has recognized that they are possible and has considered their potential impact.

All this explains why product market potential is the first area to look at after this appraisal of the past.

The remaining causes of relative decline all relate to the firm's own actions or lack of them. Some are specific errors which need unwinding, such as poor acquisitions or big projects which went wrong. Clearly the firm should do that in any case whether or not it forms part of a sharpbend. An indication of actions that might be appropriate, when assessing the period of relative decline, may be usefully given by the experience of other companies which have been more successful. It is often possible to learn from what others in the same or comparable industries have done. Frequently, scanning what is being done overseas is of substantial benefit in this respect. In most markets competitors are not just within the UK but overseas as well. Several of the sharpbenders picked up ideas in foreign markets which helped them on their way – Ellis & Goldstein from New York, Low & Bonar with the Flotex process from France, for example. The John Wood Group took this process of acquiring ideas from elsewhere further, by bringing in staff from companies involved in servicing the gas industry in the southern North Sea in order to launch their own oil-support operations.

Some of the information required may be difficult to obtain and hence the appropriate route may be to make use of consultants or information available from other intermediaries such as the Economic Development Committees (Little Neddies) which publish reports on 'best practice' here and overseas. A major characteristic which distinguished the sharpbenders from the control companies was their ability to perceive more causes of market decline and the adverse effects of poor organizational structure. It was thus not just a matter of what steps to take which sets the sharpbenders apart but the ability to be realistically self-critical and to identify areas in which there is room for improvement.

6.1.2 Product Market Potential

The most important factor for any sharpbend is for the firm to work out where it is trying to go. Many firms in a traditional slowly evolving business have been able to move forward steadily by following well-known procedures and reacting in well-established ways. Too often, then, they have failed to develop the discipline of regularly analysing their economic mission and hence find it difficult to contemplate either entering new markets or making an exit from old ones. By comparison, the sharpbenders by and large took a careful look at all the markets in which they were selling and the products which they sold in them. This enabled them to assess where profitable opportunities for growth might lie.

On the whole, successful strategies involved having a focus on particular sectors rather than a generalized approach of either having products across the whole industry or just attempting to pick good opportunities wherever they are. Thus, for example, Glaxo, although it is a large pharmaceutical company by international standards, still concentrates on a relatively limited range of products because of the investment in research and development required to bring a product on to the market. They have also assessed where the market opportunities lie, particularly in the US with its massive demand for health care and also in Japan, although this latter has proved a hard market to break into. Dawson International took a similar hard look, avoiding diversifying into 'race tracks and fish farms' and concentrating on markets where per-capita disposable incomes were high enough to afford their high-quality, expensive products.

6.1.3   Sources of Competitive Advantage

Assessing product market potential is only one dimension of trying to assess where the firm should focus, because it also has to assess what it is good at and what it can do better than competitors. Figure 6.1 illustrates one approach to analysing the relation between market potential and the company's ability to exploit it. In both cases shown as (a) and (b) in figure 6.1, there is a trade-off. In the first case not all products will sell well in all markets. For multinational firms with several production plants this will have implications for what is produced where. Even for smaller firms – such as Rotaflex – with rationalization strategies who are trying to produce only one set of products in each place, this form of assessment may have clear implications. Having sorted out which product markets seem to have potential the firm has to set this potential against its actual production abilities compared with those of its competitors and the scope for improvement in these abilities. The ideal, of course, is strong growth markets in areas where the firm has a competitive edge, say because it has strong patent protection or a good distribution network. Clearly those are areas on which the company should concentrate its expansion. However, since the firm may have existing facilities and expertise in other less promising areas it may still be highly profitable to continue with existing lines. Sidlaw followed this approach very clearly, putting resources into its oil-support operations to try to develop new ideas and opportunities while having tight cost control, and driving for maximum efficiency in its textile

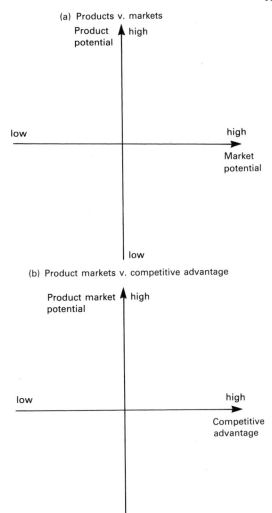

Figure 6.1 *Product market potential and competitive advantage*

division and thereby exploiting existing skills and capital advantage.

Equally as important as the identification of profitable opportunities is the disposal of businesses which will never give an adequate rate of return and hence should be disposed of. This is particularly difficult as there is always the tendency to suggest that any given area which is currently in recession is just about to turn round. We are all familiar with what Stuart Slatter describes as the 'hockey-stick' forecast – a short-term deterioration followed by quite rapid and continuous growth. Those within such areas (Drucker calls them 'yesterday's breadwinners') are perhaps the most susceptible to such optimism. The tendency to such misplaced optimism may be particularly great within a company determining to achieve a sharpbend, because those in the relatively weak areas realize that to generate the growth required there will need to be cutbacks somewhere.

Five different sources of comparative advantage are suggested by the experience of the sharpbenders.

1 Quality of Staff and their Skill Needs   Perhaps the harshest part of the initial appraisal is taking a cold look at the human capital of the firm – the people working for it and their skills and abilities. Both judgement and courage are needed to select the key managers successfully and to dispense with the services of those who are not going to cope with the new focus of the firm. The sharpbenders stressed that *people* formed the core or secret of their success. This applied at all levels from the chairman and chief executive downwards. We have observed already that most sharpbenders changed their chief executive either before the bend, which acted as the trigger, or as one of the steps to achieving the bend itself. This should not be taken to imply either that contemplating changing the chief executive would be a good idea nor that if he were changed this would enhance the chance of achieving the bend. If the company is already trying to sort out how to change on the chief executive's initiative or with his active support then the trigger for change already exists and there is no need to create another one. The probability of such a change occurring will normally be related to how poor the performance of the company has become.

The quality of people throughout the company has been shown to be important, starting with the structure of the board, requiring strong functional executive directors supported by active, participative, non-executive directors who contribute to the development of the firm from their independence of mind, experience and links with other businesses. However, uncritical non-executive directors who show little action may be little more than an unwelcome overhead. Mrs Tyrrell at Sirdar reflected this when she said that she was keen not to have 'passengers' on the board. Our impression was that experience with non-executive directors varied widely among the sharp-benders and that too often they have been selected because of their prestige rather than the contribution they would bring to effective decision-taking at board level.

The chief executives of the main operating divisions and subsidiaries also played a crucial role in the success of most of the sharpbenders. Operational decision-taking tended to be delegated to them by slimmed down head offices. It was they who actually had to deliver the output, the quality, the reduction in costs and achieve the sales through successful marketing.

However, it is not just having the right senior managers in the right place at the right stage of development which matters. The energies and skills of the staff as a whole must be harnessed and focused effectively. This involves, among other aspects, articulating and communicating a value system. Values are often communicated subtly by example rather than word, for instance by continued emphasis on the importance of attention to quality and detail, by training the after-sales staff in good customer relations and by radiating personal enthusiasm and commitment. This is not just a matter of exhortation. However, productivity of people also depends strongly on their skills, which may require experience and training. Because of the time taken to acquire such skills it is sometimes necessary to bring in new staff from competitors but they in turn need to be integrated into the company. This stress on skills, motivation and orientation among the wider workforce is similar to Peters' emphasis on 'productivity through people'. However, the central factor is 'leadership', for without it the potential of the people within the company is unlikely to be released, sustained and directed effectively.

Thus the initial appraisal has to sort out how that initial leadership is going to be applied and how the company is going to get or mould the best people for the task ahead and motivate and train them to achieve it. For without the commitment and belief in success the sharpbend is much less likely to work.

2 Sources of Cost and Price Competitiveness While all firms pay close attention to their costs in order to increase their competitiveness and profitability, for some this is the prime driving force. Porter (1985) argues that there are three generic strategies for achieving a competitive advantage. One is seeking to achieve cost leadership, the second is creating differentiated products so that they carve out their own market, and the third is to focus on specific market segments. He argues very strongly against trying to be 'all things to all people', as a mixture of aims may result in failure to achieve an advantage in any respect. Our perception is that this is too extreme a position. A firm with a differentiated product may focus upon the most profitable market segments and still be the lowest-cost producer serving its markets.

If a firm is going for cost leadership it has the opportunity to offer the lowest price and this may be the appropriate strategy where products are standard or by their nature fairly homogeneous and often where there are economies of large scale. Perhaps for this reason, selling on price alone was not a very common feature of the sharpbenders. They tended to choose either the route of differentiation, choosing high-quality products as did Dawson International, going for leadership in style such as Ellis & Goldstein, or focusing on particular parts of the market like the John Wood Group. In some cases these were combined where, for example, Ellis & Goldstein also aimed some of their products at the patrons of 'shops within shops' while still seeking leadership on style.

Pursuing the lowest-cost route entails the ability to have a favourable combination of all the cost components: low input costs, say because of ready access to materials; low overheads, either because of efficient organization or shared resources; low unit costs through large scale for example, or access to low-cost labour; low marketing and distribution costs, for example through selling to tied outlets or other parts of the group.

Before following this route to competitiveness exclusively, however, very careful appraisal is necessary. It is recognized that many British industries lack important cost advantages relative to overseas producers with very cheap labour. For instance, while Sidlaw knew that they could produce better quality jute textiles than their Indian competitors because of superior technology, even with the advantages of closeness to the customer there was no way in which they could hope to beat them on price in standard products because of the very low level of Indian wages.

The other side of price competitiveness is very important. If it is possible to charge a margin over competitors because of other non-price factors such as novelty or quality then this gives a clear advantage and the ability to spend more on marketing, investment and R&D to maintain that advantage. Bell's whisky, for example, normally sells at a premium yet still captured a significant share of the UK market in the late 1960s and 1970s.

3 Non-price Competitiveness including particularly Marketing and Quality   It is evident from macro-economic data (see Mayes, 1986, for example) that UK industry has tended to slip into selling less technological products which compete rather more on price to the other advanced countries while sending more sophisticated products to the developing countries. This seems to reflect an inability to compete effectively in the areas where high technology and quality are important. Yet it is just these areas, which exploit their skills, where the greatest gains have been made by most of the advanced industrialized countries. It is particularly interesting, therefore, that the sharpbenders tended not to share this general UK malaise and in looking for products which have greater value added, have moved up the technological league rather than down it. In many cases this has been through acquisition as much as from change within the firm.

Technological advance was reflected in improved quality and reliability, upon which the sharpbenders placed heavy emphasis. Other facets of non-price competitiveness also needed to be taken into account. Prompt delivery and good after-sales service were stressed. In most cases, effective marketing and selling were critical, the sharpbenders finding out clearly what customers wanted, establishing good relationships and working hard to maintain them. This reaps major rewards. It was not just because of competing prices, for instance, that Don Brothers kept their looms running near capacity when a depressed market for tufted carpet backing in 1986 led to severe over-capacity in their industry.

4 Goodwill Associated with Established Products or Services   The sharpbenders tended to build on the areas where they already had advantages. Thus, Whatman Reeve Angel were careful to make full use of the Whatman name, which had a strong reputation for quality. Similarly, Dawson International made full use of the prestige brand names which it had purchased, Pringle of Scotland being one of them, and concentrated its product range at the upper end of the market as a consequence. This goodwill extends not merely to the products of the firm but to the relationships which it has with suppliers and customers. Thus the formation of Whatman Reeve Angel itself out of the W & R Balston production firm and Reeve Angel International which had been marketing the products, is a clear example of how far this process of exploiting goodwill can go. Such examples of goodwill exist within the firm as well as outside it. Several of the sharpbenders were able to exploit the competitive advantage of the good relationships they had built up with their employees. Others, such as Countryside Properties, were able to exploit specific relationships, like that with the Essex County Council through their commitment to the Essex Design Guide. Associated Book Publishers stressed the importance of the nurturing of their authors as providing the basis of the flow of good products for the future.

5 Market Shares and Existence of Effective Barriers to Entry A further facet of building on positions of existing strength comes from exploiting areas where the firm already has some form of dominant position, either because it is the clear market leader and it can set the pace or because its established position confers advantages on it which others have difficulty in matching. Such an advantage could be geographical, as in the case of Sidlaw with its excellent site for oil-rig support, or through patents, as with the pharmaceutical companies. Indeed, Glaxo emphasized the importance of gaining a proper foothold in markets as the costs of entry, including certification of a new drug, are very considerable and have to be incurred in each market. Thus existing producers can have very considerable protection, which they need to make use of if they in turn are to have the resources to enter a new market or introduce a new product. In other industries, the barriers may be through existing links with customers and suppliers. For example, a publisher has to build up a stable of authors before it can actually produce new books in different fields.

Further sources of competitive advantage exist beyond the five we have indicated, but these were the most important revealed by our sample of sharpbenders. This does not imply that the other sources may not be more important in some circumstances. What is clear is the need to appraise where the competitive advantages lie and then move to exploit them.

6.1.4 Appropriate Organizational Structure

The way in which people are organized can have a major impact on their effectiveness. Thus most companies have gone for operating divisions or companies which reflect their major areas of business or product market focus.

Attaining the appropriate organizational structure was frequently associated with considerable change in the firm itself, not just in terms of horizontal or vertical integration, but in the closure of some businesses and the acquisition of others. These divestments and acquisitions signalled recognition that the new product market focus might not be achievable from the existing resources. Such dramatic changes, which led to fundamental changes in the resources to be organized, were not necessarily a prelude to success. In our study we found that the control companies made acquisitions more frequently than the sharpbenders did. Difference in success of acquisitions reflected many aspects such as the quality of the acquired company and its management, the price paid, the prospects of the markets so entered, and the effectiveness of subsequent integration of the acquired company into the organizational, planning and control systems of the acquirer. We were struck by the fact that attempts to diversify from dependence on a declining industry were not as successful when the new businesses were unrelated as when they stemmed from focused strategies.

Companies produce above-average results because they exploit effectively the business-specific characteristics of the acquired firm: the skills of their management and workforce, their operating and information systems, their market standing and relationships with major clients, and their capital equipment, plant and distribution systems. The problem confronting companies in declining industries is that these business-specific assets are tied to increasingly unprofitable markets. Whilst some may achieve profitability by staying in the business and dominating it, as Don Brothers Buist did by buying up capacity as its rivals in polypropylene textiles quit the market, such a survival strategy is not open to all. Others, like the Sidlaw Group and Low & Bonar in the textile business, properly saw a brighter future in other businesses. Yet to make a transition into a fundamentally different company with its main weight in different businesses is both painful, as faithful employees are made redundant and plants in familiar locations are closed, and potentially dangerous, because the company enters markets in which it has no distinctive advantages and relatively little knowledge. Clearly this risk is reduced the more related the new area of business is to the old, for the existing experience and skills of management are the more relevant. It is greatest where the new business is unrelated to the old, for the only skills which are then directly transferable are, in most cases, financial. It is for this very reason that diversification into unrelated businesses is normally by acquisition of a bundle of managerial expertise, operative skills, operating systems and capital equipment, i.e. purchase of a going concern. Even there, unless the acquirer has special abilities to add to those acquired it is difficult to know why it should receive an exceptional return on its investment.

6.1.5 Methods of Financial Control and Management Information

In parallel with the need for increased delegation is the need for increased control and information to be able to identify rapidly where anything is not running properly in divisions or subsidiaries. An effective, small head office needs to have concise up-to-date information on the financial performance of the various businesses in the company, their sales, market prospects and competitive positions, so it can develop a corporate strategy and monitor its success. To meet such needs both sharpbenders and controls improved their management accounting systems and provided operating rules for their subsidiaries which prevented any substantial unexpected deviations from plans.

Sound management accounting systems and financial controls seemed therefore to be what might be termed a 'hygiene' factor. Without them success was unlikely but they were not in themselves a sufficient condition for high performance. The distinctive critical factors leading to sharpbending are different. Effective, firm and purposeful leadership, the ability to give vision and direction to the whole organization and to exercise sound judgement in strategic decision-taking are what really count.

6.1.6 Financial Strategy and a Time Path for the Achievement of Change

All the previous points in the initial appraisal relate to areas where the possibility for change should be investigated. However, the order in which the realization of these possibilities is to be undertaken is crucial to the success of the sharpbend. In the first place many of the changes require expenditure: investment in new products or processes, new skills, acquisition of new companies, new computer systems for better control, for example. Furthermore, companies wishing to change will often already be in a relatively weak financial position unless they have chosen to time their move during an upturn in demand. Hence their ability to finance the changes either from existing funds, borrowing or equity, may be rather limited. Where this is so the first steps must be to generate the funds necessary to achieve the sharpbend. Costs need to be trimmed wherever possible, overheads which have accumulated with increasing numbers of bureaucratic, centralized, head-office-oriented systems over the years slashed, loss-making operations, which cannot be brought into the black reasonably quickly, divested or closed and assets not important to the future of the company sold. Such surgery is painful; familiar businesses may be lost irretrievably, faithful long-serving employees feel betrayed when made redundant; a sense of insecurity will pervade the organization. Yet this pain, insecurity and damage to relationships can be minimized where the workforce representatives have been convinced that 'rationalization' is necessary for long-term survival and can lead to better prospects of long-term employment as at the Glasgow works of Collins. Communication of its vision of the purpose of hard measures and of its concern for all its employees is an essential feature of good managerial leadership which is rightly prepared to 'grasp such nettles'.

Relationships with the company's bankers are also critically important at this stage, especially if the company has been approaching a major financial crisis, when they must be persuaded of the future viability of the company. Even where the situation is not so desperate, as with most sharpbenders, extended overdraft facilities may be necessary during the early phases of expansion.

The lags in the system can be quite long if a greenfield site has to be purchased or substantial development is required before the product reaches the market. The firm can thus be vulnerable to failure or takeover for a period over which it has undertaken expenditures and not yet got the return. For instance, the long development time of Seabug at UDI brought financial collapse leading to acquisition of the company. Similarly, the acquisition of Bell's by Guinness was probably facilitated by the impact on Bell's financial performance of the major refurbishment programme it commenced on some of the hotels it acquired when it took over the Gleneagles Group. Looked at as a whole the strategy was viable and the hotels are now making a contribution to the profitability of the company. This is small consolation, however, to Raymond Miquel and others who believed in an independent existence for Bell's!

Such vulnerability makes it essential that the initial appraisal of the path forward be realistic and that the firm's bankers and shareholders accept the strategy and be prepared to see short-run difficulties for the sake of the longer-run gain. This again is one of the reasons why the change has to be sharp. If it is prolonged, support begins to ebb and the process can be undermined. Furthermore, the longer the period of exposure the greater the chance of an economic difficulty occurring, given the relatively short length of economic cycles in the past and the rate at which competitors can also change their strategy and products. Some of the sharpbenders had to try twice to get their bend fully implemented and into sustained improvement, the first attempt having been overtaken by short-run difficulties, resulting in the need for even sharper measures later.

6.1.7   The Need for Motivation and Commitment

One of the strongest themes to emerge from our study was the need to gain the commitment, to motivate and to harness the energies of people at all levels within the company purposively. In unionized companies this meant taking the trade unions into the confidence of management on changes which would affect their members. During our fieldwork we were frequently impressed by the maturity of judgement, realism and willingness to share in hard decisions on redundancies, shown by workforce representatives who had been so consulted. Such understanding and support from unions, their members, middle and even senior managers must be earned by effective communication of the present realities, new vision and strategies and what these entail, by a leadership seen to be effective and itself committed. Change is a risky process, the initial part of it is painful and the inherent caution and conservatism of many people can readily act as enough of a brake on the sequence for the impetus to be lost.

It is essential, therefore, to arouse commitment to success. The firm which wants to change must seek sources of motivation and incentives which are positive and lead people to identify with objectives in the future. Financial rewards such as performance bonuses may sometimes have a positive effect. Fear of being out of a job can galvanize some people into action but its effect tends to be eroded as the threat recedes and it has negative side-effects. In most sharpbenders, however, no single motivational force was found to have a dominating influence, the high level of commitment being attributable to a more subtle mix of factors.

In the American-based 'excellence' literature the setting of values, 'kites', goals or whatever word is used, is a key part of trying to achieve success for the firm. Such publicly declared watchwords act as a focus of the activity of the people in the organization at all levels. This has been particularly important in industries which have a large direct service element in them, such as retailing, restaurants, airlines and other household and business services, where the attitudes and behaviour of employees to customers is crucial. It is similarly important where the company's employees are visible to the outside world as when undertaking major contracts for public authorities. However, the need to create a shared vision and to motivate the employees is far more general and the approaches successfully adopted more subtle than public slogans or 'kites'. Thus although the UK sharpbenders tended not to have such a bold outward image of goals as these American companies they nevertheless instilled enthusiasm and commitment which communicates itself via the attitudes of employees at all levels to the customer and indeed the supplier.

This is perhaps the most difficult area in which to make an initial appraisal of the appropriate way forward. There is no one approach to this which will obviously succeed. Sometimes the approach may be uniquely related to the leader, as with Miquel at Bell's, and may sometimes be peculiarly appropriate to the situation of the company. Ben Thompson-McCausland describes one approach to developing a set of shared values or 'corporate mind' at London Life, which is directed to releasing energy, achievement, confidence and teamwork. What marks his approach and that of others is the focus on *positive thinking*. Moreover, he clearly saw the important battle in revitalizing London Life was that of winning minds to participate in the more dynamic future which was required.

He set about this by institutionalizing meetings to discuss, among other things, the values of the company. What we believe to be a key factor, however, in both his case and that of the sharpbenders in our sample was the fact that the leaders were committed, had an articulated vision and communicated this by word and, above all, by example. In the early days to communicate an air of energetic enthusiasm, Ben is said to have always run up the stairs to his office two or three at a time! It was no accident that managers throughout, say, the John Wood Group or Bell's believed completely in the ethic of totally committed hard work. Both Ian Wood and Raymond Miquel showed total commitment in what they did themselves. They were at their desks earlier in the morning to later at night than other managers and yet still evinced an air of confident, energetic, positive enthusiasm.

Cases such as London Life, the John Wood Group and Bell's under Miquel illustrate the fact that, with the appropriate incentives, a great deal more can be achieved from the existing staff. Good people will produce outstanding performances when well motivated to do so. Thus planning a successful sharpbend is not just a matter of getting the right organization, with good product focus and controlled costs but it also involves getting the workforce to accept and act on the strategy and to do so in a fully committed, energetic way. In practice this process of changing behaviour may be time-consuming and often one of the most difficult to achieve. The larger the company the longer and more difficult because the corporate leader is more remote from the more junior people in the organization.

6.2 Putting the Sharpbend into Practice

All the sharpbenders stressed the importance of action. They also continued to search for new opportunities to improve profitability after their sharpbends, scanning what others were doing in both their own and other industries. Taking a leaf from their book, any manager might ask about what others have achieved and the questions, 'Can I do that?' 'Why haven't we done this already?', 'Would it work for us in our industry?', 'What would be the advantages and disadvantages?'. It is necessary to pose this as a continuing challenge. Although some dramatic steps may be necessary at the point of sharpbending, continued effort, restless search for opportunities and persistent striving for the highest performance in terms of quality, cost and after-sales service need to become a way of life to be sustained in a dynamically changing market environment.

Having said this, the very major steps often necessary at the beginning of a sharpbend rarely require repetition for some years. Mistakes made in the past need to be unwound and a major reorientation of the business including changes in key staff may be required to break the old, less effective mould. However, beyond that the focus needs to be on the longer-run commitment. Thus in addressing the steps to be taken (see chapter 4) it makes sense for companies to aim directly at achieving the characteristics of sustained, improved performance (see chapter 5). The steps taken are then directed to the goal of continuing improvement not purely short-run correction of errors which may themselves create long-run difficulties.

Thus the aim is for a future organization which embodies many of the thirteen characteristics derived in the previous chapter:

1 action-oriented management;
2 effective financial controls and management information;
3 an emphasis on 'people' within the firm;
4 good internal communications and industrial relations;
5 a simple organizational structure with a small head office;
6 incentives and motivation for employees;
7 a clear product market focus with a deliberate concentration on what the firm can do best;
8 an emphasis on customers;
9 a strong marketing focus;
10 a drive for quality;
11 delegation of operating decisions to responsible cost and profit centres;
12 regular reviews of strategy (the formality of this process tends to increase with firm size); and
13 a forward-looking approach which invests in the future through plant, equipment, R&D and training.

It is these which between them generate the flexibility and drive for continuing change which characterizes the successful sharpbend. There is value, therefore, in keeping them in mind even during the initial appraisal to identify major problems, opportunities and immediate action necessary and the first step in a sharpbend is clearly to undertake such an appraisal. This should tackle first those areas of the business which are undermining performance. It may be necessary, for instance, to eliminate or turnaround the parts of the business which are causing losses, to slash excessive stocks as at Collins, or to make a rights issue in order to eliminate crippling interest burdens. The case studies at the end of the book are replete with examples where, when the company has been in financial difficulties, it is especially necessary to obtain the support of the main financial actors, be they shareholders or bankers, for the aims of the sharpbend and to reduce the threat they perceive to their investment. Without this support the drive for change can be torpedoed at the outset, and the company exposed to a threatened or actual takeover or forced to take measures which will improve short-run cash flow and stock-market confidence at the cost of longer-run change and restructuring.

The second step is an analysis of the product market focus of the company, the kinds of businesses it should be in, covering trends in various markets, relative competitive advantages in technology, human skills, costs of inputs, including labour, quality, market shares and their rates of change. In the light of this analysis an appropriate way forward can be agreed.

This item needs to be followed by the organizational and structural changes, necessary to achieve the change in product market focus, particularly the motivation of the people within the firm, for without that they cannot achieve the sustained drive to improved performance. This will include installing the control and information systems, otherwise the activities of the company as a whole may become ill-coordinated with lower-level units pursuing their own goals to the detriment of the corporate whole. The strategies of top management may not be implemented and the performance of divisions or subsidiaries may slip unnoticed. Moreover, in delegating authority for operational decision-taking, top management must always retain levers over subsidiary business operations. Principal among these are the power to promote, sack or change the remuneration of subsidary senior managers and to control major capital expenditure. The most powerful means of influence are more subtle though, depending on the ability of the company's leadership to communicate vision, commitment and values through personal relationships.

Once the strategic direction of the company has been broadly set and the organizational structure recast if necessary, it is possible to proceed to operational actions, *viz.*:

1   developing the product market focus;
2   improving the links with customers;
3   strengthening the market and sales performance;
4   improving quality; and
5   investing in the future through:
    (a) plant and equipment;
    (b) R&D; and
    (c) training.

A variety of approaches can be adopted to achieve such changes. Each functional area may be approached by its management team, which is given specific targets to achieve against a tight timetable, or task forces may be set up to tackle each of a series of issues. Sometimes it may be desirable to use consultants, who can bring in external objectivity, and draw on wide experience. The sharpbenders chose less formal routes, tackling each of the problem areas in a more *ad hoc* fashion. Indeed among many sharpbenders there seemed to be a distrust of 'standard' approaches which emphasized critical financial ratios and other 'book' methods of running successful companies. There was certainly no wholesale adoption of the sorts of approach which fill the American literature on excellence which seems contrary to the findings of Goldsmith and Clutterbuck (1984) who cast some British companies in the same light.

Our approach too is pragmatic. Rather than list the prescriptions given in conclusions of the existing management literature to which the references section at the end of the book points the reader, we are concerned to convey the most important lessons learnt from the successful experience of others. The main reason for this is the variety of experience. In this and the previous chapters we have summarized that experience but nothing will substitute for the richness of the individual cases. Please read them, they are set out in the pages that follow. Try to see which aspects of their industries apply to you and which you could adopt. There is no one solution either for companies as a whole or for individual companies. Ultimately, managerial judgement is needed to determine which lessons from the experience of others may best be applied to the unique situation of the individual firm. We may learn from the experience of others without adopting their pattern of actions as a general prescription for success!

6.3   An Omission

If we look back to the original statement of the steps which led to sharpbending there is one clear omission from our list in this chapter, that of windfalls, since a company cannot 'seek' a windfall as such. Nevertheless, it appears that the successful sharpbenders seemed to have a larger share of good luck than the control companies. It is our impression that this was because the sharpbenders were outward-looking, seeking opportunities and continually trying out new ideas. By pressing for innovation and looking for further sources of success they actually stood a better chance of perceiving and exploiting major opportunities which occur largely at random and are open to all.

Some of these occur by being in the right place at the right time. The company's strategy is also a factor, the firm which focuses its attention narrowly on only one area of business stands less chance than the diversified company of encountering and grasping opportunities which may occur in any of several areas. Similarly the firm with a rigid structure is less able to adopt such new opportunities.

This finding of opportunities by 'luck' also depends critically on the amount of effort put into searching. The sharpbenders emphasized looking at the ideas of competitors both at home and overseas. They also put weight on research and development – trying to find their own products if they could not derive them from the work of others. Coupling the stress on new ideas with investment in new machinery and in raising the skill level of the workforce meant that they were well equipped to adopt these 'windfalls' as they arose. The emphasis on the future and *action for continuing change* paid off.

6.4   Concluding Remarks

Many firms have the potential for sharp and sustained improvements in their performance but only a few manage to trigger that change. The main emphasis must therefore be on finding that trigger if other companies are to obtain the same achievements. This is the first focal point. As we have seen in this study, most firms were pushed into change rather than volunteering in the sense of the existing management deciding to make the change without outside pressure from a decline in demand, the action of competitors (or indeed predators) or from creditors. Nevertheless if a firm can undertake a sharp bend voluntarily, success tends to be rather easier to achieve as there is not the need for urgent short-run measures to improve the short-run financial position. However, it seems an unfortunate truth that firms react more vigorously to severe pressure. Incentive alone is often insufficient, a threat concentrates the mind.

Sharpbends are based heavily on people. A change at the top is one of the main triggers for a sharpbend. Successful bends are aided by careful choice of the right people to undertake the main tasks and made much easier by motivating and involving the whole workforce.

There are no easy recipes, no single solutions but the emphasis lies on informed *action*. Recall Eric Thain's remark that there are 'the three G's' which give the route to a successful sharpbend: 'guts, good luck and good judgement.' Simply expressed but hard to do. We hope this book encourages you to try. While this is naturally a simplification it does encapsulate neatly what is required. Any strategy needs to be carefully thought out and good decisions are built on good analysis of the problems facing the company. But without the courage and determination to see things through it is unlikely that, however good their analysis of the problems, the sharpbenders in our sample would have gone on to sustain their success. The sharpbend is an episode of high human drama and large economic and psychological rewards come from such major success. Sharpbending is exciting and worthwhile but requires sustained effort and sheer, effective management too. There is no magic. It is open to all. While by definition not every firm can be *more* successful than its competitors, many more can transform their performance and unleash their potential to become winners in both the UK and international markets. The opportunities exist, as the sample of companies we have examined shows. Our hope is that this book will encourage others to follow and improve on their example.

Technical Appendix

In order to assist the readability of the text we have concentrated the exposition of the scientific background to our research in this appendix. This background has two parts, first of all the statistical basis of the analysis and secondly, the relationship with previous analytical work on the subject.

It has been our intention to achieve two main structural aims in this research. The first is to provide statistically valid tests of the wide range of hypotheses that have been developed about why companies decline, how they manage to change and what the characteristics of successful companies are. The second and perhaps more important facet is to construct a research design which enables us to distinguish the behaviour of sharpbenders from that of other companies, which although similar in size, product range and performance before the sharpbend, did not themselves achieve a similar rapid and sustained improvement in performance. It is as important to ask why these other companies did not change so successfully as it is to ask why the sharpbenders did because a large number of measures taken were common to both groups. For example, during a five-year period, most companies change their chief executive. Therefore, purely observing that most of the sharpbenders changed their chief executives during the period of the sharpbend does not of itself tell us that this change plays any causal role in the sharpbending process. To do that we have to examine the actions of new and continuing chief executives in both the sharpbenders and in the matched 'control' companies.

A.1   Sample Design

As was explained in chapter 1 our sample of sharpbenders was selected on a carefully representative basis. It was based initially on the sampling frame of publicly quoted medium to large companies (defined as more than 200 employees) in the UK over the last fifteen years. Our aim was to select the best examples subject to the overriding limit of a sample size of twenty-five imposed by the resources available for the project and to having a wide spread of industries and two firms in each industry. The industries represented cover approximately 40 per cent of GDP in the manufacturing and construction sector.

The companies were originally selected from the EXSTAT database using the nine criteria set out in table 1.2. However, nearly 50 per cent of the companies did not have data on all variables for every time period in the decade of the original analysis. This was due to data error, reporting failure, takeover or entry. The sample was therefore augmented by obtaining the relevant data on companies suggested by stockbrokers and others, and a thorough review of the financial press over three years extending the sample period from 1970 to 1984. We estimate that our sample includes between one-half and one-third of the sharpest benders in the sample frame and hence that the results of the analysis will provide very accurate estimates of the whole group of sharpbenders in that period even though there are some biases in the selection method, particularly that at the margin firms were selected for visit on the basis of geographical convenience, leading to an over-representation of Scotland.

We quite deliberately increased the range of the sample to include some smaller companies, Macallan and UDI, and two subsidiaries, Pringle of Scotland and UDI. This was to provide a second sharpbender in some industries and also to provide an indication of how the general conclusions might apply to these two groups. Clearly in this latter case we make no claims for the statistical validity of the procedure but for the main sample, drawing at worst a sample of twenty-five from a population of seventy-five we have for the estimators a sampling error of some 13–30 per cent lower than if the population had been larger. (The correction factor is $(N-n)/(N-1)$, where N is the size of the population and n the size of the sample.) However, this applies to a random sample; as our sample has been chosen to be representative this is a maximum value and the sampling variances in our case are likely to be considerably smaller. Even taking this maximum view an 80 per cent confidence interval for an estimate of, say, 30 per cent, would be 21–39 per cent. We therefore take care in the text not to ascribe any higher level of accuracy to the results. Nevertheless, this means that the large majority of our results have strong statistical validity.

However, when it comes to comparision with the matched control companies, where one is drawn for each industry – hence there are approximately half the number of controls as sharpbenders – the consideration of the sampling variances is more complex. It is not clear what the size of the parent population of 'similar' firms is. Clearly it varies by industry. However, in most cases we got the sharpbenders and stockbrokers to identify their nearest competitors. We then selected the firm which was nearest in size and structure as a control. However, while we did not receive any refusals to participate from the sharpbenders themselves, some of the control companies were second or (rarely) third choices. Thus although the potential pool of control companies appears large at first glance it is in fact small because of our requirement that the control match the sharpbender. This must, therefore, in one obvious sense entail that our estimates are likely to be relatively accurate despite the small sample size. The problem remains, however, that if these examples are to be useful they must be generalizable to the general run of companies which might wish to become sharpbenders in the future. This is achieved by the combination of the large proportion of actual sharpbenders sampled and the wide spread of industries and firm characteristics included. Clearly, when it comes to very specific characteristics, the population size itself is very small and hence will be dominated by the particular firms.

In presenting the results of our survey in the text we have not included any measures of the variances of the estimators nor indeed the results of the statistical tests performed. The more important of these results are discussed in this appendix but the full detail is too voluminous for publication here.

A.2 Estimation Method

Since most of our results come from interviews we have taken very considerable care to ensure that the conclusions drawn from them are of a high quality. In the interviews themselves there were normally two interviewers to make sure that any remarks which were unclear were clarified and to restrict the scope for bias on the part of the interviewer. Secondly, the interviews were taped which ensures complete accuracy of quotation. The whole research team could listen to all the interviews and agree on their interpretation. Thirdly, so that there was not undue emphasis on the opinions of any one person, interviews were conducted with two to four people in most firms. Stories could thus be checked. However, they were also checked against the published evidence on the firms in the form of annual reports and independent analysts' reports. Finally, the entire text of the book has been checked and agreed for accuracy by the companies themselves and has been commented on and checked by ten independent readers.

A.3 Choice of Hypotheses

Our research design, having divided the analysis into four phases according to sequence of events – *viz.* causes of relative decline, triggers for change, steps taken, and characteristics of continuing success – was to test as wide a range of hypotheses as possible. We therefore scanned the existing literature as well as developing hypotheses of our own with the help of the advisory group. This research design therefore follows what is known as the encompassing principle in econometrics in that our results include previous ideas and hence explain how these might be modified rather than purely providing a new set of our own ideas which may only partly overlap with previous work and hence provide no proper basis for checking or comparative evaluation. By this approach we hope that it is possible to move forward and build on the ideas of others rather than just provide yet another 'theory'.

The basic hypotheses derived are set out in sequential order in the table A.5. They are in the same order as the tables referring to them in the text and show the immediate source of the hypothesis although, of course, many of them will have been quoted by a much larger range of authors. Omission of these extra names does not imply any comment on the helpfulness of the research nor does inclusion imply that these are the original derivations.

However, these basic hypotheses which relate to each single event are augmented by investigating how the hypotheses in each of the four sections in the time sequence are related. Indeed, this itself is hierarchical. We begin by relating causes of decline to triggers, triggers to steps taken, steps taken to continuing characteristics and then go on to investigate the relations which occur across the first three and last three phases and finally for the whole four-phase sequence.

A.4   Relationships among Variables

In assessing the importance of each of the hypothesized relationships we have built up scales from combinations of various variables which either appear to be related in principle, e.g. that they are all measures of increasing financial control, or that are related in practice. This enables us to describe what can be called different sorts of strategies or approaches, which appear to have been used by the sharpbenders.

Taking the causes of relative decline first, it is rare for just a single cause to contribute to the companies' relative decline. They tended to occur in combination as is clear from figure A.1. Here the ten major causes of relative decline have been refined somewhat into what we have just described as scales to summarize their major characteristics.

Using simple correlations of the responses we began by checking whether there was more than one source of influence within each group. If there was, then use of only ten groups to summarize all the different causes would be insufficient and we would be discarding potentially valuable information by such an attempt. As it was, in all but three cases the correlation between responses within the group was strong. The exceptions are (a) poor quality and reliability, where only the general hypothesis of 'poor quality and reliability of product or service sold' is of any real significance; (b) poor management, which is better represented by four constituent parts (although it is rather difficult to give a clear meaning to each of these constituents), perhaps best described as: problems with chief executive, overcaution, incaution, failure to communicate; and (c) high-cost structure, which is again best disaggregated into, financial reasons, labour reasons, poor materials and working systems, excess capacity and expensive labour, and a residual category.

Four of the other categories of causes can also be beneficially divided up as they appear to show separate sets of influences. However, some of these combinations of factors seem rather heterogeneous, so that the link may be statistical rather than behavioural; such as that between changes in product technology and the influence of new substitutes on the one hand and political changes on the other as causes of a sustained drop in market demand. Nevertheless, this means that the ninety individual factors discussed in the other tables in this appendix can be boiled down into only twenty-six separate influences or scaled variables for consideration in the subsequent analysis.

In figure A.1 we concentrate on just ten major factors, rather than twenty-six, as the latter present an overcomplicated picture. Where the correlation between each of the groups is significant we have indicated this by a solid line. What is immediately apparent is that the causes are not uniformly related. Here the relations are of interest, because they identify areas which on the one hand are relatively independent of the others, such as the bureaucratic, centralized, over-large head office and ones which on the other hand are widely related such as the high-cost structure. The latter case suggests simply that firms will have a relatively poor performance if they cannot compete on costs – but that high-cost structure could have come from many sources: poor management, a fall in demand, poor financial control, an expensive failure, and so on.

The importance of the individual factors is shown in the tables in chapter 2 but here we can note that the causes themselves actually have a logical relation between

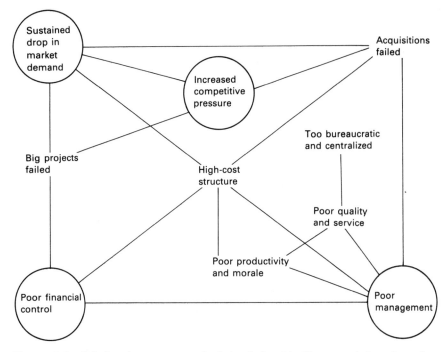

Figure A.1 *Relations between causes of relative decline (significant correlations shown by rules – 5 per cent level. Circled items could be regarded as logically prior)*

them. The four items circled in figure A.1: sustained drop in market demand, increased competitive pressure; poor financial control and poor management are likely to be logically prior to the others. For example, a sustained drop in market demand will tend to increase the competitive pressures between the companies in the market, costs will tend to rise as sales fall, and large investment projects will go wrong as they fail to achieve their expected rates of return. Similarly acquisitions will also tend to fail as the markets expected at the time of the acquisition do not fully materialize. However, these factors although logically prior are not actually necessary preconditions for the occurrence of the other causes of relative decline. A large project could fail even in the face of a sustained rise in market demand.

A.5   The Effect of Industrial Structure on Sharpbending

We also noted that the causes of relative decline could be related in more detail to the economic structure of the industry. De Jong (1987) summarizes these characteristics as set out in table A.2 for seven European industries which overlap those in which the sharpbenders lie. Reading across from the left in the table, the competitive forces bearing on a particular industry will vary according to whether the market is international, EEC-wide or national. A purely national market, say for particular telecommunications equipment which is not usually traded, can behave independently

Table A.1   *Main causes of relative decline*

1 Sustained drop in market demand	I
(i) changes in product technology, new substitutes, political changes	II
(ii) demographic and income distribution changes	III
(iii) cyclical and other causes	IV
2 Falling revenues due to competitive pressure	V
(i) technological change lowers rival's costs, threats from substitutes keep prices low, removal of protection and other barriers to entry, other competitive weaknesses	VI
(ii) High exit costs in face of falling scale, lack of strong product differentiation, lack of strong cost advantages	VII
3 Lack of effective direction, use and control of marketing and sales	VIII
4 Poor quality and reliability	
(i) poor quality and reliability of product or service sold	IX
5 Poor management	
(i) inflexible autocrat, combined chairman and MD, failure of management to communicate effectively with workforce	X
(ii) directors hold few shares, over-cautious top management	XI
(iii) neglect of core business, over-optimistic, incautious	XII
(iv) failure to communicate and create shared vision and values	XIII
6 Inadequate financial control	XIV
7 Poor organization	XV
(i) too centralized structure, too decentralized decision-making without adequate control	XVI
(ii) too formal and bureaucratic, head office too large and expensive	XVII

of fluctuations in overseas markets. Markets which are experiencing rapid growth are more likely to be able to provide a context in which a sharpbend can take place. In those like textiles where the market as a whole has not been growing rapidly, successful sharpbends tend to come from the development of niche markets as was the case with the jute spinners.

De Jong's remaining characteristics relate to:

Structural indicators – principally degree of concentration in the industry
Barriers to entry and exit
Performance indicators – innovations and pricing
Market organization.

Concentrated industries will tend to operate oligopolistically with strong competition for market share. In such circumstances firms often follow each other closely and it is difficult for any one firm to develop a competitive advantage which will enable it to achieve a sharpbend. Similarly, industries where there are higher barriers to entry may

TABLE A.2 *European market structure (average 1979–85)*

Industry sector	Market dimensions		Structural indicators[2]				Entry/Exit barriers	
	Relevant market	Market phase	C_1	C_4	Symmetry	F_m	Private	Government
Paper & board	EEC-wide; increasingly international	Stagnation to decline (UK, Italy)	Over 1000 firms, with some twenty larger ones				Economies of scale; resources in bulk less in fine papers	
Power plants	National and international	Stagnation	25-30	>60	A	Erratic	Heavy over-capacity impedes entry	National ordering; no assistance for newcomers
Telecommunications	National and international	Fast expansion	National: >80 EEC: C_1 >30; C_4 >60		A	Low	Technology; links with buyers	PTT purchases on national basis >75% of orders
Computers	EEC and international	Fast expansion	>35	>50	A	0.11	Economies of scale; vertical integration; low re-selling costs	Subsidies for major firms
Semi-conductors & integrated circuits	European and fragmented	Fast expansion	12-13 European product market shares C_4=40% in SCs and 30% in ICs	40	S	0.16-0.17	US producers in 1960s; Japanese in 1980s	Support for R&D programmes
Textiles	National and EEC-wide	Stagnation	5-6	12-15	S	0.2	In general low; very low for Third World producers	EEC frontier protection
Pharmaceuticals	Regional, national and EEC-wide	Modest expansion	25-50	25-100	A	0.15-0.20	Large R&D and advertising expenditure	Regulations

cont. overleaf

Table A.2 *(contd.)*

Industry sector	Performance indicator		Market organization		
	Innovative activity	Pricing	Competition	Co-operation	Control
Paper & board	Weak investments, excluding W. Germany	Cyclical variations	Intensity depends on boom/recession; 1974, 1979 & 1984 top years	Vertical integration prevails	Family control promoted investment; bank control
Power plants	Incremental improvements	Mostly unrewarding	European competitive power hampered by small size of firms & markets	Less than formerly; only in nuclear-fuel cycle and R&D	Important state interference, excluding W. Germany
Telecom-munications	Bilaterally induced R&D and pricing		National championship policies in nationwide markets Internationally cooperative agreements and mergers		
Computers	In hardware and software	Prices decline; price discrimination	On products, quality and prices	On standards	Dominant firm control

Semi-conductors & integrated circuits	Technological innovation & investments	Fast declines	Intensive competition	Licensing, second sourcing, and joint ventures	By international companies
Textiles	Some innovations & processes	Very flexible pricing	Intensive competition in receding market, prompted by imports	Forward vertical integration	Some mergers
Pharmaceuticals	Product innovation	Large price differences	Competition is intense for market share in therapeutic markets	Licensing agreements	Control by multinational companies

[1] C_1, C_4 concentration ratios of top one and four firms; F_m is a measure of change in market share (the greater the change the more 'competitive' the industry); symmetry (denoted S) and asymmetry (A) are indicators of relative concentration.
Source: de Jong (1987).

tend to have a more stable structure. However, where a new entrant can break in by virtue of a major innovation it may very well be able to make rapid inroads. Such barriers clearly exist in the pharmaceuticals industry because of the large amount of R&D required. However, having done the research successfully it is possible to break into new foreign markets as demonstrated by Glaxo.

It is thus clear that there are strong links between the structure of the industry and the types of sharpbend we are likely to see and, indeed, on the likelihood of bends occurring at all. Where the industry is severely controlled as it has been in certain financial markets it is virtually impossible for any particular firm to follow the sharpbending pattern of relative decline followed by sharp improvements in performance. Thus, in assessing the likelihood of a sharpbend, these considerations of industrial structure needed to be added to the specific characteristics of the firm which are brought out by their individual analysis.

A.6   Second-order Hypotheses – Relations between Phases

Moving on to second-order hypotheses – the relationships between each of the four phases in the process of sharpbending – there are now two groups which are of special note, those relating causes of decline to the steps taken (table A.3) and those relating the steps taken to the characteristics of continuing success (table A.4).

Table A.3 shows the results from regressing each of the steps taken on the causes of decline. Only results where the coefficient exceeded twice its standard error are shown. Thus, column 1 shows the dependent variable and column 2 the important independent variables, the others being omitted from the regression shown. Both dependent and independent variables are constructed as a simple scale by adding up the number of factors cited in each step or cause of decline. Thus for example there are thirteen factors in table 4.2 for step 1, changes in management. Hence the scale for step 1 for each firm has a possible range of 0–13. This is clearly a very crude indicator as the various components are not of equal importance, but nevertheless it is a clear pointer to the frequency of the various responses. Although, with a categorical dependent variable the variances will not be normally distributed, we have used the simple rule that a coefficient should be approximately twice its standard error for us to include it in the equation. However, applying a more satisfactory procedure, through F tests on the excluded variables in each equation as a group, did not lead to any important departure from this rule. Collinearity does not appear to be a problem. A further dummy variable, labelled 'sharpbenders' and holding the value unity if the company was a sharpbender and zero if the company was a control, was also included in the equation to see if the sharpbenders' behaviour differed from that of the controls.

The features of the table are discussed in the first section of the text of chapter 4. The major point to note here is the general lack of relationship.

Table A.4 is also notable for its sparseness. The variable labelled SB is the 'sharpbenders' dummy variable referred to in the case of the previous table. Here it is only in the case of the first continuing characteristic, changes in management, that the sharpbenders show behaviour different from the sample as a whole. This implies, not surprisingly, that changes in management alone are not enough to achieve the characteristics of good management observed among the sharpbenders.

It is interesting to note that reduced production costs and windfalls are the two

Table A.3 *Relation between causes of decline and steps taken*

Step taken	Related causes of decline	Coefficient	SE	R^2	R^{-2}	F
1 Change in management	Constant	2.469				
	Poor organization	1.876	(0.475)	0.366		15.604
2 Organizational change	None					
3 Stronger financial control	Constant	1.929				
	Competitive pressure	0.003	(0.001)			
	Poor marketing	1.011	(0.511)	0.239	0.181	4.090
4 New product market focus	Constant	8.163				
	Fall in market demand	−1.044	(0.593)	0.103		3.111
5 Improved quality	None					
6 Improved marketing	Constant	1.044				
	High-cost structure	0.409	(0.160)			
	Poor marketing	0.781	(0.366)			
	Sharpbenders	1.513	(0.787)	0.362	0.284	4.719
7 Reduced costs	Constant	0.515				
	Inadequate financial control	0.648	(0.185)			
	Poor quality and reliability	−2.299	(0.185)			
	Competitive pressure	0.281	(0.149)			
	Fall in market demand	0.003	(0.001)	0.499	0.416	5.992
8 Reduce production costs	Constant	1.333				
	Sharpbenders	2.449	(1.226)	0.129		3.988
9 Acquisition	Constant	1.546				
	Fall in market demand	−0.332	(0.154)			
	Sharpbenders	−0.966	(0.45)	0.349	0.299	6.958
10 Debt reduced	None					

Table A.4   *Relation between steps taken and continuing characteristics*

						Steps
Continuing characteristic	*1 Changes in management*	*2 Organizational changes*	*3 Central financial control*	*4 New product market focus*	*5 Improved quality service*	*6 Improved Marketing*
1 Good management	0.635 (0.147)					
2 Appropriate organizational structure		0.261 (0.149)				
3 Effective controls		0.197 (0.082)				
4 Sound product market posture				0.265 (0.085)		
5 Good marketing management						0.457 (0.121)
6 High quality maintained					0.448 (0.115)	
7 Tightly controlled costs				0.401 (0.155)		

Standard errors in parentheses.

steps taken which have the widest identifiable effect on the continuing characteristics. What is interesting in the case of windfalls is that two of the contributions are negative. Where there are windfall gains it is less likely that high quality will be maintained or costs tightly controlled. There is no perversity in this as the windfall in itself can provide a major contribution to the subsequent success of the enterprise. In so far as it does this it can mean that sufficiently good overall performance is achieved without the need for some of the other measures that the less 'lucky' sharpbenders have found it necessary to employ.

On the whole the relationships are as expected; management changes lead to good management, control changes to good controls, marketing and quality improves to good marketing and quality. It is not, however, immediately clear to us why windfalls should lead to an appropriate organizational structure, or debt reduction to good marketing management.

The remaining relationships are all discussed in the text and space precludes repeating the results in more technical detail here.

taken

Reduced costs 7 general 8 production	9 Acquisition	10 Debt reduced	11 Windfalls	SB	Constant	R^{-2}
				2.276 (0.914)	1.989	0.456
			0.937 (0.355)		2.562	0.194
					2.555	0.176
0.291 (0.117)			0.529 (0.292)		0.998	0.543
0.428 (0.121)		0.548 (0.283)			0.436	0.476
0.167 (0.053)			−0.313 (0.136)		0.399	0.512
0.463 (0.213)			−1.063 (0.532)		0.545	0.354

Table A.5 *Hypotheses*

A. STRUCTURE

First order
1 Causes of relative decline or stagnation before the sharpbend.
2 Stimulus for sharpbending.
3 Steps taken in achieving sharpbending.
4 Resulting continuing characteristics of sharpbenders.
 (N.B. These may be seen to be an aspect of effective implementation of 3).

Second order

5 Relationships between causes of decline or stagnation and stimulus for sharpbending.
6 Relationships between causes of decline and steps taken in achieving sharpbending.
7 Relationships between stimulus for sharpbending and steps taken to achieve it.
8 Relationships between steps taken to achieve sharpbending and continuing characteristics of sharpbenders.
9 Relationships between continuing characteristics of sharpbenders and the environmental conditions which contributed to decline.
10 Time lags between stimulus and instrumental changes.
11 Time lags between instrumental changes and success in sharpbending.

Third order

12 Relationships between causes of decline, stimulus for sharpbending, and degree of success.
13 Relationships between causes of decline, instrumental changes, and degree of success.
14 Relationships between stimulus, instrumental changes, and degree of success.
15 Relationships between time lags between stimulus and instrumental changes and degree of success.

B. FIRST-ORDER HYPOTHESES

Category of hypothesis	Number of hypothesis	Hypothesis	Source of hypothesis
1 *Causes of decline with which the company dealt relatively badly*			
1.1 Adverse changes in total market demand	1.1.1	Changing technology, economic, social or political conditions which lead to a sustained drop in demand in market served (N.B. under certain conditions this is likely to heighten price competition)	Argenti, Schendel *et al.*, Sigoloff, Slatter
	1.1.2	Cyclical decline for which the firm is ill-prepared	Slatter
1.2 Falling revenues due to more intense competition (N.B. connection with 1.5 in strategic groups in which the company operates)	1.2.1	Falling revenues, increased competitive pressure, lack of response to competitive changes	Argenti, Schendel *et al.*, Slatter
	1.2.2	Lack of product market focus, differentiation of product or strong cost advantages (see 1.6) to constrain competition	Hofer (on differentiation), Porter, Slatter
	1.2.3	Failure to develop new products	Slatter
	1.2.4	Low 'switching' costs for customer	Porter
	1.2.5	High exit costs which increase price competition in face of decline or sales	Harrigan, Porter, Sigoloff
	1.2.6	Technological change which lowers costs of rival(s)	Sigoloff
	1.2.7	High threat of potential entry	Bain, Porter
	1.2.8	Threat from substitutes prevents higher prices	Porter
	1.2.9	Removal of protection or other barriers to entry	Mayes, Porter
1.3 Lack of marketing effort	1.3.1	Lack of effective direction, use, and control of sales force, advertising, and after-sales and/or market research	Slatter

1.4	Poor management	1.4.1	Inflexible autocrat associated with stagnation or decline	Handy, Slatter
		1.4.2	Combined chairman and MD associated with stagnation or decline	Slatter
		1.4.3	Ineffective board (unbalanced boards; non-active, non-executives; no consensus; directors not major shareholders	Cuckney, Grinyer & Norburn, Slatter
		1.4.4	Management neglect of core business as (start to) diversify	Argenti, Grinyer & McKiernan, Schendel et al., Slatter
		1.4.5	Autocratic management style (and centralization of decision-taking)	Dunbar & Goldberg, Smart, Thompson, Vertinsky
		1.4.6	Overly optimistic, expansionary, incautious top management	Mayes
		1.4.7	Failure of communication from middle to senior management led to lack of top-management realism on market situation	Dunbar & Goldberg, Smart, Thompson, Vertinsky
		1.4.8	Management fails to communicate effectively with the workforce and unions: bad industrial relations	NEDO
1.5	Inadequate financial control	1.5.1	Absence or inadequacy of cash-flow forecasts, costing systems or budgetary control	Argenti, Grinyer & McKiernan, Sigoloff, Slatter, Yasai
		1.5.2	Management accounting information before top management too infrequently or too late	Slatter
		1.5.3	Management accounting information too voluminous, complex, wrong, or not that required	Slatter
		1.5.4	Top management not numbers-orientated	Slatter
		1.5.5	Centralized organizational structure hinders effective allocation of financial responsibility to operating management	Slatter
		1.5.6	Distortion of costs by arbitrary allocation of overheads	Slatter
		1.5.7	Failure to control effectively working capital, in particular stocks and creditors	Mayes
1.6	High-cost structure	1.6.1	Relatively high costs of production due to inability to exploit economies of scale	Porter, Slatter
		1.6.2	Relatively high costs of production due to inability to gain experience-curve effects	Boston Consulting Group, Slatter

	1.6.3	Relatively high costs because of absolute-cost disadvantages (competitors have tied supplies of raw materials or best channels of distribution; access to cheap, immobile labour; proprietary production know-how; favourable site locations; etc.)	Bain, Porter, Sigoloff, Slatter
	1.6.4	Centralized organizational structure with resultant head-office overheads	Slatter
	1.6.5	Poor production control, plant layout, labour productivity	Slatter
	1.6.6	Working practices, e.g. involving job demarcation, that inhibit effective deployment of labour or adoption of improved methods	Mayes
	1.6.7	Poor sales control and marketing: excessive marketing costs: high number of low-volume, expensive orders, etc.	Slatter
	1.6.8	Increased wage levels, strikes.	Patton, Riggs, Schendel
	1.6.9	Excess plant capacity and hence high fixed costs	Patton, Riggs, Schendel
	1.6.10	High bargaining power of supplier(s) has inflated costs	Porter
	1.6.11	Costs of difficulty with raw-material supplies	Patton, Riggs, Schendel
1.7 Poor quality	1.7.1	Poor quality and reliability of product relative to competitive products	Mayes
	1.7.2	Poor after-sales service relative to competitive products	Grinyer, Mayes
	1.7.3	Poor delivery times relative to competitive products	Grinyer
1.8 Acquisitions	1.8.1	Acquisition of companies with weak competitive positions	Slatter
	1.8.2	Acquisition at unjustifiably high price	Slatter
	1.8.3	Poor post-acquisition management of acquisition(s)	Kitching, Slatter
1.9 Big projects that fail	1.9.1	Underestimating capital requirements (cost estimates, project control poor or design changes or external factors inflate costs)	Slatter
	1.9.2	Start-up difficulties	Slatter
	1.9.3	Market-entry costs high	Slatter
	1.9.4	Over-estimation of need for extra capacity (see 1.6.9)	Slatter
1.10 Financial policy leads to excessive interest charges	1.10.1	Overgearing	Altman, Argenti, Slatter, Taffler

2 *Hypothesized triggers to sharpbending*

2.1	Intervention from external bodies	2.1.1	Bank, other sources of finance	Hedberg, Slatter
		2.1.2	Institutional investors	Slatter
		2.1.3	Non-executive directors	
		2.1.4	Group (if subsidiary)	Bramson
2.2	Change of ownership, e.g. acquisition	2.2.1	Acqusition – contested – uncontested	Grinyer & Spender, Hedberg, Slatter
		2.2.2	Inheritance by newcomer	Grinyer & Spender, Hedberg, Slatter
		2.2.3	Divestment by old owners: management buyout purchase by another company	
2.3	Injection of new chief executive	2.3.1	Due to above reasons (2.2)	Grinyer & Spender
		2.3.2	Due to death or retirement of old chief executive	
		2.3.3	Chief executive moves voluntarily to another job	
2.4	Recognition by management of problems and of impending or actual organizational collapse	2.4.1	This is rare due to commitment to existing recipies	Grinyer & Spender, Slatter
		2.4.2	New director(s) recruited who persuade(s) board	Bramson
		2.4.3	NEDO publications, conferences, etc., trigger recognition	Gater
		2.4.4	Publications, conferences or advisory services of DTI trigger recognition	Grinyer
2.5	Intervention by non-executive directors to replace chairman and/or managing director	2.5.1	Often more directly observable form of 2.1 where non-executives are representing interests of institutional shareholders	Slatter

3 *Hypothesized steps taken in achieving sharpbending* (assumed positively associated with improvement in performance; N.B. the general question of *risk*. Some sharpbenders may have taken high-risk actions which turned out well).

3.1	Changes in management	3.1.1a	Changes in chairman and/or managing director	Greve, Grinyer & Spender, Hedberg, Starbuck, Nystrom, Hofer, Patton, Riggs, Schendel, Slatter
		3.1.1b	New leader injects new philosophy, or vision, and values which drive the company	Grinyer & Spender, Peters & Waterman

	3.1.2	Change in key executive directors: (a) marketing or sales (b) finance (c) (more rarely) production or technical	Grinyer & Spender Slatter
	3.1.3	Change in non-executive directors (normally following 3.1.1)	
	3.1.4	Introduction of committed, positive management that encourages individual action and with 'bias for action'	Konaghan report, Peters & Waterman
	3.1.5	Key executives have ownership interests or other strong profit incentive	Cuckney
3.2 Organizational change	3.2.1	Decentralization (normally associated with creation of divisional structure and profit centres)	Slatter
	3.2.2	Reduction in size of head office (associated with 3.2.1) 'Simple form, lean (corporate) staff'	Peters & Waterman Slatter
	3.2.3	Centralization to tighten central controls: normally of cash and capital expenditure only, sometimes of recruitment	Slatter refers to centralization of fin- ancial decisions
	3.2.4	Simultaneous 'loose–tight' properties, i.e. decentralization of innovative and operating decisions whilst strong cen- tralization of issues involving key values	Peters & Waterman
	3.2.5	Introduction of corporate (strategic) planning	Cuckney
3.3 Strong central financial control	3.3.1	Introduction of (a) cash-flow fore- casts, (b) budgets, (c) management accounting data on production, (d) overhead costs, and (e) control over capital budget	Pearson, Slatter, Taylor
	3.3.2	Frequent use by managing director and board of a limited number of key financial ratios for control	Cuckney
3.4 New product market focus	3.4.1	Evaluation of existing strategy and of available alternatives and determina- tion of a corporate plan (see 3.2.5)	Slatter
	3.4.2a	Cut back to profitable core by closure or divestment of businesses, markets or products in which competitively weak	Boston Consulting Group, Hambrick & Schecter, Slatter, Taylor
	3.4.2b	Divest businesses company does not know well	Peters & Waterman
	3.4.3	Increase prices and 'harvest' busi- nesses in which competitively weak prior to closure	Boston Consulting Group, Slatter

	3.4.4	Seek 'focused strategy' by different-ial prices of emphasis to permit dom-ination of market segments	Porter, Slatter
	3.4.5	Seek to differentiate products or move into markets where strong product differentiation	Porter, Slatter
	3.4.6	Seek to enhance switching costs and other barriers to entry to the main markets in which the company operates	Porter, Slatter
	3.4.7	Seek to achieve costs leadership by: (a) gaining economies of scale (b) gaining economies of learning (c) tight control of marketing costs and discouraging high-cost customers (d) tight control of production and marketing expenses (e) control of materials and energy costs	Porter, Slatter Bramson
	3.4.8	Invest in new plant to enter new product market or give cost leader-ship in existing one	Slatter
	3.4.9	License new products from others	Kenoghan report
	3.4.10	Plan mergers and cooperative supply agreements to reduce capacity	Taylor
	3.4.11	Sell existing technology in LDCs in form of turnkey factories and systems	Taylor
	3.4.12	Create idle capacity to signal to potential entrants that growth in demand will be met by existing pro-ducers and new entry will trigger a price war	Harrigan, Porter
	3.4.13	Vertical integration to secure supplies or distribution channels	Harrigan, Patton, Riggs, Schendel
3.5 Improved product quality and service	3.5.1	Introduction or improvement of quality control	
	3.5.2	Tighter planning of production and delivery to reduce delivery delays	
	3.5.3	Introduction or improvement of after-sales service	Pearson
3.6 Improved marketing	3.6.1	Raising prices where products have price inelastic demand	Eisenberg, Pearson, Slatter
	3.6.2	Provide more competitive discounts	Eisenberg, Pearson, Slatter
	3.6.3	Analyse and rationalize the product range within the existing businesses and markets	Eisenberg, Pearson
	3.6.4	Analyse and revise distribution channels within the existing businesses and markets	Eisenberg, Slatter

3.6.5	Analyse profitability due to different categories of customers and focus on the more profitable within existing businesses and markets	Slatter
3.6.6	Analyse and revise after-sales services (either slimming, pricing to cover costs, or expanding as a marketing device)	
3.6.7	Analyse and revise advertising and promotion	
3.6.8	Change the systems for controlling salesmen, for communicating with them, and motivating them	
3.6.9	Improve marketing information to management	Bramson
3.6.10	Better control of finished stock levels and distribution	Bramson
3.6.11	'Get close to customer'	Peters & Waterman

3.7 Cost-reduction strategies (N.B. some are also mentioned under other headings but are collected here, too, for convenience)	3.7.1	Introduction zero-based budgeting or set targets for cost reduction	Slatter
	3.7.2	Introduce profit or cost centres	
	3.7.3	Cut overheads: (a) head-office staff, (b) buildings occupied, etc. (c) work in progress, materials stocks, finished-goods stocks	
	3.7.4	Cut marketing and distribution costs (a) concentrating on customers who give greatest contribution (b) concentrating on products which make greatest contribution to profits (c) rationalizing sales staff and also delivery journeys (d) rationalizing advertising and promotional activities	Hambrick & Schecter, Hofer, Patton, Pearson, Riggs, Schendel, Slatter, Taylor
	3.7.5	Reduce costs of production by: (a) seeking improved productivity via better training and higher morale (b) introducing work study or other means of reducing costs (c) tighter production and stock control to reduce working capital (d) tighter security to reduce pilferage (e) improved utilization of capacity (f) investing in new plant to reduce costs of production	
	3.7.6	Consult workers on methods of cost reduction	Bramson

3.8	Acquisitions	3.8.1	To facilitate new product market orientation: (3.8.1a) in related business (3.8.2b) by diversification	Eisenburg, Slatter
		3.8.2	Acquisition of competitors to increase competitive advantage in existing business	
		3.8.3	Acquisition of suppliers or distributive channels to secure or improve competitive position of existing business	
		3.8.4	In each of the above cases managerial action taken to effectively integrate the acquisition into company	Kitching
3.9	Debt-restructuring/new financial strategy	3.9.1	Dispose of saleable assets (including subsidiaries) to reduce debt	Slatter
		3.9.2	Sell assets and lease back	Slatter
		3.9.3	Float subsidiaries as public companies and so reduce debt	
		3.9.4	Rights issues to replace debt by equity	
		3.9.5	If private company, go public to raise new capital for expansion	Birley, Grinyer, Vaughan
3.10	Changes in the environment which remove causes of decline or benefit the firm without action by it	3.10.1	Recovery in demand in major, specific markets or segments in which relatively strong market generally due to: (a) cyclical upturn (b) secular upturn; including changes in taste, etc. (c) government policies or operation of its agencies	
		3.10.2	Reduce costs relative to competitors due to: (a) falling prices of raw materials relative to competitors (b) falling interest rates where more capital-intensive than competitors (c) falling real wages of labour relative to competitors (d) improved technology from equipment suppliers and/or lower equipment costs relative to competitors	
		3.10.3	Competitive position in the major, specific market segments served improving due to: (a) competitors going out of business (either through failure or a rationalization scheme, e.g. foundries)	

	(b)	competitors erecting barriers to entry that reduce potential competition	Caves & Porter
	(c)	changes in exchange rate or other factors making products more competitive internationally	
	3.10.4	Government agencies acting to break power of suppliers to company or buyers from it	
3.11 Others	3.11.1	Switch from specialist ⎱ in to flexible plant ⎰ declining	Harrigan
	3.11.2	Lease not buy plant ⎰ market	
	3.11.3	Strong PR efforts	Taylor, Slatter
	3.11.4	Development of financial incentives to motivate management to innovate which *this* company responds to more than others	Kenoghan report
	3.11.5	Use of consultants to pinpoint weaknesses and help refocus strategic thinking	Cuckney
	3.11.6	Infection of 'respect for people' or 'productivity through people' perspective	Peters & Waterman

4 Resulting characteristics of sharpbenders

4.1 Management	4.1.1	Energetic, top management strongly oriented to achieve good results	Grinyer, McKiernan, Yasai
	4.1.2	Top management develops and implements strategic plans	Bramson
	4.1.3	Less conservative top management	Grinyer, McKiernan, Yasai
	4.1.4	Management operate using adequate management control information	Slatter implies
	4.1.5	Communications to employees good and industrial relations healthy; company philosophy stresses 'respect for individuals'	Peters & Waterman, Slatter implies
	4.1.6	Chairman exercises controlling role over separate managing director	Slatter implies
	4.1.7	'Active' non-executive directors	Slatter implies
	4.1.8	Board does not interfere in day-to-day operations	Bramson
	4.1.9	Management at all levels has bias for action	Peters & Waterman
	4.1.10	Management at all levels keeps 'close to customer'	Peters & Waterman
	4.1.11	Top management projects strong company philosophy or values to all levels in organization	Peters & Waterman

	4.1.12	Management fosters leaders and innovators throughout company and encourages practical risk-taking	Peters & Waterman
4.2 Organizational structure	4.2.1	If company large and diversified in divisions or if company smaller and more narrow in product range is functional	Grinyer et al., Chandler, Rumelt
	4.2.2	Where market environment is dynamically changing, the organization is less formal than would be expected for its size	Burns & Stalker, Child
	4.2.3	Close links between marketing, R&D design	Bramson
	4.2.4	Where the environment is stable, and the product is at the mature stage of the product life cycle, the organization is formal and mechanistic for its size (especially where cost leadership sought)	Burns & Stalker, Child, linked with concepts of Hofer & Porter
	4.2.5	Profit (or where inappropriate cost) centres operated and decision-taking delegated to them	
	4.2.6	Centralized, large, head-office staff avoided/minimized and organizational structure is simple	Peters & Waterman
	4.2.7	Firm has different types of managers, and systems, in businesses at different strategic stages	Arthur D. Little and others
	4.2.8	'Simultaneous loose–tight properties', i.e. decentralized innovative and operating decisions, tight control, control of key values	Peters & Waterman
4.3 Effective financial and other control systems are operated	4.3.1	Timely, not excessive, and relevant management accounting information produced monthly for managing director and board	Cuckney
	4.3.2	Cash forecasts made and liquidity controlled	
	4.3.3	Effective capital budgeting system operated	
	4.3.4	Effective budgetary control operated	
4.4 Sound product market posture	4.4.1	Company is making investments in growing markets in which it has a strong competitive position	
	4.4.2	Company is 'harvesting'[1] businesses (or divesting) where it has weak competitive position and market is not growing	Boston Consulting Group and other portfolio models
	4.4.3	Company is maintaining but not investing in growth, i.e. 'milking'[2] businesses in static markets but where it is competitively strong	

	4.4.4	Company has successfully established with major businesses one of: (a) focused strategy (i.e. concentrating on specific market segments which the company can dominate) (b) differentiated product strategy (c) cost-leadership strategy which protects it from competitive pressures	Porter
	4.4.5	Company has higher bargaining power in its major businesses relative to its suppliers	Porter
	4.4.6	Company has a high bargaining power in its major businesses relative to its customers	Porter
	4.4.7	Company 'sticks to the knitting', i.e. stays close to business it knows	Peters & Waterman
4.5 Good marketing management both home and overseas	4.5.1	Marketing effort focused on high-contribution customers and products and countries	
	4.5.2	Sales force properly motivated and well coordinated	
	4.5.3	Competitive discount structures	
	4.5.4	High margins maintained in markets where company is dominant and demand is price-inelastic	Slatter
	4.5.5	Marketing management conscious of need to monitor market continuously for signals as to: (a) competitive moves (b) new products which could be substitutes (c) changing needs which could provide threats and opportunities (d) technological changes which could create threats or opportunities	After Porter
	4.5.6	Marketing management ensure good delivery time, rapid and effective after-sales services	
	4.5.7	Effective marketing information systems operated	Bramson
4.6 Appropriately high product quality maintained	4.6.1	Top management monitor from time to time deliveries, product quality, and after-sales service, e.g. analysing customer complaints	
	4.6.2	Quality control systems operated	
4.7 Costs controlled tightly	4.7.1	Cost control over raw-material costs, production costs and productivity maintained; top management regularly review cost components; shop floor also consulted	

4.7.2	Marketing and distribution costs for products and customers maintained and efforts made to minimize them		
4.7.3	Controls over pilferage maintained		
4.7.4	Technology regularly reviewed to ensure production costs minimized		
4.7.5	Production engineering, work study, and other approaches to cost reduction regularly used		
4.7.6	Productivity measured and regularly reviewed, with shop floor (N.B. this is especially important when products are mature and non-differentiated)		
4.7.7	Firm makes good use of computers, office automation, O&M, operational research, consultants, management training, NEDO advice, etc.	Bramson	

[1] 'Harvesting' is a term used in portfolio approaches to strategic management by consultants such as BCG to denote extraction of maximum positive cash flows by tight financial control, refusal to invest, and charging as high prices as possible at the expense of future market share. Capital is extracted from the business as it is run down.

[2] By contrast, 'milking' implies more careful maintenance of strong market position and productive capability in mature markets in which the company is strong. Further injection of capital to achieve growth in such markets is resisted, however, and tight financial and other control systems are operated to maximize profits which are mainly reinvested in other, rapidly growing businesses.

C. SECOND-ORDER HYPOTHESES

5 *Relationships between causes of decline and trigger for sharpbending*

Cause of decline	Number of hypothesis	Particularly associated with	Source of hypothesis
5.1 Poor management	5.1.1	Intervention from non-executive directors, banks or institutional investors	
	5.1.2	Change of ownership	
5.2 Inadequate financial control	5.2.1	Intervention from external bodies or non-executive directors	
	5.2.2	Recognition by management of problems and impending collapse	
5.3 High-cost structure 5.4 More intense competition		Not particularly associated with any trigger; could lead to any	
5.5 Acquisitions	5.5.1	Intervention of external bodies or non-executive directors	
	5.5.2	Change of ownership by acquisition	
5.6 Big projects that fail	5.6.1	As 5.5.1	
	5.6.2	As 5.5.2	

5.7	Financial policy that leads to heavy interest payments	5.7.1	As 5.5.1
		5.7.2	As 5.5.2
5.8	Adverse environmental trends		No particular trigger

6 Relationships between causes of decline and causes of sharpbending

Cause of decline	Number of hypothesis	Associated successful response	Source
6.1[3] Adverse changes in total market demand	6.1.1	Diversification by acquisition	Harrigan, Patton, Riggs, Schendel, Slatter
	6.1.2	Divestment from weak areas	
	6.1.3	Harvest	
	6.1.4	New product market focus N.B. Hofer matrix of appropriate responses increase investment to dominate niche of remaining customers in declining market	Boston Consulting Group
		Move from specialized to flexible plant and lease rather than buying assets in declining market	Harrigan
6.2[3] Falling revenue due to more intensive competition: competitive weakness	6.2.1	Strengthen market position by acquisition	Boston Consulting Group, Patton, Riggs, Schendel, Slatter
	6.2.2	Change to new product market (diversification)	Slatter
	6.2.3	Disengage (divest) from product markets in which weak	Slatter
	6.2.4	Differentiate products or focus markets	Porter, Slatter
	6.2.5	Improve marketing	Slatter
	6.2.6	Decentralize and create profit centres to lead to faster response	Grinyer, Slatter
	6.2.7	Improve quality	Slatter
	6.2.8	Where business is mature concentrate on cost reduction and efficiency: advertising and marketing expenses do not pay	Doz, Hambrick, McMillan
	6.2.9	Where market share is low concentrate on narrow product and customer base (niche) and give liberal credit terms	Doz, Hambrick, McMillan
6.3 Lack of marketing effort	6.3.1	Improve marketing	Slatter
6.4 Poor management	6.4.1	New chief executive	Slatter

		6.4.2	New other senior management	Slatter
		6.4.3	Organizational change and decentral-ization	Slatter
6.5	Inadequate financial control	6.5.1	New chief executive	Slatter
		6.5.2	New top financial management	Slatter
		6.5.3	Improved financial control systems	Slatter
		6.5.4	Decentralization	
6.6	High-cost structure	6.6.1	Cost-reduction programmes	Slatter
		6.6.2	Product differentiation of focusing	Porter, Slatter
		6.6.3	Decentralize, reduce size of head office as overhead, and place cost/ profit responsibilities on subsidiary or operating management	Grinyer
		6.6.4	Seek to gain economies of scale or learning	Porter
		6.6.5	Tighten production and stock control	
		6.6.6	Invest in more efficient plant	
6.7	Acquisitions	6.7.1	Asset reduction (divestment)	Slatter
6.8	Big projects that fail	6.8.1	Asset reduction (divestment)	Slatter
6.9	Overgearing	6.9.1	Centralize cash control and tighten capital budgeting	Grinyer
		6.9.2	Decentralize and reduce size of head office	
		6.9.3	Asset reduction (divestment)	Slatter
		6.9.4	Public flotation of subsidiaries	Slatter
		6.9.5	Rights issues and new financial policy	Slatter
			Appropriate strategies relate to trends in market (including demand) and the competitive strengths of company (Harrigan has matrix similar to Hofer)	Harrigan Hofer (see footnote)
			Raw-material suppliers costly or uncertain associated with vertical integration	Patton, Riggs, Schendel

7 *Relationship between trigger for sharpbending and steps taken to achieve it successfully*

Trigger	Number of hypothesis	Steps to sharpbend particularly associated with trigger	Source
7.1 Intervention by external bodies	7.1.1	Change in top management (N.B. 7.3 for consequential changes)	Suggested by Slatter
	7.1.2	Change in non-executive directors	
	7.1.3	Stronger financial control	
	7.1.4	Divestment of assets (and companies)	
	7.1.5	Debt restructuring	

7.2	Change of ownership e.g. by acquisition	7.2.1	Changes in top management	
		7.2.2	Changed and probably stronger financial controls	
		7.2.3	Possibly new product market position	Grinyer and Spender
		7.2.4	Divestment of redundant assets	
		7.2.5	Acquisition (new capital resources available or new owners accustomed to change of product market by this means)	
7.3	Injection of new chief executive	7.3.1	Changes in key executive directors	
		7.3.2	Organizational change (to reinforce his position)	
		7.3.3	New product market position	
7.4	Recognition by management of problems and impending organizational collapse	7.4.1	Stronger financial controls	Grinyer & Spender
		7.4.2	Improved cost control	
		7.4.3	Improved marketing (Tendency to seek to implement existing 'recipe' more effectively)	

D. TIME-LAG BETWEEN STIMULUS AND STEPS

Depends on severity of crisis and causes

Stronger financial control	weeks or months	Eisenburg, Pearson, Slatter

Change in top management	days or weeks	
Change in senior management	weeks to months	
Divestment	1–12 months	
Cost reduction	weeks to few months	Taylor et al.
Product market change	months to years	
Marketing improvement	weeks to months	
Debt-restructuring	weeks to months	

---

[3] *Hofer matrix:*

Relative competitive position	Stage of market evolution				
	Development	Shake out	Growth	Saturation	Decline
Strong	Share-increasing strategies	Segmentation and share-increasing strategies		Market concentration and asset-reduction strategies	
Average					
Weak					
Very weak	Niche marketing or liquidation strategies				

Vignettes of the Individual Companies

Arthur Bell & Sons PLC
Associated Book Publishers PLC
Associated Paper Industries PLC
Collins Publishers PLC
Countryside Properties PLC
Dawson International PLC
Don and Low PLC
Ellis & Goldstein Holdings PLC
Ferranti PLC
Fisons PLC
Glaxo Holdings PLC
Low & Bonar PLC

Macallan-Glenlivet PLC
McCarthy and Stone PLC
Pringle of Scotland Ltd
Rotaflex PLC
Sidlaw Group PLC
Sirdar PLC
TI Group PLC
UDI Group Ltd
Ward White Group PLC
Whatman Reeve Angel PLC
John Wood Group PLC

(Three sharpbenders wished to remain anonymous and are not included in this list. They are labelled A, B and C in the text.)

ARTHUR BELL & SONS PLC

This group is based in Perth, Scotland and its principal activities are the distilling, blending, bottling and selling of Scotch whisky, the manufacture and sale of glass containers, road haulage and transport, and hotel management. All comments made about the company refer to the period up to its takeover by Guinness PLC in August 1985. In 1984, there were nine subsidiary companies and the group owned five distilleries (Dufftown-Glenlivet, Blair Atholl, Inchgower, Pittyvaich-Glenlivet and Bladnoch). Statistical data relating to the company are shown in table B.1. In 1984, the turnover of £256.7m was dominated by distilling, etc. (84 per cent), with glass (10 per cent), transport (1 per cent), hotels (2 per cent). Geographically, 82 per cent of turnover is accounted for by the UK and European markets, with Africa, Asia and Australasia (14 per cent) and the Americas (4 per cent).

179

Table B.1 *Statistical data for Arthur Bell & Sons PLC (£m)*

	1974	1975	1976	1977[1]	1978	1979	1980	1981	1982	1983	1984
Total turnover (a)	60.3	81.7	117.0	43.7	152.7	201.8	202.8	233.8	245.6	246.7	256.7
Exports (b)	6.7	7.4	9.7	5.9	14.7	18.4	23.0	27.2	32.7	37.7	41.3
Profit before tax (c)	3.1	4.1	7.5	3.8	13.6	16.8	16.8	20.0	27.6	31.4	35.1
Total capital employed (d)		33.3	39.5		61.1	72.8	85.6	123.1	142.2	158.4	204.7
(c)/(d) (%)		12.3	19.0		22.3	23.1	19.6	16.2	19.4	19.8	17.1
Average no. of employees	538	1784	1789	1839	1886	1932	1965	1841	1763	1729	1989

[1] Previous year ends at 31 December 1977: figure for six months to 30 June; all subsequent year ends are 30 June.

I History of the firm

The post-war history of the group before its takeover by Guinness PLC can be divided into three phases:

(a) *Pre-1965* Up to 1965 the company was a typical, relatively small, sound, private company. It was reluctant to invest, had a very small share of the home market (which was dominated by Distillers Co.) and lacked a national reputation.

(b) *1965–83* From 1965 to 1983, the company expanded dramatically in the whisky business. It gained a dominant home market for the Bell's brand and has sustained it to the present date. In the 1970s its export sales also showed impressive growth. The company diversified vertically, acquiring Canning Town Glass Ltd to secure supplies of bottles and the Towmaster Transport Co. Ltd to meet the transport needs of the group. These account for 80–90 per cent of Towmaster's business.

(c) *1983–5* By 1983, despite continuous building projects, Bell's was still cash-rich. This was due to its highly profitable growth and also its tendency not to invest in the latest bottling technology. Consequently, it sought expansion and, by February 1984, acquired two businesses. First, Wellington Importers, with a healthy wine-importing business, was acquired in the US to provide a means of gaining licences for selling Bell's whisky in the US with the intention of gaining a more significant share of this large market. (Their own experience with distributors had been unfavourable; Bell's had captured only about 1 per cent of the American whisky market by 1983.) Second, Bell's bought the Gleneagles Group, with hotels in Perthshire, Edinburgh and London, and so diversified into a largely unrelated business.

The sharpbend may be perceived to have occurred around 1965 and to have been long-sustained. Moreover, Bell's continued to grow in the 1980s when the rest of the industry was suffering declining sales.

II Causes of the relative decline

Arthur Bell had existed throughout the 1950s with no constructed organization and with inefficient production methods. Introduced into the firm's Leith warehouse in 1956 to pursue a time-and-motion exercise, Raymond Miquel persevered over the next decade to rectify many of the traditional practices within the group and bring it up to date. In 1962, he joined the board, and by 1968, he was appointed Managing Director. On the death of W. G. Farquharson in 1982, Miquel also became Chairman of the group.

The 'relative decline' of Bell's in the 1960s was not a serious one. They could have survived as a small, traditional supplier within the industry. Their 'sharpbend' was a performance bend.

III Triggers for sharpbending

The appointment of Mr Raymond Miquel as Managing Director in 1968.

IV   Actions taken to promote sharpbending

(a) *Management style*   Raymond Miquel's hard-driving, opportunity-seeking style clearly shook up an old-fashioned board and changed the marketing and production approaches fundamentally during the second half of the 1960s.

(b) *Aggressive marketing strategy*   Inspired by Miquel, Bell's embarked on an innovative, aggressive marketing strategy in the mid-1960s in the home market:

1   promoting the product with licensees and the consuming public rather than continuing to press the major brewers to distribute Bell's through their houses; the licensees then ordered Bell's from other sources and forced the brewers to distribute it;
2   promoting via sports sponsorships and heavy advertising as well as by salesmen's visits;
3   building goodwill with the licensees by supporting holiday houses for their retired members, their charities, and organizing outings and social evenings within which Bell's was promoted. Competitors have followed most of these innovations but Bell's sought to keep ahead of the game and placed a heavy emphasis on promotion.

(c) *Investment*   Miquel pressed for a new bottling plant and new whisky storage facilities. The East Mains and the Dunfermline plants were built. At the time of building they were technologically advanced and cost-efficient, enabling a heavy reduction in labour costs to be achieved.

(d) *Financial control*   In 1964, Miquel also introduced management accounting and capital budgeting systems. Bell's were one of the first Scotch whisky firms to introduce a computerized accounting system for whisky stocks.

V   Continuing characteristics of sharpbending

(a) *Management–worker relations*   Labour turnover is relatively low at Bell's. Over the years a variety of schemes has been introduced to improve working conditions and productivity, e.g. free transport, pension, sickness insurance schemes and, since 1980, a share bonus scheme. Wages are comparable to the sector average but incentive schemes ensure that higher incomes are actually earned. There is full provision for the communication of information about the company to the workforce. It is clear that the workforce are motivated by the level of application of management (see below).

(b) *Organizational structure*   A key control innovation was introduced by Miquel for export sales in the mid-1970s and for home sales in 1980. Sales management was co-ordinated by head-office coordinators made responsible to an administrative rather than a sales director. Directors occupied the top floor of the head office. Others went there only by invitation. The idea was to divorce directors from the day-to-day operations and force subordinates to take decisions for themselves. Control was via an extensive system of reports and minutes of meetings, which then led to directors focusing on missed opportunities or problems, and discussing these in meetings with the full 'team' of overseas 'divisional directors', i.e. area representatives, or home regional sales managers. The seven-weekly sales meetings were dominated by Miquel who pointed out mistakes, lost opportunities, or poor performance to his sales-team members. He regarded this as a sharing of experience and 'training', believing it engendered 'team spirit' and strongly motivated individuals to perform better. Outsiders may view this threat to poor performers as potentially demotivating. However, the personal ingredients, involving Miquel's personality, made it effective. Subordinate managers paid tribute to Miquel's impressive memory and his ability to go quickly to the weak points of a situation. How far the system could operate effectively without Miquel is open to debate.

(c) *Managerial effort*   This organizational and control system placed enormous burdens on senior management. Miquel claimed to read all salesmen's reports and all mail going out of head office. The higher the management position the greater the amount of time expected to be spent in the company. Directors tend to work twelve-hour days for at least five days a week. There is a heavy emphasis on fitness of staff, however, and good provision for physical exercise. When we interviewed him, Miquel still ran and played squash at fifty-three years of age and claimed never to be ill. There is virtually no whisky, or other, drinking in the offices (except for visitors) and none of those interviewed smoked.

(d) *Charismatic leadership*   The highly personal control system described above, depended for its success on the charismatic leadership of Miquel. His physical fitness coupled with a period as Managing Director spanning twenty years gave him a 'halo' within the firm. This enabled him to build up a team of dedicated senior managers and directors who were loyal to him.

(e) *Nature of the business*   The nature of the distribution, marketing and technology problems is essentially simple. The main business (whisky) remains relatively small, with sixty head-office employees, eight overseas and eight UK 'divisional directors'. In 1984, there were only 626 employees in the whole of the whisky division (868 for glass and 1989 for the group total) accounting for 84 per cent of turnover and over 90 per cent of operating profits. This simplicity and smallness made it easier to control the business in a highly personalized way.

(f) *Public flotations*   In 1971, the interest of the Trust which held most of the shares became heavily diluted when 2.5 million ordinary shares were offered for sale. A further one million were placed on the market in 1975 to raise money to purchase Canning Town Glass Ltd. This widening of the shareholder base, besides providing funds for investment, led to further pressure for growth and profitability as management recognized the greater scrutiny to which it was subjected.

(g) *Pressures of increasing liquidity*   The group became increasingly liquid in the early 1980s. With this amount of liquidity (stocks and cash in 1983 were twice the level of fixed assets), Bell's was probably aware of its exposure to takeover. Indeed in September 1982 rumours were reported in the press that Bass was preparing a takeover bid for Bell's which must have drawn this danger strongly to the attention of Miquel and his board. Miquel also recognized that the high rate of growth could not be maintained in whisky alone given general trends in the market.

Hence the high liquidity provided both the means and spur for diversification. This took two forms. Following a review of acquisition possibilities in manufacturing it was decided that high returns could be generated more readily in services.

First, Miquel sought acquisition of two importers in the US to allow penetration of the market there to rise from an insignificant 1 per cent towards 7 per cent (the target given). The idea was to acquire both an existing, profitable business and also a licence to allow more effective distribution of Bell's whisky.

Second, in January 1984 Bell's made a bid for Gleneagles Hotels Ltd, and after a protracted struggle succeeded in acquiring it in February 1984. A substantial investment was required by the hotel division. For a brief period Bell's tried to manage the hotel by imposing its own brand of management control on the new, and different, businesses. There were clearly problems in the early days but these were quickly surpassed by events involving Guinness PLC.

(h) *Continued inward investment*   In April 1984, Bell's completed a £5.5m investment at Canning Town Glass, bringing their investment in the company since it was acquired in 1975 to £26m. The 1984 tranche was to fund the first recuperative furnace in the UK glass-container industry.

V   Conclusion

The sharpbend at Arthur Bell had much to do with Raymond Miquel. The whole sustained recovery revolved around his personality – built on energy, flair and physical fitness. In this sense, it can be argued that the lessons at Arthur Bell may not be generally repeatable in the wider UK industrial environment. But within the analysis, there are individual adaptable prescriptions.

ASSOCIATED BOOK PUBLISHERS PLC

The principal activities of the company and its subsidiary companies are publishing and bookselling. Books are published on general, children's, education, legal, scientific and technological subjects; periodicals are published on educational, legal and scientific subjects. The group's turnover in 1986 was £85m broken down as follows:

£49m in the UK;
£4m in the USA;
£15m in Australia/New Zealand; and
£17m in Canada.

Profit before tax was £8.3m and there were 1200 employees, of whom 550 were in the UK.

I Causes of the relative decline (experienced up to 1980 – the date of the sharpbend)

In common with the rest of the market, the company suffered a severe downturn in trade in the early 1970s. It struggled through the rampant inflation of the following years but in the later 1970s the company began to experience difficulties in certain of its main activities including trade publications. This was due to the following factors.

(a) *Overtrading* Both in (i) paperbacks in (ii) the US.

(b) *Underinvestment* During the crisis in the early 1970s, the company dramatically decreased its capital expenditure programmes. The development period of such investments in Associated Book Publishers' major activities can be as long as seven years. Hence, by the late 1970s, the company was suffering from the consequences of previous, and perhaps short-sighted, decisions.

(c) *Lack of commercial focus* Traditionally the company did not focus primarily on commercial objectives. The joys of book publishing, a love of literature, pride in high level of service to professional communities, and intellectual stimulus, appear to have given them rather greater satisfaction than the sheer pursuit of profit. The depth of recession in the late 1970s confronted them with the harsh reality of the commercial requirements of business. There had been 'twenty-five years agonizing over trying to make other areas pay'. They were 'not managing the basic flow of money in the business'.

(d) *High inflation* When coupled with publishers' long lead times, high inflation played havoc with cash flows.

(e) *Demographic trends* Associated Book Publishers' heavy reliance on the educational sector – from schools through to universities – exposes the company to changes in the birth rate. The ending of 'baby booms' in the late 1950s and early 1960s, although the booms had been smaller than those in the US, Japan and Western Europe, had a dramatic impact on the whole educational sector for a generation or more. This was compounded by cuts in funding by government throughout the education sector.

II Triggers for sharpbending

The deteriorating financial position was starkly revealed in the cash-flow figures. Major educational institutes and booksellers sharply reduced their orders, throwing the company into an adverse cash position. Turnover remained high but profits deteriorated. The sharpbend that followed was on profits rather than turnover.

III Actions taken to promote sharpbending

(a) *Rationalization* One hundred employees were trimmed from the payroll – across all levels of the business.

(b) *Commercial consciousness* The company attempted a 'big push' forward in commercial awareness. Their people were instructed to place the commercial realities of each assignment at the forefront of their thinking. This emphasis on profit was reinforced later by the introduction of a *share incentive scheme*. An ancillary aim of the scheme was to help support the morale and loyalty of employees whose dedication had always been to the literature. In the words of the Managing Director, Mr M. Turner: 'Once you start changing things in a company the good people don't like the personal upsets, the human upsets, and tend to leave.'

(c) *Decentralization of decision-making* This was introduced as far down the chain as the warehouses and distribution outlets.

(d) *Control* Action was quickly taken to straighten out the previously 'lax and cosy' purchasing policies – particularly with respect to their printers. Further control action was exerted on the cash-flow stream by adopting a marked change of stance regarding creditors and debtors.

In the short-term, we were fairly bloody both to debtors and creditors and that caused quite a lot of pain – a difficult thing to force through for about nine to twelve months because it had not been our style. We were very prompt payers, we were renowned for promptness. Many of our suppliers had relied on our cheques coming through dead on time. (M. Turner)

IV Continuing characteristics of sharpbending

(a) *Corporate planning* In 1980 plans were introduced on a one-, three- and five-year basis. The Managing Director begins by writing out a scenario incorporating the company's objectives for the next five years. The subsidiaries then prepare one- and three-year plans within this overall corporate strategy. A similar system was attempted after the fracas in the early 1970s but was extinguished by rampant inflation that destroyed the creditability of the predictions. By 1980/1, however, the top management team were committed to sustaining the rolling formal plans. Interestingly, these plans are not imposed upon subsidiaries, they tend to be based on an agreement between head-office management and the management of subsidiaries as to what is possible at each strategic business unit. This avoids publishing houses ruining themselves by forcing through unrealistically high return on capital figures.

(b) *Legal cases – databank* The company had recently utilized the advantage of developments in information technology to establish a large databank on statute law. As a legal publisher, this was seen as an exciting marketing, as well as cost-effective, programme.

(c) *Supply-side marketing* The company is actively involved in the UK Book Marketing Council, consisting of printers and publishers who exchange information on marketing problems and generate timely solutions.

(d) *Commitment to people* The company is committed to protecting their 'stars', as they view their authors, and insist that their key people, those who select topics and manage authors, look after them in a very personal manner.

V Conclusion

The sharpbend of Associated Book Publishers in 1980 is a simple, yet valuable, story. They had overtraded in paperbacks and in the US market, they had failed to monitor underlying demographic trends and had run the business with insufficient regard for commercial objectives. It is a tribute to the management that the quick actions taken – of rationalization and tighter control – enabled the company to mount its own rescue without the involvement of external agencies or the necessity to go beyond the borrowing limits. The corporate strategy that the company has embraced, by monitoring and developing markets and paying due concern to its people, should help it sustain the recovery for some years.

ASSOCIATED PAPER INDUSTRIES PLC

This diversified group has its origins in a merger between Edward Collins and Son, a paper mill in Glasgow, and Henry and Leigh Slater, an off-machine paper-coating business at Bollington in Cheshire. For the next fifty years it was involved in papermaking before diversification into aluminium-foil-lined board in 1960. The diversification programme continued throughout the 1960s and 1970s with the company entering the coating business by acquisitions. This group became Associated Paper Industries (from Associated Paper Mills) in 1985 and moved its headquarters to Macclesfield (Cheshire) in 1979. It has recently diversified into purification, air-conditioning and filtration.

The sharpbend Associated Paper Industries dipped to a loss in 1975/6, pulled back sharply to a profit in 1976/7, and suffered a further fall in profits and share price in 1979/80 when its price touched 23p. By 1985 its price was in the region of 200p in reflection of a remarkable recovery. Although over 20 per cent in 1983 the rate of return on capital employed had still, however, to reach the 30 per cent level attained in 1974.

I   History of the firm

Recent history Associated Paper Industries changed its nature fundamentally during the 1960s and 1970s from being an operator of seven paper mills to one. During this period it moved strongly into the coating and laminating business, entered aluminium-lined board at Henry and Leigh Slater in 1960, and diversified into the stamping-foil business. From 1982 to 1983, it diversified into purification, air-conditioning and filtration, by internal development and acquisition. The latter diversification has close connections with the group's existing activities that may not appear obvious. Purification Products was established as a separate subsidiary company in 1982. It combines the existing papermaking technology with the well-known properties of silica gel to produce, in sheet form, odour- and moisture-absorbing materials. This opens up a host of new markets for shoe insoles, fridge fresheners, etc. There is little indigenous competition and a strong export market.

II Causes of the decline(s) between 1975 and 1980

The underlying causes of the decline in 1976 and 1980 were largely the same, although they were worse in 1980. There was a sustained drop in demand for paper products in the 1970s and a parallel increase in competition. The drop occurred because of the development of plastic-packaging substitutes for paper bags and corrugated paper. At the same time plastic laminated boards reduced the demand for lined, laminated boards. At the very time that technological change decreased market demand, entry to EFTA and subsequently the EEC removed protective barriers, leading to more intense competition from imports. In particular, the competition from vertically integrated mills, whose costs are much lower than the unintegrated operations which Associated Paper Industries operated, eroded price margins of virtually all non-specialist papers, i.e. those with long runs.

The response of the group in the 1970s was to expand its more protected market areas (specialist papers and paper-coating) and to diversify into stamping foils. The group continued its papermaking operations however, and loss of profitability of these pulled it down in the mid-1970s.

Response to the 1976 crisis was to reinforce the change of emphasis on the one hand and to tighten production efficiency on the other. Consultants were called into the Garnett Mill and 'transformed its organizational structure [of production] and, without loss of capacity, reduced manning by a third'. Similar cost-cutting exercises, though less extensive, seem to have been undertaken elsewhere, too. Some paper mills were closed. Although Associated Paper Industries recovered dramatically, and acquired George Whiley in 1978 to expand its presence in the stamping-foil business considerably, underlying weaknesses in management remained. Moreover, its remaining paper mills were still its Achilles heel.

In 1979 the company found itself once again in major difficulties which resulted in a collapse of profits in the year to October 1980. First, the poor performance of its remaining general paper mill continued, losses mounting to £½m. Second, a major investment decision made in 1978–9 proved to be disastrous. Vale Board Mills in Lothian produced white lined chipboard for packaging. This business had faced increasingly severe competition and the company was forced to consider the alternatives of closure or major investment to improve the one large machine. A grant was obtained and favourable loan terms obtained from the Scottish Development Agency. On this basis, £1.3m was invested in updating the mill. In the event, this proved to be ill-fated, as technical problems led to the repeated shutdown of the mill and the losses at the mill mounted from £193,000 in 1978/9 to £713,000 in 1979/80. In retrospect, the Managing Director, John Graham, believes that even without these difficulties the decision to invest in a strategically weak business would have been wrong.

Third, George Whiley (acquired in 1978) continued to make losses despite its strong market position. Whiley had run into severe problems before its acquisition when it moved from three separate locations in southern England to a greenfield site in Scotland. Technical expertise was lost because skilled personnel were reluctant to move to Scotland. Levels of skill and productivity of some of the new workforce were wanting. Financial losses continued after the acquisition by Associated Paper Industries in 1978 and seemed to group management to be increasingly beyond the ability of the Managing Director (who transferred to Associated Paper Industries with the firm) to resolve. The problems at Whiley were no doubt exacerbated by the onset of the recession in 1980. The coincidence of these three problems led to heavy negative cash flows for the group: bank loans and overdrafts rose to £1.2m in 1979 and then £2.6m in 1980 at a time of high interest charges.

These problems may well have been resolved earlier, and the 1979/80 crisis avoided, had management been stronger in Associated Paper Industries as a group. However, until 1979 the group had a peculiarly weak structure. The central organization in 1970 amounted to a secretary sitting in a room in the offices of the Chairman in the City. Financial information was weak and controls virtually non-existent. In 1972 Quentin Mackenzie, now Finance Director, joined this central office and started to introduce financial controls. No head office existed, however, until the present small head office with a total of fifteen staff was set up in 1979 at the insistence of the present Managing Director, John Graham.

The lack of central direction was worsened because of the structure of executive management. There were two co-equal Managing Directors. One was responsible for the paper mills. The other, John Graham, was Managing Director of the coating subsidiary and had general responsibility for the non-paper-mill business. Relationships between the two seem to have been amicable, but each represented a collection of vested interests, and implicit bargains seem to have been struck between them with respect to items such as capital investment. With no central, overall, executive direction there was not the necessary means for pressing for disengagement from the increasingly unprofitable general paper business. This weakness was removed when, on the death of his fellow Managing Director in 1977, John Graham was appointed sole Managing Director. Not until 1979, however, was he able to persuade the then Chairman, Pat Young, to open up a small head office in Macclesfield in which the Secretary and Finance Director, with a small staff of accountants, came together in one team with the Managing Director.

III Triggers for sharpbending

The trigger for change can be seen to be the conjunction of:

1   a new Chairman. On the untimely death of Pat Young in 1979, Charles Rawlinson, then a non-executive director, was persuaded by the Managing Director to become Chairman. He, together with the team at Macclesfield, were to be the driving forces in transforming the company. They now had a Chairman who forced participative discussion of issues and insisted on action being taken; and
2   the profit crisis of 1979/80 which made urgent action necessary and provided a justification for closures.

IV Actions taken to promote sharpbending

(a) *Closures*   The necessary remedial actions were taken simultaneously. Immediate action was taken to close loss-making subsidiaries for which a secure future was not seen. Thus Vale Board Mills was closed early in 1980, and Cooke and Nuttall later in the same financial year. This left only one of the nine paper mills with which Associated Paper Industries had entered the 1970s. This was P. Garnett and Son Ltd, which specializes in poster paper and manila, in which it has a fairly high market share in the UK (over 20 per cent). Integrated mills have no advantage over it, because these products need small runs of largely flat, cut paper rather than rolls.

At the same time, having transferred its coating business to Slater and laminating business to Garnett, Associated Paper Industries sold the corrugated-paper business of Mallandain to Jefferson Smurfit in June 1980 for £1.3m. It saw no long-term future for corrugated paper without major investment in expansion and recognized the increasing substitution of plastic material for this paper packaging. Corrugated packaging moreover was an undifferentiated, low-value-added business. Also, because it had only one plant, rather than a wider network which could serve big, geographically widely spread companies, Associated Paper Industries thought that Mallandain would be better in a bigger group. The sale was in the 'nick of time' because profits slumped shortly afterwards as the demand for corrugated paper plummeted in 1981. The £1.3m raised by the sale of Mallandain reduced the net cost of sales and closures to £3.9m, a sum inflated by the need to repay grants and loans received for the earlier capital investment at the Vale Board Mill.

As a result of these actions net capital employed fell from £15.9m in 1980 to £13m in 1981 and turnover from £44.6m to £33.8m. Bank loans and overdrafts had risen from £0.8m in 1978 to £1.2m in 1979 and a peak of £2.6m in 1980, but fell back to £1.7m in 1981 and have since continued to fall. These high debts, at a time of high interest rates, meant a continuing drain on operating profits.

(b) *Rationalization of existing securities* These measures were accompanied by moves within the core business which were to remain in the group. This, as Rawlinson said in his interim statement in February 1980, was 'mainly engaged in *conversion* of paper, film, and aluminium foil into specialized products for a variety of industries and . . . the stamping-foil business in which API is now one of the leaders in the market'. Controls on cash were tightened. Capital investment virtually ceased. Consultants were employed to cut waste and increase productivity in a number of the subsidiaries, and redundancies followed. Much of what the consultants did was 'simply head-count stuff but difficult for the normal management team to do' (Graham); for example, they proposed closure of decorating and other services and buying them in. At Henry and Leigh Slater, John Graham had relinquished the role of Managing Director in 1979, and his successor, the previous Production Director, steered through these economies with determination. Discussions with the Convenor of Shop Stewards there, Mr McKernan, clearly indicated a high level of respect for him (based on long experience of his activities as Production Director), which remained despite the harsh actions he had to take. Industrial relations remained good. The one stoppage was of one hour's duration and over another issue, despite the strains that changed work practices and redundancy must have caused.

At George Whiley, as well as tightening the efficiency of production, the problem was perceived by Associated Paper Industries as top management. As action was needed urgently a main board director, Bernard Hall, was appointed Managing Director as a temporary measure. Major redundancies were declared and steps taken to build up the technical expertise lost in the 1976 move. Overseas subsidiaries of Whiley were sold or closed in many countries. This was associated with a move to selling via agents in all overseas territories except France where it was felt that the selling subsidiary was close enough geographically to allow tight control.

V   Continuing characteristics of sharpbending

These characteristics fall into three categories:

(a) *Corporate management*   This seems to be marked by:

1   a good team spirit;
2   a stress on oral communication with subordinate management;
3   a willingness to follow the action-orientation of the Chairman;
4   a stress on the importance of thinking about the strategic issues and leaving operational decisions to the subsidiary chief executives 'who can do something about them';
5   an awareness of the importance of subsidiary chief executives to the health of their operating companies and so to the group; and
6   an encouragement to travel in search of ideas and opportunities.

(b) *Organizational structure*   Head Office is kept small (fourteen to fifteen staff) with the Managing Director, Finance Director and Secretary as the senior staff, but with supporting accountants and secretaries. To keep the head office small, fairly heavy use is made of consultants, both to increase productivity or effectiveness in the subsidiary, operating companies and also to search for new diversification opportunities. Graham believes that, quite apart from keeping overheads down by avoiding the need for more central staff, consultants usually bring fresher, better-motivated, and more expert minds to bear on problems just when they are needed.

(c) *Strategic moves*   As Associated Paper Industries returned strongly to profitability it proceeded to, first, strengthen its position in the business areas in which it saw itself as having strength and a good potential growth. In stamping foils over 1983–4 it invested more than £1m, and relocated and expanded Peerless Foils in 1986. At Garnett the paper machines were computerized and new coal-fired boilers and a wastepaper-preparation plant installed. Computer controls on quality, to reduce waste as well as to improve the product, have been introduced at Henry and Leigh Slater.

Associated Paper Industries also diversified further. Garnett had expanded into charcoal and silica-gel-based paper products, such as odour-'eating' material for shoe insoles and fridge fresheners. In 1982 this activity was spun-off as Purification Products. This company has no UK rivals and has growing exports. In 1983, Diffusion, which makes 'warm air curtains' and air-conditioning equipment for offices and public buildings, was acquired. Then later in the same year Airpel was acquired for its comprehensive range of liquid filters, used in water treatment, petrochemicals, offshore oil, process plant and other industries. Associated Paper acquired with Airpel a strong product range, a good export business, and related manufacturing plant as well as a distributor of hydraulic valves, Airpel Hydraulic. Since 1983 the productive capacity of both Diffusion and Airpel has been upgraded and expanded. Both Airpel and Diffusion were selected for acquisition after a search by consultants (Research Associates) who were also involved in a brainstorming exercise to indicate the general direction in which Associated Paper Industries might develop. They also decided that 'we are good at managing small- to medium-sized manufacturing companies' and excluded 'services' from their search. Consultants were also used to study prospective acquisitions in detail.

Table B.2 *Statistical data for Associated Paper Industries*

	Paper making and converting	*Stamping foils*	*Air-conditioning, filtration and purification*
Turnover (£m)	34.6	3.0	4.0
Trading profits (£m)	3.0	1.3	0.4
No. of employees (without Airpel)	653	223	51

These diversifications should not be allowed to disguise the continuing dependence of Associated Paper Industries on specialist paper production and special coatings, where Slater has become increasingly dependent on aluminium-foil-lined board for profits as competitive pressure has mounted in the more general special-coating business, in which it has increasingly focused on smaller or very special orders with higher value added. The number of employees in 1983, and turnover and profits in 1984 within the division as shown in table B.2.

These figures illustrate vividly the continued importance of papermaking and converting; the greater profitability of the growing stamping-foil business, and the fact that the purification division is no more profitable as a percentage of sales than special paper and converting.

VI Conclusion

Associated Paper Industries have overcome what were potentially severe problems by introducing a change agent (Rawlinson) and moving away from their mature, competitive businesses to businesses where they have differentiated products, with either a high market share or a special niche; some of these are exhibiting a distinct growth. Moreover, in some, such as Whiley and Purification Products, the technical expertise required makes the entry of new rivals difficult and permits a good return on the skills employed by the company. In the year to September 1986 their sales had risen to £71m, profits to £7.5m with a return on shareholders' equity of 14.8 per cent.

WILLIAM COLLINS PLC

I History of the firm

In 1970, the printing and binding activities of Collins were located in old premises in Cathedral Street, Glasgow. Machines were somewhat antiquated. The building was multi-storey, different levels being called 'flats', and hence physical movement of work between stages of production was relatively expensive. However, morale was high, despite the fact that the large female labour force was paid low wages. The 'flats'

Table B.3   *William Collins PLC: UK financial data 1978–1982 (year end December)*

(£m)	1978		1979		1980		1981		1982	
Sales	60.6		65.1		63.7		73.1		79.7	
Trading profit	5.6	(9.3)	2.9	(4.4)	4.8	(7.6)	9.7	(13.2)	10.2	(12.8)
Post-tax profit	0.7	(5.0)	0.07	(−1.1)	0.4	(3.3)	1.5	(6.4)	1.1	(6.6)
Return on capital employed (%)	11.5		5.0		11.0		16.4		16.5	

Figures in brackets indicate per cent of sales.

created confined working environments within which social and group relationships developed strongly; indeed these groups kept largely to themselves. The workforce was drawn from the area immediately around Cathedral Street which meant little travelling time. Because of the location of the works, women workers could shop at lunchtime.

The company's move to a greenfield site in Westerhill (about four miles from the city centre on the western outskirts) in the early 1970s disrupted this world, created pressures and tensions among the workforce and revealed fundamental weaknesses in top and middle management. Table B.3 contains summary financial-performance data for the period 1978–82, demonstrating the sharpbend from 1979.

II   Causes of the relative decline to 1979

(a) *Morale*   After the move to Westerhill, the morale of the workers slumped. Older workers did not like the hygienic, open factory in its greenfield site. The old intimacy and security of the 'flats' was broken. Women found no shops from which they could buy provisions at lunchtime. Men could not get their hair cut during the lunch break or after work. Although buses were provided from the city centre, travel was longer and less convenient.

To be fair to the workers, at a time at which work was disrupted, average earnings were paid and the old piecework system abandoned. Productivity fell sharply and even after the introduction of consultants and a subsequent bonus scheme, productivity still remained uncompetitively low.

(b) *Wage costs*   At this time equal-pay legislation was beginning to take effect and the pay of the female labour in the bindery and elsewhere was rising. As the proportion of female labour in the total workforce at Collins was high, this had an adverse impact on total labour costs. In addition, within the new office buildings there was an uncontrolled expansion of clerical employees which inflated overheads still further.

(c) *Technology*   The opportunity to re-equip the factory, on moving premises, was lost. Instead, all the old, often antiquated, plant was moved from the old premises in Cathedral Street. Despite suggestions, indeed pressure, from the Fathers of the Chapel to obtain the new technology that was spreading fast in the 1970s the company failed to invest in new equipment. This further increased the trend towards loss of competitiveness.

(d) *Control*   The move to new premises, average pay, and loose bonuses all seemed to combine to undermine the authority of the foreman. Production and stock-control methods were weak which meant delivery delays and higher work in progress.

(e) *Interest costs*   The company was burdened by high interest costs, the result of the way in which the new factory had been financed by loans rather than a rights issue. This was worsened by the practice of running big editions, to get economies of long runs, which did not always sell, leaving large sums of working capital tied up in (sometimes obsolete) stock.

(f) *Weak top and middle management*   It is probable that all the above problems stem from a fundamental weakness of top and middle management. The issues of succession and conservatism applied to Collins. Production expertise had been lost in 1969 when the previous strong leader, Hope Collins, died. His successor, Jan Collins, did not run the works in the centrally focused way that he had inherited and so failed to get the commitment of the workforce.

Promotions within the Collins hierarchies was largely on the grounds of loyalty and length of service. A proven formula in many traditional family firms with a conservative management style where chiefs were not normally questioned and instructions were obeyed immediately. This rendered middle management ineffective.

III   Triggers for sharpbending

Perceptions of the causes of the sharpbend differ between management and workforce. The workforce witnessed only the dramatic events. In 1979, the Fathers and Mother of the Chapels were summoned to a meeting, the seriousness of the financial situation was exposed to them, and Jan Collins stepped down and Ian Chapman took his place as Chief Executive. Hence they see the sharpbend as imposed by financial exigencies alone. Management, too, recognized the increasing difficulty of the financial situation as the driving force behind the management changes of 1979. But pressure to obtain such a change had been mounting from May 1978, when the executive directors got together and decided that fundamental changes were necessary. George Craig (Managing Director) is seen by Clarke Paton (Group Manufacturing Managing Director) to be the main protagonist of change. Thus by 1979, when the financial results signalled the need for urgent steps, there was already a strong movement for both a change in the top management and for strong actions.

IV   Actions taken to promote sharpbending

(a) *Change in top management*   (See III above).

(b) *Rationalization*   A heavy reduction in the workforce (from 1750 in 1979 to 836 in 1985) was engineered whilst output continued to climb. Productivity more than doubled. This reduction was achieved entirely by voluntary redundancy. In 1979, the redundancies were facilitated because many members of the workforce thought the company would not survive. This programme was extended to incorporate the ineffective middle management and the burgeoning clerical staff.

Union representatives and management were united in 'the lifeboat' from 1979 to 1982. They worked on redundancies together. The Federated Chapels agreed to, and carried their members with respect to, the very unpopular measures. This relationship was a major factor in facilitating the drastic improvement.

(c) *Control* Production control was tightened up, reducing wastage and improving quality. Inventories of finished goods were placed on a computer-controlled system.

(d) *Overhead trimming* Part of the office block was 'bricked off' to lower the rates payable. This action in itself provided a significant, in-house reminder to the remaining managers to watch costs.

V Continuing characteristics of sharpbending

(a) *Technology* There has been a movement since 1983 to invest more heavily in the latest technology. Clarke Paton and his Engineering Director travel widely internationally looking at new technology which must then be justified on economic grounds. Even in 1979, when announcing redundancies, an announcement of £1.4m investment was made. The Scottish Office subsidized an investment of £10.5m between 1984 and 1985 to the tune of £1.5m above the regional grants.

(b) *Shorter economic runs* There has been a movement to a pattern of shorter runs on each edition, made more economic by newer technology, to cut working capital in stocks.

(c) *Product market changes*

1 Take-off in 1983 of the contracting service (i.e. printing for other publishers) introduced in 1979 by George Craig. This now represents one-third of turnover. The group has to bid against outsiders for work on Collins publications.
2 The major inflow of paperback printing and distribution work with the acquisition of Granada by Collins in 1983.

(d) *Managerial style* The major changes in style relate to openness of communication and accessibility. George Craig fosters an open relationship with the union officers which he began in 1979. There is now considerable trust on each side that what is said is meant and is honestly stated.

Top management also stress visibility and accessibility. Clarke Paton, for instance, has his office in the works rather than in the plush office block. He makes a point of walking around the works regularly. He, George Craig and Ian Chapman are all known by the Fathers and Mother of the Chapel by Christian name. They aim to foster a team spirit claiming that 'the ball is at *our* feet'.

(e) *Workforce involvement*

1 Union representatives, perhaps in the light of their experiences of the 1970s, seem to welcome the introduction of new technology. Clarke Paton has taken local, including Fathers of the Chapel, and regional officers to view new technology operating overseas before its purchase. The Mother of the Chapel is also involved, with some of her operatives, in decisions on new technology at an earlier stage so that the operatives could point out some of the difficulties that might occur on its introduction.

2 Responsibility has been given to line managers, supervisors, and through them the workforce, for helping to set production and quality targets and achieving them. Each level is then held accountable.

VI Conclusion

Collins is an instructive example of what management and unions can achieve in committed cooperation. The failure to grasp potential problems during their move, the weakness of top and middle management, the weak control and old technology had all contributed to the poor performance of the company.

Cooperation, harmonization, trust, openness and honesty were the key to recovery. Important product market, managerial and technological changes were achieved and suitable controls inaugurated.

Tensions still exist on some issues, such as pay, and one at least of the Fathers of the Chapel is uneasy about the substitution of capital for skilled labour. Yet there is a united realization that Collins has to be highly productive to ensure secure employment.

COUNTRYSIDE PROPERTIES PLC

The company is engaged in commercial, industrial and residential property developments in the UK, primarily within commuting distance of London.

I History of the firm

This is usefully seen in three stages:

(a) *1958–71* The firm was incorporated in 1958 and, as a privately owned company, it undertook a modest amount of development using mostly the services of outside professional firms and contractors to design, manage, build and sell its housing schemes. The firm was run largely on a part-time basis by Bob Bobroff, the founder.

In 1967, Bobroff met Alan Cherry who was then a director of Bairstow-Eves – the estate agents. With a common background in property the two decided to join forces and expanded the company up to 1971 on a piecemeal basis.

(b) 1971–5 In 1971, Countryside Properties took over the Essex-based Copthorn Group, a company previously formed by Alan Cherry before he joined Countryside, which had also been operating in a small way as residential property developers. The newly merged group then began to build up its own directly employed management and staff with the intention of expanding the business over a wider area and undertaking commercial property development.

In 1972 the company was floated on the Stock Exchange, but almost immediately afterwards the economic climate changed and the newly formed entity was faced with recession and the ensuing property crash of 1974. Tight financial control and the adoption of a marketing philosophy brought the company through this period – albeit with a heavy loss in 1975 of £1.3m.

(c) *1975–85*   This decade marks the phase of a planned and sustained recovery, with improvements in profits and sales almost annually.

Further improvements were made to financial controls via the use of computers, market research (demographic analysis especially) was improved, and administration was tightened. The company began to develop three distinct markets – residential development, commercial/industrial development and a property investment portfolio. The latter exercise is conducted by a subsidiary which was initially only partly owned, Countryside Investments. The underlying strategy of targeting the three markets is to spread the risks.

II   Causes of the relative decline to 1975

(a) *Inflation*   The company had geared itself up steadily as land prices rose rapidly in the early 1970s. When this rise halted and sales slowed this presented financing problems.

(b) *Macroeconomic environment*   Along with all firms in the sector Countryside was hit by the 1974 recessions in both the residential and the industrial/commercial sectors.

(c) *Supply/demand switch*   Simultaneously, there emerged, for the first time in many years, an excess of housing supply over demand. Although this surplus, in part, reflected a mismatch with houses of the wrong types and in the wrong places, the consequence of the excess supply was to force prices down and to constrain future building programmes. Consequently, many building contractors went into liquidation.

(d) *Collapse of sub-contractors*   Unfortunately, Countryside employed many sub-contractors on site work. Many of these individual firms were forced into liquidation or receivership, leaving Countryside with job delays, contract penalty causes and consequent higher costs per contract completion than originally planned.

(e) *Bank loans*   Bank lending to the building sector at this time can be described as easy to obtain. Countryside availed themselves of much of this and remained highly geared. Consequently, when their earnings were drastically cut back, they were still shackled with heavy outgoings to the clearing banks, producing large negative cash flows.

III   Triggers for sharpbending

The impact of these negative cash flows was a significant inducement for internal change. The financial crisis was so severe that the company's immediate future was in jeopardy.

IV   Actions taken to promote sharpbending

(a) *Financial controls*   While a form of cash-flow forecasting had been in use in Countryside since 1969, it was unreliable. The system was discontinued in 1971 and the data placed on a bureau computer and the focus of attention on the computerized cash-flow forecasting was a major feature of recovery.

(b) *Marketing*   Around 1972, Countryside became interested in marketing as a whole. Before then they did not place too much emphasis on studies of demographic trends, e.g. birth-rate profiles, single/married profiles, one-parent families, etc. However, they were inspired by the use of this kind of data in US companies and embarked on an information-gathering exercise, laying the foundations for constant surveillance of the above trends and the beginning of true market-research studies. True, the excess-demand conditions in the UK housing market up until this time had reduced the need for such studies, but this foresight proved to be a highly significant factor in the company's survival during the next decade.

(c) *Essex Design Guide 1973*   This guide was produced by the Essex County Planning Department; local building representatives, including Countryside, were invited for interview and comment. This design guide was the framework for building in Essex for the years to come.

It appears that Countryside were the first building firm to take such a guide seriously and consciously implement its contents. This inspiration probably came from Alan Cherry's involvement not only in the importance of marketing of which design would be a crucial component in this industry, but also his contribution to the guide's production. The importance to Countryside was that the publication of this guide coincided with the slump in the property market. Any company following the guide was likely to facilitate the planning permission for developments due to the elimination of red tape and problematic objections. Countryside were the only local company to capitalize on this opportunity in the immediate years after publication and hence gained a competitive edge.

The location of the first scheme under the new designs was at Brentwood. The designs and the location were excellent. Both factors drew rapid publicity for the guide and primarily for Countryside itself. For three years, the County Planning Department took visitors on guided tours of Countryside developments to illustrate the development of design in Essex.

V   Continuing characteristics of sharpbending

(a) *Design quality*   Countryside's designs were already widely acclaimed. In the subsequent years, they became market leaders in the field to be copied by larger organizations. Their designs are still outstanding and rarely fail to win annual awards and commendations.

(b) *Design guides*   To reinforce its market position, Countryside has adopted a similar strategy in adjacent counties where they have brought out design guides. Hence their initial insight in Essex, coupled with high reputations gained in the south-east in general, has helped them to be included in invitations to selective tender.

(c) *Conservation*   Public attitudes towards conservation were growing throughout the 1970s and especially in the early 1980s. Countryside have always been seen as a 'caring' builder. They do not bulldoze green acres and forests of trees. Developments are blended into *existing* landscapes producing a high 'quality-of-life' product that is respected not only by local authorities but also by customers.

(d) *Management team*   This is now a balanced blend of experience and youth. The former being Mr Alan Cherry and Mr Michael Pearce who have been together since the early days of the company's formation. The latter are hand-picked graduates who are trained to occupy highly responsible posts at young ages. The highly motivated youthful management team revels in its responsibilities and authority. The younger members of the team claim the experienced leadership helps to keep them in check and provides a reservoir of advice that prevents expensive errors occurring.

(e) *'In-house' specialists* Prior to 1976, the small head-office team used to buy-in the services of architects, surveyors and external building contractors. These services have now all been brought 'in-house' to further managerial efficiency and control.

(f) *Financial controls* In 1976, the standard set of reports and controls that had existed in the firm since the early 1970s were placed on the company's own computer system. This system has since been upgraded three times and at the time of writing is being improved a fourth time. However, it is not so much the system as the use made of it which matters. The system includes individual projections for each contract development. It consists of full reports on group cash at its four banks broken down by residential or commercial/industrial development, providing monthly, yearly and five-yearly gross-profit projections. It is a very tight rein on cash control.

(g) *Managerial succession* Alan Cherry has two sons working in the group. They know the business well, are highly motivated and are now full board members.

(h) *Counter-cyclical strategies* The three main sectors (residential, industrial and commercial, and property investment) tend to follow different cycles and hence spread risk.

(i) *Marketing* The company has continued to develop a solid marketing philosophy. This is readily apparent within the firm where PR is of an exceptionally high standard. The firm has deliberately identified niches of the market. It counters recessional conditions in two ways. First, by concentrating on the prime-demand, south-east region that appears to hold up well when general activity falls. Secondly, by designing buildings in a range of prices and styles that suit both the current demand pattern and the forecast demand pattern based on demographic-trend analysis.

(j) *Organization changes* As the company has increased its size at head office, more formalized roles have been adopted. The small teams still retain their flexibility. (Job titles, hierarchies, responsibility and accountability have all been recently ironed out to avoid duplication of work and allow for career expansion.)

(k) *Product development* The company acknowledges that the building sector is highly competitive and any design barriers to entry are only likely to be short-term. They have thus made a conscious effort to widen the product base from residential housing to include 'specials', e.g. sheltered housing.

(l) *House purchase aids* For many years, the company has operated a mortgage assistance scheme for its house buyers to cover new buyers against interest rate rises in the initial period. They have also run a part-exchange scheme since 1974.

(m) *Standardization* The company have recently begun to standardize modules in their award-winning designs without risking their reputation for quality and still being able to produce individual designs. This is to enable maximum purchasing economies in bricks, timber, tiles and other materials to be achieved.

VI Conclusion

Countryside is a tale of high gearing and external economic factors acting jointly to reduce vital cash flows. These stocked the seed-bed of success based on quality and design ingenuity. Full use of marketing research, close financial control, a neat blend of managerial youth and experience together with clever diversification have enabled Countryside to sustain a unique performance in its industry.

DAWSON INTERNATIONAL PLC

Dawson International PLC and its thirty-two subsidiary companies – the Dawson Group – is a group of specialist textile companies manufacturing high-quality products based in Kinross, Tayside. It has a strong Scottish base and operates in world markets. The group is best known for its luxury knitwear and its world-famous brand names which include Pringle of Scotland, Braemar, Ballantyne, Barrie, McGeorge, Glenmac and Gladstone.

I History of the firm

The group was built after the war by Alan Smith. He went to work for Todd & Duncan in 1946 who were cashmere spinners, and from that beginning moved on to buy up Dawson who were cashmere merchants and dehairers. In the 1960s the group became threatened by the acquisitive actions of various other textile groups in buying up Scottish firms. This led Alan Smith to buy up Pringle in 1967 and then a host of other famous Scottish brand names. Around 1971 Alan Smith handed over the Chief Executive reins to his Finance Director, Hugh Thomas, and the group started to lose momentum. It began to show interest in activities outside its own field of expertise, e.g. textile manufacturing, and was ill-equipped to deal with the recession and the oil price rise. It also became overcentralized. Alan Smith replaced Thomas and assumed the reins again himself until 1982 when he retired.

Profits fell from 1971 to 1973, enjoyed a brief recovery until a more serious decline in 1974/5 which threatened the group's very existence. The sharpbend occurred in 1975. Table B.4 contains statistical data documenting Dawson's recovery. In 1984, the £179.2m turnover was accounted for by the UK (£82.3m), EEC (£52.6m), rest of Europe (£10.6m), the Americas (£21.6m) and the rest of the world (£12m).

II Causes of the relative decline 1971–5

(a) *Sustained drop in market demand* There was a temporary collapse in market demand for luxury knitwear in 1970, and in 1974 the company suffered, in common with most of the industry, from the general recession induced by the 1973–4 oil price increases. The latter proved almost fatal to the company because of weaknesses that had grown in the previous seven years.

Table B.4 *Statistical data for Dawson International PLC (year end 31 March)*

(£m)	1975	1976	1977	1978	1979	1980	1981	1982	1983	1984[1]	1985	1986
Turnover	42.5	43.8	67.3	82.6	96.2	113.2	131.0	153.5	139.0	179.2	265.6	285.2
Net profit before interest & tax	2.2	3.9	11.9	16.3	17.0	19.7	21.5	25.6	22.3	26.8	35.1	42.1
Exports	19.0	18.7	29.2	37.2	40.3	41.4	54.0	65.8	58.2	n.a.	n.a.	n.a.
Return on capital employed (%)	9.6	17.0	59.0	62.7	42.9	37.2	34.0	35.4	23.7	25.6	n.a.	n.a.
Earnings per share (p)[2]	0.5	2.3	8.3	13.0	14.3[3]	17.5[3]	15.0	19.7	18.6	19.8	n.a.	n.a.
Employees (average no.)	5854	4856	5286	5521	5531	5983	6727	7087	6061	7066	n.a.	n.a.

[1] Including results of the German subsidiary, acquired on 5 July 1983.
[2] Adjusted for scrip issues.
[3] Comparative figure for previous year 15.5p after change in policy re-deferred tax.
n.a.: not available.

(b) *Poor management* In the late 1970s the group had expanded from its fibre-spinning and merchanting base into knitwear. The companies purchased were primarily successful up-market operations whose capable founding entrepreneurs had not provided for satisfactory succession, so that there was a lack of operating management strength. The management of the base companies lacked experience of running a larger group, and proved incapable of compensating for the deficiencies of management in the new subsidiaries. The purpose of the forward integration had simply been to protect outlets from capture by competitors. There was a lack of clarity of view about the direction in which the company should move. The group management did not identify, and hence correct weaknesses in the subsidiaries.

Sensing the inadequacy of the management to make profitable use of the company's resources, the founder retired to the chairmanship of the company and promoted his finance director to the chief executive.

The solutions the new man pursued were to build up a substantial headquarters staff, organized on a conglomerate basis with a view to diversification. The problems of the new companies taken over in line with this objective, and the planning of possible further diversification into such other fields as hotels or leisure, seriously distorted group management from the core textile business of the company. Proper establishment of communications with the management of the textile subsidiaries was hindered, and the expansion of the company outside its natural textile functions inevitably impaired the desirable creation of shared vision and values throughout the company.

(c) *Inadequate financial control* There is evidence that at the start of the decade working capital was out of control: huge stocks, particularly at later production stages, were built up when the market dipped.

Financial control was kept fairly tight after the expansion of the headquarters, with good reporting deadlines. The fault was that financial information for central management was too voluminous, and not supplemented or interpreted by an input from the subsidiary managing directors, making it harder to identify problem areas quickly.

(d) *Organization structure* The first attempts to control the knitting subsidiaries from the centre took the form of group directors sitting on all the boards and management committees of the subsidiaries. They were consequently never in their own offices, leaving a vacuum at the centre, delaying such decision-taking as was necessary and no doubt precluding the evaluation of thoughtful and co-ordinated group policies.

The second attempt to get to grips with group management, under the new chief executive, for a time seemed to have some success; profits improved in the boom period of 1972–3. However, the 1974 recession disclosed how serious were the organizational inadequacies. Foremost among these was overcentralization. Managers of subsidiaries had to ask the centre for numerous decisions which they should have been allowed to take themselves, and the top-heavy central structure, with too many functions and levels to be consulted, delayed the taking of these decisions – a serious weakness in a business were rapid response to changing market conditions is essential. These difficulties went on too long without remedy, and many opportunities were missed.

(e) *Costly acquisitions* Many of the new companies acquired in the pursuit of diversification, particularly in clothing and merchanting, were taken over merely because there was a place for them in the new divisional structure, without specific consideration of their usefulness. Almost without exception they were poorly run, and cost too much in initial purchase price and in subsequent infusions to keep them running. The group management did not manage to remedy their deficiencies, no proper return on the investments was earned, and the losses, on top of the demand collapse in the core textile businesses, were almost sufficient to bankrupt the group.

(f) *Poor quality and reliability relative to competition*   The group had ceased to pay the degree of attention to quality control necessitated by the high-price sector of the market at which many of its products were aimed.

III   Triggers for sharpbending

The financial results were so disturbing that Alan Smith (Chairman) resumed the role of Chief Executive himself.

IV   Actions taken to promote sharpbending

(a) *Change in management*   The removal of the chief executive was clearly a key step. The other executive directors proved capable to taking the necessary measures to set the group steering in the right direction, though cutting the headquarters down to a more satisfactory size and role involved the disappearance of two of them, as the new policy had no place for a central production or personnel director. Today, following Alan Smith's retirement, the central group management team consists of the chairman and chief executive (formerly the finance director), two executive directors and the finance director. It is important that all have significant textile experience.

In addition, they acquired strong non-executive directors, introduced a generous incentive scheme enabling directors of subsidiaries to increase their salaries by 30 per cent (50 per cent for Managing Directors) for exceeding targets for return on capital employed and hurried subsidiary managers into active behaviour.

(b) *Organizational change*   The principal factor which promoted sharpbending was decentralization. Responsibility for the success or failure of the subsidiaries was placed firmly in the hands of their managements. Far fewer decisions required group management approval and those that did not were implemented much more quickly. The managers of subsidiary companies were expected to run day-to-day operations, and evolve their own strategies for improving their performance.

(c) *Stronger central financial control and corporate planning*   To avoid the weaknesses of the previous era a tight system of planning and control has evolved. The new system requires each subsidiary to put up annually, and revise six-monthly, a detailed plan for the following year, and another, in less detail, covering three years ahead. The plans give relatively short time series: achievement last year, plans and latest forecast for current year, against which to assess the proposed plans. They cover output broken down into significant categories, sales by market and product, the cost of achieving this in suitable categories, capital expenditure necessary, and the foreseen benefits of the policy. After mastering the contents, the central executive team visit the subsidiary and discuss the plan in detail, probing for possible weaknesses, making criticisms and suggestions, and in a minority of cases suggesting that the plan be changed and resubmitted in the light of the discussion. Regular visits by key senior executives and the ultimate power of central management to replace a subsidiary Managing Director ensures tight control and positive action. In addition, during the year, the central management receives regular statistics of the achievement of the subsidiary compared with the plan and previous year – a weekly cash statement, quick estimate of monthly commercial results three days after the end of the month, and firm figures of sales, output, profits, overdue debts, overdraft, stocks, capital employed, etc., after nine days. Anything still not clear is investigated by a phone call from members of the central Finance Director's staff. The central management is thus informed of any problems, and will talk to the subsidiary Managing Director to probe the background and solution if it seems important enough to warrant this. The threat of a roving group auditor ensures the reliability of the submitted statistics.

(d) *Divestments and new product market focus*   The strong and weak points of the organization were no secret at its nadir in 1974–5. The parts that had no hope of becoming profitable were all the non-related subsidiaries, which were closed or disposed of with vigorous speed once the old Chief Executive left. This had the advantages of cutting the firm back to sectors it understood (in textiles) and alleviating the cash-flow position by shedding almost 1000 from the payroll.

Product policy decisions were reasonably obvious once this had happened. The knitting operations, with one significant exception, made very high-quality products, under brand names respected throughout the world, and the policy had to be to exploit this position at the top of the market. They were fed by the fibre-importing and some of the spinning operations in the group, and needed high-quality materials from them. Other elements of the group, such as a spinner of carpet yarns, similarly took the route of high-quality goods. There is great emphasis on gaining the rewards of this excellence by branding as much as possible all goods sold to consumers, and by selling widely in any foreign market where there are inhabitants of sufficient disposable income to afford their consumer products, or firms whose output requires the quality of their intermediate products.

(e) *Improved marketing*   Great pains are taken to be sensitive to shifts in taste, to analyse markets with care, to support brand names in appropriate ways. Their wide geographical sales base means there is a lot to learn, but in the end, is an advantage in expanding the sources of new ideas.

The system for marketing information between subsidiaries and the board, and between subsidiaries is largely informal – there are few bulletins or conferences or reports. But it is clear that central management has over time acquired a shrewd understanding of world markets from which to assess subsidiaries' plans and with which to suggest new possibilities. Central management also takes care to keep some contact with major customers and agents to fill out or correct what it is told by subsidiaries.

(f) *Reduced costs of production*   The firm has not hesitated to spend money on new plants wherever this can be shown to cut costs. A good relationship with customers yields a considerable proportion of long orders, which facilitates production efficiency. The end-product members of the group are expected to buy from the intermediate-product members wherever possible, and to place orders well in advance with the same benefit. Care in such ordering is encouraged by the bonus system; orders placed are invoiced, and the stock goes on to the capital of the purchasing company.

The organization is fortunate in that many of its plants are located in areas like the Border country where there is a good work ethic, labour relations are good, and productivity is readily improvable.

(g) *Acquisitions* A number of acquisitions have been important to Dawson's performance. Braemar has a making-up opportunity in the US for heavily patterned garments whose labour content was too high to stand British labour costs. The garments are knitted domestically in Hong Kong from British yarn, assembled in the Hong Kong plant and exported.

More indicative of the group's philosophy and strengths are two recent acquisitions: Kammgarnspinnerei Wilhelmshaven AG, a German spinner, primarily of hand-knitting yarns and J. E. Morgan Knitting Mills Inc., an American manufacturer of thermal underwear. Dawson's success had left it with huge cash resources, interest rates were expected to fall, and, conscious of the importance of meeting City and shareholder expectations, the board wanted to earn more on the resources. They insisted that any new acquisition must be well run; they lacked the resources to effect turnarounds, and had abiding memories of the past horrors of buying bad firms. There were few obvious British textile firms left, and anyway they welcomed the opportunity of gaining presence, experience and strength in foreign countries. They wanted companies in strong economies with stable governments, preferably close to the consumer; ideally, a firm with a strong production base whose value they could enhance by their marketing experience and techniques.

The two recent purchases met this exacting bill. The German spinner has a very low proportion of branded sales; its management wanted to expand this, but was frustrated by its owners, who preferred to extract the cash rather than make the necessary investment in building a brand strength. Dawson have revised this policy. The American company had an owner and Managing Director who had never moved his products over from a retailer-brand to a manufacturer-brand basis; Dawson put in an energetic manager, who was encouraged to do just this, with considerable success.

V Continuing characteristics of sharpbending

(a) *Strong management* Group management is pro-active. It encourages risk-taking, provides the appropriate funding, projects clear company values, provides autonomy but with close control, and has mastered the art of verbal communication. Subsidiary management can feel free from interference in day-to-day affairs and in major matters so long as performance is on target. If there is trouble, they will receive penetrating scrutiny and sympathetic help. The Chief Executive's summary of the key characteristics of a successful organization are:

1 decentralization;
2 employ the right people for all purposes, including selling agents;
3 pay attention to the market place, and be ready to innovate anywhere market requirements dictate;
4 insist on quality in every respect: people, products and equipment; and
5 have wide horizons – have a go anywhere in the world.

(b) *Appropriate organizational structure* The structure is simple and appropriate, with the minimum head-office staff to exercise control, stimulate enterprise, and carry out a very limited number of central functions, primarily financial.

Operating decisions are delegated to subsidiary companies, who very clearly function as profit-oriented cost centres. Group directors do not dissipate their energies by sitting on constituent company boards.

Intra-group troubles are relatively few. There are no transfer price problems, because all group members sell outside the group on a big enough scale for a market price to be established. If there is any disagreement which cannot be resolved, the centre arbitrates.

(c) *Sound product market posture* Dawson is a strong competitor in desirable, high-margin, quality markets, ringing the changes in their product ranges in terms of elements of fashion, for there are many competitors all over the world. They keep abreast of technology, for quality and new-product purposes as much as cost improvement. But major technological or market changes which make their products or procedures inappropriate are less likely than with most firms. In most sectors they do not face the price pressures common to most of their competitors. There is a good market for products at prices which suit them provided they can come up with the products, and market them properly. They have a well-focused strategy, and differentiate their products successfully, often by sustaining prestigious brand names. Their broad geographical base is viewed as an important defence against economic recessions.

Their own perception of the most likely source of vulnerability is a rapid increase in costs of the raw materials they buy – their specialization is in natural fibres, and they fear that they would meet resistance to attempts to pass on big increases.

VI Conclusion

Dawson have two major pieces of good fortune. First, most of their activities are located in exactly the sector of textiles that ought to flourish in high-cost countries – products that are difficult to make both technically and in terms of the fashion and sensitivity required. Second, their predecessor companies had established brand names of sufficient robustness to withstand the problems.

Their story is a strong one. A high-quality, focused market niche supported by a well-managed group structure – tight enough to ensure efficiency and free enough to ensure creativity.

DON AND LOW PLC
(trading as Don Brothers Buist PLC at the time of the study)

This company based in Forfar, Scotland is engaged in the manufacture and merchanting of industrial textiles. In 1984, it had a turnover of £39m broken down as £28m (UK), £7m (EEC), £3m (rest of Europe), and £1m (rest of world). It employs 1200 people in the three group companies.

Table B.5 *Statistical data for Don Brothers PLC (year end 31 May)*

(£m)	1978	1979	1980	1981	1982	1983	1984	1985	1986
Turnover – home	16.5	21.4	20.9	18.2	19.6	20.1	27.9	34.9	32.5
– export	5.8	5.5	7.6	6.8	7.0	8.0	11.3	16.7	15.8
Profit before tax	3.1	4.4	2.6	0.2	1.4	1.1	2.9	4.5	2.5
Return on shareholder funds (%)	13.7	19.9	8.8	6.5	5.3	6.1	9.8	17.3	5.4

I History of the firm

(a) *Structure and management* In the 1950s, Don Brothers was a speciality manufacturer of jute industrial textiles. Its position was strategically weak for two reasons. First, it lacked a marketing arm. Its output was sold through merchants and distributors of whom Low Brothers (Dundee) was one of the largest and most successful. Being cash-rich, Don Brothers was seeking to acquire a distributor to complement its manufacturing skills. In the late 1950s, the ageing management of Don Brothers brought in a younger member of the Hill family from Boots. In 1960, he persuaded Low Brothers to accept a takeover offer, and to join the management of Don Brothers. In 1963, the Smart family company (Brechin), which sold most of its output through Low Brothers, was also acquired by share exchange. A jute manufacturing and selling company with sites in four parts of Scotland, run by the Hills, Smarts and Lows thus emerged. In many respects this was the first and crucial step in achieving the sharpbend.

(b) *Nature of the market* During the late 1960s, jute was substituted by polypropylene as a carpet-backing material. Don Brothers were fortunate enough to seize on this change and, consequently, 'sharpbent' rapidly during the 1960s. This was the second step in the process. As table B.5 shows the company rode up on increasing home sales, as well as exports, to a peak in turnover and profit in 1979. This was a general feature of the polypropylene carpet-backing business in the late 1970s. The acquisition of Don Fibres in 1977 was a major boost to profitability. When the carpet industry, and home sales, slumped in the early 1980s with the flood of cheaper American and Belgian imports, Don Brothers suffered only a minor dip in home sales and had a resumed growth in export sales. Thus they were picking up the market share of other companies which were leaving the business. In this way Don Brothers kept their looms working at almost full capacity.

This was clearly at the cost of profit margins for operating profit before tax slumped from £4.4m in 1979 to £0.2m in 1981, rising to £2.9m in 1984 (see table B.5). Even then it had still not reached the earlier peak of 1978, while both home and export sales were by then some 30 per cent higher. Don Brothers chose to slim profit margins, and even to take losses, to maintain their market share in certain export markets (e.g. Greece) during the years of intense competition. They emerged as the only major British presence within the industry.

II Causes of the relative decline

(a) *International competition* The major cause was undoubtedly the decline in the domestic jute industry, due to the growing competitiveness of the Indian industry with its comparative labour-cost advantage.

(b) *Conservative management* The ageing management at Don Brothers lacked the dynamism necessary to cope with the structural decline. They delayed crucial changes in raw-material substitution that were being pushed forward by the younger managers of the newly acquired Low and Smart companies.

III Triggers for sharpbending

Eventually, the young directors persuaded the board to adopt the changes in technology necessary for survival. Their success had to wait until the conflict was resolved by the death of Lord Tayside and the appointment of William Low as his successor as Chief Executive.

IV Actions taken to promote sharpbending

Material substitution Extensive collaboration took place with the petrochemical industry to produce the appropriate materials and to develop the technology that would replace jute by polypropylene as backing for the tufted-carpet industry. Consequently, Don Brothers negotiated with an American company, Grace, to set up an extrusion facility in their own factory space.

Don Brothers were the first to enter the market for polypropylene carpet backing. They have sustained their dominance from the 1960s to the 1980s. It is important to note that the change from jute to polypropylene was evolutionary rather than revolutionary.

V Continuing characteristics of sharpbending

(a) *Marketing* Don Brothers have always stressed high quality and fulfilled delivery promises. They maintained strong machine-maintenance programmes to ensure this quality and minimize production disruption. These features have been particularly emphatic in their development of overseas markets. About 50 per cent of their output of carpet backing is exported, mainly to the Middle East, Africa and the whole of Europe. They now hold around 65 per cent of the UK market and 20 per cent of the European one. This business has always taken priority over home sales. They have stressed punctuality, strict quality control, the technical qualifications of their representatives and their ability to deliver standard products from stock.

(b) *Investment* They have invested heavily in new technology in an effort to keep costs down. They were the first in the industry to instal advanced looms with multiple loom operation by a single operator. They also moved at an early date from spun yarn to extruded tape in the switch from jute to polypropylene. During the last two years they have invested in equipment for multi-filament yarn required for industrial strappings, webbing, etc. (see below). John Smart, the Managing Director responsible for production, takes his managers to the international machinery trade fairs in search of new ideas which may not have been suggested by his current suppliers.

(c) *Vertical integration* As their polypropylene tape requirement extended, and they became the major client of the American-owned extruder at Forfar, they acquired the company (now part of Don and Low Ltd) to gain security of supplies and closer vertical integration, with strong quality implications.

(d) *Capacity* As other companies have decided to run down polypropylene, Don Brothers have acquired their weaving capacity, e.g. Low & Bonar, Sidlaw Group and Scott & Robertson.

(e) *Diversification* During the 1980s, they entered the market for 'geotextiles', the result of a discussion with a civil-engineering research establishment. These are woven polypropylene textiles used in strengthening and giving resilience to road surfaces and other structures. Over the last two years they have also entered multi-filament yarn-spinning and web-weaving to provide polypropylene strapping and similar materials for industrial use. However, the bulk of their turnover, and profits, is still derived from their broadloam backing for tufted carpets.

(f) *Tight financial control systems.*

(g) *Close management–union relations.*

(h) *Divestment of loss-making activities* During the 1970s the company entered the textile-coating business (Don Coatings), rainwear by acquisition (T. Grant (Rainwear) Ltd), woollen weaving (Strathmore Woollen Co. Ltd had been acquired in 1950) and packing (particularly presentation boxes) at Don and Low Packaging Ltd. These exercises proved to be unsuccessful. In 1982 all but Don and Low were closed or sold, extraordinary costs being carried over two years. This was partly a tidying-up operation in preparation for going public in May 1983, but they also acquired Tay Textiles who manufacture flexible intermediate bulk containers.

VI Conclusions

Don Brothers were able to 'sharpbend' because of a leap into a relatively highly technical, substitute material to replace the traditional jute used for carpet backing. It was crucial to identify the product which was high in material and capital costs and low in labour costs (on which the Indians had a comparative advantage).

This bold leap was aided by the change in Chairman and Managing Director. The subsequent adoption of polypropylene has enabled Don Brothers to sustain a strong performance over more than two decades. The secret has been marketing.

In July 1986 Don Brothers Buist was taken over by Shell and the structure of the organization, rather than the operations, altered.

ELLIS & GOLDSTEIN (HOLDINGS) PLC

I   History of the firm

Ellis & Goldstein was founded in 1912 and became a public company in 1936. In Brick Lane, London they design, purchase fabric and plan their ranges of tailored women's outerwear, which are sold through the showrooms in Kent House, London and through agents at home and abroad.

Elangol Distributors, their shops-within-stores company, has some 260 units in the UK, Eire, Denmark, Sweden and Norway retailing the Eastex and Dereta brands. They order directly from the group's manufacturing companies. Elangol also look after the DASH operation which now has eighty-five adult and twenty-five children's shops-within-stores in the UK and Germany. There is a stand-alone DASH shop in Brighton.

Their factories in Luton, St Albans and Margate, make the garments sold on the Eastex and Dereta coats, suits and casuals ranges. The majority of production is warehoused at Northolt from where they supply their high-street customers and shops-within-stores.

The chain and multiple retailers, such as BHS, C&A and Littlewoods are served by their knitwear company, Bent & Sons in Leicester and by Dukes & Marks in North Shields who supply the garments made from woven fabric.

After a period of explosive growth in the years from 1965 to 1973, this company had a relatively protracted period of lacklustre performance.

II   Causes of the relative decline

(a) *Sustained drop in market demand*   The company's products were tailored women's outerwear, geared essentially to the medium or better sector of middle-aged, middle-class customers. The market volume for this type of merchandise was slowly but steadily declining as tastes swung to more informal styles. For a brief period export success helped sustain volume, and exports as a proportion of total sales rose from 7 per cent in 1974 to 14 per cent in 1977. However, they declined over the next six years, recording 5 per cent in 1983. Important factors were the imposition of tariffs in Canada and quotas in Australia, which destroyed their markets there almost overnight.

Table B.6   *Sales and profits, Ellis and Goldstein*

	Sales (£m/year)	Pre-tax profits (£m/year)
1974–6	28.0	1.83
1977–9	35.7	1.57
1980–2	40.4	1.23
1983	47.9	2.34

(b) *Market adaptation*   During the dip in trade, Ellis & Goldstein remained market leader in its segment of the industry and held up better than most of its direct competitors. However, a great deal of revenue was lost by its failure to respond quickly enough to changing consumer tastes. In most respects, the firm was well and tightly run by experienced and capable leaders. They knew they had to think of new products to restore the firm's momentum; but they did not start the search soon enough, or award sufficient priority to its pursuit. The firm had no non-executive directors who might have been able to get management to increase the pace and consider further ideas.

They did study many projects, but for a long time came across nothing which they thought would improve their fortunes. This is strange as the company had a sufficiently strong and well-controlled financial base for expansion and diversification.

III   Triggers for sharpbending

The management knew it had to add something new to its product range; sharpbending occurred when they came across suitable products in the US. The management had the market sense to recognize an exploitable idea when it saw it, and the drive to proceed with the exploitation rapidly.

IV   Actions taken to promote sharpbending

(a) *Stronger central financial control*   As the new business became more important, a different kind of financial control became appropriate. With expansion, competition for resources became an issue – beforehand there had been plenty of cash for anything needed – and a new cash-control system was instituted. The merits of rival investment projects have now to be assessed more carefully.

But the business remains as it was – not capital-intensive, and subject to short-term changes in taste. So the managers feel that long-term corporate planning is not appropriate and is therefore not undertaken.

(b) *New product market focus*   The firm has been revitalized by adding to its old range a new and entirely different set of products. Two of their managers noticed, in New York stores, lines of active leisure wear – fashionable garments with a sporting motif, though not in fact suitable for vigorous, sporting activity, yet suitable in a formal environment. They obtained permission from a major American supplier to be allowed to sell their garments in Europe, placed orders with the Far Eastern manufacturers, and decided how to sell them through their existing outlets. The target market is younger than that for their traditional garments – it even includes children. In addition, the initial attempt to enter the men's market was launched in 1985.

(c) *Improved marketing*   By latching on to the product range initially organized by a large-scale American firm, Ellis & Goldstein are able to offer a wide spectrum of garments in related or coordinated colours, making use of a huge range of fabric types. They, themselves, have a considerable input into choices that go into the range, making the adaptations they consider necessary for the European market. The new products are marketed in very much the same way as the old, with a strong brand name and mixture of outlets. To the previous outlets (over 270 shops within department stores and wholesaling to their retailers) they are beginning to add to their own chain of retail shops a move towards formal vertical integration. These DASH outlets have grown remarkably, there were over 100 in operation in 1985. The company diversified into DASH for men late in 1985.

(d) *Rationalization of existing businesses*   Some closures and consolidations were carried out in the early 1980s. The nature of the business precludes some routes to low cost of production, since they are not manufacturers of long runs of standardized goods. However, they have been quick to source production, away from expensive domestic producers to a variety of overseas countries – especially in the Far East.

V   Continuing characteristics of sharpbending

(a) *Good management with a marketing edge*   The strength of the management lies principally in its judgement and experience of the vagaries of the British fashion market. It is actively involved in influencing what its customers will be offered – there is a new look at the range every six weeks. It prides itself on keeping abreast of what customers are interested in, and what new developments are taking place around the world which might influence its strategic choices.

Management is also keen to promote friendly competition within the firm. Care is taken with employee relations, which have always in consequence been good. Higher wages than normal in the industry are paid, and a profit-sharing scheme has recently been introduced. The company's performance is set out in a report to employees, aimed at being 'comprehensible but not condescending'.

(b) *Tight financial control*   This feature has always been paramount at Ellis & Goldstein. They scrutinize costs frequently and keep a very tight rein on cash.

(c) *Focus marketing strategy*   The company is clearly very cautious about straying outside the market it knows well.

(d) *Quality emphasis*   Ellis & Goldstein takes pains to ensure high-quality standards in its factories. Quality circles have been established at Leicester, Luton and Northolt. Each has provided a number of novel and productive contributions to sustain the high-quality profile.

VI   Conclusion

Ellis & Goldstein experienced relative decline by failing to keep in very close touch with a market known for its rapid response to changing consumer tastes. It had got stuck in a declining segment, although it remained mildly profitable. It also failed to take sufficient action when it realized what was happening. Clearly fortune played a great role in securing a sharpbend. The new leisure-wear products, coupled to overseas sourcing, have been largely responsible for the company's growth. Its sustained recovery has been attributed to a tighter product market focus, excellent financial controls (which were already in place before the bend), and a sound management style.

FERRANTI PLC

This large group of companies is engaged in the development, manufacture and sale of mechanical, electrical and electronic engineering products. Its turnover in 1984 was £452m generated by its five main business groupings – Industrial Electronic & Defence Systems (the Scottish Group, £198m), Computer Systems (£152m), Ferranti Electronics (£62m) and Instrumentation (£22m). In all, twenty-eight subsidiary companies report to the five separate groupings. The remaining activities come under Engineering Holdings (£29m).

The group depends on the UK for 68 per cent of turnover, Europe for 17 per cent, the US and Canada for 1 per cent and the rest of the world for 7 per cent.

Other statistical data relating to the group appear in table B.7. The Scottish group is the major employer with 8000 operatives out of a group total of 19,000. Just over 1000 employees are based overseas.

I History of the firm

(a) *Share ownership* Ferranti is just over 100 years old, having been founded in 1882 and incorporated in 1905. The Ferranti family dominated the ownership of the group up until recent times. It was still 90 per cent family-owned in the mid-1960s when Dennis de Ferranti, the brother of the then Chairman, Vincent de Ferranti, sold his shareholding which reduced the family domination to 56 per cent of the equity.

In September 1975, the Department of Industry acquired 62.5 per cent of the issued ordinary-share capital. This holding was then transferred to the National Enterprise Board (NEB) in March 1976. In order to liquidate a portion of the family's interest – which would have otherwise been locked into an unquoted state-owned entity, it was agreed to float some of the shares if performance targets were met. This was achieved in 1978 enabling NEB to float 12.5 per cent of the equity, reducing its holding to 50 per cent.

When the new government came to power in 1979, a decision was made to privatize the NEB stake completely. This was mainly done by placement in 1980 (raising £54m) with the residual being disposed of by distribution to employees in 1981. The net result of these transactions was to reduce the family holding to 20 per cent of the total equity. By 1987, only 8 per cent of the shares were owned by the Ferranti family.

(b) *Crisis* By 1972/3, some 30 per cent of the group operations were unprofitable. The Scottish section made more profit than the rest of the group put together. The group's projected cash requirement for 1973 was £15m on an overdraft limit of £12m. By mid-1974, borrowings had reached £20m, i.e. more than the group's equity base, ringing alarm bells with the group's bankers, who were also exposed as guarantor of performance bonds to another £20m.

The National Westminster Bank in Manchester refused to renew the overdrafts/ loans on which the group had relied for so long. The secondary banking crisis had hurt the National Westminster which, at the time, was also committing considerable expenditure to its New Tower Block of London. Its policy was to adopt a strict review

Table B.7 *Statistical data for Ferranti PLC (year end 31 March)*

(£m)	1975	1976	1977	1978	1979	1980	1981	1982	1983	1984
Turnover (a)	86.3	108.5	125.4	156.9	192.1	214.6	271.5	306.9	372.2	451.7
Net profit before interest & tax (b)	1.4	5.8	8.4	11.4	13.2	15.1	21.7	25.0	33.3	41.3
(b) as % of (a)	1.6	5.4	6.7	7.3	6.9	7.0	8.0	8.2	8.9	9.1
Return on capital employed (%)	3.7	13.2	15.8	18.4	18.0	18.4	25.4	24.6	25.2	25.7

of loan applications and the risks attached thereto. The confidence it attached to Ferranti was not great. Hence, Ferranti's run of extensive credit was over. The future of a key UK employer was in serious doubt.

II Cause of the relative decline to 1974

(a) *Family control* The retention of family control was a key part of the group strategy up to 1974. This prevented the introduction of new equity and meant that group financing was dependent upon bank loans and overdrafts rather than other means of long-term finance. Hence, when the National Westminster Bank rejected future Ferranti funding the group was crippled.

(b) *Low levels of capital expenditure* From 1968 to 1974, the group's poor financial performance limited the amount of finance available for inward investment. The family did not want to lose control and were therefore inhibited in the search for new capital.

(c) *Low morale* Due partly to the lack of inward investment and partly to their location in Manchester, morale was low within the workforce. Poor plant and machinery and the impoverished working conditions were largely due to the lack of funding. By 1974, terms and conditions of employment were below the industry average. Their location in Manchester meant that they had witnessed the demise of other giants in engineering (e.g. AEI). When, they pondered, would this happen to Ferranti?

(d) *Quality of management* Ferranti has always employed a high proportion of skilled manual workers. The quality of its management was never quite the same. Leadership from the top was weak, decisions were fudged and delayed. Indicative of the group's management style is that, prior to 1974, it had no Finance Director. As a family-owned concern, there was no regular system of planning meetings or coordination of policies.

(e) *Transformer division*
1   *National Plan*: Ever since its foundation the company had been a major producer of transformers and this continued to be the case right up to 1964 when the government changed in October.
    The National Plan announced by the new government contained some very optimistic forecasts for the growth of the economy. The demand for electricity was expected to grow in keeping with the overall growth and this in turn meant that the demand for transformers was set to increase.
    Ferranti which had a significant share of the transformer market was keen to maintain its position and invested accordingly. By the end of 1967 it was clear that the National Plan was much too ambitious and hence the anticipated increase in demand for electricity and transformers would not be realized. By the early 1970s there was gross over-capacity in transformers and the company found that its transformer division was making a loss for the first time in its history. In a period of three to four years from the collapse of the National Plan, the annual demand for transformers fell from £54m to £12m and the consequences were of course catastrophic for the industry.
    It is estimated that in the five to six years prior to 1973 the company's cash position would have been £20m for the better were it not for the transformer division. The problems of the company were compounded by the fact that North Sea gas was beginning to come on stream and much of the domestic heating market was converting to this cheaper source of fuel for heating purposes.

Hence by 1970, the transformer division was incurring substantial losses which ironically were not of its own making.

2   *Proceedings/image*: Even given the heavy losses in Section II(e)(i) above Ferranti persisted in trying to rectify the performance of its transformer division before 1973. In an effort to expand overseas, it had suffered losses of £7m and was prevented from operating in the USA because of deficiencies in the quality of the product. On tight price tenders to the Tennessee Valley Authority, it had cut corners on acceptable design limits. Subsequently, the transformers failed an impulse test and had to be redesigned and rebuilt. Ferranti incurred heavy costs due to the penalty clauses in the contract. These penalties were deducted from the original selling price and this led to Ferranti being accused of dumping on the US market. Proceedings were taken against the group – tarnishing its international image.

Arguably, a decision to close down transformers should have been taken in 1974, when it accounted for 10 per cent of group turnover (£100m) but was losing around £2m a year. Productivity had declined by 25 per cent since 1979 and there was 30–40 per cent over-manning. The division was in a technical, production and financial mess. Unfortunately, the group stayed with transformers and this was a condition of the NEB rescue. It struggled through in the face of fierce Japanese competition until 1979 when it was closed with the loss of 400 jobs.

(f) *NEB influence*   When the NEB became involved in the company in 1975 under the then Labour government, the Secretary of State for Industry, Tony Benn, was convinced that one of the conditions of government support should be the continuance of the transformer operations, primarily it seems to avoid inevitable redundancies which would otherwise arise from closure. It is clear from then on that every effort was made to rescue the division, right up to its closure in 1979, even to the extent of strengthening the top management with the additional appointment of Mr Boyle, as second in charge in 1975. The company's aim was to bring the division into profit with a view to its eventual sale.

III   Triggers for sharpbending

The main agent was the National Westminster Bank, when they refused to continue funding the group. Faced with receivership, Mr McCullum (head of the Scottish group) and two other senior executives (not Ferranti's) visited the Department of Industry to gather support from an interventionist Labour government. One of Labour's proposals was the setting up of a National Enterprise Board as the government agent for injecting funds into various sectors of the economy.

Ferranti had to endure a long delay as the government went back to the polls in October 1974 to increase its slender majority, and it was not until 1975 that an agreement of help was obtained for the group under the new NEB led by Donald Ryder.

IV   Actions taken to promote sharpbending

(a) *Change in leadership*   The NEB agreement forced a change of leadership on the group. Sebastian de Ferranti was to cease being Chairman and a new Chief Executive was appointed, Mr Alun-Jones, bringing in a fresh, more dynamic management style. Family control was ended (see Section I).

(b) *Systematic planning and control systems* The NEB insisted on proper financial control systems, an orderly management structure and a regular framework of planning and review meetings at all levels. Mr Alun-Jones drew on his previous experience with Burmah Oil in developing an effective planning system at Ferranti. The keys were autonomous profit centres, subsidiary generated objectives and regular reviews.

(c) *NEB funding/investment* The new profit-oriented management have been rewarded by increased inward investment – currently running at £30/£40m a year. Working conditions have been greatly improved.

V Continuing characteristics of sharpbending

(a) *Technical competence* Ferranti has had a long tradition of technical competence, and in fact regards itself as being in the high-tech end of developments. By definition, this operation involves both high risk and large cash resources. Ferranti have overcome these problems primarily by being heavily dependent upon Ministry of Defence sales (around 60 per cent of their output still derives from defence or government contracts). However, to continue to secure this market, Ferranti has put a great deal of effort into its design capability and technical competence.

(b) *Management training* The key stimulation for the continuing success of the company seems to be in its programme of personnel management. This entails the systematic involvement of people within the company through the regular system of planning and review meetings, together with profit accountability. This is tied in with a fairly elaborate training system, together with management conferences, which are aimed at getting people together to talk about the company, its performance, and corporate mission.

In contrast to the old days, when training was non-existent, the company now holds an annual training conference to review its objectives. The overall result of these activities has made people more purposeful in their work, motivated them and given them a sense of co-ordination and cohesion, as well as accountability.

(c) *Organizational restructuring* From 1974 onwards, the new management team concentrated on restructuring the group's organization. In 1980 they reduced the fifteen major business groupings to the five in existence today.

(d) *Divestment of loss-making activities* The engineering division, consisting of the activities in transformers and the NEB-inspired diversification into straddle carriers, was a heavy loss maker by the late 1970s. Transformer production was ended in 1979 (see Section II(e) above). The straddle carrier market suffered, like transformers, from intense international competition.

Ferranti moved into straddle carriers in 1976 to take up capacity at its ailing transformer plant. At first, they were alone in the UK and performed reasonably well, increasing the labour force from 850 to 1000. Within a few years, however, the Japanese had penetrated the world market, having diversified into straddle carriers after the collapse of the international tanker market in 1974. In addition, projected world demand for straddle carriers had fallen by 50 per cent.

By 1983, prices had collapsed worldwide, sterling was strong, Ferranti had no orders for straddle carriers and losses were over £2m. Short-term redundancies were immaterial when the world market fell back again at the end of the year and by January 1984, the engineering division was closed down with the loss of 330 jobs.

(e) *Refinement of the original NEB plans and controls*   The planning process has been refined over the course of time. It depends upon the formulation of a corporate plan, which consists essentially of two plans – one for three years and one for one year. The three-year plan stems from the NEB days. The company's present one-year plan is done in considerable detail, whilst the three-year plan has the aim of getting the operational units to look further ahead, and in the context of a ten-year horizon, which poses the question of which products the company will be in at that time.

(f) *Gate Array Technology* (GAT)   Ferranti achieved a first in GAT and for a time dominated the market. Unfortunately, five years after inventing GAT in 1974 its world market share had fallen to 30 per cent. By 1984, its share had fallen even further to 10 per cent. Nevertheless, it remains profitable despite the problems that have faced the industry over the last two years.

VI   Conclusions

Family control was no longer efficient for a group that had grown to Ferranti's size. The financing of activities had serious consequences once the group began making heavy losses. The factors aiding recovery are simple – change the management style, acquire modern management methods in planning and controlling, restructure and invest – both in equipment and people.

Ferranti is also a useful case for assessing the net effects of government intervention. Happily, the NEB were active as change agents, in the introduction of the new management and the modern management methods. Sadly, in strategic product/market matters (e.g. transformers) they were less successful, and may even have prevented Ferranti from sharpbending at a more rapid rate.

FISONS PLC

This group, based in Ipswich, East Anglia, has interests in the pharmaceutical, scientific instrument and horticultural sectors. In 1986, it had a turnover of £664m, and total profits of £77m.

I   History of the firm

Their recent history is marked by reorganization and rationalization. Their traditional business of fertilizers was facing increasing competition in the late 1970s. Fisons could not compete on equal terms with the giants such as ICI with their special access to low-cost inputs. Their profitability suffered and, coupled with poor financial controls, this led to a rapid build-up of debts and substantial overgearing.

Hence, although turnover was increasing, profitability was falling, and by 1981 the company had moved into the red. The answer lay in restructuring. First, a 50–50 merger between their agrochemicals business and Boots PLC was set up and second, they sold off other fertilizer interests to Norsk-Hydro PLC in early 1982.

The company is currently divided into three divisions, Pharmaceutical, Scientific Instruments and Horticulture, with only a small head office in Ipswich. In 1984 the Scientific Equipment division represented more than half of turnover but only 30 per cent of profits while the Pharmaceutical division had about one-third turnover, but over 60 per cent of the profits. The Horticulture division is small by comparison although expanding rapidly in the US. The 1984 figures are very different from previous years, where the Pharmaceutical division dominated, because of the purchase of an American scientific equipment company, Curtin Matheson Scientific, which trebled sales and profits in that division between 1983 and 1984.

II Causes of the relative decline

John Kerridge, Chairman and Chief Executive of Fisons in 1985, attributes the following reasons to their pre-1981 decline.

(a) *High-cost producers of fertilizers* As a relatively smaller company, Fisons could not exert either the countervailing power of a large producer on suppliers nor could they afford to integrate vertically upwards to reduce costs. The giants such as ICI had major advantages in this respect.

(b) *Delays in strategic realignment* The company had maintained the fertilizer and agrochemicals business for too long given the degree and nature of the competition. It was too slow to move away from strategically weak business areas.

(c) *Weak management control* Closely coupled with (b) above, was a relaxation in management control which had occurred when the previous Chairman and Chief Executive gave up his role and appointed his Financial Director to the post.

III Triggers for sharpbending

The financial pressures helped trigger the bend but the Chairman reaching retirement age also changed the management of the company. John Kerridge was appointed Chief Executive in June 1980 with Sir George Burton appointed to the position of Non-Executive Chairman in April 1981. He retained this post until succeeded by Kerridge in 1984.

IV Actions taken to promote sharpbending

The steps taken by Fisons reflect the general reactions to crisis:

1 selling of businesses which were either loss-making or with poor prospects (fertilizers and agrochemicals);
2 acquisition of new companies in established areas of business where prospects appeared good (continuing);
3 introduction of management accounting and tight cash control (continuing);
4 substantial management shake-up;

5   slimming of head office – finance, PR and planning were the only real functions that remained;
6   cost-reduction drive;
7   introduction of five-year rolling corporate plan and annual detailed budgeting (continuing);
8   cash and profit targets for divisions (rewards for directors for exceeding, not *achieving*, targets) (continuing); and
9   divisions left to run their own affairs within the constraints – £100,000 item limit on investment within the budget (continuing).

V   Continuing characteristics of sharpbending

(a) *Divisional autonomy with close control*   Divisions are largely autonomous and run their own marketing personnel, research, pay-bargaining programme, etc. Control is, however, through very tight cash controls. *Daily* returns are required and cash has to be rendered to the group immediately both in domestic and foreign operations.

(b) *Strategic planning*   A five-year strategic plan – incorporating considerable numerical detail – is now in use at Fisons. This plan is subject to an annual review. The first year of the plan forms the basis for drawing up the budget for the years ahead. The whole group is heavily involved with these planning exercises, the final outcome being determined through an iterative process.

(c) *Expansion funds and overseas development*   The company generated enough cash from the merger with Boots and the sales of its fertilizer business in 1982 to expand in its three remaining business divisions. Much of this expansion was overseas development with 80 per cent of Fisons sales now going abroad.

(d) *Other gains*   The steps necessary for merging its agrochemical business with Boots is a reflection of the economic scale of operations in that sector. Companies have to provide a complete product range, therefore small units, who cannot afford to do the research across the whole of this range, struggle to survive. However, Fisons had thought that the answer here was in merger, a complete sale had not been contemplated at the time. As it transpired, the whole concern was sold off to Schering AG two years after the merger, realizing a substantial cash inflow which was utilized for expansion purposes (see below). But the company was still cash-rich and managed to reduce its gearing substantially.

(e) *Strategy for growth*   Fisons utilized its cash revenue to expand by acquisition. A major step was taken in 1984 with the purchase of Curtin Matheson Scientific (see section I). Other acquisitions included Peat Producers in Canada to develop the horticulture business in the US, which Fisons see as a major growth area in the amateur segment of this market.
    The following quotation from the Chairman in the Group's 1984 Annual Report sums up the expansion strategy:

> Our aim as a company is to achieve growth, both in volume and in quality of earnings. This is being achieved by the successful implementation of our declared strategy. This strategy is based upon two precepts. Firstly, we wish to operate in industries of inherent attractiveness, which have potential for growth

and a record of profitability for successful participants. Secondly, but of equal importance, we wish to be in clearly defined business segments where Fisons can reasonably aspire to being an effective competitor by virtue of its size and its financial and managerial resources.

The group made six acquisitions in the year to March 1985 and announced a £95m rights issue in February 1985.

VI Conclusions

Fisons is an interesting example of a traditional firm refusing to accept that it ought to relinquish its traditional activities to prosper. Delay was the culprit. Planning, organization, leadership and control were the four remedies.

GLAXO HOLDINGS PLC

This international group of companies conducts research, develops, manufactures and sells pharmaceuticals (including antibiotics, vaccines, vitamins and veterinary products) and foods. Three products form the cornerstone of group sales and probably earn up to 70 per cent of profits – headed by the highly successful Zantac (anti-ulcerant) with 43 per cent of sales, Ventolin (anti-asthma) and Fortum (antibiotic). The group has subsidiary and associated companies in fifty countries throughout the world. For five years from 1981 to 1986, Glaxo outperformed every other major UK company. Turnover grew at 21 per cent a year, earnings per share 46 per cent, dividends 41 per cent and return on equity 46 per cent. Statistical data for the Glaxo Group for the period are given in table B.8. Since then turnover has increased to £1.4bn and profits have exceeded £½bn.

I History of the firm

In the pre-war era, Glaxo was a baby-food manufacturer. Milk powder, milk substitutes, and additives like vitamin D and glucose were its main products. During the Second World War Glaxo moved from baby foods to pharmaceuticals, starting with the manufacture of penicillin. In the post-war years Glaxo started making antibiotics and cortisone.

There were no real Glaxo inventions until the 1960s. The company did little research; what it was good at was product development.

Glaxo's geographical distribution was also a historical legacy – it had a presence in the UK and Commonwealth, Italy and some South American countries. Sir Alan Wilson became Chairman in 1963 (until 1973) and under his leadership research was liberated and the company made plans to expand in Europe and Japan.

Glaxo's first major success with its own product was Ventolin, and the company appeared to rest on its laurels. In 1971–2 Beecham made a takeover bid on the

Table B.8 *Statistical data for Glaxo Holdings PLC (group only)*

(£m)	1975	1976	1977	1978	1979	1980	1981	1982	1983	1984
Turnover	317.8	411.1	488.0	543.5	539.1	618.1	710.5	865.8	1027.5	1199.9
Profit[1]	49.2	81.4	95.1	94.8	80.1	75.1	99.6	148.5	199.7	268.9
Return[2] (%)	25	31	29	29	21	19	23	31	35	39
Earnings[3] (p)	6.7	10.3	12.3	12.3	14.1	12.4	17.9	23.4	29.9	45.8
Average number of employees (world)(000s)	31.5	30.7	30.5	30.9	29.8	29.2	28.2	28.1	27.8	25.1
Average number of employees (UK) (000s)	17.1	16.1	15.9	15.9	15.6	14.8	13.7	13.2	13.6	13.7

[1] Before interest and tax
[2] Return on total funds employed (based on profit before interest and tax)
[3] Per ordinary share, adjusted for scrip and rights issue in 1982 and earlier years.
Note: The figures for 1983 and 1979 have been adjusted for the changes in accounting policies for exchange differences and deferred taxation which occurred in 1984 and 1980 respectively.

grounds that while Glaxo were good at research, development and production, their marketing was weak. Conversely, marketing was Beecham's strong point and together the two would be extremely powerful. Glaxo succeeded in fighting off this challenge and appears to have entered a period of relative complacency.

II Causes of the relative decline in the late 1970s

There was a hiatus in the growth of sales during the late 1970s. Between 1977 and 1980, Glaxo sales grew by 27 per cent compared with 37 per cent for the health and household sector as a whole.

The reasons for this hiatus or relative decline were numerous; the more important ones being:

1 adverse exchange rates;
2 marketing inadequacies: there was a lack of adequate marketing organization, in particular in those countries where there was a substantial and growing demand, *viz.* Japan, Europe and the US;
3 a sense of complacency following the failed Beecham bid;
4 product succession: no major new product emerged to follow on from Ventolin; however, the decline in profits was in part due to increased expenditure on R&D and the costs of setting up a marketing organization in Europe, Japan and the US, which was expected to generate benefits in the future; and
5 acquisitions: there were acquisitions in the late 1960s and early 1970s that did not materially add to the strength of the group.

III Triggers for sharpbending

It appears that the sharpbend was the result of a gradual evolution. There was a realization that the top management had become complacent. In addition, there had been the discovery of a new drug and the time was ripe to exploit it.

IV Actions taken to promote sharpbending

(a) *Change in chief executive* The direction of the company was changed between 1963 and 1973 from an inward-looking UK and Commonwealth company to a multinational one. Under the Chairmanship of Sir Austin Bide after 1973 the company continued along this direction. The changes in leadership at Glaxo (Paul Girolami took over as Chief Executive from Sir Austin in late 1980) did not result in a change in direction. Rather, successive leaders continued along the same road, though with greater energy/determination. Much of what follows is due to Girolami's quiet, directed and determined confidence.

(b) *Research and development* Consequent upon the long-term view taken in the early 1970s, R&D continued to expand throughout the decade providing new products, such as Zantac, and product variants. Clinical development of the new products from research increased in quality and quantity and thus improved the prospects of commercial success.

(c) *Restructuring* UK operations were subjected to a major restructuring in 1978. All

UK companies were brought together under one operating company – Glaxo Pharmaceuticals. The average number of UK employees was trimmed by nearly 2000 from 1979 to 1981. Subsequently, new, discrete business units were established of manageable size.

(d) *Corporate planning* Since 1979, each subsidiary has been required to produce a five-year corporate plan.

(e) *Core business areas* The company has taken a deliberate step to focus on those businesses it knows best – ethical pharmaceuticals. In the 1960s, the company was only partly international, with unclear objectives and a mixture of business activities. They were not noted for their basic research, which was still in a state of infancy. Girolami claims that the organization was primitive and insecure. Their recent drive has been to concentrate solely on prescription drugs and as Girolami admits, 'Now we have a clear purpose. We are a worldwide company committed to ethical medicines. We are truly international in terms of our philosophy and attitudes. We are the biggest basic researchers in the world.' As part of its focus on a limited number of business areas, Glaxo sold off Evans Medical, a wholly UK-based generic and over-the-counter pharmaceuticals business, to its management team in 1986. They also disposed of Vestric (pharmaceutical wholesaler), Eschmann, Burr and Walsh (surgical equipment) and Farley Health Products (infant and health food).

(f) *Decentralization* Glaxo created profit centres in overseas companies and decentralized much of the decision-making. The top management in the more mature overseas companies is all local – Glaxo have had a long-term policy of not having a high proportion of expatriates. Central control is exercised over what products may be sold or licensed to other manufacturers, over capital expenditure and over what claims can be made for the products by the marketing teams.

Girolami believes in decentralized management because he is convinced that Glaxo now has a unity of purpose. He is not worried about autonomy leading to a loss of power or direction – 'if you all share the same purpose it is meaningless to say someone is too powerful. It doesn't matter because they are all pursuing the same goals.'

(g) *Exchange rate* The dollar/sterling rate in recent years has become more favourable to the company's international trade.

(h) *New product success/marketing flair* By far the most important factor underpinning Glaxo's growth was the success of its new product, Ranitidine – sold under the name Zantac. It was launched in 1981/2 in the UK and Italy, and in the US in mid-1983. Zantac was a similar product to Smith Kline's Tagamet which held market dominance and was an established ulcer cure. Zantac displaced Tagamet as leader due largely to the new-found flair of Glaxo's marketing policy. Ventolin – first launched in 1969 – could have been a super-drug in the Zantac mould but, sadly, it was launched slowly, first in the UK and then in Europe. Wider world markets were missed, e.g. Japan and West Germany, and the drug was not launched until 1981 in the US. Much of this was due to Glaxo's weak marketing in those years.

The Zantac story was to be different under Girolami. From the start he marketed it worldwide. Glaxo bought a small US marketing company in 1978 with a sales force of 130 for $33m. Coupled with a joint promotional venture with Hoffmann La Roche, the launch of Zantac in the US was dramatic. In the first week of its US launch it took 7 per cent of the market. In the year to 1986, sales of Zantac in the US were $768m – a third of worldwide group sales. It is possible that Zantac may generate the most profit of any export product in the world. It is now the top-selling drug internationally. It is marketed in ninety-five countries and has a market share of 50 per cent or more in the key markets like the US, West Germany, Italy and the UK.

The Japanese market, in contrast, has been a disappointment. In 1986, Zantac was the third anti-ulcerant with 28 per cent of the market. A co-marketing strategy with the giant Sankyo company has managed to make inroads but Zantac faces a major competitor in Yamanouchi's Gaster.

Zantac has been the key to Glaxo's growth. It is important to note, given Glaxo's experience with Ventolin, that a good product does not make a successful contribution without the correct marketing. True, in its displacement of Tagamet, Zantac has the advantage by not possessing the rare side-effects that can occur with high doses of Tagamet (temporary breast enlargement and impotence for men). But its wider penetration of international markets required *both* strategy and flair.

V Continuing characteristics of sharpbending

(a) *Confidence* The success of Zantac has given new confidence within Glaxo. It has proved the capabilities of the new marketing teams, provided ample liquidity, allowing it to maintain and, in some areas, increase its research expenditure. This has paid off in the launch of a new product every two to three years.

(b) *Strategy* As an insurance against the failure of R&D programmes the company has kept open its options to sell competitors' products under licence. This, in turn, helps maintain healthy cash flows.

In some markets Glaxo is prepared to license its own products to indigenous manufacturers. In Spain, recently, licences were granted to two competitors. The three companies together flooded the market, protecting it from wider competition.

(c) *R&D expenditure* As Girolami has emphasized, Glaxo are not world leaders in research. The levels of expenditure that successful products such as Zantac have made possible, act as barriers to entry to new competition. This enables Glaxo to defend a dominant position.

(d) *Success breeding success* One of the advantages of having a successful run is that new, high-quality talent is attracted to the company. No longer do Glaxo have to rely on the services of head-hunters to find recruits; the best available talent comes to them, which, in its turn, acts to promote further development.

VI Conclusion

Glaxo has experienced phenomenal growth; a growth that has been organic rather than acquisition-led. The company highlights a different kind of sharpbending. Many companies 'bend' after long periods of decreasing performance. Glaxo 'bent' after a small hiatus in an otherwise upward growth path. It 'bent' from the position of a moderate, rather than a low, performer in its industry.

It is crucial to emphasize the role of Zantac coupled with marketing flair in this sharpbend. Yet it is also crucial to realize that Glaxo is not a one-product company.

LOW & BONAR PLC

Low & Bonar is a diversified holding company with four main divisions: packaging, plastics, electronics and textiles, concentrated in four main markets; Canada, the US, the UK and continental Europe. The industry and geographical analyses of its turnover and profits are contained in table B.9.

I History of the firm

The recent history of the company contains two sharpbends. First, the diversification away from jute in the early 1970s, and second, the sharp reversal from heavy losses in the early 1980s.

The group, which evolved out of the Dundee jute industry, grew during the 1970s by acquisition. This was at the cost of falling returns on net capital employed (which was the case of most of British industry in the 1970s) from 27 per cent in 1974 to 16.6 per cent in 1979. It then suffered a heavy drop in profits in 1981 and 1982, making a loss in 1982 after interest and taxation of £2.7m. In 1983, it returned to the black with profits of £4.2m, but further major structural changes have been required in 1984–6.

The causes, triggers and actions for each recovery are worthy of separate mention.

II Causes of the relative decline to 1973

(a) *Subsidiary problems* Herbert Bonar, the Chairman and Chief Executive in the early 1970s, a son of the founding families, had taken Low & Bonar from being a jute-based textile company with African interests into both electrical engineering (with Bonar Long) and, in a minor way, packaging. At the start of the 1970s he had also acquired

Table B.9 *Statistical data for Low & Bonar PLC (percentage share)*

	Turnover		Profits	
	1985	*1986*	*1985*	*1986*
Industry				
Packaging	53.6	56.5	61.3	53.2
Plastics	5.8	12.5	4.3	8.0
Textiles	15.7	14.2	11.9	22.0
Electronics	19.0	13.8	17.5	13.6
Other	5.9	3.0	5.0	3.2
Geographical area				
UK/Europe	56.1	65.3	57.3	66.2
Canada	38.2	26.8	48.1	34.8
US	3.7	7.4	(4.2)	(0.6)
Other	2.0	0.5	(1.2)	(0.4)
Total (£m)	196	254	13.5	16.8

UK manufacturing and selling rights for a novel form of floorcovering, Flotex, but the company was in severe difficulties, facing managerial, marketing and technical difficulties. Some £3m had been poured into the company without its financial health being checked. It was deep in trouble; judicial control had been enforced. Unfortunately, the selling agreement gave Low & Bonar access only to the UK and some peripheral markets. The French company retained the major markets.

(b) *Textile thinking/organizational structure*   The group's interests were still dominated by textiles – its historic base. Most of the board members were from textiles. As there was no divisional structure, major decisions were brought from the subsidiaries to the board. The textile men became involved in operational issues of the diversified subsidiaries – businesses which they did not fully understand.

(c) *Poor central financial control*   The financial reporting and control systems were rudimentary and the financial information received by the board was inadequate to ensure effective central control.

(d) *Poor investment levels*   Sequential internal investment had been disappointingly low in both the main textile business (none for eight years in the UK!) and the diversified subsidiaries. Consequently, group interests in engineering and packaging were weak.

(e) *Decline of the jute industry*   Jute and flax interests in Dundee had no long-run future.

III   Triggers for sharpbending (1)

In late 1973, Brian Gilbert, who had been Managing Director of Nairn Williamson, became the Chief Executive, replacing Herbert Bonar. Fortunately, there was a six-month overlap with Bonar that allowed Gilbert to assess the group's strengths and weaknesses.

IV   Actions taken to promote sharpbending

(a) *Change of management – Flotex*   A new Chief Executive was recruited for the troubled Flotex subsidiary who, by shrewd management changes in marketing and the technical production side coupled to close control of costs, turned the company around in 400 days from a £700,000 loss to a £100,000 profit.

(b) *Divestment*   The jute and flax mills at Dundee were closed in 1974 at the cost of 1000 redundancies.

(c) *Organizational structure*   A new divisionalized structure was introduced for engineering, packaging, textiles and the new travel interests (see below). Later this industry-based divisional pattern was changed to a geographical base in order to encourage subsidiaries to expand within overseas markets. Gilbert lifted the parent board members off the backs of the subsidiaries and made the latter responsible to specific executive directors. The old textile directors were eased off the board, giving way to fresh non-executives who came in with the acquisitions.

(d) *Financial control systems*   Gilbert recruited a competent Finance Director who immediately introduced a wide-ranging system of control and the production of timely management accounting information for the board.

(e) *Acquisitions/joint venture*   A programme of acquisitions was introduced in packaging (e.g. Bibby & Baron) and engineering (e.g. GHP) in the mid-1970s which led to a major expansion in both sales and asset base. The reasons for these developments were to strengthen the group's UK earnings which were too low for its high UK share holdings and to develop strongly and quickly in areas in which the group was strategically weak. In the late 1970s Low & Bonar bought Nairn Travel from Unilever to gain a foothold in the growing, cash-generating travel business. It also acquired travel interests in Australia and Zambia.

During the 1970s, it was apparent that the national electricity authorities in Sri Lanka, Malaysia and Zambia were going to develop their own generator production capacity and close off the market to foreign manufacturers like the group's subsidiary, Bonar Long. The parent company therefore entered into joint ventures with local companies to retain a solid presence in those markets. To avoid overgearing, the acquisitions were financed by an exchange of shares and rights issues; thus by 1979 capital gearing was only about 25 per cent. However, Low & Bonar did raise a loan of $11m in 1979 to buy out its US partner in the Canadian subsidiary in order to expand into the wider US market where they had developed a high-quality gravure process in the packaging subsidiary. It also expanded its plastics base in North America by purchasing a rotary moulding company in the US.

By 1979, the year of expansion and reorganization seemed to have paid off as sales and profits reached new peaks in nominal terms.

V   Causes of the crisis 1980–2

As 1980 progressed there were signs of trouble and the group switched its attention to cash generation and away from expansion. The scale of the crisis was not, however, perceived at first, but as 1981 proceeded it was seen to be acute and the group made a loss of £2.7m after interest, tax, and extraordinary items. The causes of the crisis were perceived to be:

(a) *The general recession*   Destocking by clients in packaging led to heavy falls in sales; demand for the special manufactures of the engineering division plummeted as industry cut back on capital expenditure; for instance, the subsidiary, Hugh Smith, found its order book for heavy hydraulic presses and sheet-bending equipment largely disappeared, and Brentford found that demand for its special alloys and pumps were lost as the oil and petrochemical industries stopped investing. Sales of polypropylene carpet backing fell with falling sales of carpets; sales of the travel subsidiary also fell.

(b) *The strength of sterling*   This further weakened export and domestic sales because of the influx of American carpeting which reduced the derived demand for polypropylene carpet backing, and increased the cost of servicing the $11m loan taken to purchase the shares of the American partner in the Canadian packaging business.

(c) *Secular declines in some of the businesses*:

1   Hugh Smith's main competitor for specialist pumps was a subsidized Swedish company, whose prices could not be matched profitably; moreover, cheaper stainless-steel castings which Smith had pioneered were being manufactured in increasing quantities in Spain.

2   The tufted-carpet business was encountering heavy competition from Belgian and

American competitors, their sales were consequently declining, and the polypropylene backing business was found to have excess capacity.

3   Much larger networks, and turnover were necessary to secure the discounts in the Nairn travel business necessary for a profitable operation. Nairn's margins fell with the growth of 'bucket shops'. The travel agency made losses (£0.75m) forcing the group into heavy borrowings. It has since been recognized that the original purchase of Nairn, marking their entry into the travel sector, was a gross strategic error, an action that took them away from areas they knew well.

(d) *The failure of the Flotex project*   They had decided to introduce a new line in Flotex in 1979 and it took eighteen months to get the plant into operation. Then technical problems were encountered with resultant heavy costs. Runs were of 2500 metres in the printing process and quality deficiencies led to huge quantities being wasted or dumped overseas at very low prices. In one month alone in 1981 they lost £250,000 and in that year went from a £700,000 profit to a £300,000 loss. With complications in the repatriation of African earnings profits fell back and dividend payments were discontinued for 1981; share price collapsed. In 1982 share prices plunged from 214p to a bottom of 54p.

VI   Triggers for sharpbending (2)

The large negative cash flows and the plunge in the share price sparked off a number of emergency, surgical actions.

VII   Actions to aid recovery to the original sharpbending path 1983–4

(a) *Divestments*   Within the engineering division, they got £400,000 towards the cost of redundancies under the Lazard rationalization programme for the forging industry. Hugh Smith was closed along with most of the operations of Langley Alloys. Following a detailed study of the travel business, Low & Bonar recognized that Nairn had no independent future and merged it with A T Mays in 1983 in return for 35 per cent of the equity of the latter company. These divestments were aimed at focusing on the business areas that were strong and known. Future acquisitions must be complementary and not 'travel-agency' diversifications.

(b) *Rationalizations*   The head office was cut savagely; its staff were reduced from fifty-four to twelve, with specialist services like public relations and corporate planning disbanded. The Dundee head office of textiles was closed and merged into the group's new head-office building.

(c) *Cash generation*   Low & Bonar sold its 50 per cent share in a South African company, realizing £4.6m and aimed to float its Canadian subsidiary on the Canadian Stock Market to eliminate the $11m loan.

(d) *Strict control of subsidiaries*   It was impressed upon the managing directors of all subsidiaries that their own personal future depended on their company's profitability. Costs were tightly controlled and no new investments were permitted. The companies are obliged to submit detailed monthly management accounts (balance sheets, profit-and-loss accounts, budget variance analysis), participate in long-term planning – which includes the annual budgetary cycle – and stay within pre-set cash limits. Subsidiaries are regularly visited by executive directors, who are pro-active within their targeted subsidiary. These executives, as board members, receive a twenty- to thirty-page business statistics summary of all companies at each board meeting.

(e) *Barriers to entry* Low & Bonar have sunk a substantial investment into the Flotex process ensuring its relative freedom from competition. Importers cannot provide the same level of quality and service.

(f) *Company not group identity* The ethos had shifted from group to company on the basis that people are more likely to be motivated by identifying with their immediate environment. If a Managing Director believes in his firm, he will think firm and not group. In this sense, the group do not want comparisons between units, e.g. no inter-group sports competitions. They want to encourage employees to identify with their own and their company's performance.

These measures, together with a general upturn from the floor of the recession and the weakening of sterling, returned the company to substantial profitability. In 1983 the earnings per share rose from the 2p of 1982 to 33p, operating profit from £6m in 1982 to £9m, and profits after tax from £0.3m to £4.6m.

In July 1984, Brian Gilbert retired from the office of Chief Executive of Low & Bonar, while continuing to represent the company on the boards of the Canadian companies and A T Mays.

VIII Continuing characteristics of sharpbending

(a) *Strategy* The changes wrought by Brian Gilbert before his retirement proved insufficient and his successor as Chief Executive, Roland Jarvis, has taken rationalization much further. In particular he has concentrated on just four areas of business: packaging, plastics, textiles and electronics, where Low & Bonar has found lucrative niches. This has meant, primarily, a divestment of the engineering side of the business. The strength in packaging, plastics and special areas of textiles was already apparent as was the weakness of engineering. The major steps forward were first to be prepared to get rid of the remaining engineering work, much of which had only been acquired as recently as 1977, and secondly to find a new focus in the electronics field, principally in electronic power and control systems.

This reorientation was not sufficient and it was accompanied by a geographical reassessment, dropping Africa, in part by deconsolidation of the accounts, and Australasia through sale of the companies. Low & Bonar could then concentrate on the markets where they saw the main opportunities, namely, the US, Canada, the UK and continental Europe. Jarvis described the change in Low & Bonar as revolution followed by evolution. The revolution had been the switch away from dependence on jute; the changes he had had to institute had been part of the natural evolution of business 'one has to continue to seek change'. Some of the earlier diversification had been too widely spread into unrelated activities which the firm had been unable to manage. The company has a highly efficient packaging business, a reputation for high-quality printing of cartons and a patented process in this area, and a dominant market share in cling-wrapping in the UK and in plastic packaging in Canada. Its policy of concentrating investment in areas in which it has special expertise or market strength appears to be sound.

(b) *Divisional structure*   The policy that subsidiaries should have their own identity and be a focus of the loyalty of their employees (managerial and workforce), has clearly worked in a number of respects. Managerial staff seem to be highly motivated and have actively explored not only cost-cutting exercises but new business opportunities. Also, any industrial relations problems seem to have been localized and this has been one reason why large programmes of redundancies have gone smoothly. Operating decisions are also taken at divisional and subsidiary level, only requiring endorsement from the group board where major investment or new departures in terms of policy are involved; this has made the total group more efficient and more adaptive.

(c) *Action-oriented management*   Group management has operated with a style conducive to fostering hard, action-oriented, entrepreneurial management throughout the group. Brian Gilbert in particular stressed the importance of:

1   clearly identifying and confronting problems, then taking necessary action;
2   dealing orally with divisional and subsidiary management even though this has involved extensive travel; this involves, too, providing as much personal support as possible to such managers to solve their problems, whilst making it clear that continued failure must imply dismissal; and
3   this heavy emphasis on communication is linked which a personal involvement of the Chief and Deputy Chief Executive in all key divisional and subsidiary appointments.

Jarvis has developed the role with a clearer divisional structure giving managers a more focused business to run.

(d) *Tight financial control*   This management style is combined with an effective system of financial and management accounting and centralized management of cash balances. However, to achieve the development of the sectors required, the company has, as Jarvis put it, 'taken the padlock off the cash box'. As a result, after taking the harsh decision of whether to proceed with the particular company or not, the survivors have been aided effectively to achieve their potential.

IX   Conclusion

Low & Bonar have spent much time in recovery phases of late. Because they have recovered twice from precarious positions suggests that the steps taken were correct for their organization. Their case is special. Many of the changes made – of rationalization and divestment – have emphasized strategy. The other changes, at Chief Executive, board, head-office and divisional level have emphasized structure. A clear relationship is emphasized. Strategy must match structure for corporate recovery.

MACALLAN-GLENLIVET PLC

This small company (forty-six employees) operates as a 'family' firm with a single product – a malt whisky known as The Macallan. Primarily, this is sold to blenders by the cask but there is a healthy bottle trade. The company is based in Craigellachie, Banffshire.

I History of the firm

Throughout the 1970s, world trade in Scotch whisky maintained a strong upward trend, reaching an exceptional peak in 1978. From 1978 to 1983 the pattern was reversed as, in an environment of widespread recession, sales have declined. The 1978 peak is regarded, within the industry, to be artificially inflated by increased stocking in the overseas distribution chain. Even in the latest recession it has been the proprietary blends – bottled in Scotland – that have borne the brunt of decreasing sales.

Malts, on the other hand, although they represent a small proportion of Scotch whisky sales, have shown a sustained growth through the 1970s as their high quality has become more widely appreciated by consumers. Hence, distillers who were able to make the switch in the 1970s from output based on blend to output of single malts were able to switch into a growing market.

As Macallan is small it has always been fairly closely run. It had grown steadily since the Second World War with the rise in demand for whisky. While some of their whisky had always been set aside for bottled sales, particularly in the local area, in 1968 the board decided to go in for it in a bigger way and laid down larger stocks. The whisky has to mature for ten years before it can be sold in bottled form; for blending, it is sold as soon as it is distilled and put in the barrel.

Macallan made this switch in 1968 but still faced a crisis in 1974/5 when the demand for bottled blend and bulk fell throughout the industry.

Table B.10 contains recent data on turnover, profits and shares.

II Causes of the relative decline

The causes of the decline are simple:

1 depressed demand in the sector; and
2 loss of a major customer taking 30 per cent of output.

Table B.10 *Turnover and profit before tax*

	1979	1980	1981	1982	1983	1984	1985
Turnover (£m)	3.3	4.0	5.5	3.6	3.9	4.7	5.0
Profit before tax (£m)	0.5	0.4	0.6	0.5	0.7	0.8	0.7
Earnings per share (25p ordinary)	22.35p	18.4p	28.5p	22.4p	30.4p	n.a.	n.a.
Price of 25p ordinary shares (high)	535p	630p	490p	530p	640p	695p	575p

III Triggers for sharpbending

The repercussions of depressed demand ricochet through this industry at a rapid rate. Macallan soon felt the pinch with the loss of a major customer, but many other blenders at the time reduced the level of their future order for source whisky for blending.

IV Actions taken to promote sharpbending

(a) *Change of accountant/tighter financial controls* The crisis occurred within a few months of the appointment of Willie Phillips (later to become Managing Director) as Management Accountant. He had valuable experience of the tight financial controls at Pilkingtons and had played an important role in the reorganization at Scottish and Newcastle Breweries PLC. Hence, he was very valuable in the crisis. While financial control methods were already in place, he introduced much tighter controls on day-to-day cash flows.

(b) *Marketing switch* The company saw the dangers of concentrating on blenders for the bulk of their output. They decided to switch significantly to the production of single malt in bottle form. The marketing switch was simple enough to administer, given that the firm had plenty of raw-material stocks to implement the switch.

(c) *Rationalization of the labour force* There were a few redundancies in the workforce, which proved difficult to make in a tight, family-controlled firm.

(d) *Investments/advice* During the crisis the firm continued to invest in both energy-saving and labour-saving equipment. These investments were, in the main, funded by bank loans. Fortune played an important role in the recovery. The loans required were too big for both the local bank and the area office in Aberdeen to handle. The company had to deal with head office where it gained access to valuable 'consulting' advice on reorganization.

V Continuing characteristics of sharpbending

(a) *Marketing philosophy* The marketing switch made during the crisis in the recession was the cornerstone of recovery. When a Marketing Director was appointed in 1978 (Hugh Mitcalfe) he was able to initiate a staggering 30 per cent per annum growth rate for five years. Sequential attacks were made on the most promising markets via agency agreements. Such agreements allowed them to continue as a small company unhindered by the heavy cloak of administrative overheads.

More recently, the company have improved the external appearance of their distillery and prepared the new reception area for visitors. The product is promoted at the quality end of the market. Much of their quality being inherent in the water and method of distilling rather than imposed by creative marketing.

(b) *Financial planning model* The company, largely influenced by the current Managing Director (Phillips), operates detailed financial models coupled to ten-year forecasts. Because of the ten-year lag from production to sale point, such long-term speculation is essential. The model incorporates a very tight annual cash-flow plan, involving monthly reporting. The emphasis is on the control of cash rather than on the profit/loss account.

(c) *Further energy-saving investments* The company has continued its cost-cutting programme by concentrating on energy-saving investments, e.g. waste-heat recovery systems which tend to have quicker pay-backs than first anticipated.

VI Conclusion

Macallan suffered the fate of an intermediate market supplier when there was a severe depression of demand for the final product. Their rationalization, reorganization and cost-cutting strategies were such important ingredients of recovery that during the 1979/80 recession in this industry, the company was able to ease its way through with minimum disruption. A switch to a four-day week avoided a heavy redundancy programme and, as other local distillers closed, Macallan's switch in 1975 to bottled malt kept the firm alive.

McCARTHY and STONE PLC

This building company is engaged in the design and manufacture of sheltered housing schemes and managed nursing homes. They operate fifty to fifty-five building sites at any one time mostly on the mainland of the UK. There were 570 employees in 1984 (2,000 in 1987) when turnover was £21.6m and profits before tax were £6.8m (£16.1m in 1986).

I History of the firm

McCarthy and Stone began as a partnership between Mr McCarthy and Mr Stone back in 1963. At that time Mr McCarthy, who is now the principal driving force of the company, was 21 years of age. Both he and Mr Stone were carpenters by background. Their early business friendship began with the building of caravans which they did with only limited success as most of the caravan sites on the south coast were already cornered by other caravan manufacturers.

Over the decade from 1963 McCarthy and Stone grew successfully as a property-development company and by 1973 employed about 100 people.

At that time the company was deriving all the benefits of the property boom from the period of rapidly expanding money supply.

However, in 1974, the advent of the miners' strike, the collapse of the Conservative government, and the rapid rise in inflation and interest rates created a great depression in the building industry. This was exacerbated by the collapse of the secondary banking system. At the time, the building industry had got used to negotiating loans of £½m to £1m for land purchase over the phone. The new restricted liquidity of the banks put enormous pressures on the cash flow of building companies. McCarthy and Stone were faced with a situation which made them decide to cut back 75 per cent of their output in a six-month period from October 1973.

Consequently, employment at McCarthy and Stone was drastically reduced. The number of employees fell from 100 to six, plus the two Directors.

Over the period 1974-7 the company bought no land at all and took every opportunity from 1974 onwards to liquidate its landstocks. The years 1974–6 were years of considerable difficulty, which the company survived only through the urgent measures which it had taken in late 1973. In the 1974 period it had some ninety units of stock of which it managed to sell only twenty. Consequently, it had about four years supply of housing units for sale. It got through the period of 1974 by living off the fat of 1972 and 1973 together with limited bank facilities.

The final salvation came in 1975 with the introduction of the government's stock relief scheme under which it was possible to get tax relief against the inflated value of stocks held. At the same time, the UK government introduced a scheme for the purchase of private dwellings for council-housing purposes, and this enabled the company to sell a site capable of creating 111 units. This helped it to develop its cash-flow position, reduce borrowing and extricate itself from the earlier difficulties of 1974–6. There had been rumours that McCarthy and Stone had been about to fail, but these measures eventually led, together with the slow upturn in the economy, to a turnaround in the company's prospects.

Ironically, during the whole of this difficult period the company had been faced with considerable problems with regard to a particular site called the Waverley in New Milton in Hampshire. The site had been acquired back in 1972 at the time of rising expectations for the building industry, when capital was easily raised for land acquisition and building development. However, no matter how the company tried to develop this site, it found that whatever configuration was applied, whether in respect of any combination of shopping, housing or office accommodation, a profitable solution could not be found.

It was due to the persistent efforts to utilize this site that the company eventually became a spectacular sharpbender. The company's plans for this site eventually transformed the company from one which employed six people, to one which now employs 2000 people, and from one which made hardly any profit to one which recorded in its 1986 accounts a profit of £16m.

II Causes of the relative decline

The history above captures the main causes of the recession throughout the UK economy in the mid-1970s. The following factors had a particularly severe impact on the building sector:

1 high inflation;
2 high interest rates; and
3 restricted liquidity of the banking sector.

In the case of McCarthy and Stone, the situation was made more severe by the failure to develop the Waverley site.

III   Triggers for sharpbending

The enormous pressure exerted by the macroeconomic factors (see section I) in the mid-1970s on the company's cash flow almost forced it into liquidation. A crisis had developed and action had to be taken.

IV   Actions taken to promote sharpbending

(a) *Cash-flow platform*   The development of a positive cash flow, saving the company from extinction, was made possible by the sale of a large site for the building of council houses (see section I above). This cash-flow platform was the necessary base for launching the recovery.

(b) *Government Green Paper*   The Company did not cease in its attempts to develop the Waverley site by some means or another. During this search, its attention was brought to a government Green Paper on housing requirements, especially with regard to the elderly. In essence, the government was stressing the limited amount of funds available for housing needs and that the private sector should do more to meet demand in the area. The crucial aspect of the Green Paper was that it was recognized that the needs of the elderly were different from the needs of the rest of the community. Market research showed that the elderly did not need the same parking facilities as young married couples or families. This meant that the development opportunities of the Waverley site had now changed. Any proposal to build 'sheltered homes' for the elderly would not need the same proportion of parking spaces that local authorities previously required. These were, that there should normally be one and a half parking spaces per flat, but under the Green Paper proposals only one for each four of sheltered homes would be expected. Hence, the Waverley site was capable of taking a higher density of accommodation than was hitherto possible; it altered the whole question of the development opportunities of this and other sites.

(c) *Contractual strategy*   Hitherto sheltered housing had usually been operated in conjunction with or through housing associations, but McCarthy and Stone could not come to a satisfactory agreement with the local housing association and the National Association of Housing Associations, who wished to have a system of pre-emption clauses written into the contract to buy back the properties as they became vacant, and also to vet entrants to the development. At the same time the housing association was looking for a 5 per cent commission on the development. These proposals did not suit the marketing principles of McCarthy and Stone and ultimately they decided that they would pursue the development themselves whilst giving guarantees to the local authority about the manner in which the site would subsequently be managed. This gave the company more autonomy in the development. During these negotiations, they had the crucial assistance of a local estate agent, Mr Foan, who also had close links with the local housing association. This advice and local knowledge were essential to the success of the talks. Consequently, Mr Foan joined the company as a Director in 1980.

(d) *Market research*   Before developing the Waverley site the company entered into a considerable amount of market research using a consultant for a short period of time.

They also put advertisements in local newspapers to test the response. The results were mildly encouraging. A number of people actually came to its offices to enquire about the development. Nevertheless, the company was conservative about its chances of success as the market for sheltered homes was not then one which had been greatly explored.

(e) *Sheltered-housing market* The company completed the development of the Waverley site into a sheltered-housing complex in seven months – thus pioneering this 'niche' in the market. The larger builders, such as Barratt and Wimpey, had pursued properties at the younger end of the market (first-time buyers). Hence, competition in the 'elderly' market was limited.

The properties at Waverley were soon sold. This was a clear indication to Mr McCarthy to pursue his newly found 'niche' with vigour. A second development quickly followed, all other schemes were closed down in order to concentrate on the elderly market, and the company found itself on the long upward path of sustained growth.

(f) *Fortune factors*:

1 Location: the company was situated on the south coast of England where there were a high proportion of ABs in the socio-economic structure, and a very high density of elderly people who found themselves occupying and owning homes which were becoming too big for their needs.
2 Government policy (see section 4(b) above): This was now positively favouring the development of sheltered homes.

(g) *Tight financial control* This was based upon the small-company principle that all invoices, regardless of size, are witnessed and authorized at the highest level. Since 1974 the company have employed their own cost accountant whose experience during the recession was invaluable (Mr Gray).

(h) *Charismatic leader* Mr McCarthy exhibits all the qualities of an influential leader – an ability to instil motivation into colleagues, drive, dynamism, hard work, action-orientated. It was these qualities that enabled him to take the risk of pioneering the sheltered-housing market.

(i) *Pro-active use of the land bank* The normal strategy for builders is to buy up land for future use – thus restricting corporate liquidity. The company took a positive view, reversing this normal procedure, placing the emphasis strongly on cash flow. They bought land and converted it as soon as possible into saleable units of housing stock.

(j) *Technical superiority in simplicity* Mr Stone was responsible for the technically sophisticated, yet outwardly simple designs of the sheltered homes, with only three variants on design compared with over 100 for some of their competitors. Around these, they make certain internal permutations with regard to fixtures and fittings.

Such simplicity allows the use of standardized constructional processes, which together with high-quality specifications and strict budgeting cost controls ensures that its profit margins are usually greater than its competitors.

(k) *Teamwork* Man management on the site has been an important feature of the company's recovery. The key to profits is often on the construction site. Hence, control over quality, costs and scheduling has been accomplished by developing small teams who are kept together from one project to another. Their mutual understanding and experience build efficiency into site management.

(l) *Rationalization*   The workforce was reduced from 100 to six employees from 1973 to 1974.

V   Continuing characteristics of sharpbending

(a) *Improved financial controls*   As the company grew, it retained the close control of the small firm (see section 4(g)) but developed the process to meet its increased size. It utilized the services of Arthur Young in preparation for a Flotation on the Unlisted Securities Market (USM).

(b) *Management training programme (in-house)*   This was introduced to facilitate the introduction of motivation schemes and internal promotional packages. The company places a great emphasis on management quality.

(c) *Sources of funds*   These were secured by a USM flotation in June 1982 (£1m), a further £12m in December 1983 and a full market quotation in January 1984 (£12m).

(d) *Organizational structure*   As the company grew it developed a suitable geographically based structure consisting of regional offices.

(e) *Technology*   One of the first building companies to utilize CAD in the development stage of each project (1983).

(f) *Economics of standardization* (see section 4(j) above)   This has enabled the company to buy in bulk, facilitated stock control, and led to economies of construction. The latter are also aided by the use of a centrally situated crane on each construction site – a novel feature in the UK on such small developments enabling equipment and materials to be moved around more efficiently.

(g) *Corporate planning*   This was introduced with the help of consultants in 1984 to involve all managers in creating a corporate mission and a general sense of awareness of threats and opportunities. This has become part of the 'in-house' training programme (see section 5(b) above). It aims to create multi-disciplinary management teams, similar to the construction-site ones, creating units along with speed of communication and feedback.

(h) *Supportive external factors*:

1   Demographic trends – more elderly people, living longer.
2   Political – discontinuance of government policy of making 40 per cent grants available to local authorities for this type of development.
3   Local planning authorities – now more responsible for these developments than they were in the mid-1970s.

(i) *Core business areas*   In expanding, the company have not moved far away from the core business they know best – sheltered housing. They have entered the market for managed nursing homes and estate agencies.

(j) *Marketing*   Now much refined, this consists of pre-development consultations with local authorities and a close rapport with potential purchasers before construction.

VI   Conclusion

McCarthy and Stone's can be described as a crisis sharpbend. There are many facets to the case, but two in particular are important. First, the discovery of a unique market niche and the will to take the risk to pursue it. Second, the role of fortune has been highly visible in the growth of McCarthy and Stone. The lesson here is that when fortune presented the company with an opportunity, it took action to secure a return quickly.

PRINGLE OF SCOTLAND LTD

Pringle is a wholly owned subsidiary of Dawson International PLC (which is itself a sharpbender). It is engaged in the manufacture of quality knitwear and has Hawick as its main base although it has recently acquired a large plant at Arbroath with the help of regional assistance.

I   History of the firm

By the late 1960s and early 1970s, Pringle had acquired a good market name, it was strong in exports and was associated with high-quality, high-price cashmere sweaters of traditional design. By 1973/4 it was in a serious state, with substantial losses.

II   Causes of the relative decline up to 1973/74

(a) *Declining demand*   There was a movement with the general cyclical decline after the oil crisis, from the high-priced products of Pringle towards lower-priced knitwear products. The whole of the higher-quality knitwear business in the Scottish borders was badly affected.

(b) *Organization structure*   The company was poorly structured at its headquarters. There were three marketing companies, with separate managing directors and a total of twenty-six directors, all drawing on the same two production facilities. As a result:

1   overhead costs were high;
2   there was very poor coordination of production and marketing, resulting in excessive stocks yet poor delivery times; and
3   the centralized management of marketing, as well as finance, at its parent company (Dawson International) gave the managing directors of the Hawick companies an excuse for poor performance by blurring the lines of accountability.

(c) *Excess costs*   Over the years the company had developed a variety of inconsistent fringe benefits contributing to the high overheads. It was also located in more sites than necessary.

III   Triggers for sharpbending

Pringle's crisis was synchronous with, and contributed to, that of the group as a whole. When Alan Smith returned to running Dawson, he rationalized the Hawick companies. A successful, tough Managing Director had been brought from Dawson's most successful knitting subsidiary. He introduced a series of life-saving actions which shook Pringle to its roots.

IV   Actions taken to promote sharpbending

Bill McEwan, the new Chief Executive, introduced a series of parallel but related actions:

(a) *Reorganization*   He merged the Hawick companies into one. Six of the twenty-six directors were retained, the others were either moved to other senior positions or left the company. From this organizational base a much tighter coordination of production and marketing was possible. He instituted regular meetings between his six directors that still continue today.

(b) *Financial control*   Computers were utilized to tighten up the financial control systems and provide time analysis and reports.

(c) *Overhead rationalization:*

1   McEwan slashed overheads ruthlessly. One of the two production plants, and the original home of Pringle, was closed. Its management there was made redundant and production was concentrated in the remaining site.
2   Dramatic reductions were made at all levels of management. These redundancies at management level were much more severe, and proportionately greater, than on the mill floor.
3   Fringe benefits were cut for all employees, including directors, who even had to pay for their working lunches.

(d) *Labour-force rationalization*   The workforce in the mills was heavily reduced by natural wastage and redundancies in collaboration with the Union (General and Municipal). The total number of employees has been reduced by around 1000 in the last decade to the present figure of some 1400.

(e) *Investment*   After the initial reorganization, there was heavy and continuing investment by the parent company. This has been associated with the introduction of new patterned designs; the de-skilling of fancy knitwear which used to be done by hand; and the introduction of more standard lines e.g. the 'sportswear' range. The net effect has been a doubling of the number of garments produced per head over the last ten years.

(f) *Product strategy*   Bill McEwan saw the need to extend the product range from its very traditional base and to overcome the problem of slack summer sales. He was a key figure in introducing a new range of patterned pullovers (fashionable garments), and, critically, of sports pullovers (light pullovers for golfers and the like). These product developments did much to pull sales back to buoyant level by the end of the decade.

They also helped generate revenue in the early 1980s when the combined cyclical decline and effect of the strong dollar made market conditions more difficult. These conditions had an adverse impact on the profit margin rather than on sales.

(g) *Tough management style* The tough, problem-oriented style of Bill McEwan communicated itself to his managers. He used tight controls which inhibited autonomous managerial motivation. Sadly, some took jobs elsewhere. However, it was realized by the remaining employees that these ruthless cuts were necessary for survival.

V Continuing characteristics of sharpbending

(a) *Energetic, action-oriented management*
(b) *Strong customer orientation*
(c) *Adherence to core business areas*
(d) *The role of Dawson International (parent)*

1 *Formal evaluation and control*: Ronald Miller, the Dawson Chairman and Chief Executive, is Chairman of Pringle, and is their ultimate superior. He is in informal, regular contact with Brian Faulkner (the Pringle Managing Director) who consults him on major strategic decisions and problems but is left to run the business in his own way. Monthly, quarterly, and annual financial reports are sent to Dawson. Annual budgets, capital budgets, and rolling three-year business plans, prepared annually by Pringle, are sent to Dawson, and are discussed with Pringle management by 'the two Johns' (Waterton and Embry). These are seen very much as consultations with the Chairman's (Ronald Miller's) staff members rather than with supervisors and may lead to modifications to plans which necessarily remain those of the subsidiary's management.

2 *Finance*: Dawson can raise finance more easily because of its size and reputation. Hence, the investment in computers and new plant, and the cost of rationalization were met by the parent. Given its position in the mid-1970s this would not have been possible for Pringle alone. Dawson believed in the future of the knitwear industry in a way that bankers and other agents of the capital markets would not.

3 *Managerial support*: Dawson's group management concentrates on problem areas and is able to trigger change, as in the mid-1970s, by injecting new top management. It will grasp nettles and, if necessary, replace managing directors no longer performing well.

Further, the focus on the woollen textile business has meant an investment in the training of their own senior managers who are judged on internal track record before being transferred. Consequently, Dawson can often produce an appropriate top manager from within the group.

4 *Internal market*: The cashmere spinners have the advantage of a captive market within the vertically integrated Dawson group.

VI Conclusion

Pringle has the unusual distinction of being a sharpbender within a sharpbender. Doubtless one contributed to the other, but the nature of the bends is sufficiently different for Pringle to merit individual scrutiny.

If there is one salutary lesson at Pringle it relates to management style. If the financial crisis is severe then rapid action is required. The ability to implement sharp cuts, even ruthlessly, is often a critical necessity. Further, such cuts were felt throughout the hierarchy at Pringle. If anything, the cuts at managerial level were more severe. However, it is doubtful if Pringle would have survived without parental support.

ROTAFLEX PLC

Rotaflex PLC is involved, through its subsidiaries, in the manufacture of electric light fittings and systems and the manufacture of bathroom and shower appliances. It has plants in the UK, France, Belgium, Holland, West Germany, Australia and South Africa.

I   History of the firm

With a few exceptions, most luminaire manufacturers in the UK are small companies producing products for highly diverse segments of the lighting market. Many manufacturers are engaged in the export trade, concentrating on those countries where standards and certification are comparable to those in the UK – particularly in the Middle East, Far East and Commonwealth countries. In 1982, the UK was the fourth largest exporter of luminaires after Germany, Italy, and the US. However its share of this trade was declining by the mid-1980s. The major trade imbalance lay with the UK's European neighbours – namely Germany and Italy. The main barrier to entry to the European market for UK firms was the standard and certification requirements of most countries. There is a great deal of time consumed in the complex and costly process of certification. Although the ensuing process of harmonization among EEC members should ease the exporting effort of UK firms it could also lead to increased competition in the home market, which has always been considered a more open market than most with regard to standards and certification requirements.

Prior to 1976, the Rotaflex group consisted of eight companies based mainly in the UK but with some overseas interests. The group had a high reputation for design flair and consequent product pioneering but suffered from a lack of professional management. Management information systems were poor, there was little management structure and financial controls and reporting frameworks were limited. Even where they had interests in overseas subsidiaries on a 50:50 basis, the subsidiary operated on a completely autonomous basis, lacking group direction or common controls. The whole group reflected this lack of direction, especially where profits were concerned.

In 1976, Michael Frye joined the group and immediately subjected its components to a rigorous business analysis. First, he introduced a management information system to generate frequent financial reporting from all the subsidiaries. The system was so demanding that managers had to develop most of the reports themselves. They were thus personally accountable for the financial figures that had to be submitted to head office within three working days of the month end. Second, Frye reorganized and consolidated the group's strategic portfolio. Finally, he instigated a pro-active search for new, growth market segments involving a complete exploration of the residential and commercial lighting sectors. Hence, prior to the general economic recession of the late 1970s and early 1980s the group were in the process of rebuilding.

(a) *Time taken to implement the rationalization programme* The time taken for the immediate post-1976 rationalization programme was no longer than expected. Specifically, planning permission to extend manufacturing sites was delayed. Consequently, the group were caught by the onset of the 1979–81 recession without enlarged factory premises but with capital already committed to the sites and the entailed high borrowing. This delay in expansion also caused a backlog of orders and delays in the launching of new products.

(b) *Weak management* Frye strove to rid the company of slack management and establish a new, more dynamic team. However, he admits, that he was too slow to act on inefficient management in one of the subsidiaries that had adverse performance implications for the group as a whole.

(c) *General economic recession* The general economic recession, beginning in 1979, had begun to bite earlier than expected. Although the downturn in trade had been foreseen, and attempts had been made to speed up the rationalization package, it was not successful.

(d) *Overstretched borrowing* The group acquired the Linolite Company, in 1979. The acquisition was financed through borrowings. The security of these loans became crippling as interest rates rose in 1979. Further, the poor performance of Concord Lighting International and the Germany subsidiary Interlumen, meant that internal funds to service this debt were not generated in a sufficient quantity. The financial crisis was compounded by high inflation and the deterioration of the wider European markets.

III   Triggers for sharpbending

The unexpected severity of the 1979 recession, the expensive borrowing requirements to service the Linolite debt and the failure of the group to service this internally were clear signals that immediate action had to be taken to avoid dramatic losses.

IV   Actions taken to promote sharpbending

Although the rationalization programme initiated in 1976 took longer to implement than was expected, by 1979 some early results were beginning to come through in the form of positive cash flows. So Rotaflex was beginning to reap the benefits of earlier improvements by the time recession struck. It had installed rigorous financial controls and improved information systems and was entering the recession on a cost-efficient base.

In addition, Frye commissioned a number of critical actions.

1   The cash flow forecasts enabled the company to negotiate appropriate financial arrangements with banks and City institutions to confirm borrowing requirements six to twelve months in advance.

2 The firm enlisted the services of an executive from British Leyland, whose expertise lay in the field of labour-force rationalization. McGrath was with the company for only twenty-one months and, by the completion of his work in March 1980, 440 employees from a total labour force of 1185 were made redundant. Each plant was closely scrutinized for its contribution; the number of showrooms in the UK was cut back. The policy was sharp and painful and, although costly in the short term, had beneficial medium-term implications for the early years of the 1980s.

3 In parallel to the labour-force rationalization the company ran a policy of manufacturing-plant restructuring. The plants at Newhaven and Jumet (Belgium) became the two main centres of production. The plant at Havant, which was a multi-storey factory with little expansionary capacity, was closed and production shifted to Newhaven. In addition, a number of firms within the group were consolidated by re-absorption, e.g. Concord Lighting Projects was assimilaed within the activities of the previous parent 'Concord Lighting International', in an attempt to gain administrative economies of scale.

4 Capital expenditure was cut back in 1979/80 to curtail short-term outgoings. The design team was reduced from twelve to two employees and this slowed down product development to a negligible level. It was not until 1983/4 that designs began flowing from this team again.

5 Frye's personality played a critical role in coercing the subsidiaries along a rigorously controlled path.

V Continuing characteristics of sharpbending

A number of features of Rotaflex's continued performance are worth emphasizing.

1 A continuance of the strong 'cost-controlled' base.

2 Promotion and development of a professional management team. This involves encouraging young, dynamic, aggressive managers or 'performers' as they are referred to within the group.

3 The adoption of a 'minimum internal and maximum external' risk policy. Internally, risks are reduced as far as possible through tight financial controls, efficient information systems and cost-effective distribution channels. Externally, the group emphasizes taking risks in product design and development. The philosophy stems from their complacency in the early 1970s when, as market leaders, they witnessed their advantage systematically ended by competitors through their own failure to focus continually on product development. They made a further error in chopping the design staff and design budget at the onset of recession in 1979 forcing a further straightjacket on development. It was not until the early 1980s that they concentrated on a product-led recovery to record profit levels in 1984. They now focus five years ahead in product development – 'taking a big risk admittedly' as Frye put it.

4 The adoption of a decentralized organization structure with autonomous decision-making at the subsidiary level subject to stringent control criteria from a slimmed-down head office.

5 The placing of emphasis on a true flow of effective marketing information. For instance, in 1985, they completed a comprehensive mail survey of the future needs

of their customers and coupled this with an on-the-road show to invited audiences around the provinces.

6 'Only make one thing at one place.' As their main market, displays, stabilized, they aimed to retain their share and to seek out new market niches. Their carefully planned acquisitions were based on this simple philosophy of 'only make one thing at one place'. Here, the group structured their manufacturing–distribution network so that it could accommodate complexities such as UK subsidiaries selling to French subsidiaries, which, in turn, sell to Dutch subsidiaries that, in turn, eventually sell to the English and French companies. At each stage, value is added through specialist skills, and volume is thus generated.

VI Conclusions

The main causes of the sharpbend were over-borrowing (plus high interest rates), implementation delays from the rationalization programme, weak management in a subsidiary, the general depressed state of the UK and European markets, plus high inflation. The company was fortunate in respect of having not only foreseen the dip and taking appropriate action, but also in having just completed a rationalization programme which included the introduction of tight financial controls. The dominant figure of Michael Frye was central to the recovery programme. He worked out a clever European strategy and was conscious of holding and developing new markets. The group have recently introduced a substantial range of new products (one a week in 1985) and are fast regaining their old position of market leader. The group, having been shocked by the lessons of complacency, are now in a much healthier position to endure surprises and reap rewards. Pre-tax profits rose from £0.7m to £4.9m over the five years from 1979 with an average compound growth of just over 60 per cent per annum and the earnings per share went up on average at a compound rate of over 75 per cent.

SIDLAW GROUP PLC

This large diversified group has activities in textiles and oil-related services. It was once the largest jute-spinning company in the western world and remains so for fine jute yarn for carpet weaving where it has 40 per cent of the world market. It is based in Dundee, Scotland.

I History of the firm

The Sidlaw Group, formed in 1921 under the name Jute Industries Ltd by the merging of seven jute companies, became the largest jute-spinning company in the western world.

Until the late 1960s it was almost entirely a jute company, weaving as well as spinning different qualities of yarn, and its board was dominated by the older members who had grown up in the business.

At this time, Sir John Carmichael, a finance man who was Managing Director of Fisons, joined the board and subsequently became Chairman. He was a man with wide perspectives, not committed to textiles, who saw that the jute business would inevitably decline, and highlighted the need for a strategy of diversification in the early 1970s. Sir John remained as Executive Chairman throughout the diversification phase, except for a brief period when Professor Campbell became Managing Director (he died after a few months). Michael Walker took over as Managing Director in 1976 and has followed the path laid down by Sir John.

The diversification involved the acquisition of a Scottish hardware wholesaler, the financial backing for an American setting up hotels in Aberdeen, and entry to the oil-services business. The latter was achieved by taking a 20 per cent share in forming Seaforth Maritime and buying out the Aberdeen Services Company (North Sea) Ltd (ASCO) run by an entrepreneurial Scot with experience in Texas. He was based in an old whisky warehouse in Aberdeen, had entered the oil-supply business and eventually ran out of cash. The entrepreneur made Sidlaw think on a different scale in the oil scene. He helped to take them into the initial leasing and subsequent purchase of a quay facility in Peterhead from the Scottish Office which subsequently proved to be the best oil-supply base in north-east Scotland.

At the same time, an ex-Chairman of Scottish Gas was brought in as Chairman of ASCO to provide discipline and consolidate its position; non-executive directors were brought into ASCO from the oil industry to buy in contacts and experience, and since then the management of this company grew by continuing investment in land, warehousing, general port facilities and other logistic services. By 1980 it had secured four major oil companies as customers and about 20 per cent of North Sea oil-related traffic was through the base site and wharf. This business was developed with the addition of three hotels in the Aberdeen area under Skean Dhu.

To accommodate the diversifications, Sidlaw, on the advice of consultants, adopted a divisionalized structure with the group as holding company over the hardware, textiles and oil-service divisions. Eric Thain joined the group to provide central services and control. The financial system Thain inherited was inappropriate. The holding company was also an operating company with textile subsidiaries. Thain cut the holding company loose from the operating divisions and thus developed new systems appropriate to a properly divisionalized group.

The chairman of each division was a member of the board and had a degree of delegated authority *not* autonomy. The textile business was a mature mixture of business in itself; oil was totally new, having been built up from scratch; hardware lay between the two, it was already in existence but did not face the long-run difficulties of textiles. The three divisions were very different in size, textiles being the largest with its own board.

Whilst the diversified activities were being consolidated, and ASCO was building up, a major investment was undertaken in weaving. In recognition of the need to differentiate products from the commodity ones, in which either Indians were price competitive or there was excess UK and western capacity, the textile board urged that they should invest in more modern looms and go up market into wall coverings and a range of furnishing fabrics. The reasoning seemed to be:

1 this was an expanding market for differentiated products and would have high mark-ups;

2 there was available capacity: a mill stripped of other equipment could be used; and
3 a substantial government grant was available to assist with purchase of the equipment.

In accepting this proposal the board seems to have been swayed by commitment to textiles. Two graduates with MBAs were dedicated to set up the operation; looms were bought to fill the old mill (subsequently seen to be a strange basis for a capacity decision); and the operation was started in 1976.

II Causes of the relative decline

(a) *Textiles*   The continued advancement of the Indian and Bangladeshi industries provided unbeatable price competition for low-quality yarns suitable for tufted carpet backing, sacks, etc.

Similarly, the continued inroads made by plastic and polypropylene products to the markets of jute products (e.g. sacks) meant continued contraction of the total market. Hence, other than fine yarns, the spinning operations were steadily less profitable. The hammering the traditional carpet manufacturers took from tufted carpet and imported Belgian and American carpets worsened this situation.

This condition was worsened as protection for the industry was stripped away year by year, being finally removed in 1983.

Moreover the 1976 weaving project proved highly unprofitable because:

1 the management proved to be weak: it was, for example, deficient on marketing skills, and did not undertake the necessary market research; and the company failed to establish a high-quality, high-price product in the market quickly enough;
2 the workforce were not used to the quality standards required in domestic as opposed to industrial products; and
3 this was then exacerbated as the world recession reduced expenditure on such 'discretionary', high-priced wall coverings, and probably by changes in fashion too. The market collapsed after 1979.

(b) *Hardware*   At the same time the hardware wholesaler subsidiary was entering a loss-making period. With the entry of supermarkets more strongly to the hardware retailing business, the small shops traditionally served were losing their business. Further, the supermarkets wanted to trade on a UK rather than Scottish basis.

(c) *Other*   ASCO and the fine yarns remained profitable, buoyant businesses, as did the hotel interest in Aberdeen.

III Triggers for sharpbending

Management eventually recognized the gravity of the problem facing them. Even traditional textile members of the board were insisting that action was urgently required.

IV Actions taken to promote sharpbending

(a) *Rationalization*   The new weaving plant was closed together with related spinning operations, leaving only fine yarns and merchanting in textiles. Management as well as workforce were stripped out of the textile division from top to bottom. Indeed, the textile-based directors resigned from the board, in recognition of the need for sacrifices and of the fact that the group was ceasing to be predominantly involved in the area. In general, within the division, costs were slashed and no new investments made.

(b) *Divestments*   The hardware company was sold to GKN which was better able to provide it with a reasonable future. This both removed its losses and provided further capital for the continued investment in oil services.

(c) *Cost reduction*   Together with the huge cost reductions obtained in the textiles division, Sidlaw slashed head-office costs by cutting staff to the bare minimum. Chauffeurs and all other frills were removed. This was intended as a signal to the rest of the group of the severity of the cuts that had to be made.

(d) *Development and consolidation*   The economies generated by the savage cuts in (a), (b) and (c) above quickly brought Sidlaw back to the position of impressive profits. With these resources they proceeded to develop international oil-service interests by acquiring a 50 per cent share of Drexel, Oilfield Services (subsequently disposed of after the collapse in oil prices). A small excursion into the distribution of micro-computers and software-related services was also made to exploit internal skills. However, this diversification failed and was disposed of in 1986 after substantial losses. Furthermore, they carefully nurtured their fine-yarn business, having a competitive advantage in quality over the Indian subcontinent and one of price over the rest of the world (due to exchange-rate changes and lower labour costs in Dundee). Many competitors, seeing the decline of the jute industry, had invested in looms capable of weaving multi-yarns not just jute. This gave many of them the opportunity to get out of jute (much to Sidlaw's good fortune as they picked up market share in jute-spinning), and Sidlaw immediately pressed home their advantages through strong exporting efforts (export output rose from 3 per cent to 40 per cent in three years). Because their high-quality yarns are such a low percentage of the total cost of the carpet – but if they break, the consequences are dramatic – the mark-up is quite healthy.

   Moreover, Sidlaw are convinced that no-one is going to enter the jute market, so until the Indians catch up on quality they intend to extract the maximum return from the business.

V   Continuing characteristics of sharpbending

(a) *Structure*   The board now has a part-time Chairman, three executives and two non-executive directors. It is well balanced and the non-executives are valued as sources of advice to the Managing Director. None of the subsidiary chief executives are on the group board.

   Each subsidiary is a profit centre. It is expected to stand or fall on its own achievements. There is little involvement in operating matters by the head-office staff, although they stand ready for consultation.

(b) *Management through people*   The company is oriented to recognizing problems, finding solutions, and acting. It is also strongly oriented to achieving profitability through people. The Managing Director spends much time talking to his operational managers, visiting the oil-service division to learn on the spot, but making himself available to the textile operations managers on their request. Equally the company values, and has benefited from, good relations with the unions.

(c) *Financial control* Detailed management accounts are used throughout the subsidiaries, and are available to the group Managing Director and Finance Director monthly, but only balance sheet, profit-and-loss accounts, and statements on cash flow for each subsidiary go to the main board monthly. The Managing Director and Finance Director use the management accounts to bring any items of special interest to the board.

Subsidiaries prepare annual budgets and have a 'confrontation' with the group Managing Director and Finance Director then to discuss their assumptions and plans over a three- (or more) year horizon. Their budget estimates or forecasts, may be changed at any month end but they are required to either endorse or revise them, with reasons, halfway through the year.

(d) *Strategy* The approach of the companies to the subsidiaries is now very selective. ASCO is encouraged to be entrepreneurial, to invest in plant and people. The group takes considerable interest in their policy options. Textiles are run on a tight rein, costs restrained, and the managers are discouraged from thinking about investment or expansion.

VI Conclusions

Sidlaw was a company strongly rooted in a traditional, yet declining trade. The decision makers were all textile men, rooted in their experience solely to the trade at hand. New vision was essential for survival and Carmichael – whose experience was broad – provided the relevant strategies. He seized on the change from natural to synthetic yarns and began to diversify. In the latter context, fortune played a role.

The North Sea oil and gas industry was in its embryonic stage providing exciting, risky and yet rewarding opportunities for those with the nerve to enter at the outset. It was a daring move from the familiar to a non-related industry, but Sidlaw made it. They also took the decisive step of buying-in the managerial and technical know-how as required.

Once the recession struck, it forced Sidlaw to rationalize and eventually divest itself of loss-making activities. It has managed to isolate its future businesses and milk its mature ones.

More recently, the fall in oil prices has hit Sidlaw again and further painful restructuring has been necessary. This, of course, is an experience common to the whole industry and not unique to Sidlaw.

SIRDAR PLC

Sirdar's principal activities include the manufacture and distribution to the retail trade of hand-knitting yarns and related products. The company based in Wakefield, West Yorkshire was founded in 1870, and became a public company in 1954. The company is still in a nominal sense a family-controlled company, although the present shareholdings of Mrs Tyrrell, the Chairman and remaining member of the founding family on the board, are now rather small. There are two trading subsidiaries and a related company in England.

In 1986, the company had a turnover of £30m in contrast to its 1974 turnover of £10.2m. Its 1986 profit before tax was £10.3m. The company's profit before tax in 1974 was £862,000. The company in 1984 employed 1137 people, and in 1974 1535.

I History of the firm

The company had been quite successful since its foundation. In 1960 the present Chairman's father died, and Mrs Tyrrell took over the running of the company at the age of forty-two. The period from 1960 to 1970 seems to have been one of mounting difficulty, with the result that by 1970 the company was heading for some serious trouble. The profits at that time were down to about £70,000, which was the low point in the company's history.

Statistical data relating to Sirdar appear in table B.11. The turnover of £33.1m in 1984 was accounted for by the UK (£28.0m), Eire (£1.1m), Europe (£1.2m), Asia (£1.2m), North America (£0.8m), Australasia (£0.7m), and the rest of the world (£0.5m).

Since 1974, turnover, net profits before tax and exports have risen consistently, as employment has fallen. The most impressive rise has been since 1978. The profit/sales ratio increased from 1 per cent (1977) to 27 per cent (1986) while return on capital employed rose from 20 to 32 per cent in the same period.

II Causes of the relative decline to 1974

(a) *Personality problems*   Severe personality problems had developed between marketing and production which were seriously affecting performance. It appears that Mrs Tyrrell was unable to take positive action to rectify this issue.

(b) *Technology*   During the 1960s, a steady conversion from wool to synthetic yarns was under way in the industry. The use of nylon thread created a number of technical problems on the machines at Sirdar, which had been developed for use with natural fibres. The harder synthetic fibre increased the wear and tear on the hardware, and was so susceptible to climatic changes that, in certain circumstances, it became too difficult to use.

III Triggers for sharpbending

The company's answer to these mounting difficulties was to call in consultants. The consequence of their report, which was produced around 1970, was the removal of the

Table B.11 *Statistical data for Sirdar PLC (year end 30 June)*

(£m)	1974	1975	1976	1977	1978	1979	1980	1981	1982	1983	1984	1985	1986
Turnover	10.2	11.1	13.0	15.6	18.2	20.0	21.4	25.4	27.3	30.0	33.1	36.5	38.7
Exports[1]	0.7	1.0	1.7	2.3	2.0	1.8	2.6	2.7	2.4	2.3	n.a.	n.a.	n.a.
Net profit before interest and tax	0.9	1.1	1.2	1.6	2.3	3.4	3.9	5.3	6.2	7.7	9.0	9.5	10.3
Return on capital employed (%)	14.4	18.2	19.0	19.2	24.5	34.2	33.7	40.4	38.2	41.0	37.2	34.6	32.1
Earnings per share (p)[2]	1.3	1.5	2.0	4.3[3]	6.9	10.6	10.1	14.4	16.5	20.2	n.a.	n.a.	n.a.
Employees (average no.)	1535	1565	1512	1484	1457	1414	1278	1243	1212	1152	1137	n.a.	n.a.

[1] After discounts.
[2] Adjusted for scrip issues.
[3] 3.00p after change in accounting policy, re-deferred tax.

n.a. = not available.

then Managing Director (who, ironically, had himself advocated the use of consultants) and his replacement by Ken Palmer, who arrived in the 1970–1 period. Palmer was an ambitious man, and although it is said that he made a number of mistakes during his short period with the company (he died after some two and a half to three years in post in 1973/4) he did achieve a number of important changes, having clearly seen that the company faced technological difficulties, in that the equipment it possessed was incapable of using nylon effectively, and was in any case very much out of date. Also that the company did not appear to have the marketing capability to improve its competitive position.

IV Actions taken to promote sharpbending

(a) *Marketing* Palmer brought Gordon Hampton back to Sirdar from Wates (the builders) to front the new marketing effort that was necessary. Hampton undertook his marketing apprenticeship within the rigorous Proctor & Gamble school.

(b) *Acquisitions* In January 1973, Sirdar acquired Hayfield in an effort to widen their product base. This acquisition had two important repercussions for Sirdar. First, it was able to tap into Hayfield's product-development programmes. Hayfield had successfully developed a crepe nylon courtelle yarn, which was easier to use than conventional nylon yarns. With this company Sirdar was able to produce a yarn called 'Wash'n'Wear'. This became the best selling brand in the country within eighteen months of its launch. This single product transformed the competitive position of Sirdar at that time.

The acquisition of Hayfield's was brought about by necessity. It was made against the background of the Japanese determination to corner the world market for wool supplies, with the consequence that in May 1972 world market prices of wool had multiplied fourfold. The result was that Sirdar desperately needed a new yarn – by definition, synthetic yarn – with which to supplement its traditional wool-yarn business. The acquisition of Hayfield solved this problem. Moreover, the 'Wash'n'Wear' yarn was further developed which enabled the company to launch a variation in May 1975, called 'Countryside', which contained 15 per cent wool. This yarn was also outstandingly successful, and placed the company in a position of market leadership in branded yarns.

Second, the Production Director of Hayfield, Joe Stuart, not only played a leading role in the development of 'Wash'n'Wear', but completely revamped both premises and machinery for Sirdar.

(c) *Teamwork* Palmer had succeeded, within a short space of time, in removing the friction between production and marketing by drafting in Hampton and Stuart. He completed his team by adding Mr Lumb (chartered accountant) to the board – a wise move as he became Managing Director in 1982.

(d) *Investment* Largely due to Stuart, Sirdar became devoted to continuous technical improvement and innovation allowing them to move into higher-value-added products. Back in 1973 at the time of the crisis, Sirdar were not generating sufficient cash flows to fund the major changes Stuart required.

The company's turning point, in its capital investment programme, came in 1976 when Stuart succeeded in taking Harrison and Lumb to Italy to the Itma machinery exhibition. This led to agreement by the board that the company needed to invest in the latest technology. Stuart's task in getting agreement to this was made all the easier by the fact that the wool-textile investment scheme inspired by research undertaken by the Wool Textiles EDC at NEDO, was in operation, and companies could avail themselves of cash grants for the replacement of equipment. Between 1975 and 1981 the company received £1.25m in government grants. The company is now committed to new technology.

These investments in production technology over the decade have, to a large extent, been at the expense of labour. Their average number of employees was reduced by some 25 per cent over the decade to 1983.

(e) *Luck*   Coats Paton – a major UK competitor – made a series of poor decisions in the mid-1970s resulting in a marked reduction in their dominant market share. Sirdar seized upon the opportunity to increase its own.

V   Continuing characteristics of sharpbending

(a) *People and teamwork*   The people at the top of the organization all came together a decade ago, when they were all about the same age (forty to fifty years old). This team has worked well together. It possessed a lot of natural dynamism and innovative capability, and seemed to have a balance of experience in specialist fields as well as in numbers of years in the wool-yarn business.

Sirdar have attractive terms of employment for all their employees. People are important to the company but, as Mrs Tyrrell says, 'I am not one for carrying any passengers'.

(b) *Financial expertise/control*   The team is blessed with a strong financial presence at its centre. The present Managing Director is a chartered accountant, and the board had further accountancy expertise in Harrison, the Financial Director, since the early 1970s. The Company Secretary is also a chartered accountant. Consequent upon this experience, the computerized financial control systems are rigorous.

(c) *Technology*   Sophisticated, computer-based technology has been introduced for both design and manufacture. Consequently, output per head has increased markedly in the last decade.

(d) *Divestment*   Sirdar pulled out of its Nigerian business in 1982 due to poor performance, and after years of problems with its Swiss subsidiary, the board decided to close this in 1984.

(e) *Share incentive schemes*   To sustain the interest and enthusiasm of the employees, Sirdar introduced share-option schemes for all employees in 1984.

(f) *Continued investment*   In 1982, Sirdar invested £2m in a new high-efficiency spinning mill (opened in September 1984) at Wakefield to replace a large number of its obsolete buildings (many over 100 years old). This investment brought Sirdar's total investment in new machinery and factories from 1976 to 1982 to £15m. Another £3m was invested in new plant in 1983 to ensure Sirdar's position as technological leader in the industry.

(g) *Structural changes*   Sirdar have vertically integrated upwards to safeguard raw-material supply and adopted a strategy of dispersing their sourcing of raw materials.

(h) *Rationalization of shift work*   Sirdar found night shifts inefficient, with high wages, lower-quality staff, poor supervision and erratic maintenance attention. The company ceased operating these shifts to cut losses.

VI   Conclusion

Vision and fortune have played an important role in the recovery of Sirdar. Palmer had vision in building a strong management team and harnessing new technology by acquisition. Although his stay was short, it was crucial for Sirdar. He took action after a period of stultification. His successors have sustained his good work by continuing to invest in technology and people. When the opportunities have arisen – due to fortune or otherwise – Sirdar have taken them. As one director pointed out, 'It is always luck and timing and taking advantage of situations', and Mrs Tyrrell confirms, 'Success is what you make of it'.

TI GROUP PLC

This international engineering group produces a wide variety of consumer, capital and semi-finished goods, with manufacturing and marketing subsidiaries in twenty countries worldwide. In 1986, the group's main operating activities were in five main market sectors – domestic appliances (sixteen subsidiaries), cycles (twelve), specialized engineering (thirty), automotive (eleven) and steel tube (seven). Statistical data relating to the company appear in table B.12.

In 1985, the turnover of £997.1m was split as follows:

Domestic appliances	(27%)
Cycles	(14%)
Specialized engineering	(24%)
Steel tube	(15%)
Automotive	(19%)
UK	(57%)
Rest of EEC	(14%)
Rest of Europe	(4%)
N. America	(18%)
Africa	(2%)
Asia	(1%)
Australasia	(3%)
Rest of the world	(2%)

I   History of the firm

TI Group, then known as Tube Investments, was formed in the 1920s as a holding company for a number of steel-tube companies operating in the Midlands. After the war and during the 1950s, it was extremely successful and grew rapidly both by

Table B.12 *Statistical data for TI Group PLC (year end 31 December)*

(£m)	1976	1977	1978	1979	1980	1981	1982	1983	1984	1985
Turnover	716.4[1]	791.8[1]	1106.0	1213.8	1158.0	1122.0	887.2	914.3	917.2	997.1
Net profit before interest and tax	63.9	68.5	93.5	75.0	49.5	(3.8)	26.1	35.3	39.7	51.4
Return on capital employed (%)	18	17.6	20.3	14.1	9.0	—	5.3	10.5	12.1	14.5
Share price (p)	410	375	425	260	225	142	170	265	255	550
Average no. of employees (000s):UK						42.6	27.7	25.1	23.3	22.0
Total no. of employees (000s)						n.a.	33.8	31.3	29.0	27.1

[1] Aluminium interests no longer consolidated.

internal growth and acquisition. It had strong leadership in Ivan Steddiford at the centre, complemented by powerful personalities in the principal operating companies, and was characterized by minimal bureaucracy, insistence on successful performance, a high degree of decentralization, and strong technology. Although it had acquired significant interests in bicycles, electric cookers and some capital goods, it was still predominantly a steel and steel-tube company. It ranked among the top twenty or thirty industrial companies in the UK.

In 1958 and 1960, TI acquired control of The British Aluminium Company and of Raleigh. Shortly after there were major changes in top management due to retirement, and the increasing complexity of the group led to the development of a sizeable divisional management structure. Substantial cash receipts from the nationalization of most of TI's steel interests in 1966 led to further large acquisitions – Radiation, the domestic appliance group; several machine-tool companies; stockists of steel tube; and manufacturers of silencers, garage equipment and flexible tube.

By 1979 there were 60,000 employees in the UK and 8000 overseas. Profit before tax peaked at £80m, and sales of £1.2bn were made up roughly of consumer durables (30 per cent), aluminium (25 per cent), engineering products (25 per cent), and steel and steel tube (20 per cent).

The performance of the group had been barely adequate for many years, but the pressures of 1980/1 brought a collapse of profitability in all areas except domestic appliances. This highlighted the excessive exposure to commodity products like aluminium, steel and steel tube, and exported bicycles.

1981 loss of £23m plus extraordinary loss £18m.
1982 loss of £3m plus extraordinary loss £60m.

II   Causes of the relative decline to 1981

(a) *Inattentive monopoly*   The success of the 1950s enabled TI to purchase British Aluminium (1957) and Raleigh (1960). Combined with TI's own output, the Raleigh acquisition gave them 70 per cent of the market. They rested on this monopoly position which dulled their competitive edge. Consequently, when the flood of imports arrived their market share fell to 40 per cent.

(b) *Structure out of tune with strategy*   Before the acquisitions, TI had operated a divisionalized structure. As TI grew via acquisitions this structure remained static, creating poor communication and delays in crucial decision-making, and hindering financial control. The now-diffused conglomerate was suffering from top-heavy tiers of management.

(c) *Culture*   In general, the evolved TI culture was too easy-going. Targets were reasonable, not demanding. If they were missed the emphasis was on the reasons why, not on actions to correct the errors. Poor performers were given too many second chances, and management was slow to react to market changes and to encourage innovation. A false sense of security had developed with profits being inflated by stock appreciation in the 1970s.

III Triggers for sharpbending

The recession that bit in 1979 was the main trigger although the board had been discussing what to do beforehand. As TI had interests in commodities – steel, aluminium and some tubes – the recession struck them harshly.

IV Actions taken to promote sharpbending

Ronald Utiger (Chairman) splits the actions in the recovery into three phases. Phases 1 and 2 fall largely in the area of actions taken in promoting sharpbending.

Phase 1: panic actions

(a) *Reducing exposure in the most vulnerable areas*   They disposed of Round Oak Steel in 1981. British Steel bought out the TI half of a joint company to rationalize it, although in fact rationalization was only completed twelve months ago. They sold British Aluminium which had been hit by the recession and also by the rather special relationships over the Invergordon smelter. Invergordon had been built up on the expectation of low costs from a nuclear power station. In fact these costs turned out to be much more than alternative energy methods. British Aluminium was merged with Alcan in 1982 which, although it caused a large loss and heavy write-off has been very successful since. They also relinquished their interest in the commodity end of tube-making because of worldwide over-capacity. Their philosophy is 'stay in specialized areas'.

(b) *Generating and conserving cash*   They managed to squeeze £80m out of working capital. While they had set themselves a target of 25 per cent ratio to sales they got it down to 15 per cent. This in effect halved the working capital. In Utiger's view this was a key element in survival. There were almost 20,000 redundancies which caused a major cash drain. The share price actually fell below par with a debt equity ratio of over 50 per cent. Only subsequently did they realize how serious the conditions were and that if anything else had gone wrong they would have had to 'sue for peace' to rescue the company, as Utiger puts it.

(c) *Reducing costs*   This was done throughout the group in whatever manner possible, including shedding top management. Phase 2 of the recovery programme involved changing the unproductive culture that had spread throughout TI. The key to its success was the *restructuring* of the organization. The existing divisionalized management structure added nothing to what was done by operating management and by the group, while it remained a significant barrier to effective communication.

Furthermore, the divisionalized groupings were convenient administrative structures, with little market or product rationale. The divisional management was eliminated and the managing directors of the twenty-five separate operating businesses reported directly to a main board director. This not only facilitated communication but also reduced costs. Significantly, TI had examined, and approved of, similar structures at comparable companies like GKN, BTR and Tilling.

The one exception to this reorganization was the domestic-appliance business that had refused to accept the slack culture of the rest of TI and had performed consistently well during the 1980s. This was aided by the performance of the consumer-goods industry generally which held up in the recession. This division was allowed to operate under a status-quo arrangement.

Phase 2: culture shock

(a) *Communication, rationalization and motivation*   Utiger personally communicated the appalling recent performance to all the twenty-five operating managers. He stressed that this could not continue. He replaced ten out of the twenty-five managing directors and made further changes at board level, Fortuitously, he was assisted by early retirements in an effort to sharpen up the management and board. To spark them into action he introduced a bonus scheme whereby up to 30 per cent of salary could be earned if specified targets were met. Finally, in 1986 a new Chief Executive, Mr C. Lewinton, was brought in from outside the company to continue this culture change.

Both communication and control within the new culture were made far more effective by the removal of the old, administrative tier of management.

(b) *Strategy*   Their consolidation strategy was based upon a three-year plan which ran from 1984 to 1987. There were financial targets for each of the steps in terms of interest cover, gearing and return on capital. The main points of the plan were:

1 to identify publicly four major loss makers and either cure them or exit within a limited period;
2 to single out a number of internationally competitive businesses with growth prospects and put all the resources that could be afforded behind them;
3 to ensure that a number of profitable, mature businesses with strong market positions maintained their leadership positions by appropriate process and product development; and
4 to dispose of some peripheral businesses in order to fund (2).

Control methods were changed from annual budgets into a four-quarter rolling forecast. This gave a more flexible control mechanism, giving better visibility in the first six months of the second year. This was a burden on the operating staff after they had had to put up with a 30 per cent cut in their accountancy staff, but the original system was dominated by accountants and not managers. The new system made managers think about the things fundamental to the business and work on changes as opposed to levels. They had to address the question 'What can I do to effect the sales margin?' They had to think of business decisions not accounting exercises.

Phase 2 was completed successfully during 1987. TI has now entered its third recovery phase.

V   Continuing characteristics of sharpbending

Phase 3: growth strategy

(a) *Fine-tuning*   Lewinton has already made significant changes to reinforce and sustain the culture change of Phase 2. Head Office has been trimmed further and the location switched from Birmingham to London. More responsibility has been given to the operating managing directors and further changes have been made at senior management level.

(b) *Mission statement* Lewinton demanded a mission statement on his arrival. It contained two steps:

1 divest from cycles (achieved on 21 January 1987, when Derby International Corporation bought Raleigh for £18m plus purchaser to take on borrowings of £14.5m); and
2 keep either both domestic appliances and specialized engineering or just one of them.

The key to the second decision is international competitiveness. This involves technical superiority and leadership in a tightly defined product market, e.g. jet engine rings. This enables the building of protective entry barriers against competition. Appliances have 95 per cent UK output and engineering has 50 per cent exports. To make the former internationally competitive would require substantial investments in management and R&D. However, within engineering there are already six businesses with technical entry barriers and more with potential superiority on the way up.

Resources are too limited to pursue both options; engineering is the obvious selection on a cost-effective performance basis. On 27 January 1987, TI purchased a specialized European leader in small-diameter tube from Armco Inc. (US) for £27m, clearly signalling in which direction the group is heading. The domestic-appliance companies are therefore likely to be disposed of – a hard decision given their previous success.

VI Conclusions

The TI story is a powerful one. It brings the match between strategy and structure to the fore in inspiring corporate recovery. Clearly the emphasis on people – their effectiveness, communications and motivation – is a primary concern in the success of strategy. This story is a strategy-led one and it is appropriate to conclude with a close perusal of the rudiments of Utiger's business strategy:

1 in a diverse group 'bottom-up' planning by the operating units should form 90 per cent of the input;
2 simplify and focus – pursue organically related growth opportunities – be wary of sideways leaps;
3 in today's open markets a business must be *internationally* strong and competitive if it is to survive, let alone grow; and
4 mature businesses can be just as profitable as growth businesses provided you are the market leader and invest enough in technology and product development to remain the leader.

UDI GROUP LTD

UDI, originally Underwater Diving Inspection, is involved in the use of advanced techniques and equipment in subsea operations. It is based in Aberdeen and its activities include engineering and product support, system development, underwater television, and offshore surveys. They have had a variety of 'firsts' including the famous underwater vehicle, 'Seabug'. They are world leaders in the development of scanning sonars and have associated companies in the US (Houston), Middle East, Australia and England.

I   History of the firm

The recent history can be conveniently split into two periods: (a) 1972–8, and (b) 1978–80.

(a) *1972–8*   The company has its origins in a small enterprise, started in 1972, which specialized in the visual inspection of underwater pipelines (diving). As the North Sea industry began to take off in the early to mid-1970s, the company developed in two stages. First, they acquired the agency for a high-quality range of TV equipment from Sub Sea Systems Inc., in California. Second, they merged with a survey company involved in rig positioning, marking a change of direction from diving to surveying. This merged firm became UDI in 1973.

Although the company installed the first navigational package on a drilling rig, it was constrained in conducting its offshore surveys by a lack of capable sonars. The company decided to invest internally in R&D activities and build its own range of sonar equipment. For a few years profits were acceptable.

By the mid-1970s design ambitions began to dominate the firm. The company was surveying pipelines with the use of acoustic equipment and decided that a more effective way would be to employ a bottom-crawling vehicle. It decided to develop its own – the Seabug. This required a large investment in design and, consequently, the recruitment of engineers. From 1975 to 1980 the development of Seabug dominated the firm. By 1978 it had consumed a damaging level of resources, throwing the firm into severe financial difficulties.

(b) *1978–80*   Although suffering financial hardship, UDI had a sound design team with a potentially successful product in Seabug. The John Brown Group were quick to assess this potential and bought the company in December 1978.

The subsequent period up to 1980 under John Brown was one of confusion. Funds were still ploughed into Seabug. A wide variety of executives and managers were brought into UDI, each one with their own series of plans and accounting techniques. Their methods were not always appropriate for the businesses UDI were in. Consequently, the period is marked by a large turnover of UDI staff, including John Hay, one of the founder members of the original diving company. He resigned in July 1979 due to the stringent discipline imposed by the John Brown management which he found constrained the development and flow of ideas.

By 1980, UDI was in deep trouble. Seabug was not paying, morale was at a low ebb, the accounting system were still confused, and staff turnover was high. Chairman – part- and full-time – were changing, adding little stability to a traumatic position. In

Table B.13 *UDI performance data*

(£000s)	12 months to December 1978	15 months to March 1980	1981	1982	1983	1984
Turnover	—	2319	2915	5924	9645	9139
Profit/loss before tax	(191)	(870)	(388)	(272)	852	1259
Profit/loss after tax	(191)	(585)	(413)	249	431	633
Profit/loss retained		(585)	81	249	431	633
Employees					108	137

February 1980, Michael Hosking was appointed director – initially to oversee the Seabug development, but later to take hold of the reins of the company.

Table B.13 illustrates the performance of the firm during the late 1970s and early 1980s.

II Causes of the relative decline between 1975 and 1980

In the period from 1975 up until the takeover by John Brown PLC in December 1978, UDI faced a number of seemingly insoluble, yet related, internal problems. The company was dominated by three directors. Two of them, John Hay and Ian Murray, were enthusiastic design engineers. The third, Peter See, was a hard-headed manager. It was left to him to handle the bulk of the administration. There was continuous friction as the design engineers, wishing to spend money freely on development projects, faced the experienced administrator, whose task was to balance the books.

As the friction persisted, the design engineering began to dominate accountancy. The major development consumed a massive £2m in development costs up to 1980, compared with sales turnover of £2.3m in the same year. Further expenditure on numerous other research projects, including three sidescan sonars and TV equipment, made the financial position even worse. A crucial issue here was not solely the spending on design, but the fact that this vast expenditure was not monitored adequately. The company operated a simple Kalamazoo book-keeping system, which, although appropriate for a company of its size at the time, did not generate any management accounting information. In effect, the company was spending its way into receivership.

Interestingly, the role of government grant assistance may have harmed UDI's financial fortune at this time in two ways. First, the designers tended to keep to design products which would qualify for grant assistance. A market did not automatically exist for them. An example is Seabug itself. Many customers were not keen on the five-ton vehicle for fear that it would accidentally damage subsea pipelines. Second, because of the poor accounting records, the grants tended to distort the true financial picture of UDI. Heavy losses were somehow concealed for a period.

John Brown PLC bought these financial and friction problems in December 1978 and added its own brand of management confusion to UDI's problems. The large diversified engineering group imposed the rigidity of its formal planning systems on the small, unstructured design company. As Hosking pointed out 'too much formality was imposed on us too quickly'. Neither was there a sufficient concern for the business UDI were in. They were grafted onto a 'paperwork' section of the group when it may have been more effective to graft them to one of John Brown's production arms.

The problems of the marriage were made more acute by the divided loyalties of many UDI personnel regarding corporate objectives. Some decided to anchor themselves into John Brown's engulfing corporate plan, while others, including designers, wished to pursue a manufacturing strategy based on what they wished to design. The friction contained in the old UDI began to grow again. Matters were made worse when John Brown chose to focus on the Seabug as a product to sell rather than focus on the technology incorporated within it, as the designers would have wished.

Perhaps the most serious problem associated with the takeover was an accounting one. As with formal planning, John Brown, immediately after acquiring UDI, imposed its own tight accounting system on the small company. Consequently, the Financial Director before the takeover was replaced by an inflow of four accountants from John Brown. These accountants were trained in the John Brown system which concerned itself with selling man-hours and hence overhead recovery. This was probably inappropriate for UDI which was geared to selling equipment and products rather than man-hours. Further, there seemed to be no urgency in providing management accounts. They frequently came out forty days after a month end and, if this was allowed to drift even further, the reports were then delayed to be incorporated in quarterly instead of monthly figures. The consequent report was merely a profit-and-loss statement. In the same vein, sales invoices went out thirty days after the event.

One reason for delaying the output of management accounts was the concentration of effort required simply to balance the books. No-one seemed to be reconciling the accounts against the cash balance, hence expenditure continued to seep through onto development projects. In addition, John Brown were paying UDI payrolls from London – hence a huge adverse current-account balance was building up between UDI and John Brown that no-one noticed until it reached over £1.5m. Such accounting peculiarities persisted to the extent that the then Chairman, a qualified accountant, was himself confused.

Hence John Brown had not improved the unstable situation at UDI. By the late 1970s, the company was in a serious predicament.

III   Triggers for sharpbending

The immediate trigger for sharpbending was pulled by the John Brown group. Although its imposed accounting system had endured delays at UDI, eventually the bleak results on the subsidiary's financial position began to seep through to its London headquarters.

IV   Actions taken to promote sharpbending

Several critical actions were undertaken to shock UDI back into the black.

(a) *Rationalization*   Hosking initiated an axe-wielding strategy as the bleak position at UDI emerged. Administration, including sales, was chopped back. Company cars were taken away. The Marketing and Financial Directors, within whose realms the blame was placed, 'were made redundant'. Hosking's aim was to reduce employment by 18 per cent. His strategy was to lay off 10 per cent of the labour force and hope that the remainder would come via resignations. This succeeded, with employment dropping from 100 to eighty-four within a short period.

(b) *Figurehead* There was no apparent figurehead or leader of UDI after the takeover. There was a high turnover of chairmen within a couple of years. Hosking set himself up as a champion of UDI. He had two main aims: (1) to boost the morale and confidence of the remainder of his workforce, and (2) to promote and defend the UDI image, preserving a feeling of autonomy and identity as UDI, not as John Brown. He did this by changing the organization structure, to impart a company rather than a group image to UDI.

(c) *Specialization* Unprofitable activities were cut out. Numerous projects that prevailed prior to 1980 were axed. UDI focused on one (scanning sonar) and decided to persevere with Seabug.

(d) *Seabug order* After a successful operation off the Shetlands in 1980, BP became more interested in the capability of Seabug. Although Seabug I was damaged on its return from the Shetlands, BP commissioned a much larger vehicle, providing £1m of instant income.

(e) *Job specifications* Job specifications of individuals were made more precise, preventing a recurrence of the proliferation of design projects.

(f) *Financial controls* For twelve months, purchase orders were countersigned by Hosking in an attempt to control cash. He also changed the logic of the accounting system, placing heavy emphasis on the generation of punctual and high-quality management accounts. Managers were made more responsible.

The aim was to produce the management accounts within a few days of the month's end and include an integrated balance sheet, profit-and-loss account, cash-flow and budget-variance statements. In addition, emphasis was placed on the order book. The Chief Accountant, Douglas Simpson, was promoted to accomplish the task and by the mid-1980s had developed the financial control systems to an advanced level.

V   Continuing characteristics of sharpbending

As table B.13 shows the recovery was rapid and sustained. The following features are important in the later progression.

(a) *Morale* The UDI identity has been preserved and maintained at a high level within the firm. Consequently, the atmosphere is brimming with confidence and pride. This is cultivated by an open-door policy on behalf of all managers (the Chairman is also Personnel Officer, so he meets all existing and all new employees frequently). All employees are on first-name terms, contractual conditions are identical and all staff use the same canteen facilities. The chauffeur remarked that working in the company was 'like being in a family firm'.

(b) *Marketing* The prevailing ideology was changed from one incorporating a product concept to one incorporating the marketing concept. The old designers' philosophy of 'produce what we want' has been replaced by emphasis on designing 'what the customer wants'. As a consequence, both employees and customers have a firm belief in UDI products.

(c) *Fortune*   The development of scanning sonar was undertaken to assist UDI in its offshore surveying work in the North Sea. They had not planned or envisaged the wider military applications. This market has now opened up for them and is seen to be the future growth area.

(d) *Organization structure*   As employment has grown since 1980, the eight department heads were consolidated into a separate tier of management when the size reached around 130 employees. Size imposed a change in structure. The firm then had three tiers of management (including the Chairman) and this structure was in 'tune' with the current size – 155 employees (1985).

(e) *Counter-cyclical strategy*   In 1980, the operation of Seabug accounted for 70 per cent of turnover. In a cyclical offshore industry, over-reliance on one specific order was seen to be dangerous. A determined strategy to counter the cyclical process was pursued with reliance on a wider spread of orders – including much smaller ones. By 1985, Seabug accounted for only 35 per cent of turnover.

(f) *John Brown*   There are two important ways in which JB has helped UDI sustain its recovery:

1 financial backing; and
2 guarantors of major contracts – allowing UDI (a relatively small firm) to bid for large contracts that would be underpinned by the larger John Brown engineering group.

(g) *Development of financial controls*   In 1980, UDI purchased a small computer for forecasting and producing management accounts. This ran in parallel with the Kalamazoo book-keeping system. In December 1981, they purchased a more powerful machine. Software packages of sales, general, purchase ledgers, enabled the book-keeping system to be computerized. This machine's capability was upgraded in September 1983, and a further machine installed to enable compatibility with John Brown. The system is continuously improved with the search for more accurate data.

VI Conclusion

UDI has had a chequered history. It has always seen itself as a leader in ideas and technology rather than a follower. It was this paramount belief in itself to design and produce that led to the neglect of good financial housekeeping. At the time of the John Brown takeover, the company had a sound team and potentially successful products, it needed professional management. However, it suffered from a system imposed by John Brown that made a poor financial position even worse. The introduction of Hosking as an agent of change, coupled with a programme of rationalization and specialization ensured a remarkable recovery. It now commands nearly 40 per cent of its specialized survey market. It has undertaken well over 600 rig moves and numerous platform and sub-sea template positionings on a worldwide basis and installed more sub-sea cables in the North Sea than any other contractor.

WARD WHITE PLC

This group is engaged in footwear manufacture, distribution and retailing. It also has interests in the safety and sports-goods sectors.

I History of the firm

It is useful to envisage the history of the firm before the sharpbend in two parts: (a) the postwar period to 1967, and (b) 1968–75.

(a) *The postwar period to 1967* The sustained postwar growth in the UK shoe market reached a peak between 1968 and 1973 of 250 million pairs. Consequently, domestic production, which usually accounts for 80–85 per cent of the home market, peaked in 1964 and again in 1968, with output at 200 million pairs. After 1973, the growth in the national market levelled off. Throughout the 1970s, consumers' expenditure on shoes declined as a proprotion of total expenditure, partly because of the fall in volume, but also because the price of shoes fell relative to other retail prices. Imports were the main cause of falling relative prices. From a negligible 0.75 per cent of the market in the 1950s, they stood at 30 per cent in the early 1970s. Since then, with the market declining or static in size, import penetration had accelerated, reaching 60 per cent by 1984.

In the early postwar period, prior to 1967, the companies of the John White Group were involved in the manufacture and distribution of high-class footwear. Their plants, centred on Wellingborough, utilized the local, traditional supply of craft skills.

Unfortunately, although the group's products enjoyed a favourable reputation for high quality, the range of their shoe styles had remained static since 1945. This sleepy external strategic profile was compounded internally by weak, ineffective financial control. Consequently, towards the end of this period, the group's competitive position was under threat.

(b) *1968–75* Action was taken in 1968 to bring in external management consultants to rectify the major problems in productivity and develop the group's strategic profile. One of the consultants, Philip Birch, who had extensive previous experience of the industry, was eventually 'head-hunted' by the management team at John White, who were seeking to fill a vacuum at the top of the organization caused by the death of the Chief Executive. After filling various management positions, Birch became Deputy Managing Director in 1969.

Birch's immediate policy was fivefold. *First*, he embarked on a cut-throat rationalization campaign that shook the roots of every part of the group. *Second*, from 1969 to 1974, he introduced a rigorous financial control system with thirty prepared schedules per month including detailed cost breakdowns, cash flows, budget-variance analysis, etc., which has survived nearly two decades of growth and change. These statements are made immediately after the month end by each divisional manager to the full Board and thereafter, and separately, to Birch himself. *Third*, he dissected the management structure, forming a tighter, more aggressive, top management team. He imparted his own highly motivated, entrepreneurial drive to its leadership. *Fourth*, he made two significant acquisitions on behalf of the group. The first, that of George

Ward (1972) was to provide the identity of this new slim, fit organization – Ward White. The second, that of G. B. Brittan (1973) enabled the group to diversify into safety footwear and capture the famous 'Tuf' brand name. *Finally*, Birch rationalized the existing product range of John White introducing product styles leaning towards the fashion end of the market and changing the group's staid product image. By 1974, the new group was financially healthy in its new, trim and aggressive form.

II   Causes of the relative decline between 1974 and 1975

There are two main reasons for the group's declining performance.

(a) *Acquisition of G. B. Brittan Ltd (1973)*   Aware of the severe import penetration of the home market, reluctant to sit and wait for the market to be flooded, Birch chose a dual policy of product and market differentiation. For product, he chose the growing area of safety clothing and footwear. For markets, the larger, wealthier areas of the US. In order to diversify the product base, Ward White made a contested bid for G. B. Brittan Ltd, manufacturers of safety footwear and holders of the famous 'Tuf' trademark. Ward White were successful and paid £3.6m, offering a cash alternative. This however, was not the familiar cash alternative underwritten by City institutions, but one to be paid by Ward White alone. Birch argued that in his naivety of acquisition policy he was badly advised. Unfortunately, a huge 90 per cent of the cash offer was taken up, throwing Ward White into an adverse liquid position with consequent high gearing. The contingency plan was to sell off a Ward White subsidiary (Wilde's) for £2m to offset the financial crisis. But due to the general economic depression, the closest offer was only £1.6m.

(b) *The general economic depression*   The 1973/4 miners' strike in the UK, the oil crisis of 1974, and the rising import penetration of the domestic market, plunged the industry into a deep depression. Demand dropped off, causing the retailing sector to contract and leaving Ward White without a buyer for Wilde's and with extensive excess capacity throughout their plants.

The company, after having been turned around by Birch in 1969 to achieve record profits in 1972, was again facing a crisis.

III   Triggers for sharpbending

The triggers for the sharpbend were internally generated. Birch was now the Managing Director in complete control of the group's activities. He had foreseen the long-term effects of rising import penetration on the home front and had already prepared diversification plans. He had also admitted the error of judgement that led to the G. B. Brittan 'cash-alternative' crisis. This burned within him, forcing a powerful determination and drive to rectify the company's affairs. Pride can itself be a trigger.

IV   Action taken to promote sharpbending

Underpinning the actions taken to promote and sustain the sharpbend at Ward White was the existence of the well-developed financial control systems, established in the 1968–74 era, which had already begun to bite in monitoring and holding down costs, thus yielding improved margins. In addition, the acquisitions – especially, and ironically, G. B. Brittan's in the safety sector – were beginning to provide positive cash flows into the group. The specific actions immediately adopted focused on supply-side components. The cut-throat, cost-cutting policy of 1968/9 was repeated but on this occasion, aimed for overkill to eliminate all excess costs including fringe benefits. This meant a large-scale programme of plant rationalization involving nearly 1400 redundancies within the manual labour force.

The John White company has always had a convivial manager–worker relationship. Conditions of work are good with staff canteens, factory shops and evidence of clear communications on the many noticeboards. There is a happy and hospitable spirit pervading the factory floors.

During the sharpbend crisis of 1974, a 'track' system of production was in operation within the manufacturing plants. This was seen to be de-skilling and impersonal. The rationalization programme shifted the track system back to piece-work, without loss of production, but with improved efficiency and motivation. In addition, the generally depressed state of the industry had been acknowledged by many of the employees. In the closely knit, traditional community, many of them accepted the redundancies so that other jobs could survive. Further, the labour force adopted a flexible production system with those with craft skills changing tasks as the market switched from style to style. It is clear that the loyalty and flexibility of the labour force during the crisis were critical to the group's survival.

Labour rationalization did not stop at the shop floor. Some executives were fired and others demoted. The consequent cost savings of this cut-throat plant and labour rationalization package were the cornerstone of recovery.

V Continuing characteristics of sharpbending

Many of the characteristics associated with the sustained recovery process are expressed in the overall corporate philosophy. Birch has a strong background in strategy, having trained at Columbia and specialized with the Boston Consulting Group. In 1980, he formed a small planning unit at the slim head office, consisting of just three close colleagues and himself. This unit was to formalize Birch's strategic corporate thinking, and translate this into practice for the Ward White Group. The main points of this thinking are listed below:

1 aim never to have over-capacity in the group (remember the recession in 1974/5);
2 do not expose the output of any one plant to a single customer, such as a multiple store;
3 move from manufacturing into retailing as part of a marketing philosophy of 'getting closer to the customer';
4 concentrate on growing, free-market economies where substantial, successful investments can be made, e.g. more in the US, less in Australia;
5 do not over-concentrate on your competition, especially imports; concentrate on what you think you can do better and put the company's efforts behind it;
6 change the organization from its pre-1974 centralized structure to a decentralized structure with autonomous operating units coupled with close financial control from head office; and
7 continue a strategy of organic internal growth plus acquisitions. Always remain active in the assessment of opportunities but be cautious in those eventually chosen.

These should 'knit-on' to the group without time-consuming reorganization. This enables them to contribute quickly to the profit-and-loss account.

In addition, good labour relations, on a person-to-person basis with management, have eliminated the possibility of production disruptions. Even the works councils were eventually disbanded through lack of disputes. The labour force remain a strong, loyal and flexible asset – a fundamental platform for progress.

This progress has been epitomized by strong internal growth and an aggressive, but controlled acquisition strategy by Ward White in the period since 1978. Twelve companies were acquired between 1980 and 1985; four alone in 1984–5. The firm has expanded overseas, largely into the US but also into Sweden, West Germany, Denmark, Norway and Australia.

Birch's strategic thinking has witnessed the product development of the 1970s – 'a lean towards fashion' – culminating in an integrated forward plan with the acquisition of substantial retail outlets: Joseph Frisby in 1982; W & E Turner, Wyles Shoes and Preedstar in 1983. The group have concentrated on their main business and divested themselves of an unrelated, loss-making business in the engineering sector. A stronger, more dynamic and well-managed group has emerged.

VI   Conclusions

Ward White sharpbent in reaction to a poor financing decision coupled with external economic shocks. These difficulties were remedied by cost rationalization, tight financial controls and an aggressive marketing strategy. This has been sustained in the years since 1974, excepting 1979 when the recession bit into manufacturing industry, bruising the subsidiary, G. B. Brittan.

The company continues along an expansionary path under Birch's control. His blend of aggression and caution, plus his now accomplished expertise at acquisitions, should ensure the company remains a threat to the competition. The secret of successful acquisition strategy lies in both the identification of companies ripe for takeover and the instant introduction into them of proven managerial controls. The suitable candidates must first provide a synergistic component to Ward White's existing operations and, secondly, require limited attention before they make a positive contribution to profits.

The acquisition of Halfords in 1984 is a case in point. The experience accumulated from fifteen years of the successful running of the financial control system within the Ward White Group has meant that it could be easily grafted on to any acquisition and fit snugly into the group's overall reporting system. Halfords are strong in the retailing of motor accessories and cycles. They provided a 'good-fit' to the existing high-street retailing expertise of the Ward White Group. On takeover, Ward White immediately reorganized the Halfords management and introduced the proven control system. Points of sale were computer-controlled and, consequently, Halfords began contributing to the Ward White Group within a very short time.

Ward White now enjoys economies of knowledge in acquisitions, the fruits of sustained success.

WHATMAN REEVE ANGEL GROUP PLC

The Whatman Reeve Angel Group is engaged in the manufacture of industrial filtration equipment, paper and chromatography products, and the worldwide distribution of laboratory products under the 'Whatman' brand.

I History of the firm

It is useful to view the recent history of this firm through three periods: (a) 1958–73, (b) 1974–80, and (c) 1980–5.

(a) *1958–73* W & R Balston Ltd was a traditional family firm based at Maidstone in Kent. The output was almost entirely 'Whatman' filter paper – a unique and famous brand name in the trade. Production was labour intensive with limited mechanization up to 1955. The company concentrated solely on this manufacture, leaving worldwide distribution of their famous brand to Reeve Angel International, a London-based company.

In 1958, they were fortunate to attract a research chemist (C. S. Knight) who was then working on ion-exchange cellulose and paper chromatography. The eventual results constituted a unique generation of such media. During the 1960s, realizing that its traditional product (analytical filter paper) was probably obsolete, Balston invested heavily in these new developments. Further stages included entries into industrial filtration and biochemicals (diagnostic enzymes). Balston worked closely with the National Research and Development Corporation (NRDC), on the latter project and, with the promise of a large National Health Service contract, built a fully staffed and fully tooled plant at Maidstone. These developments were seen as very ambitious for a family firm at the time. Knight claims that the family were instrumental in holding the firm together, acting as a stabilizing unit, during this period of rapid change.

By the early 1970s a combination of problems came to a head:

1 the new government changed the funding of the NRDC in 1970 and the NHS contract fell through;
2 the new developments had starved the principal productive activities (papermaking and conversion) of new investment; and
3 the divorce of manufacture from sales meant that marketing, and especially pricing, were astride two corporate entities with differing ownerships and aspirations. It is generally claimed within Whatman Reeve Angel today, that Balston's output was underpriced for years by Reeve Angel International on the international scene. This depressed margins for manufacturing, further restricting new investment programmes.

The above factors combined to exert strain on the firm's financial position. Fire-fighting action saw overheads trimmed at managerial and board levels. Of the three members who left the board, two were family members. This act marked the end of family management within Balston.

There seems to be little doubt that Balston would have gone into receivership but for the subsequent merger with Reeve Angel International. Reeve Angel International were cash-rich, having just sold off some of their agencies. They had started to go into production for the first time. Their knowledge of Balston was intimate. The synergistic match was good. Although a number of previous attempts at merger had failed, this one succeeded in 1973/4.

(b) *1974–80* After the merger the new Whatman Reeve Angel Group began to put its house in order. It adopted a number of notable strategies.

1 A proper pricing system for Balston's products worldwide was paramount. Prices were pushed up, under the cloak of high inflation levels in the mid-1970s, to what the firm believed to be their true market levels. In effect, demand proved to be unresponsive to price and it was possible to 'premium-price' the goods under the highly respected 'Whatman' brand without revenue loss. The Whatman brand was exploited further. The increases in price were only one component of the improvement in margins. The improved productive efficiency through new investment (below) had a further impact on margins during this period.

2 The new pricing levels were coupled with the introduction of up-to-date marketing techniques and more importantly, a marketing philosophy within the firm. Furthermore, Whatman Reeve Angel began to incorporate its marketing strategies into longer-term corporate plans consisting of a five-year strategic plan and closely monitored one-year operational plans.

3 The organizational structure was altered to a divisionalized pattern with the following subsidiaries operating under a small parent company and subject to stringent financial controls: Whatman Paper, Whatman Chemical Separation, Balston Ltd, Balston Inc., and Whatman Biochemicals.

4 Capital expenditure at the Maidstone plant was increased rapidly. Very advanced, computerized processing and monitoring equipment was introduced into the papermaking and conversion processes. This speeded up production, increased the capital output and, therefore, productivity, extended productive capacity and improved quality and consistency. This further enhanced the Whatman brand name. The introduction of this new equipment meant that a portion of the labour force was replaced. This was accomplished over a period of four to five years through a planned programme of natural wastage (there were no redundancies among process workers although some technical and managerial staff lost their jobs), a fortuitous occurrence due to the older ages of many of the employees. At each stage of the plan, labour representatives were consulted. They sat on working committees helping to plan the change with minimum disruption. Workers felt that this involvement helped them identify with the company's efforts and objectives and to feel 'part of the plan'.

In the late 1970s, the impact of tight fiscal and monetary policies and, more important, the adverse dollar/sterling movement damaged a company that had just completed a heavy investment package and the steady return to break-even and profit. Retrenchment and consolidation were the order of the day.

(c) *1980–5* The focus on margins and cash due to the recession began to filter through into record results from 1980 to 1985. The volatile biochemical division was sold off in May 1981. A reorganization followed. The wider recognition and usage of chromatography techniques allowed the two Whatman businesses to become one. The Balston division was formed as one worldwide operation due to the marked superiority

Table B.14 *Whatman Reeve Angel: geographical analysis of sales (£m)*

	Total	UK	. Europe	North America	North America as % of total
1979	11.7	2.4	1.5	6.5	(56)
1980	13.2	2.7	1.6	7.2	(55)
1981	16.7	3.2	1.5	10.4	(62)
1982	19.4	3.6	1.9	12.2	(62)
1983	23.9	4.1	2.0	15.6	(65)

of the US companies' marketing strategy of the UK counterpart.

It is evident that the company experienced a turnaround period between 1972 and 1974. Balston would certainly have gone but for the merger with Reeve Angel International. It was after this merger that Whatman Reeve Angel began to plan ahead, reorganize and become more efficient on a firmer financial base. Hence when the squeeze came in 1979/80, the firm was able to retrench for a while, sell off a volatile subsidiary and wait for recovery. They were in good shape prior to the sharpbend. The dip in performance from 1978 to 1980 can perhaps be viewed as a hiccup in an otherwise prolonged upward growth path. Noticeably, within this firm, neither management nor financial control systems changed during the sharpbend. It is claimed that Balston always had good management and good managerial accounting information. This has continued throughout the 1970s to the present day.

II Causes of the decline between 1977 and 1979

The most significant single cause of the decline was the adverse dollar–sterling exchange rate for this UK exporting company. Their heavy dependence on North American markets during this time can be seen in table B.14.

Although sales turnover continued to increase, the wide movement of the dollar to sterling between year ends of 1.65 and 2.40 had an adverse impact on pre-tax profits. While turnover increased by 65 per cent between 1976 and 1980 the sterling/dollar rate rose by 40 per cent and profits fell from £1.4m to £0.6m. The group suffered an exchange variance of £1.5m (at £20,000 per US cent movement). This was larger than the record profits the group achieved in 1976. However, Whatman Reeve Angel are large importers of goods from the US. This acts to offset, to some degree, the adverse impact of the dollar on sales. Moreover, the dollar/sterling effect was felt almost entirely within the Whatman companies (see section I(ii)(c) above) as the Balston divisions had such a small proportion of turnover at that time.

In addition to the adverse exchange-rate movement, a number of minor ailments troubled the group. First, the biochemical division proved to be a volatile profit earner. It helped to drag down group profits in the period up to 1981 and was sold. Second, the heavy investment programme at Maidstone was nearing completion by 1979/80. The returns expected from this long capital investment programme were prematurely curtailed when the recession stuck.

III Triggers for sharpbending

The immediate and dramatic impact of the adverse movement of the dollar against sterling was sufficient in itself to activate the alarms in the boardroom.

IV Actions taken to promote sharpbending

Since the turnaround period of 1972–4, Whatman Reeve Angel had initiated formal planning systems, reorganized the group structure and established a firmer financial base. The high-calibre management had close control over the operating divisions. However, the investment programme was undertaken at a heavy cost and the group were only just making a steady return to break-even when the shock arrived in 1979/80. But internally the group was already in a lean and healthy condition.

To ease the immediate plight, they sold the volatile biochemical division. In addition, subsidiaries that had previously made losses were beginning to break-even, or at best, to make positive contributions following the recent investment programmes.

The main single cause of the recovery was the change in fortune of the exchange rate itself. The dollar–sterling rate fell from the peak of 2.40 in 1980 to 1.34 in 1984, recording a record low in February 1985 of 1.09. This turnaround fuelled the Whatman Reeve Angel take-off onto record growth paths of 25 per cent per annum in sales and profits for both its divisions.

V Continuing characteristics of sharpbending

(a) *Group reorganization*   After the sale of the volatile biochemical division in 1981, the group reorganized its divisions. The wider recognition and use of chromatography techniques allowed the two remaining Whatman businesses to become one. The group has now only the two divisions.

(b) *Exchange-rate fluctuations*   The adverse impact of the exchange-rate crisis of 1979/80 focused minds into formulating strategies to reduce the impact of such changes in the future, e.g. forward-buying, and the formation of new markets overseas to offset the heavy dependence on North American markets. This is especially evident in the Balston division that had sourced supplies worldwide to protect itself from external shocks.

Much of the ground-work for recovery had already been laid down in the post-merger period from 1974 to 1978, as is listed below along with additional reasons why the group has sustained its recovery over a prolonged period.

(c) *Returns*   Returns from the extensive capital-investment programmes of the late 1970s improved.

(d) *Corporate planning*   Corporate planning systems comprising five-year strategic plans and one-year operational plans were introduced.

(e) *Financial controls*   The tight financial control system is based on proven standard cost-accounting/budget-variance analysis which was installed at Balston in the early 1970s. Monthly reports to the board include full profit-and-loss accounts at budgeted and standard exchange rates, balance sheets, variance analyses, schedules of fixed expenditures broken down by departments (actual and budget), book-order positions and work-in-progress, employee analyses by department, schedules of capital expenditure and a summary report and prognosis. This type of tight computerized reporting system has been in use at WRA since the early 1970s.

(f) *Marketing* A strong marketing philosophy prevails throughout the group and has done so for over a decade. Both divisions possess keen marketers and marketing strategies. They are market- rather than production-oriented.

A number of distinct characteristics concerning their market operations are worthy of mention:

1 Whatman International imposes an overriding criterion on all laboratory products – they must be marketable by means of a catalogue as opposed to the requirement of an external sales force. Hence, they do not market technologically innovative products that require re-education. They distinguish themselves from competitors by improving the way in which routine laboratory methods can be practised and by searching for market niches rather than competing directly across a broad spectrum of products. In-house manufacture protects sources but, where quality can be guaranteed, they can sub-contract work to ease production schedules. This activity utilizes the Whatman brand name to its full capacity. This is brand marketing, rather than innovative technology.

Whatman's industrial business had adopted a different approach. Their innovative technology is a new papermaking process based on multi-layers of one or more fibres. In addition, their unique cellulose-based chromatography technology will be developed further for industrial applications and will be directed towards the biotechnology market. However, in both the laboratory and the industrial market, emphasis is on consumer allegiance to the brand name; only the means differ.

2 The Balston companies are similarly market-oriented. They have developed a unique selling feature that eliminates a heavy overhead but provides them with the highly trained and dedicated Balston sales force. Distributors are identified within target markets. Requests are them made to the chosen distributor that a member of its sales force becomes purely a Balston specialist. This sales person is trained by Balston, visits the firm regularly and participates in market decisions at Balston. In essence, these sales people feel as if they are Balston employees, yet their remuneration is paid by the distributor. This policy introduces a well-motivated Balston specialist at low cost and allows them to take on target 'niche' markets rapidly, while avoiding expensive and demoralizing misapplications. So far this policy has produced 100 direct sales people (1985).

(g) *Environment* It is widely claimed by Whatman Reeve Angel managers and executives that the atmosphere prevailing within the firm is supportive of individual creativity, identity and belonging. Managers often have the freedom to generate their own ideas and act alone. All employees, including those on the shopfloor, are involved in decision-making and are fully informed of company policy and strategies. There is a widespread involvement in share-option schemes. Moreover, the prevailing philosophy is that share-option schemes should be an integral part of a company's strategy. They are used to hiring, motivating and retaining individuals and linking them directly to the ownership of the firm. Retention of key executives is company policy and a record of low managerial turnover is evidence of the fruitfulness of this philosophy. Two schemes exist, an options scheme for senior executives and a general scheme under the

Finance Act 1978 in which all UK employees who qualify share equally. This environment is illustrated by the role of the Balston US and UK divisions in conducting business. They do not coordinate the divisions at the top level as most firms would. If a UK junior manager needs to see his counterpart in the US, they go themselves – the same applies throughout each hierarchy right down to the quality controllers. There are no organization charts in Balston and never have been – hierarchy takes second place to efficiency.

(h) *'Whatman' brand name*   There is a belief at Whatman Reeve Angel that for an industrial company to succeed in their highly competitive and over-capacity markets of the 1980s and 1990s it must either dominate its market or identify niches that can be exploited. The Whatman name is crucial to both approaches. In analytical filter paper, the company has a 90 per cent UK market share and 60 per cent in the US (1985). In focusing on niches the company relies heavily on the reputation of its famous brand name. Everything possible is done to keep the name synonymous with quality, consistency and service. The policy is to preserve what they claim to be their 'greatest asset'.

(i) *Management quality and staff loyalty*   The group's Managing Director, Mr Leigh-Pemberton, alleges that Whatman have always attracted managers of a high calibre. There is certainly evidence of this today. The current team are highly skilled in their functional areas. Moreover, they are dedicated Whatman people, many having climbed through the ranks. There is an evident loyalty to the firm, a caring identity with it. This is preserved by good communications, the share-option schemes, an atmosphere of creativity, a belief in people above all things. This group has a stable, high-quality and loyal management team who have been together for some ten to fifteen years with perhaps the same length of time together in front of them.

(j) *Worker participation*   The labour force are intimately involved in the firm's policies and decisions. They sit on worker committees, helping with the design and implementation of new project developments. Like management they are loyal and dedicated – long service is commonplace at Whatmans. There have never been any strikes or walk-outs.

VI   Conclusions

Whatman Reeve Angel's recent history spans the years since the merger of Balston with Reeve Angel. After a turnaround in the early 1970s, a consolidation, rationalization and investment programme during the mid-1970s, the group began to grow until it encountered the tight recession and dollar reversal of 1979/81. However, the ingredients for success had already been sown, and Whatman Reeve Angel, after some minor housekeeping on overheads and the sale of a loss-making division, came into the 1980s with a rapid rate of growth in turnover and profitability. Its marketing philosophy, prime brand name, managerial calibre and a working environment conducive to 'intrapreneurship' should ensure a sustained performance throughout the 1980s.

JOHN WOOD GROUP PLC

John Wood Group PLC, with twenty-five member companies employing 2250 people, provided over £90m of service and products to the world's energy industries in 1985. The group corporate structure has three divisions. The Engineering Division (1500 employees, £45m turnover) has activities in Offshore Services (oil-rig services, structural surveys), Workshops and Onshore Services (gas-turbine-generator services, sub-sea equipment and valve and fuel-system refurbishment) and Enterprise (heating, ventilation and mechanical services). The Oilfield Logistics and Services Division (450 employees, £28m turnover) has three modern supply bases in the UK, a full range of back-up services and the provision of fire protection and other safety equipment. The Drilling and Production Services Division (350 employees, £18m turnover) has interests in power-supply systems, computer supervisory and monitoring services for North Sea and other industries and leasing of high-grade tubing for well test and work-over, slim-hole drill pipe, collars and handling tools.

I History of the firm

In 1964 the John Wood company operated a fishing fleet and related ship-repair facilities at Aberdeen. It was well established locally, though subject to the fluctuations of the industry. Privately owned by the Wood family, it was cash-rich, benefiting not only from profits from its business but also from grants in connection with additions to its fleet. This 'traditional' business continued to generate high, positive cash flows, which were particularly strong in the late 1960s and early 1970s.

Ian Wood, only son of the founder and a graduate in psychology from Aberdeen University, joined the company in 1964 and had largely taken over its running by 1967 although his father remained Managing Director until 1970, the year in which Ian formally became Managing Director (now Managing Director and Chairman). Recognizing the cyclical nature of the fishing business, and aggressively expansionist, Ian Wood inspired diversification in the late 1960s. In 1967 a fish-processing company was acquired. In 1968, an engineering company working sheet metal for, *inter alia*, ventilation systems was added, and in 1969 a joinery company. Hence by 1970 the company was already of substantial size, in Aberdeen terms, and locally visible. Its management was young, and entrepreneurial, Ian Wood having been joined by his brother-in-law Hugh Duncan (now Group Director of Oilfield Logistics and Services Division) in 1967. Both men were in their early 30s. Ian Wood writes, 'Our success has been based entirely on a top-class management team'.

II Causes of the relative decline

John Wood & Son (Aberdeen) Ltd were an expanding company in the late 1960s and early 1970s. Their sharpbend relates to a marked upward deviation from an already expansionist path. The company was not engaged in relative decline.

III   Triggers for sharpbending

Conditions for 'sharpbending' were already present, indeed growth by acquisition had already been taking place, when the oil industry arrived in Aberdeen at the turn of the decade. The influx of oil men, often Texans with Stetsons and open-necked shirts, was conspicuous to all. John Wood made no effort to seek their business initially, but found them knocking on their door as a well-regarded Aberdeen company with ships and quayside facilities, and started providing logistic support services from their existing facilities and with their current management team. Not recognizing the scale of the opening opportunities, for a year to two they allowed a substantial share of the logistic support business to go to companies from Great Yarmouth, who had become established in the southern North Sea and opened offices in Aberdeen with experienced managerial staff.

The major growth of John Wood in oil-related services dates from 1972. Ian Wood went to Houston on a visit and realized for the first time the size of the opportunity opening to them. He returned with a powerful recognition of the commitment necessary to expand in this market. 'Pioneering', committed, willing to risk capital to gain high return, young and ambitious, he resolved to make a major commitment to the oil-services business.

The trigger for rapid growth of the John Wood Group in the 1970s can, then, be attributed to the conjunction of:

1 young, ambitious, growth-oriented top management, and in particular Ian Wood, who had an action-oriented, informal, opportunity-seeking style;
2 the chance that the oil industry came to Aberdeen and not to, say, Dundee;
3 a visit to Houston which opened their eyes to the scale of the developing opportunities; and
4 a cash-rich company, which had benefited particularly from several very good fishing seasons.

IV   Actions taken to promote sharpbending

After their Houston visit, Ian Wood and his team set about the rapid development of oil-related business. They started in services that they had already entered by developing them as businesses separate from their traditional base. Actions taken were as follows.

(a) *Acquisitions*

1 John Lewis and Sons Ltd, a ship repairer with good quayside facilities, was acquired and capital was invested in specialized plant to support the logistic supplies business.
2 By 1975, they had begun to acquire small companies established by entrepreneurial technologists who had already undertaken the early years of developing their businesses and had borne the heavy negative cash flows involved. They were frequently in financial difficulties and had often, too, revealed a lack of managerial ability. Some half of these came to the John Wood Group for financial salvation and the others were picked up because of the extensive local knowledge of Ian

Wood and his team. The recipe was to provide the financial backing of the group, the greater security to clients given by a more substantial company, and to 'bundle' services so that more and less profitable services were provided to the same customers on the same rigs.

(b) *Imported management skills*   They invested in new management with specialist knowledge of the oil-related businesses by attracting them away from the incomers from Great Yarmouth, and so acquired knowledge of the business.

(c) *Joint ventures*   They entered joint ventures, which were not always long-lived, and in this way acquired the necessary 'technology'.

(d) *Related businesses*   They developed related businesses – e.g. in painting rigs – building on their developing contacts with the oil industry.

(e) *Control*   During the 1970s, as the business expanded, they evolved an effective financial control system. Cash management is centralized and controlled on a daily basis. Reports on profits and sales are submitted monthly. Annual budgets, including capital budgets, are developed conjointly with the subsidiaries.

V   Continuing characteristics of sharpbending

(a) *Finance*   The traditional business remained a 'cash cow' and expansion was consequently entirely from ploughed-back capital.

(b) *Management style*   Ian Wood operated a managerial approach which stimulated initiative and 'application' among lower levels of managers and, critically, the general manager of the operating companies to whom all operating, but not major policy or capital-investment, decisions were delegated. He works long hours himself, believes that risks must be carefully evaluated but then taken to gain high returns, operates an 'open-door' policy to both his own managers and others who may bring intelligence about opportunities, communicates orally with his senior managers and is participative, while requiring short, succinct, written statements of all proposals. He stresses the importance of looking beyond present operations to future opportunities.

(c) *Decision-making efficiency*   Critically, the company was, and still is, able to take fast decisions. Proposals for capital investment will be taken within days of them being made by operating companies. This is due to three factors:

1   management style;
2   the relatively small size of the company by comparison with many of its competitors; and
3   as a private company managed at the top by the family, major initiatives can be made without regard to the reactions of the capital markets. In 1983, 10 per cent of the equity was sold to Scottish institutions but 90 per cent still remains with the company.

(d) *Restructuring*   After an initial period of centralization, based on the structure of the traditional business, it decentralized operational decision-taking to the subsidiaries, and evolved a divisional structure. It now has three divisions. The head office is small with only about a dozen staff. The restructuring was undertaken in 1982 to liberate the traditional business from the higher profile and more rapidly growing oil-related business, which had a demotivating effect on management in the mature 'traditional businesses'. This was also seen as an opportunity to give the John Wood Group a more focused, oil-related image.

(e) *Corporate strategic management*   The company plans at the group level, talking in terms of a corporate plan, and requires subsidiaries to produce business plans. These plans together with accompanying strategy and policy are discussed at quarterly meetings between Ian Wood, the Group Director responsible for the division, and the executive directors of the subsidiary. Decisions on implementation are made after consultation with Ian Wood and group management in the interim.

Their strategic management process has encompassed the following.

1   The introduction of a formal approach to planning, with a new Development Director, and a Development Manager. Technologies and new markets have been studied and new strategic directions determined.
2   The establishment of a new division of well-drilling and production services to take the company into areas of higher technology. This has been the vehicle for acquisitions, in particular Valtos in 1983, Completion Assemblies in 1984, and Geolograph in 1984. More acquisitions are being sought actively which will fit the intended development of drilling expertise. A tool rental service for drilling has also been developed internally.
3   The development of activities beyond the North Sea base. Geolograph in particular, in which the John Wood Group has a 50 per cent holding of the equity with an option to acquire a controlling interest, illustrates this expansion. This American company has thirty-four sales outlets in the US, has technology which Ian Wood wishes to transfer to their North Sea operations, and is the first of a number of intended American acquisitions.
4   The rationalization of the engineering division. Loss-making companies have been sold or closed or the technology sub-licensed, but care has been taken not to damage customers' interests.

VI   Conclusions

This group has undergone a rapid expansion since the late 1960s when it was a local, family-run fishing business. There are not many Scottish companies who have grasped the lucrative opportunities that the North Sea oil industry offered. John Wood belongs to a select few who utilized this 'windfall' as a springboard to international success. Fortune, ambition, drive, energy and good management have been crucial ingredients. They have enabled the company to take *action* while others watched or just played the role of small service companies. The nature of growth is important. In this case it involved carefully researched acquisitions, the realization that specialist management skills would have to be brought in, and the use of joint ventures. Fortunately, the financial base for this expansion already existed in the lucrative, cash-rich fishing base which saved the company from the cost penalties of high interest rates on borrowings.

As profits and sales peaked, the company have looked to rationalize, restructure and develop those new, higher-technology businesses that ought to sustain performance into the foreseeable future, although clearly it is exposed to fluctuations in the oil industry.

References

Aldington, Lord and Mayes, D. G. (in press) *A Future for Manufacturing*. Basingstoke: Macmillan.

Altman, E. (1968) Financial ratios, discriminant analysis, and prediction of corporate bankruptcy. *Journal of Finance*, **23**, 589–609.

Altman, E. (1971) *Corporate Bankruptcy in America*. Lexington: Lexington Books, D. C. Heath.

Argenti, J. (1976) *Corporate Collapse: The Causes and Symptoms*. New York: McGraw-Hill.

Bain, J. S. (1956) *Barriers to New Competition*. Cambridge, Mass.: Harvard University Press.

Baumol, W. J., Panzar, J. G. and Willig, R. D. (1982) *Contestable Markets and the Theory of Industry Structure*. New York: Harcourt-Brace Jovanovich.

Beaver, W. W. (1967) Financial ratios as predictors of failure. *Empirical Research in Accountancy: Selected Studies Accounting Research*, **5**, 71–111.

Bhagwati, J. (1970) Oligopoly theory, entry prevention and growth. *Oxford Economic Papers*, **22**, 297–310.

Bibeault, D. B. (1982) *Corporate Turnaround: How Managers Turn Losers into Winners*. New York: McGraw-Hill.

Bollard, A. E. and Mayes, D. G. (in press) *The New Industrial Economics*. Farnborough: Gower.

Burns, T. and Stalker, G. (1961) *The Management of Innovation*. London: Tavistock.

Caves, R. E. and Porter, M. E. (1977) From entry barriers to mobility barriers: conjectural decisions and contrived deterrence to new competition. *Quarterly Journal of Economics*, **41**, 241–61.

Child, J. (1984) *Organisation: A Guide to Problems and Practice*, 2nd edition. London: Harper & Row.

Clifford, D. K. and Cavanagh, R. E. (1985) *The Winning Performance: How America's High Growth Midsize Companies Succeed*. London: Sidgwick and Jackson.

Commission of the European Communities (1986) *Improving Competitiveness and Industrial Structures in the Community*. Brussels.

Dunbar, R. L., Dutton, J. M. and Torbert, W. R. (1982) Crossing mother: ideological constraints on organizational improvements. *Journal of Management Studies*, **19**, 29 *et seq*.

Dunbar, R. L. and Goldberg, W. H. (1978) Crisis and development and strategic response in European corporations. *Journal of Business Administration*, **9**, 139–69.

Eisenberg, J. (1972) *Turnaround Management: A Manual for Profit Improvement and Growth*. New York: McGraw-Hill.

Goldsmith, W. and Clutterbuck, D. (1984) *The Winning Streak: Britain's Top Companies Reveal Their Formulas for Success*. London: Weidenfield and Nicholson.

Grinyer, P. H. and McKiernan, P. (1987) A simultaneous equation model for growth in the UK electrical engineering industry. Mimeo. University of St Andrews.

Grinyer, P. H., McKiernan, P. and Yasai-Ardekani, M. (1987) Market structure, control of overheads, and profitability in the UK electrical engineering industry. Mimeo. University of St. Andrews.

Grinyer, P. H. and Norburn, D. (1975) An empirical investigation of some aspects of strategic planning: perceptions of executives and financial performance. *Journal of the Royal Statistical Society, Series A*, **138**, 70–97.

Grinyer, P. H. and Spender, J. G. (1979a) *Turnaround: The Fall and Rise of the Newton Chambers Group*. London: Associated Business Press.

Grinyer, P. H. and Spender, J. G. (1979b) Recipes, crises and adaptation in mature businesses. *International Studies of Management and Organization*, **9**, 113–33.

Hambrick, D. C., MacMillan, I. C. and Day, D. L. (1982) Strategic attributes and performance in the BCG matrix – a PIMS-based analysis of industrial product businesses. *Academy of Management Journal*, **25**, 510–31.

Hambrick, D. G. and Schecter, S. M. (1983) Turnaround strategies for mature industrial product business units. *Academy of Management Journal*, **26**, 231–48.

Handy, C. (1976) *Understanding Organisations*. Harmondsworth: Penguin Books.

Hay, D. A. and Morris, D. J. (1980) *Industrial Economics: Theory and Evidence*. Oxford: Oxford University Press.

Hedberg, B. K. L., Nystrom, P. C. and Starbuck, W. H. (1976) Company on seesaws: prescriptions for a self-designing organisation. *Administrative Science Quarterly*, **21**, 46–65.

Harrigan, K. R. (1980) *Strategies for Declining Businesses*. Lexington: Lexington Books, D. C. Heath.

Harrigan, K. R. (1982) Strategic planning for the endgame. *Long Range Planning*, **15**, 45–8.

Hofer, C. W. (1977) *Conceptual Constructs for Formulating Corporate and Business Strategies*. Boston: Intercollegiate Case Clearing House, No. 9-378-754.

Hofer, C. W. (1980) Turnaround strategies. *Journal of Business Strategy*, **1**, 19–31.

Inkson, K., Henshall, B., Marsh, N. and Ellis, G. (1986) *Theory K: The Key to Excellence in New Zealand Management*. Auckland: David Bateman.

de Jong, H. W. (1987) Market Structures in the European Economic Community. In: Macmillen, M., Mayes, D. G. and Van Veen, P. (eds), *European Integration and Industry*. Tilburg: Tilburg University Press.

Katz, D. and Kahn, R. L. (1966) *The Social Psychology of Organisations*. New York: John Wiley and Sons.

Kenaghan, F. (Chairman) (1983) *Encouraging New Business Activity*. Report by the New Business Panel of the BIM Economic and Social Affairs Committee.

Kibel, H. R. (1982) *How to Turn Around a Financially Troubled Company*. New York: McGraw-Hill.

Khandwalla, P. (1978) Crisis responses of competing *versus* noncompeting organisations. *Journal of Business Administration*, **9**, 151–78.

Kitching, J. (1967) Why mergers miscarry. *Harvard Business Review*, **45**, 84–101.

Kitching, J. (1974) Winning and losing in European acquisitions. *Harvard Business Review*, **52**, 124–36.

MacMillan, I. C., Hambrick, D. C. and Day, D. L. (1982) The product portfolio and profitability – a PIMS-based analysis of industrial-product businesses. *Academy of Management Journal*, **25**, 733–55.

Macmillen, M., Mayes, D. G. and Van Veen, P. (eds), (1987) *European Integration and Industry*. Tilburg: Tilburg University Press.

Mair, A. (1978) *Corporate Turnaround*. MSc Dissertation. London: City University Business School.

Mayes, D. G. (1979) *The Property Boom: The Effect of Building Society Behaviour on House Prices*. Oxford: Martin Robertson.

Mayes, D. G. (1981) *Applications of Econometrics*. Homewood Ill.: Prentice-Hall International.

Mayes, D. G. (1983) A comparison of labour practices and efficiency between plants in the UK and seven foreign countries. *National Institute Discussion Paper*, March.

Mayes, D. G. (1988) Causes of change in manufactured exports. Paper presented at ESRC International Economics Study Group Conference 1986, forthcoming in conference proceedings edited by A. MacBean.

Miller, D. (1982) Evolution and revolution: a quantum view of structural change in organisations. *Journal of Management Studies*, **19**, 131–51.

Mintzberg, H. (1978) Patterns in strategy formulation. *Management Science*, **24**, 934–48.

Modigliani, F. (1958) New developments on the oligopoly front. *Journal of Political Economy*, **66**, 215–32.

NEDO (1984a) Report of a customer survey. Domestic Electrical Appliances Economic Development Committee.

NEDO (1984b) Trade patterns and industrial change. Memorandum by the Director General, 84(21).

NEDO (1987) Research and development. Memorandum by the Director General.

Newbould, G. D. and Luffman, G. A. (1978) *Successful Business Policies*. Farnborough: Gower.

Pearson, B. (1977) How to manage turnarounds. *Management Today* April, 74–7, 134, 136.

Peters, T. J. (1986) *The Promises*. California: Tom Peters Group.

Peters, T. J. and Austin, N. (1985) *A Passion for Excellence: The Leadership Difference*. London: Collins.

Peters, T. J. and Waterman, P. H. (1982) *In Search of Excellence*. New York: Harper & Row.

Pettigrew, A. (1985) *The Awakening Giant: Continuity and Change in ICI*. Oxford: Basil Blackwell.

PEP (1965) *Thrusters and Sleepers: A Study of Attitudes in Industrial Management*. London: Allen and Unwin.

Porter, M. E. (1980) *Competitive Strategy*. New York: Free Press.

Porter, M. E. (1985) *Competitive Advantage*. New York: Free Press.

Schendel, D. and Patton, G. R. (1976) Corporate stagnation and turnaround. *Journal of Economics and Business*, **28**, 236–41.

Schendel, D., Patton, G. R. and Riggs, J. (1976) Corporate turnaround strategies: a study of profit decline and recovery. *Journal of General Management*, **3**, 3–11.

Scherer, F. M. (1980) *Industrial Market Structure and Economic Performance*. Chicago: Rand McNally.

Sigoloff, S. (1981) Lecture given to the Graduate School of Management, UCLA 27 May 1981, and reported in Slatter (1984).

Slatter, S. (1984) *Corporate Recovery: Successful Turnaround Strategies and Their Implementation*. Harmondsworth: Penguin.

Smart, G. F., Thompson, W. A. and Vertinsky, I. (1978) Diagnosing corporate effectiveness and susceptibility to crises. *Journal of Business Administration*, **9**, 59–96.

Starbuck, W. H. (1982) Congealing oil: inventing ideologies to justify acting ideologies out. *Journal of Management Studies*, **19**, 3–27.

Starbuck, W. H., Greve, A. and Hedberg, B. L. (1978) Responding to crisis. *Journal of Business Administration* **9**, 107–37.

Sylos-Labini, P. (1962) *Oligopoly and Technical Progress*. Cambridge, Mass.: Harvard University Press.

Taffler, R. J. (1981) The assessment of financial viability: an example of how financial statement data should be used. London: City University Business School.

Taffler, R. J. and Sudarsanam, P. S. (1980) Contemporary issues in financial ratio analysis: some empirical evidence. London: City University Business School.

Taffler, R. T. and Tisslaw, H. J. (1977) Going, going, gone: four factors which predict. *Accountancy*, **88**, 50–2, 54.

Taylor, B. (1982/3) Turnaround recovery and growth: the way through crisis. *Journal of General Management*, **8**, 5–13.

Thompson-McCausland, B. and Biddle, D. (1985) *Change, Business Performance and Values*. Gresham Paper on Ethics and Business, No. 1.

Vaughan, D., Grinyer, P. H. and Birley, S. (1977) *From Private to Public: An Analysis of the Choices, Problems and Performance of Newly Floated Public Companies 1966–74*. Cambridge: Woodhouse-Faulkner.

Williamson, O. E. (1970) *Corporate Control and Business Behaviour*. Englewood Cliff, NJ: Prentice-Hall.

Woodward, J. (1965) *Industrial Organisation: Theory and Practice*. Oxford: Oxford University Press.

Index

accounting systems 8, 32, 86, 143, 219, 262
acquisitions 39–41, 64, 83, 93, 95–8, 104, 107, 108, 142, 166, 171, 175, 202–3, 205, 219, 228, 252, 265–6, 276–7
advertising 26
after-sales service 90, 140, 170
Alan Jones, Derek 53
Arthur Bell & Sons 12, 13, 24, 26, 28, 29, 55, 69, 70–3, 76, 88, 89, 107, 114, 119, 122, 140, 144, 145, 146
vignette 179–84
aspiration 13–15, 60
asset restructuring 98
Associated Book Pulishers 67, 91, 94
vignette 184–7
Associated Paper Industries 30, 41, 55, 57, 103, 121
vignette 187–92

Balston, W & R 20, 52, 118, 269
banks 51–2, 144, 197, 213–15, 233
barriers to entry 21, 25, 141, 156, 230, 242
Beecham 30, 54
best practice 135
bias 54
for action 67, 68, 71, 105, 113, 117, 173, 231, 241, 276
big projects 41–4
Birch, Philip 28, 55, 60, 61, 76, 100, 101, 265–8
Boston Consulting Group 23, 119, 267
British Leyland 37, 99
British Petroleum 89
British Steel 37, 38
British Telecom 22, 23, 89

budgets 76, 79, 99, 107
building industry 7 *see also* construction industry
bureaucracy 33

CADCAM 88
capacity 209
Carmichael, Sir John 83, 246
carpets 89, 228–9
cash 257
controls 86, 99, 107, 236, 243
flow 43, 87, 98, 130, 131
management 96
Central and Sherwood 48, 100
centralisation 34–5, 75–6
champions 62
Chapman, Ian 56
Cherry, Alan 87, 196, 197–8
chief executive
change in 47–50, 59–60, 132, 223
new 54–6, 167
closures 189
clothing 7
Collins 28, 29, 31, 34, 37, 39, 51, 56, 93, 97–8, 101, 107, 121, 143, 147
vignette 192–6
commitment 8, 144–6
communication 72, 96, 113, 191, 258
competitive advantage 136–41
pressure 21–5
competitiveness
non-price 140
sources of 139–40
computers 8, 81
concentration 156–7
construction industry 81
consultants 57, 80, 148, 191, 265
contestable markets 22

contingency theory 75
contraction control 11, 12
control firm 6, 59, 63, 78, 151, 160
costs 21, 165–6
    controls 85, 125–7, 174–5, 235
    exit 21
    leadership 139
    production 110, 219
    reducing 63, 64, 91–4, 104, 107, 170, 204–5, 248
    rivals 21
    switching 21
Countryside Properties 20, 33, 81, 86–8, 90, 118, 122, 126, 141
    vignette196–200
Courtaulds 54
Craig, George 29, 56
crisis 58, 134, 213, 215
culture (corporate) 68, 73–4, 93, 256, 258
customers 89–91, 113, 114, 129, 145, 241

DASH 85, 210, 211
Datastream 11
Dawson International 12, 23, 24, 35, 52, 53–4, 67, 76, 77, 88, 94, 96–7, 100, 107–8, 115, 121, 124, 125, 136, 139, 140, 239, 241
    vignette 200–6
debt reduction 98–101, 104, 108, 133, 171
decentralisation 115, 205, 224, 244
decision-making 277
decline
    causes of 164–6
    cyclical 19, 44, 45, 228, 239
    relative 12, 18–44, 134–5, 154
    secular 18–21, 45, 228, 232
delegation 97, 113, 138
demographic trends 185
design 86–7, 198, 237
distilleries 8, 70, 88
diversification 41, 81–3, 96, 134, 176
divestment 83, 86, 100, 107, 142, 204, 209, 217, 219, 227, 229, 248, 253, 268

Don Brothers Buist 4, 55, 57, 60, 88, 119, 125, 140, 142
Don and Low *see* Don Brothers Buist
    vignette 206–9

economies of scale 25, 37, 39
electricity
    generation 20
    supply 43
electronics 7, 19, 24, 43, 213–18
Ellis & Goldstein 16, 29, 39, 49, 58, 61–2, 72, 84–5, 86, 88, 104, 115, 122, 127, 135, 139
    vignette 210–12
employment 12
encompassing principle 153
energy saving 234
estimation method 153
Evans, David 67, 90–1, 94
excellence 4
exchange rate 224, 228, 271, 272
exit costs 21
EXSTAT 11, 151
Extel 6, 7
external pressures 60, 238

failure of companies 19
family
    atmosphere 8
    firm 29
    interests 106
    ownership 8
Ferranti 3, 18, 29, 39, 43, 51, 53, 58, 89, 99, 102, 107 *see also* crisis
    vignette 213–18
fertilizers 86, 121
financial control 84, 86, 91, 165, 168, 173, 175, 182, 186, 197, 199, 202–4, 211, 227, 231, 233, 237, 238, 240, 249, 253, 263, 264, 265, 272, 277
    effective 118–19
    inadequate 31–3
    methods of 143
    stronger central 78–81, 104, 107, 108
fishing 275
Fisons 34, 37, 38, 39, 55, 83, 86, 99, 107, 114, 121

vignette 218–21
flotation 183
footwear 7, 19, 61, 265–8
Frye, Michael 61, 81, 105, 114, 242–5

Gilbert, Brian 55, 78, 81, 230–1
Girolami, Paul 55, 114, 115
Glaxo 30, 54, 55, 103, 114, 115, 120,
    136, 141, 160
  vignette 221–5
goodwill 140–1
Graham, John 55, 188–91
growth 10, 221, 258
Guinness 14, 71, 144, 179

Halfords 76, 268
hands-on, value driven 31
hardware 83
head office reduction 77, 83, 86, 87–8,
    99, 107, 116, 133, 191, 220, 258
Hofer matrix 178
Hosking, Michael 35, 43, 261–4
hotels 13, 83
housing 235–9
Hygena 20
hypotheses 9, 153, 163–78

incentives 76, 107, 113, 117, 145, 172,
    253
industrial relations 182, 267
inflation 185, 197, 235
information 143, 242
innovation 115
integration
  horizontal 142
  vertical 25, 29, 142, 209
interest rates 194, 235
interviewing schedule 9
investment 91, 93, 94, 105, 109, 131,
    182, 184, 188, 208–9, 215, 227,
    233, 238, 252–3, 270

Jarvis, Roland 81, 230–1
John Brown 12, 30, 32, 42, 53, 260–2,
    264
John Wood Group 55, 95–6, 102, 115,
    130, 135, 139, 146
  vignette 275–8

joint ventures 277
jute industry 7, 36, 125, 207, 226, 245

Kerridge, John 55, 114, 219
keyholder 65, 68
kitchen furniture 20
knitting 96
  wool 7, 19, 24

labour
  force 71
  rationalisation 223, 240, 244
  reductions 92
Lazards 99
leadership 55, 59, 69, 139, 183, 216–17,
    237
  transactional 65
  transformational 65, 66
Leigh-Pemberton, Jeremy 76
Lewinton, Christopher 258, 259
London Life 25, 31, 145, 146
Low, Bill 55, 57, 89, 125
Low & Bonar 23, 37, 38–9, 40–1, 42, 43,
    44, 55, 58, 67, 77, 78, 80, 98–9,
    116, 117, 119, 120, 135, 142
  vignette 226–31

Macallan-Glenlivet 3, 8, 26, 52, 67, 72,
    88, 91, 105, 107, 121, 125, 152
  vignette 232–4
McCarthy & Stone 20, 81, 84, 86, 90,
    92, 100, 103–4, 105, 126
  vignette 234–9
McKinsey 31, 75
management
  changes 65–74, 104, 107
  good characteristics 113–16
  style 242
market demand 18–21
market power 24
market research 236–7
marketing 64, 131, 182, 186, 197–8,
    199, 204, 208, 211, 212, 224–5,
    233, 238, 252, 263, 268, 270, 273
  improved 89–91, 104, 108, 110,
    169–70
  lack of 25–6, 164, 176
  management 123–4, 174

Marks & Spencer 24, 121
materials 208
mergers 13
Midland Bank 25
Miller, Ronald 77, 241
minimum efficient scale 23
Miquel, Raymond 28, 55, 69, 70, 71, 72, 114, 144, 145, 146, 181–4
mission statement 259
Mitcalfe, Hugh 67
morale 193, 215, 263
motivation 69, 127, 133, 144–6, 258, 273

National Enterprise Board 53, 99, 213–18
Newton Chambers Group 48, 100
NHS 20, 269
non-executive directors 29, 51, 60, 138, 167
NRDC 20, 269

objectives 56
offshore oil industry 7, 19, 275–78
oil industry 7, 19, 246
 North Sea 55, 63, 103
 support 83, 95
ordinary least squares 12
organisational structure 33–5, 65, 75–8, 105, 108–9, 116–18, 141–2, 148, 168, 173, 182–3, 191, 199, 202, 203, 206, 217, 227, 231, 238, 239, 264, 270
overborrowing 245
overcapacity 18
overgearing 177
overheads 77, 98, 195, 240
overtrading 185
ownership
 change in 48, 53–4, 167
 family 8

paper making 7
 and board 24
Paton, Clarke 56
people 65, 138–9, 186, 248
performance measures 9–12, 128

Peters & Waterman eight characteristics of excellence 34
pharmaceuticals 7, 121
pilot survey 6
planning 53, 76, 86, 99, 107, 116, 186, 203, 217, 218, 220, 224, 238, 267, 272, 278
 permission 84, 87, 198
potential 130–50
 product market 135
Pringle of Scotland 12, 22, 23, 35, 52, 67, 72, 93–4, 96, 141, 152
 vignette 239–42
privatisation 22
procurement 20
product
 cycle 120
 differentiation 21, 122
 market 195
 market focus 21, 63, 81–6, 104, 107, 108, 110, 112, 131, 147, 168–9, 204, 211
 market posture 119–122, 173–174, 206
 market potential 135–136
 strategy 240
production control 194, 195
productivity
 capital 10, 12
 labourk 10, 12
profits 10
 centres 84, 116, 117
Pro-Ned 51
protection 21
publishing 7, 90, 141, 184–6

quality 110, 115, 166, 169, 205, 212, 247, 274
 improved 86–9, 108
 maintained 124–5, 129, 174
 of staff 138–9

rate of return 10
raw materials 38
R & D 38, 103, 104, 109, 121, 160, 223, 225, 260
Rawlinson, Charles 57, 189, 192
redundancy 94, 105, 106, 131, 244

restructuring 277
risk management 244
Rotaflex 61, 81, 105, 114, 127, 136
  vignette 242–5

sampling 151–2
  error 152
Seabug 42–3, 89, 144, 260–1, 263–4
service 86–9, 108, 110, 168
shareholders 10, 101
sharpbender, definition 1–3
Sidlaw 39, 40, 51, 55, 83–4, 100, 117,
  122, 125, 127, 136, 139, 141, 142
  vignette 245–9
simultaneous loose-tight
  properties 75–6, 117
Sirdar 19, 57, 64, 88, 99, 105, 138
  vignette 250–4
skills 131, 138–9, 188, 277
small firms 52
Smith, Alan 200–2, 240
standardisation 238
sticking to the knitting 40, 86, 120
stockbuilding 21
stock control 31, 194
stress 46
strikes 132
structure 256
  change 253
  industrial 155–60
substitutes 19, 21, 24

takeovers 11, 13, 30, 131–2, 183–4
  bid 93
  threat of 48
targets 76
teamwork 145, 237, 252, 253
technological change 21, 57
technology 19, 20, 93, 193–4, 195, 218,
  238, 250, 253
telecommunications 24, 155
Telfer, Walter 67, 78, 80
textiles 79, 83, 142, 207–9, 247
Textline 7

Thain, Eric 150, 246
Thompson-McCausland, Ben 68–9,
  145–6
TI Group 7, 100
  vignette 254–9
track record 132
trade union 94, 144–5, 195
training 217, 238
travel agents 79–80
triggers 13–16, 45–62, 150, 167, 189,
  194, 216, 250, 252
turn-around 4, 13, 19, 45, 48, 55, 92,
  100, 131, 133
Turner, Michael 94, 186
Tyrrell, Mrs 57, 105, 138, 250

UDI 12, 30, 23, 25, 42–3, 48, 53, 89,
  99, 100, 104, 118, 144, 152
  vignette 260–4
Unlisted Securities Market 100
unquoted companies 12
Utiger, Ronald 257

value systems 68, 71, 113, 138–9
vision 69, 70, 71, 72, 143

Walker, Michael 55, 117, 127
Ward White 28, 35, 37, 39, 55, 60, 61,
  76, 89, 100, 101, 121
  vignette 265–8
Whatman, Reeve Angel 20, 52, 60, 76,
  88, 99, 105, 118–19, 123, 140, 141
  vignette 269–74
whisky 8, 52, 70, 71, 179–84, 232–4
windfalls 63, 101–4, 108, 149, 162, 278
Wood, Ian 55, 95–6, 146, 275–8
wool 57
Wool Textile Investment Scheme 99,
  253
workforce involvement 195–6, 275
working capital 32, 93

Z score 9
Zantac 103, 221, 223–5